KU-460-716

THE FAMILY

SECOND EDITION

 THE FAMILY:

A SOCIOLOGICAL INTERPRETATION

BERT N. ADAMS
University of Wisconsin, Madison

 RAND McNALLY COLLEGE PUBLISHING COMPANY/CHICAGO

MAIN LIBRARY   POLYTECHNIC
WOLVERHAMPTON WV1 1LY

Rand McNally Sociology Series

0528680579

95414   306.8 ADA
301.42 ADAM

Current Printing (last digit)
15 14 13 12 11 10 9 8 7 6 5 4 3 2 1

Copyright © 1975 by Rand McNally College Publishing Company
All Rights Reserved
Printed in U.S.A.
Library of Congress Catalog Card Number 74-27274

To my socializing agents:
Beulah R. and William W. Adams

When I started working on the second edition of this text, I believed some chapters would not require revision. I was mistaken; the literature review which preceded the rewriting convinced me that *every* chapter would require at least some reworking. Yet, useful new materials have not been distributed evenly throughout the major subdivisions of family study. Five areas of major advance in scholarship stand out, and are reflected in this edition. First, the "new family history" has demanded an almost total reconsideration of the often conjectural generalizations about the colonial and early industrial family found in the first edition. Second, the response of black (and white) scholars to the Moynihan report has continued to produce ideological and empirical material on the black family in the United States. Gratifyingly, the new historical and black family literature have more often than not corroborated the inferences of the first edition, drawn as they were from the sparse evidence available in 1970.

A third area of progress in family study has resulted from the feminist-humanist, or women's liberation, movement. Questioning just how "free and equal" men and women are, even in the middle-class family, this new literature on women's roles, women's status, and marital power relations has been the basis for major changes and additions to the chapters on marital roles and marital adjustments, and has prompted the inclusion of a new section on sex-role socialization in Chapter 7. Fourth, the alternatives to the monogamous nuclear family, almost totally ignored in the first edition, have received extended treatment in the closing of the second chapter, as part of the discussion of the family's future. Spouse swapping, or swinging, staying single, the arrangement, and communes are all commented upon in Chapter 16, in the attempt to make this book better reflect "where it's at" today.

The final area of advance, and perhaps the most satisfying, has been in family theory. The 1970s have seen a major push beyond the "conceptual frameworks" for family study to efforts at explaining "how," "why," and "under what conditions" events occur in families. These new theoretical insights, referred to specifically in Chapter 1, are presented whenever appropriate throughout the volume. The new theoretical emphasis in family study, it should be noted, has only just begun.

In preparing this second edition, I have tried to be sensitive not only to the direction of family scholarship, but to positive and negative criticisms, by friends and colleagues, of the first edition. It is my hope that, without sacrificing either brevity or clarity, this new edition will even better meet the need to understand the structure of and changes in families today.

Bert Adams

Madison, Wisconsin
November 1974

CONTENTS

LIST OF FIGURES

LIST OF TABLES

THE FAMILY

Introduction
to Family Study

This book is about one of man's basic institutions, the family. At one time or another most Americans have been told that the three great institutions of the community are the home, the church, and the school—with the word *institution* left undefined. An institution may be defined as an organized aspect of man's social existence which is established and perpetuated by various norms* or rules.[1] Family and kinship; the economy; political, legal, educational, religious, and scientific structures—these are some of the more important institutions, or organized aspects, of modern society.*

In many ways the family is the most remarkable of these. The state or political structure concerns itself with social control and mobilization; economic institutions regulate the production and distribution of goods and services; religious organizations seek to relate man to the supernatural and to ultimate values. Yet, basic to these types of social organization *historically* has been the family, that institution pertaining to sexual relations, marriage, reproduction and childbearing, socialization or child training, and the relating of the individual to the other institutionalized aspects of society.

The key word in the previous sentence is *historically*. Is the family in modern industrial society still of central importance? Is it dominant? is it

---

[1] Terms followed by asterisks are defined in the glossary at the end of the text.

specializing and adapting to the contemporary world? or is it disintegrating? This complex question lies at the heart of current preoccupation with the family, which is reflected in Margaret Mead's statement that the "American family is at the center of American concern at the present time; its strengths and weaknesses, its past and its future are being subjected to every kind of scrutiny, pessimistic and optimistic."[2]

The interpreters of and commentators on the modern family are as varied in their assumptions and views as they are numerous. To some it is the object of serious *criticism*. The radical may claim that the contemporary family is the greatest single hurdle to be overcome before social equality, personal freedom, and self-realization can be achieved. In 1884 Friedrich Engels expressed it thus: "The modern individual family is founded on the open or concealed domestic slavery of the wife, and modern society is a mass composed of these individual families as its molecules."[3] Radicals are not, however, alone in their criticism of today's family. Edmund Leach, a British social anthropologist and provost of King's College, has asserted that "far from being the basis of the good society, the family with its narrow privacy and tawdry secrets is the source of all our discontents."[4] Some of these discontents have found expression in current experiments with "alternative forms of intimacy," ranging from communes to middle-class "swinging." In Chapter 16 we will look in some detail at the experimentation with alternatives.

Many of those more favorably disposed toward the family nevertheless find it a source of *dismay*. Individuals from sociologists Carle Zimmerman and Pitirim Sorokin to newspaper columnist Ann Landers observe with concern the practice of marriage at an early age, the high divorce rate, the prevalence of premarital sex, and the generation gap. An inference often drawn by such people is that the institution of the family is decaying and, with it, the nation. Among the pessimistic are those who feel that, far from being the *source* of discontent, the family is an unwitting victim of rapid social-cultural-technological change, having little control over its own destiny.

A large number of practitioners address themselves to the family as an object for *advice*. A few indicative book titles would include: *Making the Most of Marriage, Understanding Your Teenagers, Growing with Your Children, The Art of Dating,* and *The Macmillan Guide to Family Finance.* The advice directed at the modern family ranges from the advocacy of complete

---

[2] Margaret Mead, "The American Family," in Huston Smith, ed., *The Search for America* (Englewood Cliffs, N.J.: Prentice-Hall, 1959), p. 116.
[3] Frederick Engels, *The Origin of the Family, Private Property, and the State* (New York: International Publishers, 1942), p. 65.
[4] *Wisconsin State Journal,* November 17, 1967.

sexual freedom to a return to the family farm as the panacea for individual and family problems.

Preoccupation with the family is manifested in at least two other ways among Americans. Because one of the means by which men cope with strains and tensions is humor, the relations between family members are often handled in this fashion. *Jokes* about the mother-in-law and the hen-pecked husband are ubiquitous in the family humor of American society. Finally, in addition to being the object of criticism, dismay, advice, and humor, the family is currently the focus of serious and substantial efforts to describe and *understand* it. Research studies, and authors' interpretations of them, comprise a large segment of the literature on the contemporary family. Seeking to avoid any judgment as to the "goodness" or "badness" of the family in its contemporary form, the writers who present and interpret such studies attempt to report what the family is like and how it functions.

There are, therefore, several bodies of materials on the family which are available to the text writer. First, there are *factual materials,* drawn from empirical studies of various sorts. Sometimes their results reinforce each other, while at other times they appear to be contradictory. Second, there are *interpretations and explanations* of the facts. How, why, and to what extent has the family changed? What is the larger significance of the family's characteristics? How can the differences between research results be reconciled? Several of the best available sociological texts on the family assemble vast amounts of research findings but explicitly avoid taking interpretive positions on the open issues.[5] In fact, the scientific study of the family is currently long on data and short on interpretation and explanation. Third, there are *social criticisms or critiques* by such recent writers as Paul Goodman, Barrington Moore, and Edgar Friedenberg, as well as by Karl Marx and Sigmund Freud and their followers. Finally, there are abundant *suggestions* for family improvement and change which have been articulated by both professionals and nonprofessionals concerned about today's family.

The majority of twentieth century family texts have focused on either factual materials or suggestions, and have been called "sociological" and "functional" texts, respectively. The reasons for the dominance of these two approaches will become more apparent as we review the history of family study. We, however, have determined to emphasize *interpretation* instead, using suggestion and criticism quite selectively, and introducing those re-

---

[5] One of the very best empirically based but noninterpretive sociological texts on the family is Gerald Leslie, *The Family in Social Context* (New York: Oxford University Press, 1973 ed.). An exception is Bernard Farber's *Family: Organization and Interaction* (San Francisco: Chandler, 1964), in which the author posits two types of family systems and interprets data on the modern family according to these types.

search studies that seem most useful for understanding the contemporary family. These interpretations should not be accepted as final; you will find yourself agreeing with some and disagreeing with others. Their purpose is to get you to think *sociologically and interpretively* about the family in its historical and cross-cultural context.

Section One

THE HISTORY OF FAMILY STUDY

Systematic study of the family did not begin until after the middle of the nineteenth century. Until then, interest in the family had been expressed by means of folklore, proverbs, moralisms, and laws. The family's importance in the structure of society was affirmed in much of the early wisdom literature of China, India, and the preexilic Hebrews. The beginning of the movement toward systematic understanding of the family can be traced roughly to the appearance of Charles Darwin's *Origin of Species,* in 1859. The years from 1860 to the present may be profitably divided into three thirty-year periods and one twenty-five–year period, each characterized by a particular emphasis with respect to the family.[6]

1860–1890: Social Darwinism

From 1860 to 1890 numerous writers attempted to apply Darwin's biological evolutionary scheme to the course of human history. Discussions of origins, coupled with notions of evolution and progress, were found in the writings of Lewis Henry Morgan, Friedrich Engels, J. J. Bachofen, Edward Westermarck, and others. Did the family begin in a primitive horde? Was marriage originally by capture? How did monogamy arise, and what will be its fate? Such questions interested those influenced by Darwin's theories when they wrote about the family. Their treatises were macrocosmic, or large-scale, and cross-cultural, attempting to devise universally applicable laws of societal development. Their scholarly techniques were often intuitive, involving the somewhat unscientific approach of drawing a conclusion or developing a theory and then mustering evidence from diverse sources to support it. Yet, despite the inadequacy of some of their methods, the writings of the Darwinists aroused the kind of interest in family and kinship which eventually gave rise to efforts to empirically investigate families in relation to their societies.

---

[6] For a discussion of the history of family study that uses a somewhat different temporal framework, see Harold T. Christensen, ed., *Handbook of Marriage and the Family* (Chicago: Rand McNally, 1964), pp. 3–32.

During this period there were exceptions to the eclectic, large-scale approach to family analysis, a prime example being the work of Frédéric Le Play, a Frenchman. The methods he used to study the families of European workingmen foreshadowed later developments in the use of both the interview and participant observation in data collection. He lived in many workingmen's homes, and took notes on his observations as he participated in family activity. On this basis, Le Play distinguished three types of families in France. The "unstable," or nuclear, family consisted of husband, wife, and young children; in the "stem" family one married child stayed in the parental home; and the patriarchal family included the aging parents and their male—and sometimes their female—offspring and their spouses and children. Thus, Le Play can be viewed as a forerunner of later attempts at scientific study of the family.[7]

1890–1920: Social Reform

The second period, especially in America, was dominated by an urgent concern with social problems and reform. Industrialization and urbanization had resulted in a heightened awareness of poverty, child labor, illegitimacy, and other problematic or problem-producing aspects of family life. Furthermore, the "accepted" Victorian morality diverged in obvious ways from actual behavior. The Chicago school of sociology, with its journal, *The American Journal of Sociology,* founded in 1894, became a spokesman for reform. The school's underlying assumptions, not always expressed, were that "we understand both the family and the effects of urban and industrial developments; what we must do is solve the resulting problems and strengthen the family." However, the problem and reform orientation gave rise in the early 1900s to another viewpoint, to the effect that "maybe we don't know as much as we need to about the conditions and characteristics of the modern family." Some academics at institutions other than the University of Chicago, such as Ernest Groves at the University of North Carolina, were able to embody both the "reform" and the "research" orientations in their work. However, the new research orientation likewise had its focal point at Chicago.

1920–1950: Scientific Study

The thirty years from 1920 to 1950 are best characterized as the years of scientific study of the family. In the early years of this century, even while reform movements held sway, statistical techniques were being developed and

---

[7] Frédéric Le Play, *Les Ouvriers Européens* (Tours: Mame Libraire, 1855); and *L'Organisation de la Famille* (Paris: Dentu, 1870).

social psychologists such as W. I. Thomas and Charles H. Cooley were focusing on individual personality adjustment. Both Thomas and Cooley were influential at the University of Chicago, but it was under the leadership of Ernest Burgess that the study of the family became a major sociological endeavor. Burgess conceived of the family as a "unity of interacting personalities," as he stated in an article published in 1926; through Burgess and his students, the study of the family became more than speculations about origins or pleas for social improvement. With major researches on marital adjustment in the 1930s, '40s, and '50s, Burgess' various studies fostered efforts to understand the factors involved in choosing a mate in the United States, the forms of interaction between family members, divorce and breakup, the position of the aged, and so on. By 1950, and perhaps earlier, it was proper to speak of a body of scientific facts about the family.

1950–Present: Attention to Family Theory

Since 1950 research activity has continued to accelerate, but in addition there have been renewed efforts to interpret and explain the family and its forms and changes—attempts to go beyond mere description. Harold Christensen, in his *Handbook of Marriage and the Family*, designates these years as the period of systematic theory building.[8] This label, however, appears a bit presumptuous, at least for the decades prior to the 1970s. Instead, the twenty-five years from 1950 to 1975 might best be described as the period of summarization of findings, of conceptual frameworks, of complaint about the lack of a comprehensive theory, and—most recently—of substantial theorizing. It might, in fact, be instructive to view the 1960s as dominated by conceptual frameworks, and the 1970s as oriented toward codification and theory building. Currently, much comparative research, synthesizing, and reworking is being done so as to bring the sociology of the family into the mainstream of the sociological discipline. Men such as William J. Goode, Reuben Hill, Ira Reiss, F. Ivan Nye, Wesley Burr, and Bernard Farber are in the forefront of these activities.

Christensen reports seven dominant trends in family study from its beginning to the present: (1) There has been increasing acceptance of the scientific viewpoint. (2) The field has been increasingly respectable within sociology. (3) Increasing attention has been paid to personal adjustment within the family context—a result of Ernest Burgess' influence. (4) Substantive reports or empirical studies have been proliferating. (5) Organization programs concerned with the family have been developed. Of special importance in this connection is the National Council on Family Relations (NCFR), whose

---

[8] Christensen, *Handbook of Marriage and the Family*, pp. 3–32.

official publications are the *Journal of Marriage and the Family* and the *Family Life Coordinator*. (6) Research methodology has been increasingly refined. (7) Concern over theory building has been growing. This last trend Christensen uses to characterize the period from 1950 to the present.

Three of these trends require extended comment before we close our brief history of family study. The first two, acceptance of the scientific viewpoint and increasing respectability, are closely related. As we have said, the study of the family in the United States in the early years of the twentieth century was problem- and reform-oriented. Many professionals were involved: lawyers, doctors, psychologists, clergymen, and others were seeking to cope with the effects of urban life on the family. Gradually, the impact of scientific thinking resulted in a separation between the practitioners and the researchers, as a result of the consolidation of the practitioners, first into a subfield and then into the separate discipline of social work. Today there is a form of family course that is consistent with the approach of each of the major parties to this separation. First, there is the problem-oriented, or "how to," course, sometimes called the *functional* course. This type of course ordinarily uses a suggestion-centered textbook, is often taught through the home economics or social work department, and may explain how to rear well-adjusted children, how to plan and maintain a family budget, or the mechanics of an adequate sexual adjustment. The extreme *sociological* family course, oriented toward factual materials, may simply catalog the findings of sociological researchers, without espousing a particular stance with respect to family values and often with little interpretation of the facts.

Since sociology as a discipline seeks to be objective and scientific, perhaps you can see why Christensen's first two trends are closely linked. The more that students of the family have espoused a scientific orientation, the more respectable family study has become among sociologists in general, since they regard themselves as trying to be scientific. However, it must be added that, as long as practitioners of various sorts see the family as good and important, it is hardly likely that the problem orientation will ever be completely dominated by the scientific approach. The National Council on Family Relations well illustrates the dual orientation of family study up to the present. The NCFR's statement of purpose, printed on the inside front cover of the *Journal of Marriage and the Family,* reads as follows: "Its purpose is to advance the cultural values now principally secured through family relations for personality development and the strength of the nation. It seeks to unite in one common objective persons working in all the different fields of family research, teaching, and welfare." On the same page is a description of the *Journal* and its contents: "The *Journal of Marriage and the Family* is a medium for the presentation of original theory, research interpretation, and critical discussion of materials related to marriage and the family. The *Journal* does not assume any responsibility for the written content of articles." This is, of course, the typical disclaimer of media presenting fact and opinion. During the 1960s, the NCFR's division of labor resulted in its sponsorship of two journals—the aforementioned *Journal of Marriage and the Family*, which emphasizes scholarly work, and the *Family Life Coordinator*, which is more action-oriented.

The point is simply that, although the trend toward scientific study of the family has increased the respectability of the field, it is unlikely that the family, at least in the foreseeable future, will become strictly a subject of scientific investigation. Personal and societal values will continue to support a particular form of family system. The present volume seeks to avoid the numerous suggestions of the practitioner at one extreme and the stultifying effects of fact without interpretation at the other.

Let us now look at Christensen's seventh trend, theory building, which he uses to characterize the period since 1950. Granted that there has been great concern with understanding the family and its relation to man's social existence, it is nevertheless true that until the 1970s the theoretical inroads were limited. The previous decade began with Reuben Hill and Donald Hansen's paper on the five *conceptual frameworks*,[9] and for the next ten years the frameworks were added to, subtracted from, criticized, and used. These frameworks, said Hill and Hansen, are not theories or explanations, but are viewpoints from which to analyze and describe family structure and behavior. An analogy from the physical sciences might make clear what Hill and Hansen mean by a conceptual framework. Suppose a scientist were to begin studying the common earthworm. He might investigate (1) its chemical properties; (2) its internal structure; (3) its reaction to stimuli; (4) its relation to the phyla, orders, families, genera, and species of the animal kingdom; or (5) its position in both the organic and inorganic environment. Each of these five approaches would provide a *description* of the earthworm from one perspective—whether that of the biochemist, biologist, taxonomist, or animal ecologist. A theory, however, might *explain* how the earthworm acquired its characteristics or the nature of its significance within the animal kingdom. Conceptual frameworks, in short, are descriptive standpoints from which to view some portion of reality—they are not theories.

According to Hill and Hansen, five clearly definable frameworks are being utilized by students of the family. The *interactional* approach focuses on family members in intimate contact. Since it is concerned with the relation between the individual and the family group, it is a social psychological approach. Beginning especially in the work of Burgess, its emphases include psychological and interpersonal adjustment in the family, the roles that

---

[9] Reuben Hill and Donald A. Hansen, "The Identification of Conceptual Frameworks Utilized in Family Study," *Marriage and Family Living* 22 (1960), 299–311.

family members play, and the kinds of relationships that develop in a family setting.

The *structure-functional* framework, a second approach, is employed in the work of William J. Goode, Meyer Nimkoff, and Robert Winch. What different sorts of family structures are there? How does the family articulate with such other societal institutions as the economic, educational, and religious? What functions does the family perform on behalf of the individual or his society? This is an ahistorical approach which assumes that at any given point in time the various structures of a society tend to be coherent and consistent, and to perform specific functions. A problem with this approach is the "ideal-real," or normative-actual, fallacy, which will be referred to in Chapter 2.

The *developmental* framework is simply a technique for observing changes that occur, not in the society, but in the family life of the individual as he is born, grows up, marries, raises his family, and dies. The time span is the life cycle of any nuclear family, and the units of analysis are the stages—childhood, adolescence, marriage, adulthood, and old age—which can be demarcated within the life of an individual and his family. Most textbooks on the family utilize this framework at least to some extent, and ours will be no exception.[10]

Hill and Hansen's other two frameworks, the situational and the institutional, have been criticized and virtually dropped, as being special cases of the interactional and structure-functional approaches, respectively. The situational approach has to do with adaptation and problem-solving in the family unit, while the institutional approach—exemplified in John Sirjamaki's history of the American family—views the family-in-society as it changes historically.[11]

There is, then, nothing immutable about the conceptual frameworks identified by Hill and Hansen. Two of their frameworks have fallen into disuse, while additional frameworks, such as the economic, psychoanalytic, and anthropological, have been identified by other writers.[12] A result of these discussions was that by 1970 some scholars were convinced that we had moved beyond conceptual frameworks, that their identification had become relatively unimportant.[13] Others, however, such as Ivan Nye and the present writer, continue to feel that an awareness of such perspectives makes both

---

[10] For an example of a cross-cultural application of the developmental framework, see Kiyomi Morioka, "Life Cycle Patterns in Japan, China, and the United States," *Journal of Marriage and the Family* 29 (1967), 595–606.

[11] John Sirjamaki, *The American Family in the Twentieth Century* (Cambridge, Mass.: Harvard University Press, 1953).

[12] See F. Ivan Nye and Felix M. Berardo, *Emerging Conceptual Frameworks in Family Analysis* (New York: Macmillan, 1966).

[13] Carlfred B. Broderick, "Beyond the Five Conceptual Frameworks: A Decade of Development in Family Theory," *Journal of Marriage and the Family* 33 (1971), 139–59; and Wesley R. Burr, "Some Notes on Future Theorizing and Research" (paper delivered at the

the writer and his readers cognizant of the standpoint and biases from which the author is approaching his material.[14] Conceptual frameworks are not a sufficient basis for current theorizing, but are the stage setting or foundation on which theory building takes place. In the present volume, for example, the chapters on cross-cultural variations, family and society, and historical antecedents take an approach that is primarily structure-functional/institutional. Much of the material on the contemporary family, with its parental roles, husband-wife interaction, and crises, is concerned with adjustment—an interactional/situational issue. Finally, the bulk of the volume follows a developmental outline, beginning with early socialization of the child and carrying him through adolescence, mate selection, adulthood, and old age. This developmental viewpoint, Carlfred Broderick feels, will provide the basic framework for most future theorizing about the family.[15] The important thing to note, however, is that these are not theories of the family, but are simply viewpoints from which to try to describe reality.

Is this, then, as far as current developments in family study have taken us? No; the 1970s have seen the appearance and codification of several theories which have been applied to the family institution. Broderick, for example, in noting the current state of family theory, reports that *exchange* theory now has numerous advocates among students of the family. This theory, which is based on the economic terminology of profit-cost-reward-alternative, has been applied particularly to the husband-wife relationship and to divorce.[16] Even more important, however, than the actual theories extant in the 1970s are developments in the methodology of theorizing. In the hands of Wesley Burr and other scholars, these have already produced numerous insights—incorporated into the present volume—and seem likely to bear considerably more fruit in the years ahead.

The data on the family, Burr argues, are massive. Recently the methodological tools developed by Hans Zetterberg, Jerald Hage, and others have become available.[17] Thus, these data should be reworked using the newer tools. Basically the new methods involve deductive theory, with the following

---

Family Theory Workshop, National Council on Family Relations meetings, Portland, Oregon, October 1972).

[14] F. Ivan Nye, "Discussion of Burr's 'Some Notes on Future Theorizing and Research'" (paper delivered at the Family Theory Workshop, National Council on Family Relations meetings, Portland, Oregon, October 1972).

[15] Broderick, "Beyond the Five Conceptual Frameworks," p. 153.

[16] John Scanzoni, *Sexual Bargaining* (Englewood Cliffs, N.J.: Prentice-Hall, 1973); and George Levinger, "Marital Cohesiveness and Dissolution: An Integrative Review," *Journal of Marriage and the Family* 27 (1965), 19–28.

[17] Hans L. Zetterberg, *On Theory and Verification in Sociology* (Totawa, N.J.: Bedminster Press, 1965); and Jerald Hage, *Techniques and Problems of Theory Construction in Sociology* (New York: Wiley-Interscience, 1972).

components: variables are carefully defined and are combined into propositions which identify relationships. Since these are cause-and-effect relationships, explanation is logically deduced on the assumption of ceteris paribus, or other things being equal.[18] There is more to the relationships between variables, however, besides their existence. For example, says Burr,

> relationships can differ in *direction, shape,* and *amount of time* involved in them. In addition, there is one other characteristic of relationships that . . . has received very little attention elsewhere. This is variation in the *amount of influence* that occurs in relationships.[19]

This kind of theorizing, then, requires the development of propositions which are then linked together into a multivariate model,* positing the relations between many independent or causal variables and dependent variables, whether mate selection, marital satisfaction, or the family's reaction to stress. As in any area of social theory, the simpler theories of an earlier time become more complex, and Burr and Broderick agree that such "complexification" is both necessary and inevitable. Broderick puts it thus: "Family theory will increasingly have to deal with complex, multivariate models . . . and with the specification of richer typologies[*] of family structure and developmental sequences."[20] The key word is *specification,* as earlier propositions are qualified according to the conditions under which they are correct. For example, a simple proposition might be that people do not marry across racial lines. This, however, in the light of research might be specified or qualified to read: people do not tend to marry across racial lines, unless (a) racial distinctions are not salient or important to them, or (b) they have had frequent and equalitarian contacts with members of other races.

Burr believes, furthermore, that the reworking of existing theories and data is not the end of the theory building process. Rather, it is necessary at this stage in the development of family theory. The kind of deductive propositional model building which he and others have been attempting in the 1970s, he feels, "should be viewed as a process that occurs at one particular period in the history of a science, and much if not all . . . [of it] will subsequently be revised."[21]

The tentativeness of Burr's and Broderick's conclusions will, of course, not deter us from drawing upon them. It will, however, be well for the reader to keep in mind that the family field is still long on conceptual frameworks and short on definitive theory. A major purpose of the present vol-

[18] Wesley R. Burr, *Theory Construction and the Sociology of the Family* (New York: Wiley, 1973), p. 22.
[19] Burr, *Theory Construction and the Sociology of the Family,* pp. 10–11.
[20] Broderick, "Beyond the Five Conceptual Frameworks," p. 152.
[21] Burr, *Theory Construction and the Sociology of the Family,* p. 40.

ume, like that of Burr, is to supplement summaries of research results with explanation and interpretation. The setting for the interpretations includes the various types of family *structures* found around the world, the *functions* performed within family and kinship units, and the other internal aspects of *family culture.** Family systems—and families within the same system—vary in terms of their structures, including marital linkages, household members, and residential location vis-à-vis kin. The issue of family functions, or what the family does on behalf of the individual and of the society, has also been analyzed by scholars. Other aspects of family-kin culture include descent and inheritance, husband-wife authority and roles,* approaches to mate selection, and the cultural emphases in child rearing. While all of these are important in preparing the reader to understand the modern family, treatment of the family in the United States will focus upon the last three issues: husband-wife relations, mate selection, and child rearing.

Within the setting of the structural types, functions, and other internal culture, two basic concepts will be employed to help the reader understand the family against a historical and cross-cultural background. These concepts, *institutional embeddedness* and *personnel embeddedness,* mirror the two orientations of family and kinship: toward society and toward the individual. The first idea, that of institutional embeddedness, is well expressed by David Schneider:

> In many primitive and peasant societies a large number of kinds of institutions are organized and built *as parts of the kinship system itself.* Thus the major social units of the society may be kin groups—lineages perhaps. These same kin groups may be property-owning units, the political units, the religious units, and so on. Thus, whatever a man does in such a society he does as a kinsman of one kind or another.[22] (Italics added.)

In such societies, the other institutions are "embedded" in, or undifferentiated from, the kinship system, so that economic-productive, political, religious, medical, and other activities take place within, and as aspects of, the kinship organization of the society. Thus, the head of the kin line may also be the political ruler, performer of religious ritual, primary educator, and leader of the kin division of labor. A second form of institutional embeddedness is present if a "nuclear" unit (a set of parents and their children) is the seat of multiple societal activities, but is emancipated from the larger kin group. One of the key questions toward which this volume is directed concerns the extent to which other institutions have become differentiated from—are no longer embedded in—either the kin groups or the nuclear families of the contemporary United States.

---

[22] David M. Schneider, *American Kinship: A Cultural Account* (Englewood Cliffs, N.J.: Prentice-Hall, 1968), p. v.

Personnel embeddedness, or the relation of family and kin to the individual, is a second major focus of this book. There are societies in which individuals and nuclear families are embedded in and serve the needs of the kinship system. Personnel embeddedness involves interaction patterns, solidarity, and values. If, for example, a conflict between the wife and her mother-in-law is resolved by sending the wife away, this would seem to indicate that the husband-wife unit is of secondary importance to the kin group. In some societies the nuclear family unit has been little distinguished from other forms of kin solidarity or in terms of interaction. In these societies the major emphasis in child rearing is that one develop into a good kin-community member. There are actually two levels of personnel embeddedness: (1) the individual and the nuclear family are interactionally embedded in, and of secondary importance to, the kin community; or (2) the family unit of parents and children may be emancipated from kin dominance, but the individual may still be subservient to, and operate primarily within, the nuclear family. If the alternative to institutional embeddedness is institutional differentiation, the alternative to personnel embeddedness is individualism. Therefore, a second key question in the present volume involves the extent to which the individual is still embedded in the nuclear family, and the family within the kin group, in modern U.S. society.

This introduction of institutional and personnel embeddedness has been both brief and somewhat premature, for the understanding of these concepts requires a level of cross-cultural and definitional sophistication that the reader may not have yet attained. The author, however, feels it important to introduce these concepts early; they should become increasingly clear as the reader moves through the cross-cultural and historical materials of Chapters 2 through 5. Particularly in Chapter 5 will these and other theoretical issues in family study be confronted directly. It is the author's conviction that explanation and interpretation, however tentative, is preferable to simple fact gathering. The reader must judge the outcome for himself.

Section Two

STUDYING THE FAMILY

Studying the family in one's own society, it may be well to note, is different in one crucial way from the study of theoretical astrophysics, the classical background of English literature, or the use of path analysis in social research. This difference is due to the fact that most readers are familiar in their daily lives with, and thus to some extent experts on, the phenomenon we call "the family." This familiarity and expertise in family relations can be both a help and a hindrance to the sociological study of this institution. It is a help because a certain amount of understanding can be assumed.

When the reader sees the word *family,* he will think of two parents and one or more children whom they are rearing. Seeing the term *marriage,* he will think of two individuals of different sexes, legally joined together for the sake of sexual access, procreation, and the sharing of a common residence—though perhaps not in these terms. *Divorce* he will understand to be the legal separation of these two individuals. When *courtship* is mentioned, the sharing of time and activities with a member of the opposite sex will come to mind, perhaps in terms of dating or going steady.

Yet this very familiarity may likewise stand in the way of an attempt to step back and consider the family either objectively or in terms of generalizations. The majority of families in the United States may or may not closely resemble his own. However, even if the reader's family is rather typical, it is important to be aware of the tendency to feel that the way his own family does things is the only, or at least the best, way. It would be improper to condemn such feelings; it is quite proper to be aware of them. In order to gain some sense of perspective and objectivity, this discussion shall begin with some examples that illustrate the great diversity of family systems throughout the world.

A generation ago, Robert MacIver defined the family as "a sex relationship sufficiently precise and enduring to provide for the procreation and upbringing of children."[23] This definition, while descriptive of essential elements in the family, is inadequate for use in this volume. Our purpose is to interpret family experience within the context of contemporary society. This study will concern itself with the rearing of children, the adolescent experience, and premarital relations between the sexes, as well as with marriage itself. The subject is the modern family, its history and change over time, its relation to the society of which it is a part, its formation and dissolution, and its internal relationships. The foundation for this superstructure includes cross-cultural and historical variations in structure, functions, and internal culture. This setting or foundation is the focal point of the next four chapters, beginning in Chapter 2 with structural principles and types and certain other aspects of kin-family culture.

---

[23] Robert MacIver, *Society: Its Structure and Changes* (New York: Long & Smith, 1931), p. 112.

The different types of family structures which have existed in various societies, and the principles which underlie them, are almost innumerable. In this chapter the most important structural principles, and the types produced thereby, are introduced. These principles include marital and blood linkages and residential clustering. In addition, other factors useful for distinguishing family systems are introduced: descent and inheritance, family authority, and types of nuclear families. Special attention is given to three problems in family study: (1) the difference between norms or expectations and actual behavior in a family system; (2) types or typologies and their use; and (3) the incest taboo and its relation to social structure.

Family Structures and Varieties

Section One

FAMILY STRUCTURAL PRINCIPLES[1]

In United States society a young male and female decide to marry. His name is added to her maiden name, and they affirm that their marriage is for as long as they both shall live. If possible, they move into a dwelling separate from both sets of parents, and they begin to plan for the coming of children. Their parents and other kin are interested in them and help them when the need arises, but the young couple is generally expected to be independent, to go it alone. In an introductory textbook written in the Western world, the word *family* is likely to signify what we have just described. Technically, this

[1] For a parallel but somewhat divergent treatment of family structural variations, see Meyer F. Nimkoff, *Comparative Family Systems* (Boston: Houghton Mifflin, 1965), chap. 2. Perhaps the most insightful introduction to cross-cultural differences in family and kinship is Robin Fox's *Kinship and Marriage* (Baltimore: Penguin, 1967). Fox points out clearly how *unimportant* marriage is in many societies compared to various consanguineal kin linkages. In this chapter we have treated marriage as more central than it actually is cross-culturally, because most Western readers have grown up in a marriage-centered and nuclear family–centered system. The interested reader may, however, want to move on to a book such as Fox's.

unit, consisting of a male, a female, and their offspring, is called the *monogamous nuclear family,* and it is, of course, the prevalent and legalized form of family in the contemporary United States. Common residence, which is typical for this unit, facilitates the sexual access of the married couple, care for the offspring, and a familial division of labor. A distinction is made in everyday speech between this unit and one's kin; when an American says, "I want you to meet my family," he ordinarily means the unit of parents, brothers, and sisters, or else (if he is one of the parents) the unit consisting of his spouse and children.

This, then, is the type of family with which Americans are most familiar. Yet, when family structures are viewed cross-culturally, the variations from this pattern are seen to be enormous. These variations are based upon such structural issues as the number of persons of each sex who are allowed to marry; the expected household composition, including both marital units and blood kin; and the pattern of residential clustering of kin. An understanding of these structural principles, and of the types of kin-family systems produced by them, should give the reader a better sense of the U.S. family system as but one type among many. In addition, we shall try to make it clear that expectations and reality often diverge—that the way people expect to, desire to, and say they behave are not necessarily the same as the way they actually behave. The last point, while drawn in this chapter from cross-cultural illustrations, will be seen to be important when husband-wife decision-making, treatment of the aged, the position of the working wife, and other issues in the U.S. family are confronted.

Marriage Arrangements and Types

Marriage in the United States is monogamous, meaning that only one male and one female are allowed to be married to each other. Though it is quite natural for the individual without cross-cultural experience to assume that this is the way marriage "should" be, when marriage in the United States is compared with marriage in other times and places, monogamy is seen to be but one type among others. The other possibilities, all involving more than one member of one or both sexes, are together called by the term *polygamy,* or multiple marriage. The polygamous possibilities are three. Two or more females may be married to one male; the term *polygyny,* or "many wifes," refers to this. Or two or more males could be married to one female, in which case the term *polyandry,* or "many husbands," is used. Theoretically, two or more males might be married to two or more females, which would be *group marriage.* Therefore, polygyny + polyandry + group marriage = polygamy, as distinguished from monogamy.

The frequency with which these four types of marital arrangements occur normatively, that is, as expectations or desires, in various societies is interesting because of the light it sheds on man's sexual and economic nature. In a world sample of 554 societies, George P. Murdock finds polygyny to be normative in 415 of them, monogamy in 135, polyandry in 4, and group marriage in none.[2] A thesis proposed to account for the prevalence of polygyny is that men are generally governed by internal sex drives and are disposed toward sexual variety to a much greater extent than are women. If this is so, then men are subjected to a greater strain in monogamous marriages than women are.

Two cautions should be added regarding the prevalence of polygamous marriages. A distinction must be made between the normative marital arrangement in a society, or that dictated by its ideology, and the frequency with which specific arrangements occur empirically. In some societies, such as the United States, monogamy is required and multiple partners are prohibited. Yet in many, if not all, of the 415 societies in which polygyny is normative, monogamy predominates numerically. Suppose, for example, that in a normatively polygynous society each male married but two females. If the sex ratio (the number of males per 100 females in a population) of the society were approximately 100, half the males would have to remain unmarried. A partial solution to the statistical problem in some polygynous societies is that the man often marries late, and marries a girl considerably younger than himself. This means that, with a relatively short life-span, a larger proportion of men can marry polygynously. However, a result of this practice is that such societies also contain considerable numbers of widows. A large proportion of men could also be polygynously married if the sex ratio were extremely low or if large numbers of males were killed in warfare. These, however, are infrequent occurrences, and the result is that most males are married to more than one female in only a few polygynous societies.[3] It is well to note at this juncture that some of the early anthropologists who visited exotic places and asked informants how things were done there came away with the normative rather than the actual structural arrangements. The resultant difference is comparable to that between the impression a visitor from Mars would receive if he accepted our account of what families are like in the United States, and his impression if he went into our houses to observe those living there. We shall return again to this normative-actual distinction.

---

[2] George Peter Murdock, "World Ethnographic Sample," *American Anthropologist* 59 (1957), 686.

[3] On the prevalence of polygyny in normatively polygynous societies, see Vernon Dorjahn, "The Factor of Polygyny in African Demography," in William R. Bascom and Melville J. Herskovits, eds., *Continuity and Change in African Culture* (Chicago: University of Chicago Press, 1959), pp. 88–112.

There is more than a logical-statistical reason why monogamy predominates in many societies that ideologically favor polygyny. Most men in a polygynous society are simply too poor to afford more than one wife. The important or high-ranking male takes additional wives to validate his superior status and to aid him in the care of the fields, the raising of cows, or other economic ventures. He must, however, be able to afford the bride-price, the cost of purchasing her from her parents. In such societies, wives are considered economic and status assets if they can be afforded, with sexual access being a secondary motivation for polygyny, if it is a motive at all. Polygyny is normative, therefore, for what it signifies, but it is far from behaviorally dominant in the 415 societies that accept it.

Household Arrangements

In the United States, a couple, following marriage, may live for a time with the parents of one of them. This arrangement is usually temporary, for the desires and expectations of the pair are ordinarily for housing apart from all other kin. The nuclear family is not, however, the normative household unit in all societies. On the contrary, the number of nuclear units may be compounded, as indicated above, by the addition of marital partners and their children in the various forms of polygamy. The household may also be compounded by the addition of other blood (consanguineal) kin. Perhaps the two best-known examples of consanguineal household extension are the three-generation extended family and the joint family. These may be compared with the monogamous nuclear family by means of Figure 1.

Figure 1
Three Types of Household Arrangements Based on Consanguineal Ties

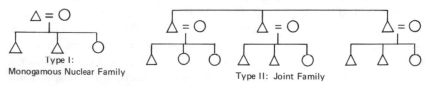

Type I:
Monogamous Nuclear Family

Type II: Joint Family

SYMBOLS
△ : male
○ : female
= : marriage
⌐⊥ : children

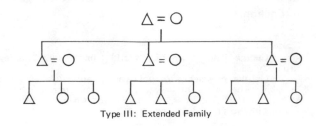

Type III: Extended Family

Each of the three parts of Figure 1 depicts a household type based on blood ties. Type I is, of course, the typical household in the United States, consisting of a parent of each sex and their children. Type II shows a joint family composed of three brothers, their wives, and their children. The best-known example of such a family pattern is the traditional Hindu family of India. Type III depicts the extended, or three-generation extended, family. Here the aging parents live with their sons and the sons' wives and children. Classical China is frequently used as an example of a society in which the extended household pattern was prevalent.

Once again, two qualifications should be added to the delineation of normative household arrangements according to consanguineal ties. First, it will be noted that both the extended and the joint family were diagramed with the brothers living together and their sisters presumably having married into other such units and having left home. There is no logical reason why the diagram should not have shown sisters living together with their husbands and children, with their brothers having married and moved out. The only reason for depicting these consanguineal arrangements as we have is a statistical one: the pattern in which brothers live together after marriage is normative in a larger number of societies than is that in which sisters live together.

Second, the important distinction between norms or expectations and actuality or behavioral variety can be profitably reinforced in this connection. In classical China, the ideal in the upper echelons of society was for the aged patriarch to keep his family together and continue to wield authority over them as long as he lived. As in the case of normative polygyny, however, extended-family households were in the minority. Historical data indicate that in reality the great majority of pre-Communist Chinese households were rather small, averaging about five persons. The family ideology, especially among the literati, and actual family patterns are again found to be divergent.

A study of an Arab village, reported by Henry Rosenfeld, may illustrate and help to explain the great disparity between normative and actual family structures. Upon entering this community, the researcher asked what sort of family system they had. The uniform response was that they were an extended-family village. Then, rather than stop with the verbal expression of norms, he went from door to door to see the household composition himself. Here is what he found:

17 complete extended families, consisting of grandparents, their sons, and the sons' wives and children;
27 partial extended families, one or more brothers having left;
15 joint families with the grandparents deceased;

11 unmarried brothers living alone or with their mothers, their fathers being deceased;

205 nuclear family households, consisting of a male, a female, and their children.

Are the 205 nuclear families unhappy and longing for the norm or cultural ideal? The answer is simply no. If anything, the tendency is for more of those involved in extended or joint households to desire the nuclear arrangement than vice versa.

What, then, keeps some of the extended and joint families together? The religiocultural norm of filial piety or obligation to parents is still quite strong and influential. However, the primary reasons for the continuation of extended and joint households appear to be economic. Extended, partial extended, and joint families are most prevalent under two opposing conditions. First, if the family is economically *prosperous*, the aging father may attempt to keep his family together for reasons of prestige and authority and for reasons of economy—to help him do the work. The male offspring, on their part, may be willing to accept this subordinate position during the father's lifetime for the sake of the inheritance that will eventually come their way. At the other extreme, the *poor* are likely to stay together out of economic necessity. They must pool their resources in order to survive. Unquestionably, the overall movement in the village is toward more nuclear households, though the people, when asked, will still express the traditional extended-family ideology.[4]

It is necessary, we are suggesting, to examine not only the cultural ideal but also the variations and the direction of change when studying the family system of a given society. The fact is that different ideals may even be operating within the same culture. Some of Rosenfeld's villagers desire, for very good reasons, to preserve the traditional extended-family household and economic unit, while others, for what they consider to be equally good reasons, prefer the monogamous nuclear family. When we turn to the family in the United States, we shall once again see multiple normative principles at work, and we will be concerned to discover the direction and speed of change.

The monogamous nuclear family, polygamous marriage, and the composite consanguineal unit—these are three basic structural distinctions among marriage-family-household types. One further word regarding these distinctions is instructive. Meyer Nimkoff, as well as several other writers, in making the same general threefold distinction (see note 1), simply uses the term *nuclear family* to refer to the monogamous nuclear family. Our purpose in

---

[4] Henry Rosenfeld, "Process of Structural Change Within the Arab Village Extended Family," *American Anthropologist* 60 (1958), 1127–39.

adding the word *monogamous* is to indicate that there are nuclear units within each of the structural types. The monogamous nuclear family has but one nuclear unit, consisting of two parents and their children. In a polygynous family, a man who has three wives is simultaneously a member of three nuclear units, each consisting of himself, a wife, and their children. Likewise, in a composite consanguineal household, multiple nuclear units live under the same roof. The classical Chinese ideal, for example, might comprise four nuclear units: the grandparents and their sons being one nuclear family, and each of the sons and his wife and children being another. Thus, if the term *nuclear family* is used to describe the first structural type, that type is not mutually exclusive from the two composite types. But the addition of the marital designation *monogamous* makes the three structural categories mutually exclusive.

Residential Clustering and Location

Besides the typical marital linkages and household units described above, other structural principles differentiate family-kinship systems. One pertains to residential clustering from the perspective of the nuclear family. When a man and woman marry, they may be expected to locate with or near his kin, her kin, both sets of kin, neither set of kin—or they may spend part of their married life near his kin and part near hers. Among the possible arrangements, the ones that occur most frequently may be reduced to five. The single most prevalent residence pattern cross-culturally is that closely related to Figure 1: settling with or near the husband's parents following marriage, a practice that is called patrilocality. Other common patterns include matrilocality, living near the parents and kin of the wife, and neolocality, settling apart from both sets of parents. The last is the normative pattern in the contemporary United States. Some young couples in the United States may live for a time with one set of parents or the other, but this is usually out of necessity; the ideal, or desired, arrangement is a separate, or neolocal, residence not governed by the location of either set of kin. Two other patterns occur in enough societies to be worthy of mention. In one of them, called "bilocality" by Murdock, the newly married couple may choose whether to reside near the husband's or the wife's parents. Avunculocal residence, the fifth pattern, signifies that the young couple is expected to live with or near the husband's mother's brother (the husband's maternal uncle).[5]

Other aspects of residential clustering involve, not the location of the nuclear family, but of persons, such as aging parents, single adults, and so

---

[5] Murdock, *Social Structure* (New York: Macmillan, 1949), pp. 15–17

on. The major issue here is the way in which the nuclear family is related structurally to household and kin clusters.

Section Two

SELECTED CULTURAL DISTINCTIONS AND THE USE OF TYPES

Thus far we have introduced the marital, consanguineal, and residential clustering principles that help to shape the various family-kin structures. These principles, and the types of structures produced thereby, give us some sense of the U.S. family within the larger context of societal variations. At this point we shall turn to some additional cultural distinctions that are useful in defining the setting and background of the U.S. family. Rules of descent and inheritance, family authority, and types of nuclear families will be discussed.

Descent and Inheritance

Descent and inheritance are closely related, but not synonymous. Descent has to do with the formal manner in which the individual is related to his kin. Inheritance involves the property, goods, and obligations that are passed along through specified kin. The three most prevalent types of descent groupings are patrilineal, matrilineal, and bilateral. Patrilineal descent is traced through the male line; matrilineal descent is traced through the female line. Bilaterality signifies normative equality in affiliation with both the mother's and the father's kin, although in actuality kin ties in a bilateral system tend to be overbalanced in favor of the preferred kin.[6] Inheritance follows the same types of patterns, but is generally more complex than the determination of descent because multiple items tend to be inherited, as we shall see below. The U.S. family is basically bilateral in descent; that is, we trace descent through, and consider ourselves equally related to, both parental kin groups. Only in the practice of adding the husband's family name to the wife's at marriage, does the U.S. family retain a vestige of patrilineal inheritance.

Although descent lines tend to be relatively clear-cut, neither descent nor inheritance ordinarily operates in either-or terms. Patrilineal descent does not mean that an individual is related to his father's male kin to the exclusion of interaction, obligation, and intimacy with his mother's kin. In fact, intimacy in a patrilineal society is often greater between an individual and his maternal kin simply because there are "no strings attached." In the

---

[6] Murdock, *Social Structure*, pp. 15–17.

case of inheritance, even more than in the case of descent, involvement with the two kin groups tends to be a matter of degree or kind rather than of exclusiveness. For example, J. B. Christensen reports that, among the Fanti of West Africa, along with membership in a matrilineal clan (matrilineal descent) goes the right of property inheritance, the use of clan land, succession to a position of political authority, and a proper funeral and burial. Thus, the Fanti might easily be considered a matrilineal society. Yet the father's line among the Fanti is also a source of certain types of inheritance. From the patriline, the individual receives his military allegiance, his father's deity, and his soul; physically, he regards his father as the primary source of his blood. Christensen concludes that the Fanti are, in fact, characterized by double descent (from our perspective—"double inheritance"), receiving certain benefits and obligations from each of the two kin lines.[7] While inheritance is not always as equally divided as it is among the Fanti, many unilineal, that is, either patrilineal or matrilineal, systems are characterized by a secondary inheritance and by close relationships with members of the opposing kin group or line.

If an offspring desires to inherit property when a parent dies, he may be obliged to help care for that property while the parent is alive. For this and other socioeconomic reasons, it is not surprising that a fairly high correlation exists between residential clustering and descent-inheritance patterns: patrilocality with patrilineality, matrilocality with matrilineality, and neolocality with bilaterality. These correlations are, however, far from perfect. Under certain conditions, for example, matrilocal residence may occur in combination with bilateral or patrilineal descent rather than with matrilineal descent. In order to understand the bases for the relation between residential clustering and descent-inheritance in a particular society, one must understand the overall societal configuration—not just the kinship system, economy, polity, religion, or geography. Our discussion of the Nayar, Papago, and Chinese family systems in Chapter 3 should make apparent both the viability of and strains in systems very different from that of the United States.

Authority

Authority, status, and decision-making patterns in the family and kin group may be profitably divided into three ideal types. The most familiar pattern historically and cross-culturally is patriarchy, or father rule. A matriarchal society is one in which the mother makes the decisions and wields the authority in the family. Equalitarianism signifies approximate similarity between the

---

[7] James Boyd Christensen, *Double Descent Among the Fanti* (New Haven, Conn.: Human Relations Area Files, 1954).

husband and wife in status, in authority or control, and in decision-making. In this pattern, equality in the last area is effected either by coming to an agreement or by dividing areas of influence. In unilineal descent systems a single aged individual in each kin unit usually wields great authority, with varying amounts of inequality between husbands and wives within the various nuclear families. One important effect of the nuclear family's emancipation from the larger kin group, or its freedom from personnel embeddedness, is that, at first, the authority of the husband tends to be heightened. Thus, it is under a system of nuclear family centrality—both institutionally and in terms of personnel—that normative patriarchy within the nuclear family appears to reach its zenith. Among the topics that will engage us throughout this volume are the extent to which the typical American family has changed from a patriarchal to an equalitarian authority pattern and the relative prevalence of the patriarchal and equalitarian patterns in different segments of the U.S. population.

Types of Nuclear Families

The diagrammatic presentation of the patrilineal extended family in Figure 1 shows that, within this household type, the adult son is simultaneously a member of two nuclear families. One of these comprises his parents and brothers (as well as any sisters who may have married and moved away), and the other consists of his wife and their children. Several years ago W. Lloyd Warner made a valuable terminological distinction between these two types of nuclear families. Referring to Warner's distinction, Murdock asserts, "Every normal adult in every human society belongs to at least two nuclear families —a family of *orientation*, in which he was born and reared, and which includes his father, mother, brothers, and sisters, and a family of *procreation* which he establishes by his marriage and which includes his" spouse and their children.[8] Whether the members of a nuclear unit are living together or apart is irrelevant to the definition. The sisters who have married and left home (and are therefore omitted from Figure 1) are still members of the adult son's family of orientation, although the residential component may be clarified by the use of the term *kin of orientation* to indicate a nondomestic unit. The neolocal U.S. pattern means that the adult ordinarily lives with his family of procreation and apart from his family (kin) of orientation.

The Use of Types

Types of family structures based on marriage, consanguineal ties, and residential clustering have been introduced, as have descent-inheritance links,

---

[8] Murdock, *Social Structure*, p. 13.

The family systems of the Nayar of South India, the Papago Indians of southern Arizona and northern Mexico, and the Chinese of pre-Communist China are discussed and interpreted. The discussion centers on lengthy quotations from Kathleen Gough, Ruth Underhill, and Maurice Freedman. Three problems in family study are highlighted by these three examples: (1) the universality of the nuclear family; (2) the popular question, "How could such a system work?" and (3) the use of historical sources.

Family Varieties Exemplified: Nayar, Papago, Chinese

The great variety of family structural possibilities is apparent from the structural and cultural principles discussed in the previous chapter. Family-kin systems do not, however, exist in isolation, but in complex relations with the societies in which they function. These variations and complexities may come alive for the reader as he confronts specific examples of social systems different from his own.

The family systems of three societies are described at length in the pages that follow. The societies are those of the Nayar, the Papago, and the Chinese. The Nayar are one of several subcastes living in Kerala State, South India, and are sometimes characterized as traditionally practicing group marriage, but more often as polyandrous. The arid region of southern Arizona and northern Mexico is the rather inhospitable home of the Papago Indians, a society which at the turn of the twentieth century was normatively polygynous. Chinese civilization is an ancient and proud one, traditionally viewed as patrilineal and patriarchal in family structure. None of the three societies has escaped change in recent centuries, but in a consideration of their "classic," or traditional, organization, we may gain insight not only into their ways but into several crucial questions in family study.

Whether or not marriage and the family are universal depends upon how one defines the terms. The Nayar are an exceptionally valuable case study, around whom discussion of the family's universality has revolved. A second question, especially troublesome for the beginning student of the family, is, "How could such a system possibly work?" The questioner may be referring to arranged marriage, exogamy, polygyny, or any other pattern that differs greatly from his own. But regardless of the specific aspect which intrigues him, he is likely to see it as at least strange, if not unworkable. In describing the relations of the groom and the family of the bride-to-be in two societies, Leo Rosten, in Feature 1, expresses both the strangeness and the fascination which differing family customs hold for the outside observer. The Papago Indians illustrate arranged, polygynous, village exogamy (marriage outside one's home village), and may aid the reader in perceiving how such a system can "make sense" to the people who practice it. The material on the Chinese family once again points up the ideal-actual distinction, but the reasons for its inclusion in this chapter are both to indicate the problems encountered in using historical materials and to illustrate the distinction between *nuclear family* institutional and personnel embeddedness (in the Chinese) and *kin* embeddedness (in the Papago).

Section One

THE NAYAR OF SOUTH INDIA

The nuclear family of father, mother, and their children has been considered by Murdock and others to be virtually universal in human societies, being found without or within the composite marital and consanguineal structures

---

FEATURE 1

Grooms: Two Ploys. 1. In the back-country of Pakistan a young groom-to-be must appear before his future in-laws—who roundly revile, berate, and insult him. Why? Because if the groom can take expert abuse he is thought ready to enter holy matrimony—hardy enough, that is, to take whatever billingsgate his beloved may hurl at him sometime or other in the connubial years ahead.

2. But in Bosnia and Herzegovina, prospective grooms are lavishly dined and tanked up by the bride-to-be's family. The gal's parents, however, never say a word ("Yes," "No," "Agreed," or "Never!") to the anxious suitor.

How, then, does the palpitating lad know what the family verdict is? Most clearly: After the feast and palaver about dowries-shmowries, coffee is served. If the coffee is sweet, the young man has been voted okay for the marital match. But if the coffee is bitter, the guy realizes he has been given the heave-ho.

I am greatly relieved that this custom never reached our fair shores. Judging from the coffee I have been served in otherwise civilized homes, American swains would be in a hell of a muddle.

Leo Rosten, "Customs à la Mode," *Saturday Review–World*, April 6, 1974, 37.

referred to in Chapter 2. However, at least one prime example of a family system without the father as a continuing member has been found, namely, the Nayar of the Malabar coast of India, prior to British rule (before 1792). The best-known research on the Nayar is that of E. Kathleen Gough; much of the ensuing discussion is drawn from her writings.[1] (The use of the past tense indicates that the practices being described have long since been substantially altered.)

The Nayar were matrilineal and matrilocal. Between the ages of seven and twelve, or prior to puberty, Nayar girls were ritually married to a male of the appropriate subcaste. After four days of celebration, during which defloration of the bride by the ritual husband was permitted, the husband left the house and had no further obligation to his bride.

A bride in turn had only one further obligation to her ritual husband: at his death, she and all her children, by whatever physiological father, must observe death-pollution for him. Death-pollution was otherwise observed only for matrilineal kin.

After the ritual marriage, the bridegroom need have no further contact with his ritual wife. If both parties were willing, however, he might enter into a sexual relationship with his ritual bride about the time of her puberty. But he had no priority over other men of the neighborhood group. . . . There appears to be no limit to the number of wives of appropriate sub-caste whom a Nayar might visit concurrently. It seems, therefore, that a woman customarily had a small but fixed number of husbands from within her neighborhood, that relationships with these men might be of long standing, but that the woman was also free to receive casual visitors of appropriate sub-caste who passed through her neighborhood in the course of military operations.

A husband visited his wife after supper at night and left before breakfast next morning. He placed his weapons at the door of his wife's room, and if others came later they were free to sleep on the verandah of the woman's house. Either party to a union might terminate it at any time without formality. A passing guest recompensed a woman with a small cash gift at each visit. But a more regular husband from within the neighborhood had certain customary obligations. At the start of the union, it was common although not essential for him to present the woman with a cloth of the kind worn as a skirt. Later he was expected to make small personal gifts to her at the three main festivals of the year. These gifts included a loin-cloth, betel-leaves and arecanuts for chewing, hair-oil and bathing-oil, and certain vegetables. Failure on the part of a husband to make such a gift was a tacit sign that he had

---

[1] E. Kathleen Gough, "The Nayars and the Definition of Marriage," *Journal of the Royal Anthropological Institute* 89 (1959), part 1; reprinted in Norman W. Bell and Ezra F. Vogel, eds., *The Family* (New York: Free Press, 1960), pp. 76–92. See also Gough, "Female Initiation Rites in the Malabar Coast," *Journal of the Royal Anthropological Institute* 85 (1955), 45–80; and Gough, "A Comparison of Incest Prohibitions and Rules of Exogamy in Three Matrilineal Groups of the Malabar Coast," *International Archives of Ethnography* 46 (1952), 82–105.

ended the relationship. Most important, when a woman became pregnant, it was essential for one or more men of appropriate sub-caste to acknowledge probable paternity. This they did by providing a fee of a cloth and some vegetables to the low-caste midwife who attended the woman in childbirth. If no man of suitable caste would consent to make this gift, it was assumed that the woman had had relations with a man of lower caste or with a Christian or a Muslim. She must then be either expelled from her lineage and caste or killed by her matrilineal kinsmen. I am uncertain of the precise fate of the child in such a case, but there is no doubt that he could not be accepted as a member of his lineage and caste.

Although he made regular gifts to her at festivals, in no sense of the term did a man maintain his wife. Her food and regular clothing she obtained from her matrilineal group.

In these circumstances, the exact physiological fatherhood of a child was often uncertain, although, of course, paternity was presumed to lie with the man or men who had paid the delivery expenses. But even when physiological paternity was known with reasonable certainty, the genitor had no economic, social, legal or ritual rights in, nor obligations to, his children after he had once paid the fees of their births. Their guardianship, care and discipline were entirely the concern of their matrilineal kinsfolk headed by their *karanavan* [or the oldest male of the group]. . . .

All the children of a woman called all her current husbands by the Sanskrit word *acchan*, meaning "lord." They did not extend kinship terms at all to the matrilineal kin of these men. Neither the wife nor her children observed pollution at the death of a visiting husband who was not also the ritual husband of the wife.[2]

The rationale for the Nayar system, so far as it pertained to the men, was that they were employed as mercenary troops, often being absent from their village in wars against neighboring kingdoms. The family system, of which they were not expected to be permanent members, meant that their loyalties were not divided between family and military service. The women held land as tenants for a raja or other landlord, to whom they paid rent. The land passed from a mother to her female children; this matrilineage was buttressed by the absence of the males, which prevented them from laying claim to their wives' goods. Whether the Nayar system is called "group marriage," since several males and several females appear to have had sexual access to each other simultaneously, or "polyandry," since the women were the permanent residents and entertained several husbands, is relatively unimportant. However, of crucial importance is the absence of the male as a permanent family member, in conjunction with the necessity of having some

---

[2] Gough, "The Nayars and the Definition of Marriage," in Bell and Vogel, *The Family*, p. 80.

male assume legal paternity in order to legitimate the child. This last point—legal paternity—deserves some elaboration. The term *father* may have any of three connotations. It can mean the physiological progenitor of the child, the legal father, or legitimator, of the child, or the socializer of the child—the person with specific responsibilities for passing along family culture. In the case of the Nayar, fatherhood is restricted to legitimation, with no implication of duty as a socializing agent and little direct connection with biological parenthood. There are other societies in which the physiological and social concepts of fatherhood are separated, with the category "father" being more social than physiological.[3]

Is the Family Universal?

The answer to this question must, of course, rest upon one's definition of "marriage" and "family." The *Notes and Queries* definition of marriage, published in 1951, states that "marriage is a union between a man and a woman such that children born to the woman are recognized legitimate offspring of both parents."[4] It can be seen that the family form this definition assumes is the nuclear family, as it was defined earlier. The Nayar are often cited as an exception to the rule that nuclear marriage and the nuclear family are universal, or are found in every human society. We emphasized in preceding pages that coresidence in marriage is normative, facilitating sexual access, child care, and economic cooperation. The Nayar do not fit this pattern. Nor, as Ira Reiss and others have pointed out, do the Israeli kibbutzim, the matrifocal families of Jamaica, or certain other systems.

When it is claimed that the nuclear family is not universal, is this the same as saying that the family is not universal? The responses of Gough and Reiss to this question are negative. The problem is that, for cross-cultural purposes, the nuclear family cannot be thought of as synonymous with "family." Therefore, Gough suggests that marriage be defined as follows: "Marriage is a relationship established between a woman and one or more other persons, which provides that a child born to the woman under circumstances not prohibited by the rules of the relationship, is accorded full birth-status rights common to normal members of his society or social stratum."[5] For her, then, the key is not the idea of mating and common residence, but the legitimation of offspring.

---

[3] Gough, "The Nayars and the Definition of Marriage," in Bell and Vogel, *The Family*, pp. 81–83.

[4] *Notes and Queries on Anthropology*, 6th ed. (London: Routledge and Kegan Paul, 1951), p. 24.

[5] Gough, "The Nayars and the Definition of Marriage," in Bell and Vogel, *The Family*, p. 90.

Reiss notes that Murdock postulated the nuclear family—functioning for socialization, reproduction, economic cooperation, and sex relations—as universal. Citing evidence, Reiss states that in some societies the family system does not perform these four tasks. He then posits this definition of the family: "The family institution is a small kinship structured group with the key function of nurturant socialization of the newborn."[6] Gough and Reiss, in short, are saying that, cross-culturally, marriage should be viewed as an institutionalized means of legitimating offspring, while the family is the institutionalized means of raising them.

While these definitions provide valuable insights (we shall return in Chapter 5 to the issue of family functions), their principal effect is to relocate the argument regarding the universality of the family away from the nuclear unit. The difficulty with this relocation is that the posing of definitions of "family" which might be universally valid has no logical limit. One might claim that the family is "a unit involving two or more persons who share an intimate sexual relationship and a common residence," but in so doing one would be including even the homosexual liaison. Thus, in 1971 Andrew Weigert and Darwin Thomas again tackled the issue of defining the family. Viewing the family as a "conditional universe," they concluded that its minimum necessary structure is "self-plus-infant," a unit which, obviously, can take many forms. We must not, they asserted, base a universal concept like "family" on posited biological or social links which may be broken by culture or technology. Neither marriage nor parturition (childbirth) are the ultimate dyadic links which perpetuate society; rather, it is perpetuated by any individual plus a growing infant.[7]

The point of all this is simply that one's decision regarding the universality of the family may easily become a function of how he personally defines it, with the debate becoming endless. Of greater value, it would seem, is the question of whether or not the *nuclear* family is universal, since the addition of this restriction provides a common denominator for discussion. Cross-cultural indications are that such a unit is not a universal phenomenon, though it is of central importance in a book that focuses primarily upon the family in the modern industrial world. Furthermore, as Weigert and Thomas note, the proper task is empirical: to document and analyze the types of families that exist throughout the world and not to be overly concerned with the issue of whether or not the family per se exists in a given society.[8]

---

[6] Ira L. Reiss, "The Universality of the Family: A Conceptual Analysis," *Journal of Marriage and the Family* 27 (1965), 449.

[7] Andrew J. Weigert and Darwin L. Thomas, "Family as a Conditional Universe," *Journal of Marriage and the Family* 33 (1971), 188–94.

[8] Weigert and Thomas, "Family as a Conditional Universe," pp. 188–94.

Section Two

PAPAGO FAMILY AND KINSHIP

The Papago Indians of southern Arizona and northern Mexico present a noticeable contrast to both the Nayar and the U.S. family in the centrality of their kinship organization and in the extent of both institutional and personnel embeddedness in the kinship system. Until the early 1900s, they were rarely disturbed by Spaniards or by whites from the United States. Their location was the semidesert region spanning the Rio Grande, land that none of the invaders seemed to want. The raising of crops on scant rainfall had resulted in close and cooperative relations among the Papago. For three or four summer months each year, the Papago lived in small thatched-roof villages of about two hundred, raising corn, beans, and squash. The other eight months or so they scattered to the isolated mountain springs to hunt.[9]

A Papago village consisted almost entirely of kin. In conversation, cousins were designated by the same terms as one's brothers and sisters, although a terminological distinction between cousins and siblings could be made if necessary. The father, besides being economic head of his family, and co-owner with his lineage, was also teacher and governor. The village council, composed of the adult males, was about all the government the Papago had, there being no higher-level tribal government. The council met only in the summer, when the village was occupied; leadership was more religio-ritualistic than political or jural. From time to time a person who misbehaved might be ostracized or cast out of a village, the result of which would be either his death in the wilds or his adoption by another village. Ordinarily, however, the council's function was to symbolize community solidarity.

Marriage was exogamous in terms of one's own village, being arranged by kin units of neighboring villages. Almost before any sexual urge arose in the child, his parents would make an appropriate pairing. What developed between couple members after marriage was loyalty, rather than what we would call romantic love.

At marriage the girl often showed fright, and perhaps she even ran away during the ceremony. It was her mother's responsibility to bring her back if she took flight. One reason for the girl's fear—whether real, ritualized, or both—was that, during most of the twenty-four hours of a day, males and females were separate. The sexes tended to remain apart not only in the division of labor, but even for conversation in the evenings. Thus, the girl's contact with males, including her father, had been infrequent, often fleeting,

---

[9] Ruth M. Underhill, "The Papago Family," in Meyer F. Nimkoff, ed., *Comparative Family Systems* (Boston: Houghton Mifflin, 1965), p. 149.

and authoritarian. Now, however, she was to be sexually intimate with a male. Even more important, she knew that her marriage meant moving from her own kin village to one consisting of strangers and a few former members of her village of birth.

Polygyny was the preferred marriage form among the Papago. How, we might ask, could this work without jealousy and constant friction between wives of the same husband? For the Papago it was relatively simple. First, as we have said, the wife married into a village other than her own, and was a stranger there. Second, the marriage was arranged, making problematic the romantic feelings which would be likely to give rise to feelings of jealousy. Third, and most important, polygyny among the Papago was most often "sororal," that is, sisters married the same man. Would this not, however, intensify rather than mitigate feelings of jealousy? Underhill responds to this question with the following quotation from a Papago woman: "After you have slept on the same mat with your sister for ten or twelve years, of course you are glad to have her come to your new home."[10] Sisters actually appeared to get along well as cowives—a sign that the nuclear family was quite embedded in, or overshadowed by, the kin system. As might be expected from our earlier discussion, the majority of Papago males had only one wife, but, due to village exogamy and the clear division of activity between the sexes, the normative practice of polygyny seemed to work satisfactorily when it did occur.

Virtually the entire organization of Papago society was kin-based at the village level. Child rearing was strict, separation between the sexes extensive, and cooperation among kin imperative for survival. This reference to cooperation should not be interpreted to mean that the Papago were friendly to everyone. During the course of the year the marauding Apache would steal their animals and generally pester the Papago. Therefore, about once a year the Papago organized a raid in which they burned a few Apache huts as a reminder of who controlled the area. Maintaining the regional balance of power was as necessary for survival as was cooperation.

The Workability and Value of Normative Practices

We have shown that sororal polygyny seems to have worked fairly well among the Papago. Is the point of our discussion, you might ask, the acentric notion that one way of organizing a society and its family system is as satisfactory to its members as another, provided that the arrangement is normative or expected? This would be an incorrect interpretation of the Papago example, and of material on normative arrangements in general.

---

[10] Underhill, "The Papago Family," in Nimkoff, *Comparative Family Systems*, p. 152.

William Stephens, writing about a number of polygynous societies, states that there is often jealously among polygynous wives. "In most known cases at least some co-wives seem to suffer rather intensely from jealousy, and a good many of the polygynous families are strife-torn."[11]

Stephens' comment indicates that the distinction between workability-acceptance and value-satisfaction should be kept in mind. It might be said that any system that is accepted as normative by a particular people is workable, whether it is polygyny, head-hunting, or the extended family. This is not, however, the same as saying that everyone who accepts a particular system as normative, or "the-way-things-are-supposed-to-be," is consequently happy and satisfied with it and his position in it. Nor is it the same as saying that one system makes for about as many problems as another. The discontent fostered by a given arrangement is one of the seeds of social change, of the rethinking by each new generation of the society's familial and other structural arrangements. It is discontent with lineages and extended families that gives rise to the "nuclear family revolution" in many developing countries of the world, and it is discontent with the nuclear family that gives rise to experiments with communes and other alternatives in the modern industrial world. Many different kinds of systems can and have worked passably well, historically and cross-culturally; our task is to *understand* their rationale and workability, not to conclude that all systems are equally "good" in some absolute sense, or equally satisfying to their constituents. When we confront such issues as premarital sex in U.S. society, the question "How can a specific system work?" will once again arise.

Section Three

THE CHINESE FAMILY IN HISTORICAL PERSPECTIVE

Many writers have referred to the society of pre-Communist China as one dominated by family and kinship organization. The large family unit with the aging patriarch ruling the household has sometimes been pictured as typical of classical China. Recently, however, scholars have recognized that classical China had a strong state organization and a complex, though primarily agrarian, economy, and thus should not be thought of as an example of total institutional embeddedness in the kin group and lineage. Furthermore, in terms of numbers, classical China was not characterized primarily by the large landed lineage, but by the nuclear family households of the peasants. A con-

---

[11] William N. Stephens, *The Family in Cross-Cultural Perspective* (New York: Holt, Rinehart and Winston, 1963), p. 63.

sideration of Chinese society and its family-kin system allows us to raise the issues of historical change and the use of historical sources. This consideration also allows us to ask what it means for a kinship system to be functionally central to its society. In an insightful account of the Chinese system, Maurice Freedman clarifies some of the dimensions of family and kinship, and the relation between them and the political and economic realities of the larger society. In this section, Freedman will be allowed to speak for himself at considerable length.[12]

The patrilineage was normatively the key kin unit in classical China; however, it hardly incorporated all the other institutional activities of its society. In fact, even among high-status Chinese, it would be proper to ask whether the patrilineage dominated the state, whether the state dominated the patrilineage, or whether the two institutions were actually in a power balance. Furthermore, we might ask whether the strong patrilineage and its patriarch were characteristic of the entire Chinese population, or only of high-status persons. Let us assume, says Freedman,

> that the problem is to decide what strength or potency lay in kinship relations as a whole. We may take China as it was in the last hundred years of its existence as an imperial state. The question resolves itself into an analysis of how the solidarities and values of kinship were enmeshed in a political and economic order which required of individuals that they owe allegiance to a state and participate, despite the dominance of agriculture, in a wide-ranging economic system.
>
> From the point of view of the state, a man's obligation to it were in fact both qualified and mediated by his kinship relations. They were qualified in the sense that obligations springing from filial piety and mourning duties were held to modify duties owed to the state. An official who lost a parent was supposed to retire during the mourning. People related to one another in close bonds of kinship were so far regarded by the written law to require solidarity among them that the Code provided that certain relatives might legitimately conceal the offenses of one another (except in cases of high treason and rebellion), either escaping punishment altogether or suffering a penalty reduced in accordance with the closeness of the relationship; and that it was an offense generally for close kinsmen to lay even just accusations against one another. There was built into the system the principle that close patrilineal kinship set up special rights and duties standing apart from the rights and duties between man and the state. . . .
>
> In the eyes of the state, then, a man stood posed against it in a network of primary kinship duties. But the state also regarded kinship units as part of its system of general control, so that a man's duties to it were mediated through his membership in these units. The family is the clearest case. The Confucian emphasis on complex families and the

---

[12] Maurice Freedman, "The Family in China, Past and Present," *Pacific Affairs* 34 (1961–62), 323–36.

legal power vested in the head of a family to prevent its premature breakup are aspects of a total political system in which some authority is delegated from the administrative system to what, in a metaphorical sense, we may call natural units. The Confucian moralizing about the family, the stress put upon filial piety and the need for solidarity among brothers, the underlining of the importance of domestic harmony—these reflect a political view in which units standing at the base of the social pyramid are expected to control themselves in the interest of the state.

But the family is not the only case. It was morally right for men to align themselves on the basis of their common patrilineal descent and to form lineages. Lineage organization implied ancestor worship, a Confucian value of high order. It implied the promotion of schools and mutual help; in these the state could take pleasure. It implied, finally, an organization which could be used by the state for political and fiscal control. And at once we can see the dilemma faced by the state when it tried to make use of the lineage and encourage its prosperity. To be of use to the state, the lineage must be organized and strong; but strength might grow to the point at which what was once a useful adjunct of government now became a threat to it. Where the lineages grew in numbers and riches they fought with other lineages. This was objectionable enough, but clearly what frightened the central administration more than anything else was the tendency for patrilineal organization to snowball. A lineage was justified by a genealogy; people began to produce longer and wider genealogies to justify more extensive groupings, going so far—and this "excess" excited very great official indignation—that attempts were sometimes made to group together in one organization all the lineages in one area bearing a common surname. It is important to realize that genealogical rearrangement and the grouping together of lineages makes perfect sense, given the logic of the patrilineal system, and that the objections raised by officialdom, although they might be couched in terms condemning the falsification of genealogies, were essentially political. That is to say, strong nuclei of local power were being created which constituted a threat to state authority.

From the political point of view, then, kinship organization entailed a balance of forces with the state. . . .

On the role of kinship in economic life we have no systematic and large body of information on which to rely, but we can make a general argument. If we start from the assumption that kinship relations and values predominate in the conduct of economic affairs, we must expect that enterprise will take the form of what is often called the family business. Now, of course, there is plenty of evidence to show that Chinese economic enterprise has tended strongly to be organized so that people associating their capital, or capital and labor, are related by kinship or affinity. But what is the real significance of this fact? Is it that the moral imperatives of kinship impel people to seek out kinsmen with whom to work? The answer is no. Given the nature of the capital market, given a legal system which offers little protection to business, given the tendency to rely on people with whom there is some preceding tie, we should expect that kinsmen would be associating with one another in economic activities. What is really involved is that these activities are made to rest on highly personalized relationships and that a man's circle of relatives is likely to contain the greater number of individuals apt for selection. It is important to remember that, outside the family, a kinsman has few specific economic claims, that he can be approached as a landlord or creditor, and that in general we must not look to see preference being shown to a kinsman in economic matters on the grounds simply that he is a kinsman.

We have so far been concerned with the question of how far the family in "pre-modern" China can be said to have been the basic unit of society. The argument has taken the form that family and kinship together provided one method of balancing the power of the state and that kinship was not *in principle* basic to economic life. If we confined our attention to the family in the strictest sense of the term, we might be able, by noting how much of the ordinary individual's life is lived within it, to assert that we were dealing with something fundamental. But in doing this we should be ignoring the whole range of wider institutions without which the family can in fact have little meaning.

We must now turn to the inner structure of the Chinese family before modern times, placing emphasis on two things: first, the nature of the tensions inherent in it, in order to see whether they can help us in our understanding of modern developments; and second, the linkages between the family and the wider society, so that we may look for changes in the family which may correspond to changes in society at large.

It has become an accepted fact, says Freedman, that the average size of the traditional Chinese family was no more than five or six. Of greater importance currently would seem to be the question of

why it was that some families were very large and others very small, with many gradations between these extremes. Let us go back to the political point that the state looked to the family as the first unit of social control. The ideal family from this point of view was one in which large numbers of kinsmen and their wives were held under the control of a patriarch imbued with the Confucian values of propriety and order. Some families came close to this model, several generations living under one roof. They were powerful families. We may consider the power they wielded in terms both of their control of economic resources and of their command over other people. They were rich. They owned much land and other capital resources. By renting land and lending money they could exert influence over other people. They could afford to educate their sons and equip them for membership in the bureaucratic elite. They often (perhaps usually) entered into the life of this elite, making use of their ties in it to control both less fortunate families and their own subordinate members. Such a family may be looked upon as a large politico-economic corporation with much power vested in its chief member. But this corporation could not grow indefinitely in membership, for with the death of its senior generation it split along the lines laid down by the constitution of the next generation, every son having a right to an individualized share of his father's estate on that man's death. However, despite the partition which took place every generation, high status families were able to remain large. The passing of the senior generation was likely to take place at a point when the men in the next generation were themselves old enough to have descendants sufficient for complex families of their own. At this level of society fertility was relatively high, the chances of survival were higher, adoption was easy, the age of marriage was low, and plural marriage was possible.

At the other end of the social scale the family was, so to speak, scarcely Confucian. Poverty and powerlessness produced, instead of a strong patriach, a weak father. He could rally no support from outside to dominate his sons. He had few resources to withhold from them. In fact, he might well have only one son growing to maturity. If, however, he had two or more sons reaching manhood, only one would be likely to stay with him, and perhaps even this one would leave him too. Demography, economics, and the power situation at this level of society ensured that families of simple structure were a constant feature of the landscape.

Changes in social status promoted changes in family structure. Upward social mobility was partly a matter of increasing the complexity of the family, both because changing demographic, economic, and power conditions entailed complexity and because the ideal Confucian family was a model towards which people strove when they were moving upwards. And we should note that downward social mobility brought with it a corresponding decline in complexity.

The relations between the sexes and between the generations were dependent on differences in family structure. It will be convenient to start from a feature of Chinese family life which has always attracted the attention of outsiders: the unhappy position of the daughter-in-law. She may be looked upon from three points of view: as a woman, as a member of the family by incorporation, and as a member of a junior generation. It needs no stressing that being a woman was a disadvantage. Every aspect of her society and its values left the Chinese woman in no doubt on that score. In the family into which she was born she might indeed be well and affectionately treated, but this favorable treatment rested on the paradox that she was merely a temporary member of it. Certainly, her marriage would call upon the family's resources, for it would cause her father to assert his status by sending her off in such a manner as to narrow the status gap between him and the father of the groom. But her marriage cut her off economically and as a legal person from her own family and transferred the rights in and over her to the family receiving her. In this new family she was at once a stranger and a member—the former because she was new and the latter in that, henceforth, the rights and duties in respect of her would lie with her husband's people. From the day of her marriage she must begin to think of her interests as being inevitably involved in those of her husband and the members of his family. She had no secure base outside this family from which to operate, because, while she might try to bring in support from her family of birth to moderate oppression, she could not rely on it. To a large extent physically, and in all degrees legally, she was locked within her husband's gates.

Her husband's mother was her point of contact with the new senior generation to preside over her—whence the tears, for she had to be disciplined into a new role in a new family. In fact, however, the difficulties faced by the daughter-in-law were only one aspect of a broader configuration of difficulties. Men in Confucian morality were urged to reject the claims made by their wives on their attention and their interests, and to stand by their brothers against the threat posed to fraternal solidarity by their wives. Women were troublemakers, partly because they were strangers. Her mother-in-law represented for the wife the female half of the family into which she was firmly thrust if her husband refused to come to her aid. Mother-in-law, daughter-in-law, and unmarried daughters formed a battlefield on which any one daughter-in-law must fight for herself and, later, for her children.

Now if in fact the married brothers in a family did stand together, refusing to listen to their wives' complaints, it was because they were posed against their father. And this father was a strong figure whose power rested on the economic resources he controlled and the command he could exert on the world outside the family. It will be seen, therefore, that we have been dealing with the characteristics of a family of high status. Because of riches, life might in one sense be easy for the married woman (she had servants and other luxuries), but she was distant from her husband and at the mercy of the other women in the house until she was herself senior enough to pass from the dominated to the dominators.

In a family of low status and simple structure the elemental relationships of father and son, brother and brother, and husband and wife formed a different pattern. The father's control was weak and the brothers highly individualized among themselves. Each brother stood close to his wife, so that while the wife might be made miserable by poverty and hard work, at the lower levels of society she had greater strength as an individual. Here she was far less likely to need to cope with other mature women in the house.

From this summary analysis we may conclude that the probability of tension between the generations and the sexes increased with a rise in social status, and we may look forward from this point to the attempts made in modern times to remedy what seemed to be the difficulties and injustices of the Chinese family system.[13]

The reform attempts, as Freedman summarizes them, actually involved change in the structure of the high-status family, making it more similar to the historical form of the low-status Chinese family just described. That is, much effort was expended in the first half of the twentieth century (and was continued under the Communist regime) to weaken the control of the powerful lineages, thereby increasing the status and power of women and children in relations with men. Moreover, in conflicts of interest between the family and the state, the state now holds sway, to the extent that a parent who disregards a regulation of the state may be in danger of being reported by his own children.

---

[13] Freedman, "The Family in China," pp. 328–29.

The major change is therefore that the

family now lies open to the state. It has little property to hold it together. Its ritual bond has been removed. Its head can call on few sanctions to support him in the exercise of authority—his wife can divorce
him, his children defy him. The allocation of tasks in economic life is
not now in any important respect a family matter. The whole range of
activities once covered by the family is now reduced to a narrow field
in which husband, wife, and children associate together in the interstices,
so to speak, of large institutions—the work group, the dining hall, the
nursery—which have taken over the functions of economic coordina-
tion, housekeeping, and the rearing and education of children. The family has become an institution for producing babies and enjoying the
leisure time left over from the major pursuits of everyday life.

Now, as soon as we formulate our account of the contemporary
Chinese family in this fashion—and of course the account may well be
overdrawn, which in fact strengthens the argument to follow—we can
no longer rely on the assumption that the family is to be destroyed. The
more we look at this picture the more familiar it will seem to us, for it
contains features from the Western experience of family life. For most
of the inhabitants of an industrialized society the family is a small residential group from which many of the major activities of life are excluded. The factory, the office, and the school separate the members of
one family for many hours of the day and provide them with different
ranges of relationships and interests. What they unite for as a family is
a restricted number of activities of consumption, child care, amusement,
and emotional exchange. True, if we are to believe what we are told,
the Chinese family in the commune has gone further in reducing the
minimal functions we associate with family life, but it has not necessarily departed in principle from a pattern which we know to be intrinsic to the modern form of society.

If we begin a discussion of whether the family now exists in China
with a definition of the family which lists a number of functions, it is
possible that we shall deny it to present-day China, just as some people
have denied it to collective settlements in Israel. If instead we look in
the family for a configuration of relationships between spouses and between parents and children, a configuration standing out from other patterns of relationship in which people are involved, then we should have
little difficulty in satisfying ourselves that the Chinese family has survived.

But there is more to it than that. We can argue that the family has
survived not *against* the wishes of the people responsible for policy in
Communist China but rather in accordance with their desire to see the
institution persist and flourish. The persistence is of course on their
terms, but what they may seek to perpetuate is necessary for the orderly
working of their society. Marriage may be potentially fragile, but marriage there certainly is. Its purpose is to provide a locus for the raising
of useful citizens. Children are not going to be produced on an assembly line; they must be linked to parents before they can be linked to
society. In the early years of their control the Communists gave the appearance of waging a war on the family. Since about 1953, the war having been won to their satisfaction, they have been at pains to stress such

of the value of family life as they regard as important in the institution as it now is. Old people must be looked after by their children; the young must be respectful; there must be a harmonious relationship between husband and wife.

It would appear that the form taken by the family in recent years is essentially the same as that which we have seen to have characterized the greater part of the Chinese population before any of the modern trends began. That is to say, the family is either a unit of parents and their immature children, or it includes, in addition to those people, the parents or surviving parent of the husband or the wife (of the former rather than of the latter). The "solution" produced by the Communists is in reality an old one, and in arriving at it the Communists were continuing a process of change which had started many years earlier at the higher levels of Chinese society. In fact, it could be argued that just as the Communists worked on peasant hunger for land to bind the mass of the people to them in the early days of land reform, so they commanded the allegiance of many people by playing on the stresses inherent in complex family organization. The resentment of the wife and the son, and the strains between the sexes and the generations, were material on which politics could work to create opinion favorable to its general aims.[14]

What conclusions can be drawn regarding the importance of the family in classical China? What is the nature of recent changes? According to Freedman, classical China was characterized by a balance of power between strong patrilineages and state authority. The vast majority of the population, however, lived on the land in nuclear family units, free from the complexities of highly developed patrilineal organization.

Much of the historical literature on China has, of course, focused on the life of high-status people. The nucleation and weak kin linkages of the poorer segments of the population have hardly been noticed. The trend in the Chinese system toward a decrease in the importance of lineages in favor of nuclear family units has in fact been a trend toward a pattern already typical of low-status families. The primary political result of this trend has been to weaken the powerful intermediate lineage structures, thereby providing state leaders with more immediate access to and control over the nuclear units.[15]

A second way of viewing the changes in Chinese society pertains to the embeddedness of the economy in either the kin group or the nuclear family. Although Freedman says little about this, it is nevertheless true that in

---

[14] Freedman, "The Family in China," pp. 333–34.

[15] For an extended treatment of the process of weakening the intermediate structures of family, kinship, and religion, so that in modern society the individual lies more open to state control, see Robert A. Nisbet, *Community and Power* (New York: Oxford University Press, Galaxy Books, 1962 ed.).

many land-based economic systems conjugal and kin units are important loci of productive activity. In classical China, the lower-status population has for centuries been primarily a series of nuclear units within which productivity was embedded. The change in the higher-status population has been away from lineage-based production to nuclear-based production, with the agrarian economy now centered to a great extent in nuclear units. With the increasing industrialization of modern China it is predictable that the nuclear unit will likewise give way to the individual worker as the main productive unit. Meanwhile, however, most of the Chinese population still consists of family units working the land.

When we turn in Chapter 4 to the antecedents of the modern family, the reader should watch for the similarities and differences between the family in pre-Communist China and the family in the colonial United States. At no point in history has the *typical* Chinese pattern been a high degree of institutional and personnel embeddedness in the kin group, though a minority of high-status lineages could be thus characterized. Nor is classical China a pure example of institutional embeddedness even in the nuclear family. For centuries the political organization of China was counterposed to the kin-family organization of the society, the link between the state and the family being certain powerful patriarchs who played both political and kin authority roles. The complexity of agrarian China was such that, on the one hand, the nuclear family was more important to the functioning of society than we found it to be among the Nayar, but, on the other hand, kin group and social organization could not be considered virtually synonymous as we found them to be among the Papago.

Section Four

SUMMARY OF CHAPTERS 2 AND 3

Some of the major principles by which family and kinship structures may be distinguished include marriage patterns, consanguineal ties, and residence location. In addition, descent and inheritance and authority patterns differentiate the family cultures of various societies. Among the most significant types produced cross-culturally by these principles are: (1) monogamous, polygynous, and polyandrous marriages; (2) monogamous nuclear, joint, and extended households; (3) patrilocality, matrilocality, neolocality, bilocality, and avunculocality; (4) patrilineal, matrilineal, and bilateral descent and inheritance; and (5) patriarchal, matriarchal, and equalitarian authority. Such types are, of course, group constructs that are useful for comparisons but are in reality simply abstractions and points on a complex continuum of societal expectations and empirical reality.

The married person is simultaneously a member of two nuclear families, the one into which he was born, called his family of orientation, and the one which he establishes by means of marriage and parenthood, called his family of procreation. The incest taboo, which designates certain categories of kin as unavailable for sexual intercourse or mating, is a virtually universal aspect of human societies, though there are substantial differences from one society to another in the specific relations falling under the taboo. Even sibling and parent-child mating have been considered legitimate in certain societies.

Three societies were used to exemplify some of the problems in cross-cultural family study. The Nayar of South India, a quasi-polyandrous people, were the focal point for discussing the universality of the family. These people appear to have traditionally lacked the husband as a permanent member of the household. Thus, if the question concerns whether the *nuclear* family, with father, mother, and child as permanent members, is universal, the answer is probably no. If, however, "family" is redefined as a mechanism for legitimating or rearing offspring, it is very likely universal.

A Western observer understands his own family system and considers it "natural." But how, he might ask, can a "totally kin-embedded" system work which includes polygyny, arranged marriage, and village exogamy as attributes? Among the Papago it seems to function fairly satisfactorily. For one thing, the majority of household units are monogamous rather than polygynous. More important, sororal polygyny, or the marriage of the male to sisters, is apparently pleasing to the Papago female who is living as a stranger in her husband's village. This does not mean that polygyny does not cause problems. Instances of jealousy between cowives are reported in the literature. Rather, the point is that any system can function, once established, although it may include within it the seeds of discontent and eventual destruction.

Classical China was considered for many years to have consisted of a series of large family-kin households. Freedman's discussion illustrates the difficulties in using historical sources, in speaking of family-kin "importance," and in determining the direction of changes over time. In the case of China the problem is that many authors have written about the high-status family as if it were typical. The recent trend in China toward greater nucleation of families has actually been a movement toward the small household that characterized the poorer masses during the classical period. The kin-lineage system was important to classical China in the sense that among the wealthy it acted as a political balance against the forces of centralized state authority and as a major unit of agrarian economic production. Today the nuclear unit is the seat of agricultural production, but industrialization is, in China as elsewhere, weakening even this form of economic embeddedness in the family. But more will be said later on this last point.

Precolonial influences on the family in the United States include the beginnings of privacy; the appearance of a strong repressive sex code and the notion of sanctity; increased awareness of women's low status in .the family; and the development of the romantic love concept. The sex code and the sanctity concept were in direct conflict with the looser norms of the late Middle Ages. Prior to and during the colonial period, other institutions were to a great extent embedded in the nuclear family, not the kin group, although an increasing number of specialized functionaries were operating outside the family unit. In the colonies, romantic love began to be linked with mate selection. The family was characterized by patriarchal economic-legal authority. During the period from about 1800 to the present, certain aspects of the family in the United States—such as household composition, personal choice of a mate, and residential mobility—changed but little, while others—such as women's status, sex codes, and institutional embeddedness—underwent substantial alteration.

Antecedents of the Modern U.S. Family

PRECOLONIAL INFLUENCES

Until recently, attempts to investigate and understand the antecedents of the modern family have confronted the difficulties referred to by Freedman in his discussion of the Chinese family. The vast majority of historical sources have been descriptive of the high-status family or have been written from a normative perspective, that is, they tell how people *should* behave instead of how they *do* behave. Now, however, a flurry of historical research activity, utilizing census records, parish registers, tax records, and legal and political documents, has begun to dispel the cloud of uncertainty which blocks our understanding of the behavior of "average" families in precolonial and colonial days.[1]

These new historical studies have, of course, not resolved all the issues which they have raised. There are several reasons for this. First, historians and historical sociologists have ordinarily worked from data for a particular town or area at a particular point in its history. This limits the generalizability of their results, which often run counter to the conclusions reached by other scholars who have studied other times and places.[2] Second, even working with the same data does not necessarily lead different historians to the same conclusions or interpretations. David Rothman, for example, in presenting an alternative interpretation of child rearing in the colonies to that of John Demos, states that

> many historians have experienced that middle-of-the-night panic when contemplating how thin a line separates their work from fiction. But on this score the study of childhood seems especially nerve-wracking, threatening to turn us all into novelists.[3]

Third, the farther back into history one wishes to delve, the more tenuous his conclusions are likely to be. Lutz Berhner notes that only after 1800 were there attempts to describe working-class family life accurately. In general, he concludes, the farther back in time one goes, the higher up the social ladder he must look to find people who are literate and about whom adequate source material for family study survives.[4]

Thus, we enter upon a discussion of the modern family's antecedents with enthusiasm for the "new family history," but also with caution. It is tempting, furthermore, to begin by dwelling at length on such early antecedents as the family of the ancient Hebrews, the Greeks, the Romans, and the early Christians. Our discussion, however, will be restricted to a few of the more important characteristics and developments during and following the medieval period, with detailed accounts left to other sources.[5]

---

[1] Peter Laslett, cofounder of the Cambridge Group for the History of Population and Social Structure, has been a key figure in the "new family history"; see Laslett, *The World We Have Lost* (New York: Scribner's, 1965); Laslett and Richard Wall, eds., *Household and Family in Past Time* (New York: Cambridge University Press, 1972). Michael Gordon, *The American Family in Social-Historical Perspective* (New York: St. Martin's Press, 1972), is an excellent summary of research on American family history up to 1970.

[2] Rudy Ray Seward notes such discrepancies in the estimates of family size made by various historians, in his article "The Colonial Family in America: Toward a Socio-Historical Restoration of Its Structure," *Journal of Marriage and the Family* 35 (1973), 58–70.

[3] David J. Rothman, "Documents in Search of a Historian: Toward a History of Childhood and Youth in America," in Theodore K. Rabb and Robert I. Rotberg, eds., *The Family in History: Interdisciplinary Essays* (New York: Harper & Row, 1971), pp. 181–89.

[4] Lutz K. Berhner, "Recent Research on the History of the Family in Western Europe," *Journal of Marriage and the Family* 35 (1973), 395–405.

[5] Several excellent accounts of the antecedents of the modern family may be consulted for a fuller picture. These include Panos D. Bardis, "Family Forms and Variations

During the early Middle Ages, the nuclear family and its kin-community were highly embedded in each other in terms of personnel. That is, the nuclear family had little existence either structurally or attitudinally apart from the kin-friend-neighbor milieu in which the individual functioned. The nuclear family seldom operated as a separate entity, and it did not arouse strong feelings of allegiance among its members. Among those of higher status this meant that lineages were strong, and in many areas of Europe, such as central France, there were large kin-based agricultural communities.[6] Among those of lower status it simply meant that family and nonfamily, kin and nonkin, were not easily distinguished—nor was it felt necessary to distinguish them. The flow of kin, friends, children, and nuclear family members into and out of the home meant that nuclear family members had virtually no privacy from one another or from other members of the social network and that affective feelings flowed fairly freely through this broader network.[7]

In the early medieval Church, religious ordination, but not marriage, was considered a sacrament; the family was not a holy union but a concession to the weakness of the flesh. Thus, sex in the family was only slightly more acceptable to the religious leaders than was sex outside the family. Such negativism regarding sex in general, when coupled with the broader range of intimate relationships and the lack of strong nuclear family values, means that sexual promiscuity (by later standards) was very likely quite prevalent. The nuclear family was simply embedded interactionally in its wider social network.

A second possible form of embeddedness involves the relationships between the family or kin group and other societal institutions. In a society such as that of the Papago, in which all economic, religious, political, and other functions are performed as aspects of kinship organization, one can speak of total institutional embeddedness in the kin group. However, in medieval Europe this was clearly not the case. There were separate functionaries set aside in political, religious, and economic institutions. And yet there was a great amount of embeddedness of these and other social in-

---

Historically Considered," in Harold T. Christensen, ed., *Handbook of Marriage and the Family* (Chicago: Rand McNally, 1964), chap. 11; Philippe Ariès, *Centuries of Childhood* (New York: Random House, Vintage Books, 1965 ed.); Morton M. Hunt, *The Natural History of Love* (New York: Knopf, 1959); Gerald R. Leslie, *The Family in Social Context* (New York: Oxford University Press, 1973 ed.), chaps. 6–7.

[6] William L. Parish, Jr., and Moshe Schwartz, "Household Complexity in Nineteenth Century France," *American Sociological Review* 37 (1972), 155.

[7] Ariès's book *Centuries of Childhood* is important for its insights and ideas. It is, however, based primarily on interpretations of artistic works and architecture, and many of its conclusions regarding the family are therefore somewhat inferential, especially when they are applied to the "common" family. Also, since the book deals with the French family, the picture it presents cannot be taken as a perfect representation of the English family prior to the establishment of England's American colonies.

stitutions in the kin-friend network. Education took place, for the masses, in the home with kin and friends. Religion had its separate location, but its reinforcement was often left to the family unit. In the early Middle Ages the economy could hardly be called either nuclear family–dominated or kin-lineage–dominated. It was, rather, male-dominated, and this domination ordinarily occurred within a kin-lineage system among the higher strata of European society and within a nuclear–social network system among the lower strata. Generally speaking, then, in the early medieval period the nuclear family was not a clearly distinguished societal entity in its relation either to the individual or to the other institutions of society.

The changes that had occurred by the late Middle Ages in Europe had a profound effect on the family in the American colonies. Underlying many of the other changes was the developing concept of the privacy and sanctity of the nuclear family. In earlier centuries sociability had meant that the home was open to kin and friends almost as much as to spouse and children. Rooms had not been set aside for specialized functions; family and nonfamily members had interacted in various circumstances. The concept of privacy was twofold. It meant the separation of the family from the outside world and the separation—if they so desired—of family members from one another. This developing separation (not completed in the Middle Ages)[8] was accompanied by the glorification of family life and the appearance of the moral notion of marriage as a sacrament. Monogamy was already the legalized form of marriage, with important economic motives behind such legalization. Now came a distinction in the sex code which said that, although sex within marriage was blessed by the Church, outside of marriage it was a sin. Devoutly religious people still frequently felt considerable guilt about sex, even within marriage, but the distinction between sex inside the nuclear family and sex outside the nuclear family was now clear. One important long-term effect of this new emphasis on the nuclear family unit was to reduce the personnel embeddedness of the nuclear unit in its social network; another was to alter the institutional embeddedness, in terms of functions performed, away from the network and toward the nuclear family.

One aspect of the change toward the privacy and sanctity, in short, the self-consciousness, of the nuclear family during the Middle Ages had to do

---

[8] Barbara Laslett, "The Family as a Public and Private Institution: A Historical Perspective," *Journal of Marriage and the Family* 35 (1973), 480–92, notes, in fact, that the *private* family, an institution characterized by relatively limited access and greater control over the observability of behavior, did not become an accomplished fact in the United States until this century, when the separation of work from family activity came to characterize an overwhelming majority of American families.

with household composition. Lineage systems, with their patriarchal extended or stem family households, had been prevalent in the early Middle Ages, but by the eleventh century these systems had begun to decline in France. Even among the upper classes the extended family household, consisting of aging parents, their sons—and sometimes their daughters—and their sons' wives and children, had weakened during the thirteenth century.[9] The stem family, in which one offspring, often the eldest male, continues in the household so as to inherit most of the immovable property, persisted in France, England, and much of the rest of Western Europe throughout the Middle Ages. However, by the seventeenth century even this household type—a result of agricultural-based economy, long-term landownership or tenantship, illiteracy, and regional traditions—had been far outnumbered by nuclear family units. The result, then, is that by the time British and French colonies were established in the "New World," it was unusual to find households containing more than two generations in the countries from which their colonists came. Neolocality, or movement out of the parental home at marriage, was the rule.[10] "In short," says James Henretta, "the England from which the settlers of Dedham came was at the end of a . . . process of transition which had largely destroyed the earlier peasant society."[11]

The stem family, it should be added, did not automatically provide large numbers of urban migrants during the late Middle Ages, because its fertility was often low and its child mortality high.[12] However, the predominance of nuclear family households by the beginning of the seventeenth century meant that a mobile labor force would be available when the industrial revolution occurred nearly two centuries later.

Two points need to be made about women's status during the medieval period. First, if a woman had no brothers she and her husband were likely to inherit family property. However, in the more likely event that she had brothers she could offer little economic incentive to an eligible man of her own status. Emily Coleman reports the outcome of this situation:

> At the same time, her very status—without the economic inducement of land—would offer positive motivation to a man in a lower social position. In other words, a man would marry up for psychological reasons or with the conscious intention of improving the status of his progeny;

---

[9] Parish and Schwartz, "Household Complexity in Nineteenth Century France," p. 155.

[10] Seward, "The Colonial Family in America," refers to several studies done in the 1960s which report neolocality and the two-generation household as predominant.

[11] James A. Henretta, "The Morphology of New England Society in the Colonial Period," in Rabb and Rotberg, *The Family in History*, p. 193.

[12] Parish and Schwartz, "Household Complexity in Nineteenth Century France," p. 171.

a woman would marry down due to the force of economic circumstances.[13]

Thus, due to the woman's lack of economic control and the man's dominance and status striving, the class structure was gradually transformed.

The second point concerning women's status has to do with its change during the course of the Middle Ages. This change, resulting from the increasing self-consciousness of the nuclear family and the concomitant change from institutional embeddedness in the social network to embeddedness in the nuclear family, was that the husband's dominance over his wife became more obvious. In the sixteenth century, the wife's position was such that "any acts she performs without the authority of her husband or the law are null and void."[14] Some have argued, as does Philippe Ariès, that changes during the Middle Ages actually served to worsen the woman's position. The present writer would argue that what nucleation did was to make increasingly evident the subordinate position that women had traditionally held. This awareness, along with other factors, eventually gave rise to the women's rights movements of the nineteenth century. However, the normatively patriarchal pattern of the family's legal-authority structure was carried over into the American colonies, and will be referred to again.

Another factor that influenced the family in the American colonies was the development of the concept of romantic love as distinct from other forms of love. In the upper strata of society in the early Middle Ages, parents commonly arranged the marriages of their offspring to members of appropriate kin groups. During this period, codes of etiquette and chivalry became highly developed in the courts of European nobles. These codes were dramatized in the games at which the valiant did battle for the favor of a particular female.

Chivalry and arranged marriage were not, however, sufficient to produce the idea of romantic love as something different from the ordinary love resulting from sharing and companionship. As long as male sexual experimentation outside of marriage was relatively easy to accomplish (due to personnel embeddedness in the kin-community), romantic love was not distinguishable as a separate entity. However, with the strengthening of the nuclear unit and the clear normative demarcation between sex with one's spouse and with all others, the arrangement of marriages in the upper strata began to be accompanied by heightened frustration. Romantic love, ordinarily occurring after marriage and with a person other than one's own spouse, was often unrequited or frustrated, and involved idealization and

---

[13] Emily R. Coleman, "Medieval Marriage Characteristics: A Neglected Factor in the History of Medieval Serfdom," in Rabb and Rotberg, *The Family in History*, p. 12.

[14] Ariès, *Centuries of Childhood*, p. 356.

strong emotion. In late medieval Europe, among those of high status, romantic love came to be a technique of rebellion against familial control of mating. In short, the historical factors most immediately responsible for the development of romantic love as something unique or different from ordinary love included the practice of arranging marriages, the courtly games and etiquette codes, and the increasing separation of the nuclear family—sexually and otherwise—from other societal groupings, in accordance with the official morality. During this period, romantic love was distinguishable primarily in the upper strata and had little direct relation with either marriage or the selection of a mate.[15]

We have been speaking of the upper strata of the late Middle Ages. Among those in the upper strata, marriage was planned as a link between two important lineages (and, later, households). Mating among the masses, it should be noted, was frequently a matter of choice and had a strong emotional element. Here, then, is an instance of what Freedman refers to in discussing the Chinese family. A characteristic of the common people, seldom written about by the literati of the time—specifically, personal choice of a mate—came to be a goal for people at all levels of society. There were, however, a few differences between personal choice and love among the masses of medieval Europe and the romantic love concept of the twentieth century. Affectional ties were not the sole basis for most marriages and could not be described by the romantic notions of "love at first sight," frustration, or idealization. Marriage was likely to be between two people who had known each other for years, and it was often based on economic considerations as well as emotional attraction.

The increase in the rate of illegitimacy, and the changing *relational* basis for it, between the sixteenth and nineteenth centuries is further evidence for the spread of romantic love in European society. Edward Shorter observes that the explosion of bastardy during these centuries may be seen

> as the supplanting of peasant-bundling and master-servant exploitation by hit-and-run and true-love illegitimacy as the predominant types. This transition came about because popular premarital sexuality shifted from manipulative to expressive, thus elevating the number of conceptions, and because inconstancy crept into the couples' intentions toward each other.[16]

These changes, especially the change from master-servant illegitimacy to "hit-and-run," had only begun prior to the seventeenth century, and the prevalence of the "true-love" type was still three centuries away. Thus, we

---

[15] For more on this, see Hunt, *The Natural History of Love.* Literary illustrations can be found in Alfred Tennyson, *Idylls of the King* (Boston: Ticknor and Fields, 1859).

[16] Edward Shorter, "Illegitimacy, Sexual Revolution, and Social Change in Modern Europe," in Rabb and Rotberg, *The Family in History,* p. 55.

shall return to this issue in the sections which follow. Suffice it to say, however, that the beginnings of romantic love as the predominant basis for both mate selection and illegitimacy occurred in the late Middle Ages in European society.

In summary, it can be said that the upper strata of the late Middle Ages were characterized by planned marriages and an increased emphasis on extramarital romance; while, among the majority, marriage was by choice, but was based on a complex of factors which did not yet include romantic love as a definable type. Privacy and normative sanctity; the increasing demarcation between familial and extrafamilial sex; increasing institutional embeddedness in the nuclear family rather than in the social network; and patriarchy—these are some of the late medieval influences that most affected the family in the New World.

Section Two

FAMILY LIFE IN THE AMERICAN COLONIES, 1611–1800[17]

Family life in the American colonies was shaped partly by the European traditions of the settlers and partly by the challenges of an unexplored continent. There were, as among Rosenfeld's Arab villagers, two sets of norms at work. The norms of the official religiopolitical morality stressed the sanctity of the nuclear family and its position as separate from the social network, while the norms of the common people retained many elements of the personnel embeddedness in which the nuclear family was little distinguished—sexually and otherwise—from its social milieu. However, the mobility that characterized the settling by Europeans of the American continent served to weaken network ties, as nuclear units moved from place to place, and thus prepared the way for the ascendancy of the nuclear family during the Victorian era of the 1800s.

Though romantic love was already a popular theme of the literati of Europe, it was not yet directly or consistently linked to courtship and mate selection. Two factors in the early history of the colonies began to effect this connection. First, the colonists were overwhelmingly from the lower strata of European society. This meant that they brought with them a

---

[17] We must admit that the date used to indicate the close of the colonial period—1800—is more arbitrary than most. Other possibilities were 1776, the year in which the colonial period ended politically, and 1850, by which year the industrial revolution was in full swing in the United States. The year 1800 is merely a compromise, indicating the beginnings of a new country and incipient industrialization, though marking no specific event and no specific break with the past.

tradition of personal choice in marriage, though parents—with an eye out for an economically advantageous arrangement for their son or daughter—ordinarily influenced the choice. Yet, in general, parental influence had to be exerted by subtle means, since choice was the rule.[18]

The second factor that began to link romance to mate selection was the shortage of European women in the colonies, especially on the expanding frontier. To put it in economic terms: when any commodity is in short supply, the desire for it becomes more compelling. The feeling is likely to be: "I've got to have that (one)!" When that feeling is projected toward a human being of the opposite sex, the internal reaction is not very different from that of the medieval courtier to the unavailable lady. The internal pain of the courting male (or males) was in fact the emotional response that had already been labeled by the literati and the upper strata as romance or romantic love. It ordinarily settled upon one love object, and was a forerunner of the idea that one can love only one person at a time. Literature, both fiction and nonfiction, describing the plight of the competing males, publicized this approach to mate selection.[19] Thus, the combination of a tradition of choice, the shortage of females, and the increasing emphasis upon the nuclear family apart from its milieu began to link romantic love and mate selection in the American colonies. This link was in contrast to the previous situation, in which such love was simply a sort of free-floating emotion that could strike at any time, under any conditions, but most often after and outside marriage. While long-term acquaintance and economic considerations kept romantic love from becoming the sole basis for marriage in the colonies, romantic-love choice as *the* precondition for marriage was well on its way.

Not only did the seventeenth and eighteenth centuries see an increasing link between romantic love and mate selection in the colonies, but they very probably saw a parallel rise in the hit-and-run sex relationship, based on expressive needs and romantic feelings. Such hit-and-run sex was, in turn, accompanied by a dramatic rise in illegitimacy. Hit-and-run illegitimacy in Europe, says Shorter, "typified a period when young people swooned romantically through a social landscape of disorder and flux." And this flux, coupled with imperfect means of birth control, "raised illegitimacy to

---

[18] Daniel Scott Smith, "Parental Power and Marriage Patterns: An Analysis of Historical Trends in Hingham, Massachusetts," *Journal of Marriage and the Family* 35 (1973), 419–28, notes that in Hingham, a stable New England community, parental involvement in mate selection declined gradually from 1700 until the twentieth century, but that the level of such involvement was still considerable in 1800.

[19] Washington Irving, *The Legend of Sleepy Hollow* (London: Macmillan, 1920). For other literature, see the footnotes to Herman R. Lantz et al., "Pre-Industrial Patterns in the Colonial Family in America: A Content Analysis of Colonial Magazines," *American Sociological Review* 33 (1968), 413–26.

historic heights." Thus, the years just before and after the end of the colonial period were the peak period of illegitimacy in virtually every community and society of Europe.[20] We may infer that Shorter's findings for Europe are not too inaccurate for the New World as well.

Perhaps the best-known feature of official colonial morality is its ethic of severe sexual repression. One reason this was of great importance to religious and community leaders was, in all probability, the great gulf that separated the official morality from common practice. Premarital sex and pregnancy occurred increasingly among the populace, but the official attempts to curb such practices—attempts that had become noticeable in late medieval Europe—were continued into the colonies. In New England, premarital sexual relations were punishable by public denunciation and extramarital sex often meant dismissal from the Church. Being thus excluded was intended to make one a social as well as a spiritual outcast, since the Church was both a social and a religious organization. Yet the fact that only a small proportion of the population belonged to the Church very likely made dismissal less than completely effective. In some cases of premarital intercourse, the couple were obliged to marry; in most cases, some sort of penance was required, at least of the female.[21]

Although the official norms are generally acknowledged to have been severe and repressive, it is extremely difficult to discern their direct effect on common behavior. In fact, as the historian Charles Francis Adams points out, no one knows with certainty whether or not the harsh code, the public and sometimes severe punishment, and the penance leading to reinstatement acted as deterrents even among the devoutly religious. It is possible that the combination of "forbidden fruit" with the emotional satisfactions that must have accompanied the completion of penance and reinstatement increased the behavior that the code purported to control. Be that as it may, it should be added that while it has become popular to speak of the preoccupation with sex in the present-day United States, the colonists were apparently also engrossed in the subject, though the official stress among colonial spokesmen was upon repression. We shall return to this topic in upcoming pages.

Moving now from courtship, sex codes, and sex behavior to the colonial family itself, we can see much internal similarity between that family and the common European family. The father was the actual and legal head of the family, dominating the normative decision-making processes. A content analysis of colonial literature revealed about three references to

---

[20] Shorter, "Illegitimacy, Sexual Revolution, and Social Change in Modern Europe," in Rabb and Rotberg, The Family in History, p. 57.

[21] There are even scattered reports of capital punishment for sexual sins. See Hunt, The Natural History of Love, p. 230.

overt male power over decisions for every reference to overt female power. In addition, the authors found numerous sources noting the use of subtle power by the female, which they saw as "a reaction to or a way of dealing with male authority."[22] Such subtle influence on the part of the female is precisely what one might expect in a system that is legally and normatively patriarchal. The female gave up legal title to any resources she brought into marriage; they became resources at her husband's disposal. As the eighteenth century wore on, however, some variations in property-holding by sex began to appear, with certain colonies giving women somewhat more control over property. Likewise, accounts of female attorneys and married women in business become increasingly frequent in the last quarter of the eighteenth century—an involvement which has not been fully recognized.[23] Nevertheless, the wife's usual lot in the colonial family was to bear and care for the couple's children and, under difficult conditions, to supervise the household. An excerpt from one written record in a family Bible from this period reads as follows:

> He had sixteen children. When the first child was a year and a half old the second child was born. The baby was but four days old when the older child died. Five times did that mother's heart bear a similar cruel loss when she had a baby in her arms; therefore when she had been married but nine years she had one living child, and five little graves bore the record of her sorrow.[24]

The mother's domestic, reproductive, and socializing (child-rearing) role was one of physical hardship, drudgery, and normative subjection to her husband; it is hardly surprising that she took great pride in those of her offspring who survived to adulthood.

A single illustration from a family Bible is not enough, however. The decline in the rate of population growth during colonial days was a function of both an increase in childhood mortality and a decrease in fertility. In Andover, Massachusetts, for example, Henretta reports a drop in the average number of births per marriage from 7.6 in 1700 to 4.2 in the 1770s.[25]

How, then, did colonial family size compare with that of later periods? Studies by Demos, Greven, Wells, Lockridge, Norton, and Higgs and Stettler show a range from 4.64 children per family to 7–8 per family.

---

[22] Lantz et al., "Pre-Industrial Patterns in the Colonial Family in America," p. 419.

[23] Herman R. Lantz, Raymond L. Schmitt, and Richard Herman, "The Preindustrial Family in America: A Further Examination of Early Magazines," *American Journal of Sociology* 79 (1973), 586.

[24] Arthur W. Calhoun, *A Social History of the American Family,* vol. 1 (New York: Barnes & Noble, 1945), p. 106.

[25] Henretta, "The Morphology of New England Society in the Colonial Period," in Rabb and Rotberg, *The Family in History,* p. 198; Seward, "The Colonial Family in America," p. 65.

Rudy Seward, in summarizing these studies, notes that, being longitudinal, they give a much larger number of children than the census, which is cross-sectional. He therefore concludes that the number of children per family has been exaggerated, and that the actual number was very likely not too different from that for the first half of the twentieth century.[26] It seems to this author that these writers are in danger of confusing the three key factors which affect family size: that is, number of births, childhood mortality, and number of survivors to adulthood. In the seventeenth century, births were high, and mortality and survival were moderate. In the eighteenth century, the birthrate decreased, the mortality rate rose, and survivorship dropped to a low level. It is this level, then, that compares favorably with that of today, a time when the birthrate and mortality rate among children are both at an all-time low.

The child's position in the colonial family has been characterized as one dominated by the three R's of repression, religion, and respect, although one might add that religion was often primarily used to increase the other two. A child's basic tendencies were considered to be sinful; it was his parents' task to set him straight. Legally, the child was no better off than the wife. The "father was entitled to his child's services, and he could demand that the child work for him without pay. If the child worked for an outsider, the father was entitled to his earnings."[27] Discipline, while stern, also included the first expressions of a new concept of the child. Up to this time he had been viewed as a small adult; in the colonial family, however, playfulness and mischief were sometimes dismissed with the assertion that "boys will be boys"—an expression of the belief that children are somehow different from adults and should be treated differently. But, for the most part, childishness merely served to increase parental concern about the youngster's wantonness and sinfulness. Not only was the child expected to be submissive, but he was to do his fair share in the family economy, whether with the crops, the flocks, or the housework. Adult roles were learned by the young from parents and persons like them, including older brothers and sisters. As a small adult, when the child was "off duty" he was allowed a substantial amount of freedom to roam and govern himself. In short, the child's life was dominated by his role in the family division of labor and by a repressive discipline, though he often found—or was given—time to escape temporarily into mischief and fun.

In discussing child rearing in Plymouth Colony, Demos' *A Little Commonwealth* reports indulgence of the infant during the first year of life,

[26] Seward, "The Colonial Family in America," p. 62.
[27] Herma Hill Kay, "The Outside Substitute for the Family," in Seymour M. Farber, Piero Mustacchi, and Roger H. L. Wilson, eds., *Man and Civilization: The Family's Search for Survival* (New York: McGraw-Hill, 1965), p. 6.

with the second year characterized by rapid weaning, the arrival of a sibling, and harsh and restrictive discipline. Demos notes, as we have, that the child's willfulness had to be curbed, his spirit broken, and his autonomy limited. As Demos moves beyond this to an interpretation of the relation of child rearing to adult personality in Plymouth Colony, his conclusions, as Rothman noted, become open to alternative views. Yet the character of Puritan discipline seems clear.[28] Straightforward, harsh, and buttressed by legal and moral authority, that discipline appears to have become weaker as the seventeenth and eighteenth centuries went by. The Handlins, in particular, note that the mobility of late colonial society was such as to begin the undermining of parental authority.[29] We shall return to this subject in the next section.

The relation of the family unit to the external world, the other institutions of the colonies, bore a great resemblance to that of the late medieval European family. Partial embeddedness of the various institutions in the nuclear family, not in the kin-friend network, characterized the colonies. The economy focused on family subsistence farms, from 70 to 90 percent of the colonial population being in such agricultural units. The colonists built homes, made furniture and clothing, and raised food. There were trade centers where individuals could take their surpluses and exchange them for what they lacked, and where certain specialists, such as the blacksmith, had their shops; but, for the most part, the family was an economically self-sufficient unit. Religion, while having separate functionaries and, usually, a separate meeting place, was frequently employed for socialization or disciplinary purposes in the home. In fact, families that did not employ religion within the home, very often ignored the religious organization and its leaders as well. Recreation, when the colonists found time for it, tended to be home- or church-based, involving the entire family unit in many instances. The educational process was even more home-based than was recreation: it involved training in homemaking and motherhood for the females and the learning of farm work or an apprenticeship in some trade for the males. Formal education outside the home, even for males, was not universal, and it did not last many years for those who received it. Protection in the colonies demanded cooperation among various family units for mutual defense. The most common type of health care was the "home remedy." In short, the nuclear family was functionally central to the

---

[28] John Demos, *A Little Commonwealth: Family Life in Plymouth Colony* (New York: Oxford University Press, 1970); Demos, "Developmental Perspectives on the History of Childhood," in Rabb and Rotberg, *The Family in History*, pp. 127–39; Rothman, "Documents in Search of a Historian," in Rabb and Rotberg, *The Family in History*.

[29] Oscar Handlin and Mary F. Handlin, *Facing Life: Youth and the Family in American History* (Boston: Little, Brown, 1971), p. 18.

economy of colonial society: the male family head held property, and the family, as the unit of production, joined in a well-defined division of labor. Other institutions—religious, recreational, educational, protective, and medical—all were embedded in the nuclear family to a substantial degree. That is, the activities that characterized these institutions generally either took place within the home or involved the family unit as a whole. Only in the political sphere was there almost no direct tie between the institutional activity and the nuclear family unit.

The question of functional centrality, or institutional embeddedness, which came up in the discussions of the Papago and Chinese families, arises again in observing the American colonial family. Two questions implied in the various discussions of institutional embeddedness are often left unanswered. They are: (1) Is it the kin group or the nuclear family that is thought of as central to the functioning of a particular society? (2) Is this family-kin unit essentially political or economic in its centrality? In classical China, for example, Freedman speaks of the masses as nuclear family units on the land, with a balance of political power afforded by certain influential lineages. In colonial America, as in China, we find large numbers of economically important nuclear units working the land, but we don't find the politically strong kin units that were present in the Chinese upper classes. Thus, the institutional centrality of the colonial family system may be thought of as lying somewhere between the virtually total institutional embeddedness in the kin group of small, kin-based societies, such as the Papago, and the institutional differentiation of the family in modern industrial society, which is the focus of the present volume. That is, institutional embeddedness in the colonial family may not be thought of in any total or absolute sense.

An important concomitant of the colonial type of institutional embeddedness in the nuclear family was the increasing concern in the colonies with keeping family units intact. The growing demarcation between the nuclear family and its social network and the importance of the family, economically and otherwise, were such that divorce laws came to be strict and narrowly delimited, with adultery (particularly on the female's part) being the single most prevalent—and often the only legal—ground for divorce. Although an intolerable family situation could be escaped by desertion (perhaps by "heading for the frontier"), the norms and sanctions were such that this was apparently a less frequent occurrence than legalized divorce is in contemporary U.S. society.

Having considered institutional embeddedness and differentiation in the colonial nuclear family at some length, we must now briefly mention personnel embeddedness. The colonial period was characterized by nuclear family households, often supplemented by one or a few additional kin or nonkin. These "extra" household members, however, followed no traditional pattern, but were idiosyncratic results of specific needs. The "official" morality of the day viewed the nuclear family as of central importance, and this unit was still moving toward its period of greatest ascendancy, that is, the Victorian era of the nineteenth century. However, the high level of residential mobility and neolocality, and the frontier and achievement mentalities, were simultaneously laying the foundation for a later emphasis on individualism. By the end of the colonial era, the individual was still fairly well embedded in the nuclear family, interactionally and attitudinally, but one could already perceive the beginnings of the coming struggle between family and individualistic values—about which more must be said later.

We shall close this discussion with a brief summary of the character of and changes in the colonial family. During the colonial period these major changes took place: (1) romantic love moved ever closer to being the prime basis for mate selection; (2) family size, in particular the number of children surviving to adulthood, diminished as a result of both fewer births and higher mortality rates; (3) institutional embeddedness, divorce laws, and personnel embeddedness all shifted toward a greater focus on the nuclear family's sanctity, societal importance, and inviolability. James Henretta puts very succinctly this increased institutional and personnel embeddedness in the nuclear family:

> The decline in community was paralleled and to some extent offset by the rise of the family. During the eighteenth century the basic social unit took on more of the tasks of socialization and acculturalization. . . . It was the family, likewise, which became the prime economic institution in the society.[30]

In addition, the seeds were planted for a later individualism. Two areas of family life saw only the beginnings of change during the colonial period: (1) the Revolutionary War opened new opportunities for women, and (2) residential mobility and neolocality began to weaken the parents' control over their offspring. In both areas, it was only at the end of the eighteenth century that signs of the weakening of patriarchy, or father-husband dominance, became very evident. A final factor which deserves mention is that sex attitudes became considerably stricter during the colonial period, and this seems to have had the effect of reducing *extramarital* intercourse. Whether it had the same effect on *premarital* intercourse, however, seems more problematic and less likely. Let us now turn to the nineteenth and twentieth centuries.

---

[30] Henretta, "The Morphology of New England Society in the Colonial Period," in Rabb and Rotberg, *The Family in History,* p. 209.

CHANGES IN THE AMERICAN FAMILY, 1800–1970

Many discussions of changes in the family since colonial days have been plagued by one or more of the following problems. The first difficulty, which has been clarified and, to a great extent, corrected by recent writers, is the tendency of many historical accounts of the colonial family to present an idealized, or normative, conception of earlier days. The picture of a series of family units living happily in a kinship network on adjoining farms, with little or no sexual promiscuity or other internal difficulty, has been labeled by William J. Goode the "classical extended family of Western nostalgia."[31] It is, of course, impossible to discuss changes that have occurred unless one can first piece together a basically accurate picture of the past.

A second problem has been that the issue of change was, until recently, consistently posed in terms of the relation between industrialization and the family. The capitalist market economy, the political ideology of the United States, urbanization, the knowledge explosion, communication growth, agricultural productivity, and other changes that are not completely subsumed under the "industrialization" label, may all relate to the family in distinct and important ways. Moreover, not all students of recent history agree that the family is necessarily the dependent variable* in the causal chain. It has been argued that neolocality and the development of nuclear family privacy vis-à-vis its social network may have been preconditions for many of the economic-technological changes that characterized the industrial revolution.[32] Be that as it may, the posing of the issue as one existing between the family and industrialization simply ignores a whole series of related developments—technological and ideological—which may have been associated with family change not directly connected with the industrial revolution itself.[33]

The third difficulty with much theorizing about historical changes in the family is that, in one source or another, as many as fifteen different features of the family—such as husband-wife power relations, sex codes, romantic love, courtship, women's status, and divorce—have been linked

---

[31] William J. Goode, *After Divorce* (New York: Free Press, 1956), p. 3.

[32] H. J. Habakkuk, "Family Structure and Economic Change in Nineteenth-Century Europe," *The Journal of Economic History* 15 (1955), 1–12.

[33] Among the best treatments of the issue of industrialization and the family are: Sidney M. Greenfield, "Industrialization and the Family in Sociological Theory," *American Journal of Sociology* 67 (1961), 312–22; Frank F. Furstenberg, Jr., "Industrialization and the American Family: A Look Backward," *American Sociological Review* 31 (1966), 326–37; William F. Ogburn and Meyer F. Nimkoff, *Technology and the Changing Family* (Boston: Houghton Mifflin, 1955).

to industrialization. The results of choosing certain aspects of the family and ignoring others have been three divergent conclusions regarding the family and change: (1) industrialization caused change *X* or changes *XYZ* to occur in the family; (2) since no change occurred in feature *A* or features *ABC* of the family, the industrial revolution apparently had no effect; (3) characteristics *LMN* of the family's structure were the cause of certain changes that occurred in the economy. (The last is the least frequent interpretation.) The argument over change, cause, and effect has raged, but has been persistently contaminated by an *idealized view* of the colonial or pre-industrial family; by *ignoring important developments* other than industrialization which influenced the family; or by the *selective use of family features* on the part of the individual researcher or writer.

An attempt is made here to avoid such pitfalls by asking at the outset, "What changes have and have not occurred in the American family since colonial days?" instead of the more difficult question, "What effect did the industrial revolution and the Western nuclear family have upon one another?" Subsequently, we shall raise the issue of whether certain changes were in fact related to the industrial revolution. A second strategy for avoiding the pitfalls inherent in discussing change is to compare current conditions to those which existed at the end of the previous period, that is, 1800, instead of talking in a vague manner about the contemporary family and the "colonial" family. The American family of 1630 was "colonial," and so was that of 1770—and we have just noted the kinds of changes which occurred between those two points in time. We are, therefore, comparing —as well as the sources will allow—the U.S. family in 1800 with that of today. Several excellent sources which have appeared since 1960 discuss changes and stabilities;[34] from them and from the author's own investigation, the preliminary list shown in Table 1 was devised. The various family features listed in the table can be subsumed under three general headings: (1) *family formation,* or premarital relationships and mate selection; (2) *unit characteristics,* or *internal* family relationships; and (3) relations with the *external* world of social network, community, institutions, and society.

The *formation* of nuclear family units in the United States involves personal choice, romantic love, the mechanisms of courtship, and the issues of premarital sexual norms and behavior. As indicated earlier, personal choice of a mate was already typical of the colonists upon their arrival

---

[34] Lantz et al., "Pre-Industrial Patterns in the Colonial Family in America," and Lantz, Schmitt, and Herman, "The Preindustrial Family in America"; several of the articles in Rabb and Rotberg, eds., *The Family in History,* especially those by Shorter, Wells, and Rothman; B. Laslett, "The Family as a Public and Private Institution"; Smith, "Parental Power and Marriage Patterns"; of crucial importance is still William J. Goode, *World Revolution and Family Patterns* (New York: Free Press, 1963).

Table 1

Approximate Degrees of Change in U.S. Family Features from 1800 to the Present

Degree of Change		Family Feature
Little or No Change	(1)*	Personal choice of a mate
Slight Change	(1)	Romantic love in mate selection
	(2)	Nuclear household composition
	(3)	Residential mobility
Moderate Change	(1)	Premarital sexual behavior (probably curvilinear)
	(2)	Husband-wife power norms and behavior
	(2)	Marital breakup
	(2)	Personnel embeddedness in the nuclear family (probably curvilinear)
	(2,3)	Women's status
Major Change	(1)	Courtship patterns
	(1)	Premarital sex norms
	(2)	Husband-wife roles and adjustments
	(2)	Socialization of children (child rearing)
	(2,3)	Divorce laws
	(3)	Institutional embeddedness in the nuclear family
Unknown	(2)	Marital happiness

* These numbers indicate the categories into which the various family features are divided in the subsequent discussion. Category 1 concerns family formation and premarital relationships. Category 2 pertains to family unit characteristics, or internal relationships. Category 3 involves relationships between the family and the external world.

in the New World. Then, as now, there were extremely small numbers of high-status families attempting to keep direct control over mating, but even the arranged marriage of the small American elites has never been the prepubertal linkage that has characterized some societies. For the most part, mate selection in the United States has been controlled by residential patterns and value systems, with personal choice as the norm. Daniel Smith, for example, notes that the decline in parental involvement in mate selection in Hingham, Massachusetts, which began in the eighteenth century, has continued up to the present. In fact, in 1850, 48.2 percent of Hingham marriages were between two Hingham residents, and this had declined to 25.8 percent by 1950.[35] The only change with respect to romantic love was that it was becoming more and more common as the basis for mate selection. Lantz, in his study of magazine articles written between 1791 and 1825, reports that the glorification of emotions was a dominant orientation. He likewise finds that by 1825 the motivations for marriage were al-

---

[35] Smith, "Parental Power and Marriage Patterns," p. 426.

ready beginning to be focused in romantic love.[36] This was accompanied by significant alterations in courtship behavior. Dating (unchaperoned heterosexual activity and experience) was not even a part of nineteenth century vocabulary. Until the early 1900s, courtship had centered in the social gathering or the home, with the couple having little unchaperoned time and lacking the freedom, transportation, and places to go which eventually gave rise to dating as *the* U.S. form of courtship. Another change in courtship has been the direct appeal of the female for the interest of the male, by means of more revealing clothing and self-styled makeup. The womanly "wiles," involving coyness and indirectness, which were so appropriate to chivalry and the double-standard morality, have taken a back seat to more obvious mechanisms of attention-getting.

Along with the appearance of dating as the focal point of American courtship, major changes occurred in the sexual codes governing premarital behavior. Much has been made of the colonial practice of bundling and its possible implications for premarital sexual intercourse.[37] Historians such as Charles Francis Adams have noted how the officially strict norms and sanctions may have increased rather than limited premarital sex. The crucial element in premarital sex norms and behavior, however, is the rise and fall of the nineteenth century Victorian era, with its great stress on the nuclear family and sexual continence outside of marriage, especially for the female. One effect of the Victorian era's emphasis on female continence was to strengthen the double standard. Men divided women into "good" and "bad," so that once a sex object had been degraded into the "bad" category, erotic feelings could have free play. The perverseness of this system was such that, since sex relations degraded a woman, a man might choose as his wife a woman who did not arouse sexual desire in him, says Bryan Strong.[38] However, along with the increasingly apparent double standard of sexual morality, an opposing development was occurring. The hit-and-run premarital intercourse and illegitimacy of the eighteenth century gave way in the nineteenth century to what Shorter calls "true-love illegitimacy," with a concomitant reduction in the illegitimacy rate. As Shorter puts it, the stabilization of nineteenth century society, and the greater integration of the lower and working classes into it, removed the transient quality from many romantic relationships. Legitimation of offspring increased greatly during the last third of the nineteenth century, "a sign that couples who coalesced briefly for intercourse were staying together with con-

---

[36] Lantz et al., "The Preindustrial Family in America," p. 579.

[37] On bundling, see Henry Reed Stiles, *Bundling: Its Origin, Progress and Decline in America* (New York: Book Collectors Association, 1934).

[38] Bryan Strong, "Toward a History of the Experiential Family: Sex and Incest in the Nineteenth Century Family," *Journal of Marriage and the Family* 35 (1973), 463–64.

nubial intent."[39] Such hit-and-run intercourse, we should add, appears to be on the increase again at the present time. The increasing strictness of the official norms from colonial days through the mid-1800s, followed by a wholesale questioning of this position during the twentieth century, seems, then, to have had the result of decreasing slightly the incidence of premarital sex by the mid-1800s and increasing its prevalence again in this century—even beyond its incidence in colonial days. Though we can only tentatively conclude that premarital sexual behavior followed this curvilinear pattern, with noticeable twentieth century rises in the 1920s and since 1965, we do know that society has moved toward an overt and often positive attitude in dealing with sexual matters. In particular, this has meant a more positive attitude toward female sexuality and a substantial movement away from the double standard. Sex education, sex research, popular literature, motion pictures—these and other media have brought about the frank and public consideration of all manner of sexual practices—a drastic departure, even from the treatment of sex in the early 1900s. An example of this change is that the pros and cons of premarital intercourse are being openly debated, not simply rejected by invoking an absolute, by many of the country's religious or moral leaders.[40] The white settlers and their colonial progeny did not ignore sexual matters. Nevertheless, the emphasis in official quarters is no longer on denunciation, control, and guilt, but has moved toward freedom, permissiveness, and openness.

Internally, the family has generally undergone moderate-to-great changes over the past two centuries. Perhaps the least change has occurred in the actual structural composition of the household. Well before the colonists came to America, the European household had taken on a nuclear character. The majority of nuclear families lived apart from the other members of their social network, this being an aspect of the privacy motif referred to above. The little change that did occur in household composition between the seventeenth and twentieth centuries was a decrease in the proportion of extremely large households, although the modal size category remained about the same. Another possible difference, based on the greater tendency in colonial days to incorporate an aging parent or parents into the household, has been balanced by the greater likelihood today that parents will live until their children reach maturity.

Much has been written about greater permissiveness in child rearing and about the decline in parental authority. It seems, however, that the

---

[39] Shorter, "Illegitimacy, Sexual Revolution, and Social Change in Modern Europe," in Rabb and Rotberg, *The Family in History*, p. 58.

[40] A good example is an article by a Protestant chaplain, Ronald M. Mazur, "Commonsense Sex," *Redbook* (July 1969), in which the author discusses premarital sex as a viable moral and ethical option.

major changes in socialization center on the division of labor in the family and a more continuous, developmental concern on the part of the parents. The family is no longer the basic economic producing unit, a fact that frees the child from the kind of patriarchal authority that could be asserted over someone in a clearly defined and inferior economic role.[41] Yet the child's role in the colonial family's division of labor, buttressed by moral training in absolutes and a tendency to perceive the child as a small adult, included a substantial permissive or self-directive element. That is, the colonial child, when "off duty," or free of responsibility, was often on his own—with internalized absolutes left to suffice. Today parents lack strong economic-labor authority and are less likely to be buttressed by absolutes, but they tend to be more consciously and continuously concerned with the child as a developing person—with achievement and other aspects of socialization. Rothman makes the clearest statement of the modern child's freedom-from-patriarchy-without-autonomy. "In the middle classes," he states, "parental authority may have maintained itself through a shift in tactics. The manipulation of the child, rather than his outright coercion, became more prevalent in Jacksonian America." Let us allow Rothman to speak at greater length concerning child rearing in the nineteenth century:

> The normative literature of the period insisted that strict obedience be the ultimate goal of parental training, but now authors had a wider variety of fresh strategies to recommend before resorting to the rod. Although they counselled greater displays of affection than their eighteenth-century counterparts, they were no less insistent on denying the child autonomy.

Typical interpretations, says Rothman, have viewed age-grading and affectional display as evidence of increasing concern for child welfare and freedom. But there is another side to it:

> Age-grading may have been part of an effort to lockstep the child into rigid and predetermined modes of behavior. The change looked not to his benefit, but to the rationalization of childhood so that behavior would become more predictable and manageable.[42]

Thus, only a portion of the apparent greater permissiveness is due to reduced parental authority; the remainder is based on a heightened parental awareness of and concern about individual personality and child rearing in toto.

---

[41] One of the most generally agreed-upon observations is that the father, and parents generally, have lost *formal* authority over their offspring since the mid-eighteenth century. On this, see Neil J. Smelser, "The Social Challenge to Parental Authority," in Farber, Mustacchi, and Wilson, *Man and Civilization*, pp. 70–71; Henretta, "The Morphology of New England Society in the Colonial Period," in Rabb and Rotberg, *The Family in History*, p. 202. As Henretta puts it: "Patriarchy had given way to parental solicitude and aid."

[42] Rothman, "Documents in Search of a Historian," in Rabb and Rotberg, *The Family in History*, pp. 188–89.

Child rearing, then, is a matter of a lessened formal or traditional parental authority, a greater use of indirect persuasion, a constant oversight of the child's development, and a greater concern for individual personality development (this final point going counter to part of Rothman's interpretation). We shall return to this in Chapters 7 and 8.

The curvilinear change in personnel embeddedness posited in Table 1 is closely related to the socialization issue just discussed. In the late medieval period, we have noted, the nuclear family began to be distinguished from its social network. Emphasis on the nuclear family, at the expense of the kin-friend network, continued through the colonial period and culminated in the Victorian era of the mid-1800s.[43] Already, however, a new emphasis on the individual was increasing; it was embodied in the conception of home architecture which made possible the privacy of family members from one another. Thus, the move from the Victorian era into the Progressive era was characterized by a decrease in nuclear family values and an increase in concern with the individual and his needs for adjustment, understanding, personality development, and uniqueness. Shorter's description of the rise of more liberal sexual attitudes can be used to characterize the rise of individualism as well. It "probably flowed from heightened ego awareness and weakened superego controls."[44] Precisely where we are today in nuclear embeddedness versus individualism cannot be determined until later in the present volume, but it is a question that the reader should keep in mind (see Figure 2).

Figure 2
Changes in Personnel Embeddedness from Colonial Days to the Present

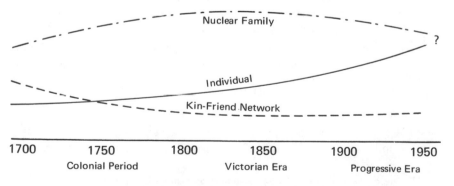

[43] Strong, "Toward a History of the Experiential Family," p. 458, notes that from the early eighteenth century the family became more important, due to the emotional dislocations caused by the societal changes of that period.
[44] Shorter, "Illegitimacy, Sexual Revolution, and Social Change in Modern Europe," in Rabb and Rotberg, The Family in History, p. 63.

Husband-wife power relations in the family are extremely difficult to ascertain for two primary reasons. For one thing, legal and normative authority may, as Lantz et al. observe, be circumvented or overridden by subtle means of influence.[45] Furthermore, there is the nagging question in the study of power anywhere, not just in the family, of whether *not* doing a task or making a decision means that the individual lacks power in that area, or whether it means he has delegated power or authority to the one doing the task. We do know that wives may have substantial influence in a normatively patriarchal family system. We also know that, in the modern couple that is seeking to make decisions democratically, the father may, because of his achievements or the resources he controls, find himself with veto power in many key decision-making situations. Despite these facts, it seems likely that some change has occurred in husband-wife power behavior, allowing an increase in the *direct* and *acceptable* influence of the wife. Lantz's two studies show that this change was already under way at the beginning of the present period, his data indicating more female power in the marital relationship during 1794–1825 than during 1741–91.[46]

Firmer ground is reached in looking at changes in power norms or expectations rather than behavior. Patriarchy, or husband-dominance, was the general expectation in the colonial family; today this norm is competing with the norm of conscious equalitarianism and democracy in the home. The reason for speaking of moderate rather than great change in this area is that *conscious* power equality in the family is increasingly characteristic, not of the entire U.S. family population, but of one major segment: those "white-collar" or middle-class families that are financially fairly well off.*

Another change affecting the family has to do with the position of women in society,[47] and the concomitant alteration of husbands' and wives' roles. As late as 1850, in many states a wife had no legal control over personal property; all her belongings were legally at her husband's disposal. However, the democratic ideal, plus the growing awareness of females that they could make a living in urban, industrializing society, resulted in the birth of the women's rights movements. Within the past hundred years, women have gained legally and politically: ownership of property within marriage and the right to vote are two examples of these gains. They have gained educationally. In colonial days even a grade school education was thought unnecessary for a girl. A century later, the distinction was drawn at the secondary school level. High school—and in high-status families, col-

---

[45] Lantz et al., "Pre-Industrial Patterns in the Colonial Family in America," p. 419.

[46] Lantz, Schmitt, and Herman, "The Preindustrial Family in America," p. 577.

[47] This subject should more accurately be introduced when changes in the family's relations with the external world are treated, but is raised here to prepare the reader for the "internal" issue of husband-wife roles in marriage.

lege—was deemed valuable for males, but impractical for females. The twentieth century ushered in the period of "coeducation," with about one-third of today's American college graduates being females. Women have likewise gained substantially in the economic sphere. Not only do some 25 million U.S. women hold jobs, but they have advanced to the point that salary differentials for men and women doing the same work diverge but slightly. One must be cautious, however, not to overstate women's gains in the United States. For one thing, as we shall see in greater detail in Chapter 11, women lost status in the industrial world before gaining it. That is, industrialization removed the husband from the home to play his major economic provision role elsewhere, thereby giving him economic control over the domestic unit in a way not possible in agrarian society. The domestic captivity of the wife, then, is considerable in the nuclear, industrial family. For another thing, even now job-holding by women has *supplemental* connotations economically, since a wife tends to make less money than her husband, and more income means more spent for consumer goods. In addition, job discrimination against females is still strong, both in terms of bars to advancement and in terms of virtual exclusion from many professional and business fields. In fact, after World War II, the glorification of wifehood and motherhood by the mass media undid to some extent the former gains of the feminists. Thus, the female today is in a difficult position: her rise in status has been accompanied by the tendency to play down her traditional role—to speak of being "just a housewife." And yet this remains her dominant life goal due to the influence of tradition and the systematic, yet subtle, discrimination that she confronts in society.[48] Many of the positive changes in women's status are thus yet to come.

The change in the status of women in society is related to the changes in courtship practices discussed above, as well as to changes in husband and wife roles and adjustments. The basic movement has been away from predestined economic and familial roles toward an open, free-choice approach to being a husband and father or a wife and mother. In colonial days, a man was expected to run the economic machinery of the family and to be a stern and able disciplinarian; a woman was expected to marry, raise children, and provide for her husband's needs. In the nineteenth century, under the influence of Victorian glorification of the family, the husband and wife often fell far short of the kind of intimacy extolled by the moralists of that day. With sex viewed as sinful, the married couple were likely to have a strained relationship, while manifesting a surface or "pseudo" mutuality.

---

[48] At least one author has argued quite persuasively, by means of occupational and other statistics, that women have actually lost status in recent years in comparison to men. See Dean D. Knudsen, "The Declining Status of Women: Popular Myths and the Failure of Functionalist Thought," *Social Forces* 48 (1969), 183–93.

This strain, in turn, caused the wife to turn to her children for gratification.[49] A result was the kind of watchfulness discussed above—the "smothering mother" syndrome still referred to in the popular press. However, even pseudomutuality and smothering do not capture the essence of the wife-mother position in the nineteenth century family. During that same period, as families became smaller and longevity greater, couples found their lives after their children had left home becoming a major part of their life cycle.[50] This, when combined with the other two characteristics of the period, placed an added burden on the wife, whose psychological existence was more completely tied to family and children than was the husband's. Today, the options have multiplied and traditional norms are questioned. How should the father operate: as disciplinarian, provider, or buddy? How much of himself should a man invest in activities that are internal to the family and how much in community and occupational affairs? Should a woman be "just a housewife," or should she balance her domestic responsibilities with employment elsewhere or with various forms of community service? The crucial element in all the various role decisions men and women must make is openness, the weakness of traditional expectations, a lack of predetermination. This, of course, heightens the importance of adjustment between wife and husband; each couple must work out its own role definitions, though equality of choice between the sexes is still far from complete. The intricacies of these role options and the adjustments required are one of the major foci of the present volume, particularly of Chapters 11 and 12.

The notion of family adjustments brings us to one of the more intriguing dimensions of the "classical extended family of Western nostalgia." It is often assumed that the family in colonial days was a happy, close-knit unit in which conflict and indecision were far overshadowed by stability and tradition. Yet, as we have indicated, the colonial family was kept together by various legal and traditional mechanisms for the sake of the economic and other functions which the nuclear unit performed. Thus, personal happiness might vary greatly from one family unit to another. It is not that unhappiness did not result in the breakup of some colonial family units; it is rather that some units very likely stayed together, despite unhappiness, for the sake of their other functions. The twentieth century American family, by contrast, lacks many of the cultural or normative supports for the unit which characterized an earlier day, and finds itself held together primarily by the quality of internal relationships. Under such circumstances, happiness, satisfaction, or adjustment becomes the overt goal of the married couple. While it is

---

[49] Strong, "Toward a History of the Experiential Family," p. 461.
[50] Robert V. Wells, "Demographic Change and the Life Cycle of American Families," in Rabb and Rotberg, *The Family in History*, p. 93.

impossible to determine how happy colonial couples were, it seems quite possible that the actual "happiness quotient," or level of happiness, of married couples is higher today than it was in colonial times, for two reasons: first, married couples work so hard at it today; second, more unhappy marriages weed themselves out today than was formerly the case. Whether or not this interpretation is correct, let us not make the mistake of referring nostalgically to the "happy, traditional colonial family."

The prevalence of marital breakup is one of the more frequently used indicators of the purported "decay" of the American family. We know that the number of legal grounds for divorce increased substantially in the nineteenth century and that this was followed in the first half of the twentieth century by a rise in the divorce rate.[51] However, it is difficult to determine the extent of the increase in all forms of family breakup since colonial days. For one thing, family units in colonial days that might eventually have been disrupted by desertion were often broken up by the premature death of one spouse or the other. For another thing, some of the rise in the divorce rate is nothing more than an increase in the tendency to legalize marital separation. Thus, while the divorce rate has risen, the rates of premature family breakup by death, desertion, and separation have declined. In short, the change in the laws governing divorce has been greater than the change in total rates of premature marital breakup. Yet the strictness of the norms and laws, and the concern of the colonists to keep families together for the sake of their economic and other functions, meant that husband-wife relations had to be worse in colonial days than today before a couple would *voluntarily* separate.

Turning to the relations between the nuclear family and the *external* world, which include the already discussed position of women, we find a close connection between personnel embeddedness, the dimensions of the household, and the amount of residential mobility. One of the reasons for the increasing separation of the nuclear unit from its social milieu, in terms of values and household composition, is the residential mobility of families. This mobility is not, however, so much a difference between colonial days and the present as it is a pervasive characteristic of U.S. history. The history of white colonization and colonial expansion on the American frontier is, in fact, the history of residential mobility. Henretta asserts very simply that "the structure of the colonial American family . . . facilitated geographical mobility and economic expansion," and he notes the rapid decrease over the seventeenth and eighteenth centuries in the proportion of sons who inherited land

---

[51] A case could be made both for considering the increase in the divorce rate to be internal to the family and for considering it to involve relations between the family and the external world.

—immovable property—from their fathers.[52] We may grant that a substantially larger proportion of colonial persons inherited farms or settled on land near their kin, but this is offset to some extent by the large numbers of working-class persons who in the nineteenth and twentieth centuries clustered together in the same city with their kin. The number of multiple moves by any one family unit in modern society may have increased, but this is a characteristic of a minority of the population—primarily certain professional and executive persons and their families. Furthermore, twentieth century mobility is neither uniformly unaffected by the location of kin and friends, nor does it entail—as mobility often did in colonial days—virtual isolation from kin and former friends. Too much has been made of the modern family's pursuit of industrial and managerial work opportunities; the overall picture is more one of slightly greater freedom to choose one's residential relationship to his kin and of somewhat greater frequency of residential movement.

The European and colonial American family systems were already basically different—in terms of institutional embeddedness—from such societies as the Papago, in which the family-kin network and social organization were almost synonymous. In the colonies, legal and political institutions were quite separate from kinship and family ties, and economic, religious, and educational institutions had special functionaries as well as strong ties to the nuclear family. Nevertheless, great changes in embeddedness have occurred since colonial days. The industrial revolution, centered in the development of the factory system, directly effected one of these changes by transferring the economic-productive function from the family unit and the home to a separate location, to which one or more family members go to work to provide for their family's economic needs. The family as a unit is no longer both producer and consumer, but merely consumer. Yet in the capitalist market economy, the family's role as consumer is extremely important, and the business community of today is quite cognizant of the value of having a strong nuclear family system.

Other activities that were handled by the family in an immediate and often rudimentary fashion have undergone expansion and spatial separation. Recreation, once a family activity at home or church and an individual pursuit around the home, has become increasingly specialized along age lines and centered in various locations other than the home. The protective function (except for a few private fallout shelters) has ceased to be a cooperative-familial responsibility, being instead the concern of the police, firemen, and other community specialists. Health care has become the responsibility of

---

[52] Henretta, "The Morphology of New England Society in the Colonial Period," in Rabb and Rotberg, *The Family in History,* pp. 201–9.

the doctor, the drug store, and the hospital, with the family as coordinating agency. The home remedy, once the key element in medical treatment, has become nothing more than the butt of jokes.

Except for economic productivity, the educational function is perhaps the most dramatic example of expansion and parceling out. Today the law makes it impossible, except under extreme extenuating circumstances, for parents to keep their children at home to educate them. At five or six years of age the child is removed from the home for thirty to forty hours a week. Simultaneously, however, parents supervise and give continuing attention to their children's development.

The religious function, once of great importance to socialization and discipline, has seen its roots in the home become weakened, with its activity restricted to specific times and places apart from the home. The lessening of the carry-over between the religious institution and the home makes it possible for commentators to note a fourfold to fivefold increase in church membership since colonial days and, at the same time, to refer to the increasing secularization of society. All these developments may be referred to as institutional differentiation or the weakening of institutional embeddedness in the nuclear family; we have avoided the often-used term *loss of family functions*.[53] The reason for this is that the term, although in common usage since the 1930s, has overtones that might cause some to think of the contemporary family as "twiddling its collective thumbs" for want of responsibilities or activities. This, however, is an incorrect representation on two counts. First, the family is still very much involved in the coordinating of physical care and of socialization. Second, while much family unit interaction occurs in the interstices of other societal institutions (as Freedman puts it), there is an increasingly overt and central involvement of the family unit in meeting the psychological needs of its members. But more on the functions of the family today shall be reserved for Chapter 5.

Section Four

SUMMARY AND CONCLUSIONS

The most striking changes in family formation or premarital conditions since colonial days have been in courtship and sex codes, with an increasing link between romantic love and mate selection. The major change—in reality, a complex of changes—in relations between the nuclear family and the larger

---

[53] On the term *loss of family functions,* see William F. Ogburn, "The Family and Its Functions," in *Recent Social Trends* (New York: McGraw-Hill, 1933), chap. 13, and our discussion of Ogburn's view in Chapter 5 of this volume.

society is in the expansion and parceling out of certain traditional functions to other agencies and locations. By far the most numerous large-scale changes have occurred within the family itself. These have included an increase in the number of role options and definitions open to both sexes, with a concomitant multiplying of the number of necessary adjustments, and a loosening of divorce laws, making it easier to dissolve a given family unit.

Only a few of these developments can be directly related to the industrial revolution. Most important is, of course, the influence of industrialization upon institutional embeddedness—especially the economic-productive function. Industrialization also seems to have had some effect on the status of women and husband-wife roles and adjustments, though these were also influenced by democratic ideology. Otherwise, it becomes extremely difficult to perceive direct linkages between the family and industrialization.[54]

The "new family history" has made it increasingly possible to paint with broad strokes the characteristics of the colonial family, and to compare it with the family today. This historical reconstruction is not complete, and historians will continue to illumine additional facets of the colonial family experience. Of particular concern to the present author in attempting to generalize about "the colonial U.S. family" is the knowledge that much of what has been discovered about the family in Dedham, Plymouth, and Hingham may very well not hold for Charleston, South Carolina, or Richmond, Virginia. It is generally accepted that in the South there were more kin-based landholdings—more lineages—and that these were more dominant politically and economically than were such units in the North. This difference, it might be added, did not stop with colonial days but continued into the present period. Much, however, remains to be done in investigating the southern family system, and in comparing it with those of New England and the frontier. In discussing classical China, Freedman spoke of two organizing principles: that of high-status people and that of the masses. Rosenfeld likewise found two cultural ideals at work in the Arab village: the traditional and the modern. The same issue must now be raised regarding our depiction of changes in the American family since colonial days; when we speak of "sex codes" or "husband-wife power codes," the question arises, "Whose codes?" Are they everyone's codes, or are they the codes of one important group within the society? The answer, to which we shall return in detail in subsequent chapters, might be inferred from the previously made comment that "conscious power equality in the family is increasingly characteristic, not of the entire U.S. family population, but of one major segment: those 'white-collar' or middle-class families that are financially fairly

---

[54] On this, see Morris Zelditch, Jr., "Cross-Cultural Analysis of Family Structure," in Christensen, *Handbook of Marriage and the Family*, pp. 492–97.

well off." This equality is the norm of those who dominate American culture, that is, the middle classes. The term *dominate* is used here in much the same sense as in the discussion of polygyny. It does not mean numerical *predominance*; rather, it refers to that cultural style which, due to the key position of its proponents in government, education, and the mass media, receives the widest dissemination among the populace as a whole. In a society such as the United States, there are active subcultural principles as well as the dominant ones. Chapter 6 is devoted to the delineation of the various subcultural principles at work in the United States and the historic interrelations among them. Furthermore, we must keep our eyes open for conflicting norms even among the middle classes, and for inconsistencies as well as integration within the family system. As Rothman asserts, it is "at least as appropriate to search for discontinuities as for neat matches."[55] One way to view the nuclear family unit and its activities is as a unit that is becoming more specialized in a society of specialists. This issue and the crucial theoretical problems concerning it will command our attention in Chapter 5.

---

[55] Rothman, "Documents in Search of a Historian," in Rabb and Rotberg, *The Family in History*, p. 189.

Literature has accumulated on the subjects of family structure, function, and variety; in this volume we deal with all three. One strand of writing has sought to determine which tasks the family performs in every society. This concern with universal family functions may be more usefully employed for our purposes by transforming these functions into variables. A second strand, derived from Ogburn and others, notes the family's loss of functions to other institutions and its affective function today. Using Durkheim's view of societal integration, the affective function is placed in societal context and guiding propositions are developed. These propositions include: (1) the family's specialized affective function; (2) its specific function as economic consumer; (3) its general role in socialization; (4) the complexity and inconsistencies in society and its family system; (5) the divergent family cultures in U.S. society, or the subculture concept. Finally, five continua are developed to deal cross-culturally with family formation, socialization, marital roles, institutional embeddedness, and personnel embeddedness, in order that the current character of, and direction and speed of change within, the U.S. family may be better understood.

The Family in a Differentiated Society: Toward a Theoretical Perspective

A review of Chapters 2–4 shows that the three major foci of attention have been family structure, family functions, and family varieties. In the present chapter we propose to tie together many of the loose ends from the foregoing analysis, and to develop a quasi-theoretical* framework that will be utilized throughout the remainder of the volume.

· The structural concerns thus far presented revolve around the degrees of institutional and personnel embeddedness in various societies, including such issues as household composition, relations between the nuclear family and the kin group, and relations between the family system and other societal institutions. These factors will be discussed further in the present chapter, and will continue to be major emphases throughout the book.

The concept of function, as it has been employed in the sociological literature on the family, is multidimensional, having at least three distinct meanings. These three meanings may be exemplified by the following statements:

"The family is functional for society in several ways."

"The functions of the family have changed."

"The family functions in the following manner."

In the first statement, the term *functional* has to do with the *good* or *benefit*, perpetuation, or integration of society. The idea of universal family functions, such as reproduction and socialization, is closely related to the issue of the family's universality, referred to in Chapter 3. This idea concerns the way in which the family furthers certain goals of the society in which it is operating. The second use of the idea of family functions has to do with *tasks* performed, so that when we speak of the functional centrality of the family we are saying that the central tasks of a given society are performed within the family setting.[1] The third statement, which changes *function* from a noun to a verb, is simply concerned with describing how the family actually *operates*. The kinship system in the United States, we might say, functions for affective ties and a certain amount of obligation. Or one can speak of certain parts of the family system as functioning, that is, operating, in an inconsistent or conflicting fashion. For example, the norm that says the American should be independent is inconsistent with the one that says he should honor his aging parents; the way in which these norms are reconciled is the way society functions at that point.

The first of the three uses of "function" is not a major concern of this volume, though we shall discuss it briefly in the next few pages. The question of changing family tasks is a basic issue in this chapter and, like the structural questions, continues to be raised in subsequent chapters. Finally, the large mass of materials describing adolescence, dating, husband-wife relations, and other aspects of the family simply depicts the way in which a particular family system—that of the United States—operates.

Thus far, the concept of family varieties has been exemplified crossculturally by the use of materials on the Nayar, Papago, Chinese, and other family systems. In turning more exclusively to the United States, the issue of variety is redefined as one of subcultures and subsocieties. Are there peoples within the United States who are sufficiently different culturally or separate

---

[1] Robert F. Winch and Rae Lesser Blumberg, "Societal Complexity and Familial Organization," in Winch and Louis Wolf Goodman, eds., *Selected Studies in Marriage and the Family* (New York: Holt, Rinehart and Winston, 1968 ed.); and Murray A. Straus, "Family Organization and Problem Solving Ability in Relation to Societal Modernization," *Journal of Comparative Family Studies* 3 (1972), 70–83. These authors use the word *function* very clearly and well to mean "tasks performed." Kin networks, as Straus puts it, "vary tremendously in the number and importance of the functions they perform."

socially as to be distinct from the dominant members of that society? This question will be the focus of Chapter 6, and will also arise from time to time throughout the remainder of the book.

We shall begin to synthesize the ideas of function, structure, and variety by referring briefly to the notion of universal family functions.

Section One

UNIVERSAL FAMILY FUNCTIONS

One strand of theoretical, or explanatory, writing about the family generalized the question regarding family functions in the following manner. There are certain goals that any society must accomplish in order to continue existing. It must reproduce individuals to replace the dying; it must protect its boundaries; it must motivate persons to take positions of leadership; it must solve the economic problem of physical survival; and so on.[2] Among these necessary functions are some that appear to be performed by the family in every society; these are called "universal family functions," or functions that the family has always carried out everywhere. Kingsley Davis speaks of reproduction, maintenance, placement, and socialization (or raising the young) as universal family functions. George P. Murdock says the universal functions are reproduction, socialization, economic cooperation, and sexual relations. Ira Reiss claims there is but one universal function of the family—the "nurturant" socialization of the newborn. Other functions are often, but not always, performed by the family or kin group.[3] A particular author's *definition* of the family is, of course, closely related to the functions he sees it as carrying out. Thus, a close link exists between the discussion in Chapter 3 of the universality of the nuclear family and the idea of universal family functions.

A distillation of a list of family functions devised by William J. Goode yields three functions, which can be viewed from the standpoint either of the family itself or of the family-in-society. First, there is the *reproductive* function, which is dependent upon age at marriage, fertility, and other factors. From society's perspective, this might be called the replacement function. That is, for a society to survive, new members must be produced to replace those who are dying off; this occurs within families. The second function is *status placement*, which means the determination of the indi-

---

[2] D. F. Aberle et al., "The Functional Prerequisites of a Society," *Ethics* 60 (1950), 100–111.

[3] Ira Reiss summarizes the views of Davis and Murdock, as well as his own, in "The Universality of the Family: A Conceptual Analysis," *Journal of Marriage and the Family* 27 (1965), 443–53.

vidual's life chances within his society. From the standpoint of society, this is the integrative or maintenance function. It simply means that family background has historically and cross-culturally been a major determinant of one's career achievement or status in society. Third, the family, as Reiss indicates, performs the *socialization* or child-rearing function. In the family, the individual learns what to do and what not to do in order to get along in his society, in order to be consistent with its demands and expectations. Thus, from society's standpoint, this is the social control function—a result of the family's embodying and imparting the society's culture.

Goode rightly cautions the reader against assuming that the three functions he lists are universals in the sense of being constants.[4] Though the discussion of "universals" is valuable in its own right, Goode feels that such functions should be thought of as *variables,* with the family system of a given society meeting more or less of a specific need. For example, in some societies one's life chances are predicated almost entirely upon the family unit into which he is born. In other societies, such as the United States, the possibility of individual achievement means that the family might be better described as the base, or beginning point, defining certain limits upon status. A careful review of the literature might result in the conclusion that in the United States about 40 percent of status placement is determined by family background. Or, the reader might conclude that in one society 90 percent of socialization occurs within the family and kin group, while in another society the figure is less than 50 percent. Thus, the universal functions may profitably be transformed into variable functions for the sake of comparing societies.

Bernard Farber goes even further in criticizing the notion of universal family functions. When you start by saying, "Here are the things which must be done for society to survive, and these are the things which the family does for its society," you are defining the goals of a society, as well as talking about tasks. In speaking of the family as doing certain things for the benefit of society, or as furthering societal ends and integration, two value judgments must be made. First, we must ask whether the family is doing a good or a poor job of performing its functions in a given society, thereby drawing a judgment regarding its quality of performance. Also, we are likely to make the inherent judgment that equilibrium is better than change, that stability is better than alteration of society and culture. Rather, we should be reminded that, as families carry out their reproductive, status-placing, and

---

[4] William J. Goode, "The Sociology of the Family," in Robert K. Merton, Leonard Broom, and Leonard S. Cottrell, eds., *Sociology Today* (New York: Basic Books, 1959), chap. 7.

socializing functions, they may or may not be contributing to societal integration and perpetuation. It is quite possible to conceive of high fertility, low status placement, and socialization for change in a particular segment of a society as leading to upheaval rather than maintenance.[5] A difficulty arises, then, in the discussion of universal functions when one moves from the general notion of family functions to their specific implementation, that is, how the family system of a given society is doing in this regard. This obstacle is not insurmountable, for the careful student may profitably seek to discover the goals and values of a society and the relation of family functioning to those goals.[6] That is not, however, a key purpose of this book. When you read in subsequent pages about the functions of the American family, keep in mind that we are not describing how well a set of universal functions is being performed, but are merely noting the ways in which the family in the United States has historically articulated and currently articulates with this particular society and its other institutions.

Section Two

THE FAMILY AND ITS CHANGING FUNCTIONS: THREE VIEWS

Leaving the attempt to discover universal family functions to such writers as Davis, Murdock, and Reiss, let us turn instead to three authors who have summarized the transformation of the family in Western civilization in recent times. William F. Ogburn, Ernest Burgess, and Bernard Farber have each made a contribution to understanding the modern family. Ogburn, writing in the 1930s, described the family's loss of functions. Industrialization and urbanization have resulted in the transferral of one traditional family function after another to specialized institutional settings. The economic producing function has been transferred to the factory and office; the educational function has been moved to the schoolroom; the religious function has been left almost entirely to the church or synagogue; the recreational function has gone to the theater and stadium; the medical function has been transferred to the doctor's office and the hospital. In most cases, family members go to these places individually, not as a family unit. The result has been that the

---

[5] Bernard Farber, *Family: Organization and Interaction* (San Francisco: Chandler, 1964), pp. 23–28.

[6] Harold Christensen, "The Intrusion of Values," in Christensen, ed., *Handbook of Marriage and the Family* (Chicago: Rand McNally, 1964), pp. 974–75, points out that the scholar "can use some goal or desired end (value) as the criterion against which to measure its phenomenon—but of course without making any judgment as to whether the end itself is good or bad."

family is left to provide affection and understanding for its members, but little else.[7] In short, with the increasing differentiation and specialization of society, the family has also become a specialist. No longer functionally central, it now specializes in gratifying people's psychological needs.

Ernest Burgess, while more interested in describing what takes place among family members than in relating the family to the larger society, nevertheless parallels Ogburn in his conception of the family. The family, says Burgess, is moving from an institution to a companionship. Recalling our definition of an institution from Chapter 1, we can readily observe with Burgess that the institutional family is ideally one whose "unity would be determined by the traditional rules and regulations, specified duties and obligations, and other social pressures impinging upon the family members."[8] Its institutional characteristics include authoritarian or autocratic power, stability and permanence, the perpetuation of culture, compliance with predetermined roles, and the carrying out of numerous tasks, such as economic, religious, and recreational ones, *as a unit*. The U.S. family—or, more generally, the modern industrial family—has, over the past two centuries, moved away from an institutional character and toward a "unity which develops out of mutual affection and intimate association of husband and wife and parents and children." The characteristics of this emerging type include equalitarian decision-making; individual choice of a mate, based on affection and personality; concern with happiness and adjustment in marriage; and a great modification of the family's historic functions. "The external factors making for family stability, such as control by custom and community opinion, have been greatly weakened. The permanence of marriage more and more depends on the bonds of affection, temperamental compatibility, and mutual interests," in sum, on companionship.[9] Although the modern family has not yet arrived at the companionship type, it is currently heading in that direction.

The family, according to Bernard Farber, is moving from orderly replacement to universal, permanent availability. *Orderly replacement* refers to both persons and culture content, but the emphasis is on the latter. It means the passing along of family culture from one generation to the next with as little change as possible. Today, however, orderly replacement is giving way to *universal, permanent availability*. In using this term, Farber focuses, not on socialization, but rather on mate selection or the formation and dissolution

[7] William F. Ogburn, "The Family and Its Functions," in *Recent Social Trends* (New York: McGraw-Hill, 1933), chap. 13.

[8] Ernest W. Burgess, Harvey J. Locke, and Mary Margaret Thomes, *The Family*, 3rd ed. (New York: Litton Educational Publishing, 1963), p. 3, by permission of Van Nostrand Reinhold Company.

[9] Burgess, Locke, and Thomes, *The Family*, p. 4.

of family units. The individual, Farber believes, is becoming increasingly free to choose as a mate any individual of the opposite sex with whom he comes in contact. That is, members of the opposite sex are becoming "universally available" as potential mates. They are, furthermore, becoming "permanently available," so that if one marital linkage proves unsatisfactory, it may be terminated and another begun.[10] Personal choice of a mate, loosening sex codes, frequent divorce—all three are consistent with the expectation of happiness and meaningful relationships in the family, and, Farber feels, are indices of the movement toward universal, permanent availability.

Each of these three authors notes that in a society in which the family is functionally central, or is the prime economic and socializing unit, there is apt to be great concern for keeping the individual family unit intact. Thus, in the institutional, functionally central family concerned with orderly replacement, sex is controlled (if possible), divorce is difficult to obtain, and mate selection is pretty much in the hands of the adult generation. However, when functions are expanded and parceled out from the family unit, the cultural mechanisms for maintaining the boundaries of any given family unit are weakened. This weakening is felt to be a part of the family's recent history.

Loss of family functions, movement toward a companionship basis for marriage, and universal, permanent availability of members of the opposite sex for mating—these are some of the conceptualizations that have been developed to summarize the changes discussed in the preceding chapter. Although valuable, these conceptualizations are somewhat misleading and overdrawn. Thus, in Section Three, we shall—with the aid of the French sociologist Émile Durkheim—extend and clarify the issues raised by the three authors referred to in this section.

Section Three

DIVISION OF LABOR AND THE FAMILY: EXTENSIONS AND CLARIFICATIONS

In the late nineteenth and early twentieth century, Émile Durkheim presented a view of society and the direction of social change which, while incorrect in some of its predictions and conservative in its ideology, is of help in understanding family change. Durkheim's major emphasis throughout his writings is the nature of societal integration, or what it is that ties people together in society. Historically and cross-culturally, many societies (the

---

[10] Farber, *Family: Organization and Interaction*, pp. 106–9.

Papago, for example) have been composed of relatively self-sufficient family-kin units, each of which carried out approximately the same activities as any other. The members of these self-sufficient and similar units are not obliged, out of necessity, "either to remain united or to perish. On the contrary, since they do not need each other, as each contains within himself all that social life consists of, he can go and carry it elsewhere."[11] What, then, is it that links persons together in such societies and keeps each subunit from wandering freely and self-sufficiently? For Durkheim, the answer lies in the strength of the behavioral norms and the interpersonal bonds—the expectations and the collective sentiments ("we" feelings) that are developed. The simple, or undifferentiated, society is held together by careful specification of the acceptable, serious punishment of the unacceptable, awareness of the ways in which "our" behavior differs from that of the people "in the next valley," and the identification of persons in a family-kin unit with their larger society. Both norms and bonds are a part of the collective conscience; the development of a strong collective conscience is necessary to societal integration in a society in which the family-kin units do not actually need one another. This, says Durkheim, is "mechanical solidarity."

Societies in the modern world are very different from such undifferentiated societies. They are characterized by an ever-expanding division of labor. The individual family-kin units are no longer self-sufficient and identical; rather, there is an organic solidarity or integration among them. That is, they are linked together like the parts of an organism, each with a specific function to perform and each very much dependent upon the others for its survival. Civilized and industrialized society is held together not so much by the feelings of the units toward one another as by necessity.

While these ideas from Durkheim are of some interest in themselves, a certain amount of extension is necessary before they begin to illuminate the internal nature of the family. Durkheim's efforts, we have said, were directed largely toward understanding society. Seldom did he turn his attention to what goes on within the family-kin units.[12] However, a few hints can be pieced together from the following references. In the mechanically solidary or undifferentiated society, "the farmer's life does not extend outside the familial circle. Economic activity, having no consequences outside the family, is sufficiently regulated by the family, and the family itself thus serves as occupational group." But in the organically solidary society, in which the family-kin units are no longer self-sufficient, "the family, in losing the unity

---

[11] Emile Durkheim, *The Division of Labor in Society*, trans. George Simpson (New York: Free Press, 1964 ed.), p. 151.

[12] For some of Durkheim's lesser-known references to the family, see Herbert Bynder, "Emile Durkheim and the Sociology of the Family," *Journal of Marriage and the Family* 31 (1969), 527–33.

and indivisibility of former times, has lost with one stroke a great part of its efficacy. As it is today broken up with each generation, man passes a notable part of his existence far from all domestic influence."[13] This transformation is elsewhere described in this way: "The family, in truth, is for a long time a veritable social segment. . . . Instead of remaining an autonomous society alongside of the great society, it becomes more and more involved in the system of social organs. It even becomes one of the organs, charged with special functions. . . . It is, indeed, a law without exception that the more the social structure is by nature segmental, the more families form great, compact, undivided masses, gathered up in themselves."[14] So the family, says Durkheim, comes to be more and more of a specialist among specialists, dependent upon other such units and upon a differentiated economy for survival. Yet Durkheim has only hinted at the character of the family-kin units themselves. One key hint, for example, is the term *undivided masses,* from the above quotation. Let us, therefore, expand upon the familial references contained in Durkheim's writing.

In "mechanically solidary" societies composed of self-sufficient family-kin units, what is the internal nature of those units? Cross-cultural study has led anthropologists and other social scientists to conclude that, no matter how simple a society is in terms of technology and division of labor, there is role differentiation on at least two bases: age and sex. Morris Zelditch, for example, reports this from a survey of literature on 56 societies. Males and females, adults and children are assigned different roles, tasks, authority, and privileges in the institutionally embedded (mechanically solidary) society. This differentiation is centered in the various family-kin units, although each of these units is relatively similar, as Durkheim points out, to every other. The care and detail with which the family-kin division of labor is spelled out is most appreciated by one familiar with anthropological literature.[15] In ideal-typical language, we are suggesting that, in a society integrated by mechanical solidarity, the subunits—family-kin groups—will tend to be internally, or "organically," integrated by a clear division of labor. This division of labor, and the organic solidarity of family-kin units, was noted briefly in our discussion of the Papago family system. The strength of the family members' bonds to one another is not as important to its internal functioning and maintenance as is the strength of the norms and bonds that contribute to integration *among* families. Also, whether the nuclear family can be easily dissolved is dependent upon the extent of personnel embeddedness. If a larger kin unit, such as a patriline, is the chief unit of economic

---

[13] Durkheim, *The Division of Labor in Society,* p. 17.
[14] Durkheim, *The Division of Labor in Society,* pp. 210, 292.
[15] Some of this literature is summarized and excerpted in William N. Stephens, *The Family in Cross-Cultural Perspective* (New York: Holt, Rinehart and Winston, 1963), chap. 6.

production and other functions, the marital relationship may be somewhat tenuous. If, however, the nuclear unit is the seat of many institutional functions, but is not greatly embedded in a larger kin unit (as was generally true in the colonies of the New World), divorce may be difficult to obtain due to the nuclear family's perceived importance.

When the division of labor and other institutions cease to be primarily embedded in either kin or family units, and begin to involve specialization in institutions and differentiation among the units, a change in the internal nature of the family-kin unit occurs as well. To put it categorically, as society moves from mechanical to organic solidarity, its family-kin units move from organic to mechanical solidarity. That is, the family division of labor becomes less distinct and is predicated more on choice than tradition, with relations within the family increasingly based on strong norms and (especially) bonds. The family in the specialized society is kept together more by the development of behavioral expectations and by strong affection than by either its members' need for one another or society's need for stable family units. Thus, if affectional bonds are weak, the unit may dissolve.

The family, then, has come to be the seat of, and to be based on, primary relationships. As defined by Charles H. Cooley and refined by others, a primary relationship is one involving: (1) *Response to whole persons* rather than segments. The doctor sees modern man as a patient; the grocer sees him as a customer; the teacher sees him as a student—but who sees and knows him as he is? This is expected of the nuclear family. (2) *Communication of oneself:* with whom are pleasures shared and upon whom are troubles unloaded? Presumably this occurs within the family, with a few additional kin or friends also being confidants. (3) Personal satisfaction, or the *relationship* is seen *as an end in itself.* One's relations on the job, at school, or even socially may be for the sake of success or some other goal. But a primary relationship is maintained for its own sake; this, likewise, is expected to occur in the family. The modern industrial family has become, as the cliché might have it, a refuge from a segmented and impersonal urban life. According to the authors referred to thus far in this chapter, modern families are ideally characterized by primariness, by companionship, and by mechanical solidarity.

The word *ideally* is used advisedly, for several qualifications must now be added to the foregoing analysis. First, you will have noticed that the unit of analysis has been left vague throughout, both structurally and temporally. The nuclear family and kin group were not distinguished by the present author; Durkheim seldom refers directly to the societal subunits of which he speaks; Ogburn refers primarily to the nuclear family. One reason for leaving this vague is that the kind of historical discussion contained in the preceding pages is both ideal-typical (as Burgess admits) and highly condensed. One passes over much history—the strengthening of the kin group in agrarian societies, its subsequent weakening in favor of the nuclear family, the parceling out of functions by the nuclear family—if he refers only to the notion of a historical change from mechanical to organic solidarity in society. The issue is one of temporal or historical vagueness. Durkheim is comparing the "simple" society with modern industrial society; Ogburn is discussing preindustrial and industrial families; Burgess' ideal types are the patriarchal family and the modern industrial family; Freedman describes a classical Chinese system in which kin groups were buffers between state and family. The difficulty in synthesizing these ideal-typical summaries lies in their tendency to overestimate the changes that have occurred. Ogburn, for example, has been incorrectly interpreted by some as saying that the preindustrial American family was a perfect example of the functionally central family system because the institutions of the larger society were totally embedded in the family. However, the changes that have been the subject of Chapters 3, 4, and 5 might best be defined by a series of six types, ranging from total institutional embeddedness in the family to total differentiation and specialization (see Figure 3).

In Type 1, the division of labor is encompassed by the nuclear family, with interaction including other members of the hunting-gathering band. Economic, political, and other separate functionaries are nonexistent. Type 2 also has few separate functionaries in institutions other than the family. However, with agriculture or herding, corporate kin groups tend to develop, with personnel and institutions embedded in them; for example, the Papago. Type 3 is found in the classical China depicted by Freedman. Here the nuclear family is somewhat less embedded in the kin group institutionally, but kin provide a balance of power vis-à-vis (the now-separated) political and religious functionaries. In this type, the marriage tie may be less binding than the blood tie; the same is true for Type 2. Type 4 is exemplified by the colonial American family described in Chapter 4. The kin group is no longer central to economic and other functions, nor does it play the role of political buffer. However, much economic, educational, and other activity still involves the nuclear family as a unit, or else takes place within the home. It should be pointed out that there were a few Type 3 kin groups in the American colonies, especially in the South, and that the typical pre-Communist Chinese family was very similar to Type 4. Thus, the difference is not that Type 3 is Chinese and Type 4 colonial American, but rather that Type 3 is high status and Type 4 low status. The difference between the Chinese and the American examples arises from the fact that, with a long agrarian history, Chinese society had more—and more powerful—units of Type 3 than did the New World colonies. It is, further, noteworthy that Types 1, 2, and 4 are actually curvilinear in terms of institutional and personnel em-

Figure 3
Types of Relationships Among Family, Kin Group, and Other Institutions

Type 1: Personnel and institutions
embedded in nuclear family; age
and sex division of labor in
family (Durkheim's merchanically
solidary society: e.g., hunting-
gathering band)

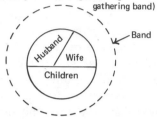

Type 2: Personnel and institutions
embedded in kin group; age and
sex division of labor in kin group
(typical of agricultural and pastoral
societies: e.g., the Papago)

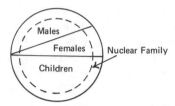

Type 3: Some institutional differentiation;
kin group as buffer between state and
family (e.g., high-status classical China)

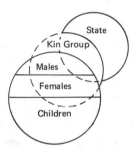

Type 4: Some institutional differentiation,
including economic; personnel
embedded in nuclear family
(e.g., colonial America)

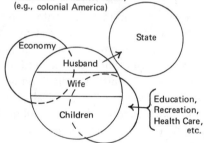

Type 5: Little institutional embeddedness;
personnel embeddedness variable (modern,
industrial society: e.g., contemporary U.S.)

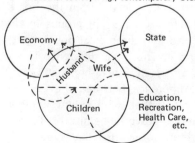

Type 6: Complete institutional differentiation;
family serves the individual (Durkheim's
organically solidary society)

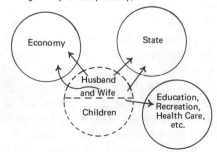

beddedness. The nuclear family is basic in the simplest hunting and gathering bands and again in the early stages of industrialization, with the kin group most prominent in agricultural and pastoral societies.[16] Type 5 is modern, industrial society, with the family unit still playing a substantial role in education, recreation, and religion, as it tries to give general direction to the socialization process, but seldom acting *as a unit* in economic production. In addition, the wife may or may not engage in occupational employment; the stress may be variable between the family unit's importance and that of the individual in terms of personnel embeddedness. Type 6 is basically hypothetical, although certain systems, for example, the kibbutz in Israel, have attempted to establish a differentiation closely resembling this one.[17] The historical confusion arises when an analysis such as Ogburn's is viewed as describing a change from Type 1 to Type 6, whereas in reality the change he is referring to was from Type 4 to Type 5. Thus, a necessary clarification of the ideal-typical discussions of Ogburn, Burgess, Farber, and Durkheim involves the further specification of the structural and temporal units of analysis.[18]

Another important point regarding the six types in Figure 3 is that, on a worldwide basis, there is a predominant trend from Types 1 and 2 toward Type 5. This has been noted by many authors, among them Goode, Zelditch, and Straus, not merely as a process but as a process *desired* by the world's people. "Modernization," including the move away from extended families and lineages toward the nuclear family, "is a world wide aspiration and, barring a planetary catastrophe, it is unlikely to be halted."[19] The issue of whether or not such a goal is worthy, or *good* for people, is another matter. Suffice it to say that, while it may be easy for one who knows the modern

---

[16] Sources which postulate the curvilinear pattern of nuclear family dominance in the band, corporate kin group dominance in agricultural and pastoral societies, and nuclear family dominance again in the industrial state are M. F. Nimkoff and Russell Middleton, "Types of Family and Types of Economy," *American Journal of Sociology* 66 (1960), 225; and Winch and Blumberg, "Societal Complexity and Familial Organization," in Winch and Goodman, *Selected Studies in Marriage and the Family*, p. 92; and Blumberg and Winch, "Societal Complexity and Familial Complexity: Evidence for the Curvilinear Hypothesis," *American Journal of Sociology* 77 (1972), 898–919.

[17] For a discussion of the kibbutz family and some additional references, see Yonina Talmon, "The Family in a Revolutionary Movement—The Case of the Kibbutz in Israel," in Meyer F. Nimkoff, ed., *Comparative Family Systems* (Boston: Houghton Mifflin, 1965), chap. 13.

[18] Note that the six types depicted in Figure 3 should not be considered as a unilineal continuum through which all societies must pass in the process of change. Note furthermore that the types describe society in terms of the family perspective. The same individual plays multiple roles; but the issue here is whether he plays them as a member of the family and within the family setting, or whether he plays them in separate locations and at specific times. The interwoven fabric of the individual's life in society is not captured in Figure 3.

[19] Straus, "Familial Organization and Problem Solving Ability in Relation to Societal Modernization," p. 71.

industrial world from the inside to criticize its economic and familial structures, it is extremely difficult to convince the peoples of the developing world that they should not want to "nuclearize" and industrialize.[20]

A second point of confusion, which we have tried to avoid (and which is actually an extension of the above concern), lies in Ogburn's term *loss of family functions* and its misinterpretations. Ogburn's point is that activities that traditionally took place within the home or involved the whole family now take place elsewhere and engage family segments. The problem with the term, however, is that it can convey the impression that the family now has little to do. The actual process has been one in which activities that were performed in a simple or rudimentary fashion within the family have expanded to the point where the home can no longer encompass them. This process has been referred to above by the terms *expansion* and *parceling out* of functions. Yet, as Clark Vincent points out, even this leaves the picture one-sided. "It is interesting to speculate," says Vincent,

> about what might have happened if students of the family (a) had kept in mind Ogburn's central interest in social change and (b) had emphasized that it was the *traditional content and form* of given functions, rather than functions *qua* functions, that were being performed decreasingly by the family.[21]

The family may no longer be an economic producing unit, but its function as consumer has been heightened. More important, the family as a unit plays an increasingly important role in *adaptation*. By this, Vincent means that the organically structured, or specialized, society requires individuals who can adapt to residential movement, to varied demands, and to rapid changes. It is within the family that one learns—or doesn't learn—this vital aspect of modern life. While we may argue with Vincent's point regarding the economic function (since the family has always been a consuming unit for whatever the economy had to offer), his notion of the family as teacher of adaptability is a valuable one. The knowledge explosion and specialization have made it virtually impossible for a given family unit to encompass the educational demands of its offspring—and the laws have made it illegal for a family to try. Yet, it is within the family that direction is given to the socialization process, that a style of confronting society's expectations and opportunities is developed. The problem is not so much that the term *loss of*

---

[20] While teaching in East Africa, the author had the experience of trying to "warn" his students of the perils of capitalist industrialism and nuclear familism, only to be met with the response: "We want to learn those 'problems' for ourselves."

[21] Clark E. Vincent, "Mental Health and the Family," *Journal of Marriage and the Family* 29 (1967), 26; see also Vincent, "Familia Spongia: The Adaptive Function," *Journal of Marriage and the Family* 28 (1966), 29–36.

family functions is incorrect as that it is incomplete, leading one to view the family as inactive and of less significance than it is.[22]

The concept of the family's loss of functions necessitates a third qualification as well. Some social analysts, especially during the years when industrialization and urbanization were being decried as resulting in social disorganization, expressed the fear (or the view) that the loss of traditional functions would mean the disintegration of the family as we know it. No longer the economic, educational, and religious center of society, the family has lost its reason for being. In rejoinder, the suggestion has been made that, concomitant with the specialization of society, the family has become a specialist in gratifying people's psychological needs—needs for understanding, affection, and happiness.[23] But, it might be argued, what about the high rate of divorce? Does this not indicate that all is not well with the family? In answering these questions, let us first note that to say that the family, ideally, is a focus for primary relations is also to indicate where its problems will arise. The demand to gratify people's needs for love, companionship, and emotional release is a heavy burden for any social group to bear. This pressure is even greater since neolocality and decreased family size have reduced the numbers of persons sharing intense day-to-day relations. It should not, therefore, be surprising to find that those who do not achieve satisfactory relationships within the family are likely to break ties and try again, especially if the economy's needs are not such as would necessitate keeping them together. The rate of divorce, in other words, may be viewed as either a problem or a solution, depending on one's perspective.

It should be noted, moreover, that the expectations that characterize the companionship family, that is, happiness, adjustment, and primariness, tend to retard to some extent the movement toward what Farber calls "permanent availability." "Availability" connotes access to an individual for marriage, for sex, for intimacy. Yet, divorce and extramarital sex tend to be limited by the specific happiness-adjustment function the family is expected to perform. A couple may, for example, have decided that they might be happier if they divorced but may decide against divorce for the sake of the adjustment or perceived needs of their offspring. Or the individual who considers himself "intellectually free" to engage in extramarital sex may perceive that his marital happiness would be detrimentally affected thereby, and therefore forgo the exercise of his freedom for the sake of greater personal

---

[22] For a further critique of the "loss of family functions" conception, see John N. Edwards, "The Future of the Family Revisited," *Journal of Marriage and the Family* 29 (1967), 505–11.

[23] Frank Musgrove, *The Family, Education, and Society* (London: Routledge and Kegan Paul, 1966), pp. 31, 35–40, 99, discusses this phenomenon.

adjustment, happiness, and primariness within his marriage. The point is simply that the family's "affective" function is, at present, a crucial deterrent to rapid change.

The questions of distintegration and change must not be dismissed on the basis of the preceding generalizations. In fact, much effort in the present volume is expended toward the goal of defining the direction of change within the family system of the United States. To this end, several continua, on which current characteristics and directions of change may be located, are posited in Section Five. But before these continua are presented, the historical and functional strands of Chapters 4 and 5 will be synthesized in several propositions.

Section Four

QUASI–THEORETICAL PROPOSITIONS ABOUT THE U.S. FAMILY

Several characteristics of the contemporary family in the United States emerge quite clearly from the last two chapters, while others may be inferred therefrom. The first three characteristics pertain to the family functions that have been the subject of Chapter 5. The family unit performs two specific functions in U.S. society. (1) Its *affective* function is a central basis for both the formation and the continuation of individual family units. The people of a society, like those of any group, perform tasks and establish relationships. If the family or kin unit is primarily a task group, as in the undifferentiated (institutionally embedded) society, the development of relationships within that unit is problematic, since the bases for the persistence of the unit are tradition and functions as well as affection. When, on the other hand, many societal tasks are performed outside the family unit, much of the family's effort is focused on meeting its members' needs for affection and understanding, and the ability of the family to provide for those needs is a key determinant of whether a given unit will persist or dissolve. Furthermore, males in such a society are more likely to take an active role in providing primary relations than they are in a society in which the family involves a stringent division of labor by sex. Yet, providing primary relations, or affectivity, is but one of the crucial functions of the contemporary U.S. family.

(2) A second specific family function is to serve as *economic consumer* and *reservoir of unpaid labor*. The two key dangers to the capitalist system are too little consumption and too many producers. One reason why the larger society fosters nuclear family values is because the family unit plays so great a role in consuming the goods of the market. As far as the

capitalist market economy is concerned, in a society in which families are not the units of economic production it is permissible for individual family units to dissolve, as long as—at any given point in time—most people of marriageable age are married to someone and raising families. And, it should be added, the proportion of married adult Americans has been higher in the twentieth century than ever before in our history. Too much production, on the other hand, is only a problem if there are not enough consumers or if too many people are doing the producing, are drawing wages. For this latter cuts down on profit. Therefore, the family has, since the industrial revolution, become an increasingly useful means of keeping people out of the "job market," as machine efficiency and automation have lessened industrial manpower needs. Women have been unpaid and economically unvalued members of society, as "housewives," while early retirement and mass college attendance increasingly serve to keep other large portions of the population from being producers and wage earners. All this, while hardly satisfying to the individuals affected, has meant that the family and education have served capitalism by keeping the ratio of producers to consumers at a low level. This function of the family is under great fire today, from feminists-humanists especially, but also to some extent from the elderly and those who would free the male from his traditionally aggressive—economically competitive role.[24]

In addition to the specific affective and economic functions performed by the family, this unit plays (3) a general, though somewhat reduced, role in *socialization*. Other institutions, such as recreational and educational ones, meet many specific needs that individuals have for learning their culture. Nevertheless, the family, with its current concern for the developing individual, tends to coordinate and give direction to the influence of such institutions. Thus, for example, one family may further the goals of the school system by encouraging achievement and cooperation, while another family may attempt to negate or neutralize the efforts of the educational institution by belittling its goals and practices. There also appears to have been some reduction in the distinction between the father role and the

---

[24] Kathryn Clarenbach has pointed out in personal conversation that, while women have been restricted to a marginal role in economic production, their dominant role as housewives has been unvalued economically. The best way to see this is in the case of divorce. In most states the law permits a woman to claim only that portion of the family estate which is commensurate with the proportion of the family income she has earned. If she has been a housewife, she must depend on alimony—a handout—which keeps her in a subordinate position vis-à-vis her ex-husband. Warren Farrell, to whom we will refer again in Chapter 11, is a spokesman for "Men's Liberation," a movement to free men from the burden of traditional competitive masculinity. Oscar Handlin and Mary F. Handlin, *Facing Life: Youth and the Family in American History* (Boston: Little, Brown, 1971), p. 237, notes the way in which colleges serve the economy: "The college kept the unwanted high school graduates off the labor market, as the WPA had in harder days."

mother role in socialization. Parents still try to "orderly replace" their culture from one generation to the next; the major difference is in the influence of other institutions in reinforcing or altering the culture (values, beliefs, norms) transmitted by the parents.

The themes covered in these three propositions are a response to such questions as: "What functions does the family perform?" and "How does the family relate to the rest of its society?" These questions appear to bespeak a strongly functional perspective—a perspective that assumes a great amount of consistency and integration both among the parts of the family system and between that system and the total society. Explanation, therefore, appears to originate in function performed and consistency assumed: a characteristic is sufficiently explained by what it does and by its articulation with other characteristics. There are, however, two further propositions that act as correctives upon an overly functional stance regarding the family. (4) The family in modern society includes *inconsistent aspects and fragmentary changes*—it is not entirely coherent. Our brief description of the family in recent history, in Chapter 4, would lead us to conclude that the various aspects of the American family system have not changed at the same rate of speed; nor, as Rothman pointed out, are they necessarily consistent with one another at a given point in time; nor are they well integrated, at every juncture, into the larger society.[25] The basis for the formation and persistence of family units, it has been argued, is love; yet, up to now, the cessation of love has not been a legal ground for their dissolution. The individualistic value of independence and achievement and the familial value of honoring one's parents are at odds from time to time, especially when the parents reach old age. It is not necessary to spell out all the loci of stress and inconsistency at this point, but the reader should be on the lookout for such discrepancies throughout the remainder of the book.

(5) A corollary of the realities of inconsistency and stress is that there are in fact *subcultural varieties* within the contemporary United States. The author's view of society is not based on the kind of consensual model which says that the middle-class style of life is pervasive in the sense that all social change is in that direction since all people strive to be middle-class. Rather, the middle-class style is considered *dominant* in the sense that middle-class people are most able to enact their norms into law and to disseminate their views on what is right, proper, and expected behavior— whether in the family or elsewhere. This dominance is not even necessarily

---

[25] David J. Rothman, "Documents in Search of a Historian: Toward a History of Childhood and Youth in America," in Theodore K. Rabb and Robert I. Rotberg, eds., *The Family in History: Interdisciplinary Essays* (New York: Harper & Row, 1971), p. 189.

a numerical *pre*dominance, but is due to the key positions of the middle class in government, education, and mass communications. However, there are subcultural varieties with their own ideals and expectations; as Rosenfeld pointed out in his study of the Arab village, the influence of these ideals is not necessarily unidirectional. History and diversity must, in short, be taken seriously. A part of this seriousness involves consideration of the inconsistencies alluded to above; another part involves the consideration of divergent principles. It is quite possible, for example, that not all portions of the U.S. population believe that the father should take a major role in affectivity and in socialization. Do ethnic, racial, religious, and socioeconomic categories signify major cultural and social cleavages, or only minor differences? The concern of Chapter 6 will be to outline briefly the key varieties of cultural principles found in the United States and to indicate where their problems lie and in what areas changes are taking place.

The general quasi-theoretical stance produced by these five summary propositions is based on notions of function, change, and variety. The stance acknowledges that much can be learned by asking about functions performed and the bases for their existence among a dominant segment of the population. It also admits that explanation requires an understanding of history and subculture as well; and that a society and its families will manifest disjuncture and variety as well as articulation and integration. In order to discern the mix among these elements, we shall employ Goode's suggestion that functions and characteristics should be treated as variables, or continua, rather than as constants. By developing five continua to deal with major family characteristics, we should be able to locate the contemporary American family in terms of its basic features and to define its direction and speed of change.

Section Five

FAMILY SYSTEM CHARACTERISTICS: FIVE CONTINUA

In Chapter 4 the various aspects of the family in American history were grouped together under three headings: family formation, internal family relations, and the family and the external world, or other institutions. Internal family relations can be broken down into socialization, marital role structure, and personnel embeddedness; all of these aspects, with their logical extremes, are illustrated in the five continua of Figure 4.

Looking at the continua one at a time, it is possible, as indicated in Chapter 2, to conceive of a society in which marital arrangements are made by the parents and incestuous and exogamous prohibitions leave the in-

Figure 4
Five Ideal-Typical Continua on Which to Locate Family Characteristics and Changes

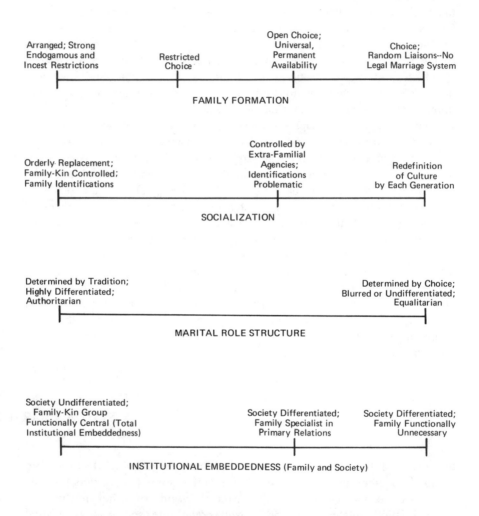

FAMILY FORMATION

- Arranged; Strong Endogamous and Incest Restrictions
- Restricted Choice
- Open Choice; Universal, Permanent Availability
- Choice; Random Liaisons--No Legal Marriage System

SOCIALIZATION

- Orderly Replacement; Family-Kin Controlled; Family Identifications
- Controlled by Extra-Familial Agencies; Identifications Problematic
- Redefinition of Culture by Each Generation

MARITAL ROLE STRUCTURE

- Determined by Tradition; Highly Differentiated; Authoritarian
- Determined by Choice; Blurred or Undifferentiated; Equalitarian

INSTITUTIONAL EMBEDDEDNESS (Family and Society)

- Society Undifferentiated; Family-Kin Group Functionally Central (Total Institutional Embeddedness)
- Society Differentiated; Family Specialist in Primary Relations
- Society Differentiated; Family Functionally Unnecessary

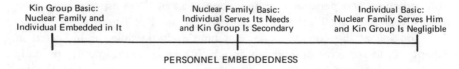

PERSONNEL EMBEDDEDNESS

- Kin Group Basic: Nuclear Family and Individual Embedded in It
- Nuclear Family Basic: Individual Serves Its Needs and Kin Group Is Secondary
- Individual Basic: Nuclear Family Serves Him and Kin Group Is Negligible

dividual with only one category of persons within which to find a mate. Or the prohibitions may be fewer, resulting in a wider range of marital possibilities, but with the parents still working out the pairings. Restricted choice, as in colonial America, is characterized by the individual's choosing his own mate, but with residential immobility, religious and racial status, or other restrictions severely limiting the range within which his choice operates. The notion of open choice, or universal, permanent availability (as indicated earlier), is that all the members of the opposite sex in one's society are potentially available to him for mating. They are, furthermore, permanently available, so that an unsatisfactory relationship can be terminated and a new one begun at any time. This is where Farber feels the American family system is rapidly heading in terms of mate selection. The logical end of this continuum also involves universal, permanent availability, but without the legalization of either marriage or divorce. This we have labeled "random liaisons." The issue here, as far as the modern family is concerned, is whether its current mate selection is most accurately described by the term *restricted choice* or by the term *universal, permanent availability*.

The socialization continuum has, at one extreme, the society in which culture is redefined by each succeeding generation only enough to be consistent with small technological advances, in which the family and kin group control the learning process, and, thus, in which the individual is likely to find his crucial positive identifications with other family–kin group members.[26] At the other extreme is the society in which each generation completely rethinks and reworks its culture, that is, in which socialization, or the passing along of culture, does not take place. Somewhere in the middle would be the society characterized by some redefinition, in which extrafamilial agencies control the socialization process, so that identification with a family member is as problematic as identification with a football coach, a movie star, a teacher, or any other significant member of one's society. How closely, we might ask, does the extrafamilial socialization model fit the contemporary United States?

Family roles may be traditionally determined, so that the society includes only one definition of what it means to be a father, a mother, or a son or daughter of a certain age. In this case, there are no role definition options open to the individual. Such a society, as noted earlier, tends to have as part of its traditional definition of family roles a carefully worked out division of labor and an authoritarian control of resources and decisions.

---

[26] By "positive identification" is meant the attempt to model one's behavior after that of another person. The process of identification is both complex and important, and will be referred to in greater detail in Chapters 7 and 8.

At the opposite pole is the society in which definition of the father or mother role is determined by choice. The choices are such that the members of the family unit are likely to share equally in decision-making and control of resources; they may divide economic, socialization, and affective roles in any way they see fit—since tradition dictates no predetermined family division of labor. The question concerning family roles which will engage us throughout this work is the extent to which there is freedom of choice in the contemporary U.S. family.

The fourth continuum is really a reduction of certain aspects of Figure 3. The extremes are the undifferentiated society, with all functions totally embedded in the family (Type 1) or kin group (Type 2), and the totally differentiated society, whose family system is therefore functionally unnecessary (Type 6). In between are Ogburn's modern family, specializing in primary relations, and Burgess' companionship unit. To what extent, we might ask, do major functions now take place outside the home and involve subsegments of the family? Has the family stabilized at the companionship level, or is its present character merely a stage on the way to eventual disintegration?

The final continuum is related in many ways to the preceding four. Yet the multidimensional nature of the "personnel embeddedness" concept demands that we spend a bit more time with it. There are two stages, or types, of personnel embeddedness, each with an interactional and a value element. *Kin group embeddedness* means that the kin group is the primary milieu for social interaction and is valued more highly than either the nuclear family or the individual. The nuclear family in this situation has little existence apart from, or privacy within, its kin group; and kin solidarity takes precedence over that among nuclear family members. To put it briefly, both the individual and his nuclear family operate within and serve the needs of the larger group. A second form of personnel embeddedness is found if the kin group and its community are weak, but the individual is still expected to operate primarily within, and to serve the needs of, the *nuclear family*. "He is the black sheep of the family"; "He has disgraced us": such expressions indicate that "the family" is actually considered more important than the individual and his needs. However, if the family is viewed as basically serving the needs of the individual, and as concerned with his unique welfare, and if both family and kin interaction are less important than extrafamilial activity, one cannot speak of personnel embeddedness, but of *individualism* and independence. "Where did we fail him?" "What makes for achievement?" Such questions bespeak an individualistic orientation within the society. It is generally acknowledged that the culture of the contemporary United States is not characterized by kin group dominance, with the nuclear family and the individual highly embedded in the kin group. The difficult question, however (and one which will occupy us throughout this volume), is whether the correct representation of the present-day U.S. family depicts the individual as operating within and serving the needs of the nuclear family or depicts the family as serving the individual's needs and helping him to operate as a unique individual. Looking at the continuum as a logical system, and recalling the ideal types of Figure 3, we should note that the simplest band is characterized by nuclear family embeddedness, with the more complex agricultural and pastoral societies closer to the left-hand end of the continuum than either the band or modern industrial society.

Many of the issues raised by these five continua will arise time and again in the chapters on socialization, mate selection, husband-wife interaction, kinship, aging, crisis, and family dissolution. However, we must first expand upon the theme of definable subcultural types within the contemporary United States.

Family Subcultures and Subsocieties in the United States

In this chapter we describe middle-, working-, and lower-class models of family behavior. Subsequently, religious, ethnic, and racial subdivisions are introduced, and the key problems facing them are noted. For the religious subsociety, the problem has been to stay separate in a society that tends to assimilate its parts. For the European ethnic groups, the problem has been to keep their cultural heritage alive and meaningful in the face of their desire for, and ability to gain, assimilation. For blacks and other racial minorities, the problems have been their inability to achieve equality in the dominant economic structures and white resistance to accepting them into the dominant society or to accepting their cultures as viable alternatives to the dominant culture.

The United States is a society characterized by a Western, urban, and industrial form of culture. Within that society certain familial attitudes and practices are so common as to be considered virtually cultural universals.* Among these cultural forms are monogamy, legal marriage, legal dissolution of marriage prior to remarriage, joint residence of spouses and their dependent children, and responsibility of the parents for the care and rearing of their children. Legal and social sanctions of various sorts tend to restrict deviation from these universals. Whether such "universals" should be sanctioned so as to restrict deviation is a question currently being debated, especially by minority group politicians and policymakers, and this issue will be noted again when we discuss the black family.

There is, however, an order of deviation that, as Ruth Cavan puts it, "is subordinate to the basic culture and gives a quasi-organization to aggregates of people who accept the basic culture but are distinctive in the ways in which they implement it, or in less fundamental phases of culture."[1] Thus, within the basic culture, there may be great variation in the acceptance or rejection of birth control, husband-wife role relationships, the socializa-

---

[1] Ruth Shonle Cavan, "Subcultural Variations and Mobility," in Harold T. Christensen, ed., *Handbook of Marriage and the Family* (Chicago: Rand McNally, 1964), p. 536.

tion of children, the importance of kin, and other aspects of the family. These variations tend to divide the society into subcategories of persons whose intensity of interaction with one another is greater than it is with those whose culture differs substantially. Nevertheless, the congruence between subcultures (particular configurations of attitudes and behaviors) and subsocieties (networks of interacting persons) is not perfect. "The subcultural system of the United States," says Cavan,

> is a composite of social classes and of ethnic-religious and racial groups. They are combined into a vertical hierarchy according to general principles of relative status and along a horizontal spacing according to the degree of mutual acceptability. When groups are unacceptable to each other, they tend to form parallel social-class systems.[2]

This "horizontal spacing" is, in fact, the division of society into subsocieties, whose cultures may in some instances be virtually identical. On the other hand, persons within a subsociety may be characterized by great cultural diversity.

The approach of the present chapter is to begin by outlining three subcultural models that are found in American society. Subsequently, the notions of religious, ethnic, and racial subsocieties will be introduced, in the hope that several key questions regarding such categorizations may be resolved, and the problems confronting these groups made plain.

Section One

MIDDLE-CLASS AND LOWER-CLASS FAMILY MODELS

Much has been said already about the middle-class family in the United States. The changes between colonial days and the present, listed in Chapter 4, are for the most part comparisons of the colonial family with the modern, middle-class type. While this approach is valid, due to the dominance of middle-class forms today, historically it is only partially correct. This is because the modern urban middle-class, working-class, and lower-class family systems can be traced back to colonial days, with certain similarities and certain divergencies. Thus, beginning with the middle-class model, we shall attempt to clarify the historical processes and connections.

During colonial days, the vast majority of Anglo-American families lived at or near the subsistence level. They were agricultural, following the cultural patterns described in Chapter 4. With the industrial revolution began a

---

[2] Cavan, "Subcultural Variations and Mobility," p. 541.

whole complex of developments that eventuated in the formation of the urban middle, working, and lower classes, the first becoming dominant. The move from agriculture to industry and the cities was spearheaded by a small number of creative Anglo-American Protestants, who embodied the individualism-work-success motif idealized, but not ordinarily realized, by the eighteenth century colonists. Along with the industrialists, large numbers of people came to the city to work in the factories. However, the nineteenth and twentieth centuries did not belong simply to the wealthy industrialists and their workers; this was also the period of the emergence of the middle class. Beginning as a small number of independent businessmen, the middle class grew with the differentiation and expansion of government, education, and legal and medical services, and with the vast increase in commercial and office personnel in the industrial complex. These persons—professionals, managers, salesmen, and clerks—are occupationally typical of that category known as the middle class. Economically, these are the persons who, along with their families, have risen above the subsistence level, enabling them to turn their attention to self-respect, experience and personality needs, and child development. It was the women within this group of predominantly white Anglo-American Protestant urbanites who found the time and the rationale for the women's rights movements. This push for sexual equality had substantial impact upon relationships within the family as well as outside it.

What, then, are the basic aspects of the *middle-class family style* as it developed during the nineteenth and early twentieth centuries? (1) Economic and work values are central, including, if need be, residential mobility in pursuit of opportunity. Such values are somewhat more typical of professional and managerial families (often referred to as the upper middle class) than of sales and clerical families, but are often used to characterize the entire middle class. (2) Husband-wife relations are predicated on happiness, communication, and mutual gratification. Even in the sexual sphere, in which formerly only the husband sought pleasure, the stress on equality and mutual needs has resulted in a concern for mutual satisfaction. Love is expected to be fundamental, not only to the selection of one's mate, but to the household as well. (3) Socialization of children emphasizes sheltering during their younger days. The world of childhood is insulated to some extent from the woes and cares of adults. In addition, the child is taught that he must get along with other people and that he should learn to do things for himself. He is expected to internalize the value of deferred gratification, or putting off immediate goals and pleasures for the sake of greater goals in the future, for example, postponing marriage for the sake of a college education. Getting along, initiative, independence, deferred gratification—these are, after all, the values that middle-class parents believe have gotten them where they are.

This middle-class configuration is oriented toward success and respectability as defined by the official societal values. Children learn to identify with their parents more as general symbols of success than in terms of the specific occupational or other roles they play. The intensity of emotional ties among family members is great; punishment is likely to center here. This family differs at many points from the typical colonial farm family; three keys to its divergence are the fact that the husband's economic role is "white collar," or nonmanual, and is played outside the home, and that the family's focus of attention is no longer subsistence or survival.

The first point of divergence between middle-class and colonial families, that is, nonmanual versus manual work, also distinguishes the middle class from the urban working and lower classes. During the nineteenth century, large numbers of unneeded farm laborers moved into the cities in quest of work. Some found it in the growing industries, as foremen, skilled craftsmen, and assembly line workers. Such members of the urban working class are likely to believe that the middle class does not do "real" work, and to value physical rather than intellectual modes of expression. Because occupational advancement is limited, they tend to redefine the success goals of U.S. society in achievable terms. Owning their own home, an automobile, and other possessions—especially possessions related to leisure pursuits—and education for their children are important to the working class.[3]

The working-class family model is the most direct descendant of the colonial type at several points, but the change from rural to urban has caused substantial alterations. (1) Segregation of roles between husbands and wives is quite similar in the modern working-class and the colonial families. Sex is the husband's pleasure and the wife's duty. The husband expects to take little hand in household tasks and child rearing, since these are "women's work." (2) A second point of similarity between the colonial family and that of the modern, urban working class is in socialization. The primary concern of the parents is to teach their children order, obedience, honesty, respect for adults, and limits; within this framework, the children are given considerable freedom. This freedom is not the kind of supervised independence training that characterizes the middle class, but is a freedom from adult supervision for periods of time.

Changes or differences between colonial and modern working-class families include the following: (3) The husband, in both cases, perceives himself as patriarch, or as dominant, having delegated household and child-rearing responsibilities to the wife. However, when his economic provision for his family is somewhat limited and his economic role is played outside

---

[3] Jack L. Roach, Llewellyn Gross, and Orville R. Gursslin, *Social Stratification in the United States* (Englewood Cliffs, N.J.: Prentice-Hall, 1969), p. 181.

the home, the husband finds himself less able to assert consistent and *acceptable* authority within the home. That is, the husband's actual status in the home is likely to be lower in the urban working-class family than it was in the colonial farm family. This status, however, depends on traits of character as well as economic well-being, so that our generalization accounts only partially for the lower status of working-class husbands. (4) Much urban manual work does not provide those who do it with a sense of inherent worth, although the differences between their attitudes and those of the farmer tilling the soil have probably been overdrawn. It seems that the shorter workweek makes it possible for members of the urban working class to pursue leisure activities with the money provided by stable employment. Kin and friend groups, neighbors, and informal work groups provide much of the social interaction that gives meaning to their lives—and this also has some similarity to the colonial pattern, though the specific leisure activities have changed. Deferred gratification and success striving are more characteristic of the middle-class family than of the working-class family, though the major difference here is that in the middle class the striving is by the parents themselves, while in the working class it is expressed in the hope that the children will "get somewhere."

The lower class is felt by some observers to be simply the lower reaches of the working class, since, like the working class, its occupations are manual. What distinguishes the lower class is minimal education, little skill to "sell" in the economic market, and a living standard at the poverty level. The members of the lower class are individuals who have never really made it in the industrial world, though they live in an urban, rather than a rural, environment. Surrounded by affluence, they perceive the cards as stacked against them in their struggle for survival. Economic marginality is at the heart of their life-style, which often includes the following characteristics. (1) Lower-class individuals have low aspirations and strive for immediate gratification. (2) Their families tend to be unstable, and include many broken homes. In colonial times the legal system, social sanctions, and the family unit's functions were likely to hold economically marginal families together—though some, of course, did separate. Of considerable note today, then, is the number of poor families that do stay together despite weak cultural supports. (3) Their child rearing tends to be harsh and erratic, swinging from spontaneous punishment to ignoring or rejection. Much of this stems from a lack of time or energy to spend on children.[4]

In many of its characteristics the lower class is unquestionably a logical extension of the working class. The working-class husband may have some trouble exerting authority; the lower-class husband is apt to have even more

---

[4] Roach, Gross, and Gursslin, *Social Stratification in the United States*, pp. 198–200.

trouble. The working-class breadwinner may not find great satisfaction in his work, but this is more likely to be true of the unskilled lower-class worker than a skilled working-class craftsman. It may, in fact, be that the lower class simply consists of those who, due to multiple problems and minimal preparation, can't and don't make it rather than of those who lack aspirations. Be that as it may, the urban middle, working, and lower classes are sufficiently different to be distinguishable as modal types, or as points on the socioeconomic status continuum.

Here, then, are three models of family life today.[5] Each has some roots in the colonial family and other roots in the urban-industrial revolution. One stresses equality, personality, respectability, and success; another stresses role segregation, order and freedom, and the social network; the third stresses survival. But how are such cultural themes or configurations related to specific societal categories within the U.S. population? We have already indicated the relationship between the middle-class style and the white Anglo-American Protestant population. But what of the other religious, ethnic, and racial divisions of society? These are the foci of attention in the sections that follow.

Section Two

THE RELIGIOUS SUBCULTURE AND SUBSOCIETY

Some religious subcultures, such as that of the Mormons, have been adaptable and willing to change in the face of pressure from the dominant culture and societal changes. For that matter, the Mormons were never as "deviant" as their detractors and critics wanted to believe. Even polygyny, which was normative and acceptable among them, was practiced by only a very small portion of their population.

In this section, however, we are concerned primarily with the groups of religious immigrants who have kept themselves both culturally and socially apart from the peoples around them. Cavan refers to them thus: "Certain subcultural groups achieve almost complete and relatively permanent isolation, for example, the Amish, Doukhobors, and Hutterites, and,

---

[5] For more on the middle-class model, see Gerald Leslie, *The Family in Social Context* (New York: Oxford University Press, 1967), chap. 9. On the lower-class model, see Arthur Besner, "Economic Deprivation and Family Patterns," in Lola M. Irelan, ed., *Low-Income Life Styles,* Department of Health, Education, and Welfare, Welfare Administration Publication No. 14 (1966), pp. 15–29. On families of the working class, which is between the middle class and the lower class on the socioeconomic ladder, see Mirra Komarovsky, *Blue-Collar Marriage* (New York: Random House, 1964). For a brief introduction to upper-class family patterns, see Leslie, *The Family in Social Context,* pp. 304–7.

in the past, the Shakers and the Oneida Community."[6] The Amish and Hutterites are perhaps the best-known examples of such groups. We shall briefly describe the latter.

The Hutterites "are not only an ethnic group," says one of them, "but also one of the world's important religious minorities which have in recent years come under the close observation of sociologists and others."[7] Hutterite colonies are located in the Dakotas and Montana and in Alberta, Manitoba, and Saskatchewan, Canada.[8] The Hutterites are one of three surviving Anabaptist groups, and are able to trace their history back to early sixteenth century Europe. Their pacifism, civil disobedience, and communal economy—all viewed by them as New Testament Christian principles—caused them to be persecuted and driven from Moravia and the Tyrol of Austria to the Ukraine and then, in the 1870s, to the United States. They have a social organization that can be adapted to the grazing and crop areas of any nation. The Hutterites are large-scale farmers who are generally quite economically successful in raising draft horses, cattle, pigs, sheep, geese, ducks, turkeys, chickens, bees, and crops such as wheat and oats. They have not hesitated to sell surpluses to those in the "outside world," nor have they rejected the technological advances that make their economic endeavors more profitable. About their economic success and social forms, a Jehovah's Witnesses missionary commented: "Them Hutterites are a case where religion is just something to keep the economics going." John Bennett notes that, while such a view is mistaken, it does illustrate the point that "the colony's religious activity is sometimes less conspicuous than its economic and decision-making apparatus."[9] To this, Paul Gross, himself a Hutterite, responds:

> Most of our critics are unable to look beyond the sphere of dollars and cents. To them we appear to be economic competitors who deliberately plan our way of life so as to compete more efficiently with our neighbors.
>
> But serious students of our way of life have discovered that the basis of our communal existence is not economic but religious. Take

---

[6] Cavan, "Subcultural Variations and Mobility," p. 536.

[7] Paul S. Gross, *The Hutterite Way* (Saskatoon, Canada: Freeman, 1965), p. 1.

[8] Besides Gross, *The Hutterite Way*, see John W. Bennett, *Hutterian Brethren* (Stanford, Calif.: Stanford University Press, 1967); John A. Hostetler and Gertrude Enders Huntington, *The Hutterites in North America* (New York: Holt, Rinehart and Winston, 1967); S. C. Lee and Audrey Brattrud, "Marriage Under a Monastic Mode of Life: A Preliminary Report on the Hutterite Family in South Dakota," *Journal of Marriage and the Family* 29 (1967), 512–20; Hostetler, "Socialization and Adaptations to Public Schooling: The Hutterian Brethren and the Old Order Amish," *Sociological Quarterly* 11 (1970), 194–205.

[9] Bennett, *Hutterian Brethren*, p. 108.

away our colonies within which we are insulated from the crime and disease of the world, and our young people would soon be forced to give up their faith and join the mad world in its headlong plunge into perdition.[10]

Are the Hutterites to be numbered among the Protestants? While the historical and temporal answer would seem to be yes, they themselves deny any such identification. In addition to their strict adherence to the communal form of organization, there are at least three other respects in which they differ from most Protestant groups: they refuse to bear arms, they refuse to take legal oaths, and they refuse to assume civil authority to uphold what they regard as unjust and barbarous laws.[11]

The decision-making apparatus, to which Bennett refers, centers in a council of five to seven men. The council always includes the ministers, householder, and field manager, and usually one or two heads of economic departments as well. Council members sit in order of rank and "make practical day-to-day decisions, grant permission for travel, judge minor disagreements, and help the colony to run efficiently by making many semiroutine decisions."[12] A Hutterite colony consists of an elaborate set of functionally differentiated roles; status distinctions are commensurate to these roles. Paradoxically, however, the colony is at the same time an extended set of kin, involving male relatives and their wives and children in a brotherly and egalitarian network. While the bureaucratic and kinship principles often seem to be at variance with each other, the group identifications with which colony members have been imbued since birth tend to keep strains and conflicts to a minimum.[13] The way in which group identification and decision-making actually work is well illustrated by Hostetler and Huntington's description of the yearly meeting:

> The various enterprises are carefully considered by the colony at the yearly meeting. Whether to expand, mechanize or diminish one enterprise, such as hog or turkey raising, will be important for the welfare of the whole colony. Important factors entering into decision making for the productive enterprises are: the cleavage between the old and young men, since the younger are more prone to support mechanization; the ability of the person in charge of a given enterprise; and the ability of the group to arrive at an amicable consensus. Since consensus is more important for "the good of the colony," than sheer efficiency, the Hutterites have refrained generally from speculative production.[14]

---

[10] Gross, *The Hutterite Way*, p. 3.
[11] Gross, *The Hutterite Way*, p. 6.
[12] Hostetler and Huntington, *The Hutterites in North America*, p. 29.
[13] See Bennett, *Hutterian Brethren*, p. 109, on these two principles.
[14] Hostetler and Huntington, *The Hutterites in North America*, p. 40.

The three groups of Hutterites—who call themselves Schmieden Leut, Lehrer Leut, and Darius Leut—are endogamous, not only with respect to the outside world, but with respect to each other. Though there have been a few exceptions (a member of one Leut marrying one from another Leut), the slight but important differences in styles of dress and technology stand in the way of Leut intermarriage. Within a Leut, the rule is colony exogamy, that is, a male from one colony will ordinarily marry a female from another. One reason why kin ties seldom conflict with the system of social ranking is that kinship, as in the urban-industrial world, serves primarily to provide primary relationships. While these relationships may be somewhat more intense among the Hutterites, they nevertheless are not the basis for the colony's division of labor. Seldom, for example, does an offspring inherit his father's role in the colony.

Perhaps the best way to understand the Hutterite in his family and colony life is to follow him from birth until death—in summary fashion. The socialization process prepares the individual for two key events: baptism and death. Baptism, at about age twenty, is more than an expression of religious faith; it is the act by which the Hutterite identifies with the colony and its way of life. The success of socialization for incorporation "is evidenced not only by the stability of the colonies as social systems, but also by the extremely low rate of defection."[15] Arthur Mange notes that during the fifty-year period from 1900 through 1949, when the population increased from 500 to nearly 4,000, only 98 males and 7 females—mostly late teenagers—left the Schmieden Leut colonies.[16]

Until the age of three, children stay at home as "house children." They learn early that the colony comes before the individual. Punishment or discipline is usually physical and occurs frequently; however, the child also learns through petting and fond attention that he is very much wanted. A "good" baby, says Hostetler, "has two major attributes. He sleeps a lot, at least during colony work periods, and he will go to anyone. In other words, he does not disrupt the colony time schedule and he accepts all colony members."[17]

From ages three to five the child attends kindergarten or nursery school. Here: (1) he begins to be weaned from his family; (2) he becomes acquainted with his peer group, with whom he will spend his life; (3) he learns to respect authority; (4) he learns to tolerate a restricted environment; and (5) he is rewarded for cooperativeness and passivity. Self-control and obedience are inculcated as basic principles; the child is now expected to

---

[15] Bennett, *Hutterian Brethren*, p. 110.
[16] Arthur P. Mange, "The Population Structure of a Human Isolate" (Ph.D. diss., University of Wisconsin, 1963).
[17] Hostetler and Huntington, *The Hutterites in North America*, p. 60.

be quiet around adults. "The child can easily interpret these changes as rejection. He has fallen to the lowest status group within the colony, but he has also started the steady, rewarding climb up the steps that lead to full, responsible membership in the colony."[18]

For the ten years following kindergarten, the young Hutterite attends both the German and the English school within the colony. Many of the functions of the kindergarten are merely continued and intensified during this period, cooperativeness and respect for authority being especially crucial. Children are expected to make mistakes and misbehave during this period, for that is their nature. They must be willing to accept their place in the social structure, caring for those younger than they are and reacting obediently to those older. The English school is only one of several "schools" in the young person's life, and it is not the one from which he learns how to "live." When a teacher is assigned to the colony for the first time, he is given a lecture by the preacher at the beginning of the school year. English school schedules are governed by colony time patterns and work schedules. In short, the English school—though an outside influence—is encapsulated by the colony pattern, and its influence is bounded by Hutterite culture.[19]

At age fifteen the young person assumes adult work responsibilities, but he does not reach full adult status until baptism. Between age fifteen and baptism there is some experimentation with the "ways of the world." Comic books, radios, nail polish, jewelry, even cigarettes may be obtained surreptitiously and stored, particularly by girls, in special places. The young person is left free by the adults to compare these objects with the communal life he sees around him; in most cases he eventually chooses the latter. The expectation of both personal and economic security

> is undoubtedly one of the main causes of the relatively high stability of Hutterian life, and the low rate of defection. As one outspoken young Hutterite put it: "Well, it's a pretty good life, you know. You go away from it once in a while, but you always come back. Where else can you get a good deal like this for a lifetime?"[20]

The main reason that experimentation is allowed during youth is, of course, that the adults are quite sure that Hutterite culture has been reinforced sufficiently during the early years and that the young person has already internalized or accepted the Hutterite norms and values and will return to them.

Dating begins sometime after age fifteen and is likely to last for two to six years. The freedom surrounding Hutterian courtship is seen in the great variation both in parental control or permissiveness and in the openness or

---

[18] Hostetler and Huntington, *The Hutterites in North America*, p. 67.
[19] Hostetler, "Socialization and Adaptations to Public Schooling," p. 198.
[20] Bennett, *Hutterian Brethren*, p. 129.

secretiveness of premarital relationships. Dating is facilitated by the interchange of labor between colonies, which enables eligible young men and women to be together. Much of this period of courtship, experimentation, and responsibility can be viewed as providing the young person with an opportunity to evaluate himself with respect to the peer group, the opposite sex, and the colony. His interest in the outside world aids him in understanding what it means to be a Hutterite.

Prior to marriage, the young person makes the decision to be baptized, thus becoming a full member of the colony. "The goal of child rearing among the Hutterites is the individual's voluntary decision to submit himself to the *Gemein*. All the child's life has been, in effect, a preparation for this major rite of passage."[21] While each stage since kindergarten has brought the growing Hutterite closer to his parents, baptism results in their treating him as both an offspring and a colony member. He has now chosen the colony's way of life, has rejected the world, and is thus almost removed from the young people's circle. The last step is, of course, marriage.

Mate selection is, in fact, quite similar to that in the urban-industrial United States. It is based on individual choice and love, with parents and kin exerting pressure in the same way as they do in the outside world, that is, by verbal encouragement or discouragement and by arranging meetings, but without force and with few sanctions. The key difference is in the range of interactional possibilities; at this point the comparison breaks down. "In contrast to the long, rigorous preparation for baptism, the preparation for marriage is incidental."[22] While the wedding is a joyous occasion—even more so if several occur simultaneously—postwedding adjustment for the groom is negligible. His brothers may simply move out and his bride move in. For the bride, the adjustment involves the drastic step of leaving her colony to live among a few other former members of her colony of orientation and a large number of strangers.

The separation of the sexes in adulthood is a separation of status and of function. This distinction has been summarized thus: "Hutterian men are colony citizens first, executives and managers second, and laborers third; Hutterian women are housewives and mothers first, light laborers second, and citizens third."[23] Males are believed to be both physically and mentally superior to females. Thus, the women do not participate formally in colony decision-making or produce economically for trading in the outside world. Their economic responsibilities, perhaps for the raising of geese or chickens, involve only goods being raised for colony consumption. Yet, as pointed out by Lantz et al. in discussing the colonial family, such women have much in-

---

[21] Hostetler and Huntington, *The Hutterites in North America*, p. 81.
[22] Hostetler and Huntington, *The Hutterites in North America*, p. 84.
[23] Bennett, *Hutterian Brethren*, p. 114.

direct influence on decision-making, and their patently inferior status gives them a certain amount of freedom.

The men of a Hutterite colony are very likely to be known and referred to according to their functional roles: John may be the turkey man and Paul the hog man. Minute status gradations accompany these economic tasks and help the individual to understand his place in the colony. Several observers have noted the effect that these distinctions and the stress on consensus have on primary relationships. In the lifelong struggle to avoid conflict and to develop consensus, a certain amount of spontaneity is lost. Even in the relation between brothers, since openness of expression and communication may lead to dissension, the only safe practice is to hold fast the reins on self-expression.

When a person can no longer contribute a full day's labor to the colony, he is retired. Although the aged lose the status which accrues to a specific functional role, the traditionalism of the Hutterites causes them to be greatly respected by the younger members of the colony. Death is seen, not as the end, but as the beginning of a new day; predeath anxieties regarding property and inheritance disposal are minimized by the Hutterian way.

What is the crucial problem that the Hutterites, and similar separatist subsocieties, face in the modern United States? It is the problem of *staying separate in a society that tends to reach out and assimilate its parts, culturally and socially.* How effective are the Hutterites in avoiding that assimilation? Hostetler, for one, feels that for two prime reasons they have been more effective than the Amish and most other isolationist religious subsocieties. First, they are communal rather than familistic. This communalism helps them to avoid the individualism that is so destructive of religious isolationism. The Amish family, on the other hand, has a less inclusive discipline to employ in keeping its youth in line than that afforded by the Bruderhof of the Hutterites. Second, bringing the English school into the colony, rather than attending the public school, gives the Hutterian colony control over "alien education." The Amish were afforded the same control as long as one-room schools, dominated by Amish children and parents, were prevalent. But with school consolidation, the Amish parent, according to Hostetler, felt it necessary to rebel. Several Amish parents were taken to court over their attempts to keep their children out of the public schools. The following propositions, Hostetler feels, apply to the isolationist subsociety, or what he calls "the little society": To the degree that a secular educational system is forced upon the little society, that society must either resist or perish. The extent to which the little society can control socialization patterns is directly related to its viability.[24]

---

[24] Hostetler, "Socialization and Adaptations to Public Schooling," pp. 204–5.

Section Three

THE ETHNIC SUBCULTURE
AND SUBSOCIETY

Throughout the previous discussion, the terms *subculture* and *subsociety* have been employed, and the terms *ethnic group* and *minority* have been avoided. Yet, because the latter terms are descriptive of many elements in American society, some understanding of them is essential. The most useful definitions can be found in Shibutani and Kwan's book *Ethnic Stratification*, in which minority groups are described as the "underprivileged in a system of ethnic stratification," and as "people of low standing—people who receive unequal treatment and who therefore come to regard themselves as objects of discrimination."[25] An ethnic group, say the authors, "consists of those who conceive of themselves as being alike by virtue of their common ancestry, real or fictitious, and who are so regarded by others."[26] Thus, a minority may or may not be an ethnic group, depending upon whether or not there is a sense of corporate identity, and an ethnic group may or may not be a minority, depending upon whether or not it is discriminated against in society.

Historically, the groups in America that have been most often defined as ethnic are the non-Protestant European immigrants—including Irish, Polish, and Italian Catholics and the Jewish people—though the latter are hard to distinguish analytically from a religious subculture. According to most observers, the history of such groups in America is that of a movement from ethnic minority status to ethnic group to quasi-ethnic group. Speaking of their patriarchal family system, for example, Ruth Cavan asserts that "this type of family organization has faded under the strain of urban-industrial life and the acculturation of immigrants and their children into the prevailing patterns of Anglo-American culture."[27]

But what is "this type of family organization"? what is the historical ethnic model Cavan sees as having faded? Oscar Handlin, drawing especially upon data on the Irish in the nineteenth century, has posited a characterization somewhat as follows. Their premigration homes were primarily peasant villages, where they had patrilineal, patriarchal, extended families, with the agricultural economy embedded in the nuclear unit. In the New World, they confronted both social and economic stresses. The social stresses included an urban life involving density, poor sanitation, disorganized ghettos, and

---

[25] Tamotsu Shibutani and Kian M. Kwan, *Ethnic Stratification* (New York: Macmillan, 1965), p. 35.
[26] Shibutani and Kwan, *Ethnic Stratification*, p. 47.
[27] Cavan, "Subcultural Variations and Mobility," p. 549.

the impingement of other religions, and the results were mental illness, disease, and criminality. The economic stresses included a lack of skills, low wages or unemployment, woman and child labor, a longing for the soil, and a lack of social or geographic mobility. The effects of these stressor conditions on the family, according to Handlin, were the breakdown of paternal authority, the isolation of the nuclear family from the lineage and extended family, family instability and breakup, and eventual assimilation by the dominant society.[28]

When the data of other writers, such as Miller, Rischin, Vecoli, and McLaughlin, are compared with Handlin's model, it becomes clear that there were variations from ethnic group to ethnic group, from city to city, and from region to region. The Germans, Jews, and Irish in Cincinnati, described by Zane Miller, were not victims of ghetto life or of the impingement of other religions. These groups were able to effect a greater amount of upward mobility than that depicted by Handlin, and were able to avoid the kind of assimilation posited by Cavan and Handlin.[29]

Moses Rischin, writing about the New York Jews during the period 1870–1914, notes first of all that, as traders, they had a tradition of urban residence. In coming to New York City, they found no problem with religious pluralism—or the impingement of other religions—and, given their urban tradition, they had low rates of disease and criminality. Furthermore, they did not lack the skills necessary to compete in an urban environment, and although they were assimilated economically they were able to remain separate socially.[30] E. E. LeMasters adds to this portrayal that one mechanism for survival and, we might add, success among both Jews and Italians in the city was

> a process of doubling up—new arrivals moved in with relatives already established; mothers held outside jobs; older brothers and sisters helped younger children to get a start. This system of mutual aid seems to be extremely functional for low-income families. Resources are shared until each family can care for its own.[31]

Thus, the family did not necessarily become either internally fragmented or isolated from its extended network of kin and friends.

The Italians, as described by Rudolph Vecoli and Virginia McLaughlin, were likewise not peasant farmers, but came from the smaller cities of Italy.

---

[28] Oscar Handlin, *Boston's Immigrants* (Cambridge, Mass.: Harvard University Press, 1941); Handlin, *The Uprooted* (Boston: Little, Brown, 1951).

[29] Zane L. Miller, *Boss Cox's Cincinnati: Urban Politics in the Progressive Era* (New York: Oxford University Press, 1968).

[30] Moses Rischin, *The Promised City: New York's Jews, 1870–1914* (Cambridge, Mass.: Harvard University Press, 1962).

[31] E. E. LeMasters, *Parents in Modern America* (Homewood, Ill.: Dorsey Press, 1974 ed.), p. 104.

The family, says Vecoli, was father-dominated, but mother-centered in terms of activity.[32] While it was subjected to economic stresses, these did not result in the undermining of the father's authority or in the breakdown of the family or its kin ties. As McLaughlin puts it:

> Although the Italian family had its share of poverty and unemployment, it did not develop a characteristic frequently associated today with lower-class life—a female-headed family system. In fact, there is little evidence of family disorganization among Buffalo's Italians.[33]

Just how complete, then, is the fading of the ethnic culture patterns depicted above?[34] Paul J. Campisi feels that, within a period of twenty to twenty-five years after arrival, the Italian immigrant family was almost completely assimilated by the dominant society and its culture. This assimilation occurs as the younger generation grows up and as their aging parents begin to realize that success is predicated upon becoming like the "old Americans."[35] Features of the family, from patriarchal control to rejection of birth control, are altered radically under the influence of the Anglo-American style.

Will Herberg, in his book *Protestant-Catholic-Jew*, describes a more complex and less complete process of assimilation through which the Catholic and Jewish immigrant groups have passed. The first generation, which arrived after 1840, attempted to hold on to the ways of their fathers and became an enclave within their new society. Language, family forms, and belief systems were retained, and awareness of differences was intensified, by the tendency of these groups to cluster together residentially, especially in the growing urban centers along the East Coast. The result was considerable persecution of and discrimination against these groups by the Anglo-American Protestants among whom they settled.

As the members of the second generation moved out into the school system and the peer culture, the conflict of old and new was no longer only intergroup, but became intergenerational and intrafamilial as well. "Frequently, though not always, the man of the second generation attempted to resolve his dilemma by forsaking the ethnic group in which he found himself."[36] The struggle for incorporation into the American social, economic,

---

[32] Rudolph John Vecoli, "Chicago's Italians Prior to World War I: A Study of Their Social and Economic Adjustment" (Ph.D. diss., University of Wisconsin, 1962).

[33] Virginia Yans McLaughlin, "Patterns of Work and Family Organization: Buffalo's Italians," in Theodore K. Rabb and Robert I. Rotberg, eds., *The Family in History: Interdisciplinary Essays* (New York: Harper & Row, 1971), p. 125.

[34] The author wishes to thank Samuel Sheppard, graduate student in history at the University of Wisconsin, for bringing to his attention several of the sources on which the previous section is based.

[35] Paul J. Campisi, "Ethnic Family Patterns: The Italian Family in the United States," *American Journal of Sociology* 53 (1948), 448.

[36] Will Herberg, *Protestant-Catholic-Jew* (Garden City, N.Y.: Doubleday, 1960), p. 28.

and political system was long and hard, but it was successful because of the second generation's ability to assume the dominant cultural forms and because of the willingness of its members to aid one another educationally and otherwise. Mutual aid and a mutual rejection of many key aspects of the old culture occurred simultaneously.

It is at this point that Campisi's discussion of the assimilative process ends. Herberg, however, notes that a further change occurred after 1920. At this point, the stream of immigrants ceased, and the third generation appeared. This generation

> became American in a sense that had been, by and large, impossible for the immigrants and their children. That problem, at least, was solved; but its solution paradoxically rendered more acute the perennial problem of "belonging" and self-identification.

Herberg then goes on to describe how this problem was resolved:

> They wished to belong to a group. But what group could they belong to? The old-line ethnic group, with its foreign language and culture, was not for them; they were Americans. But the old family religion, the old ethnic religion, could serve where language and culture could not.

With modifications, this religion could be made to serve the American value system and still be used for identification, confirming

> the tie that bound them to their forebears, whom they now no longer had any reason to reject, whom indeed, for the sake of a "heritage," they now wanted to "remember."[37]

As far as the family is concerned, the problem for the third and subsequent generations has been twofold. On the one hand, many of the ritual practices by which the ethnic-religious ties had been reaffirmed have been emptied of their former significance and lack a meaningful content. On the other hand, the dominant value system continues to beat away at the remaining features of the old system, for example, birth control among Catholics. A lingering sense of ethnic solidarity and identity remains, but there are few points—with the exception of continuing strong kin ties—at which the family culture of these ethnic groups does not resemble that of either the middle-class or lower-class model described above. What, then, is the central problem for these groups at the present time? First, it must be stated that, unlike the Hutterites, the Amish, and other separatists, they have desired economic and some cultural assimilation—and have found it possible. *Their key problem has been to keep alive any of their ethnic subcultural characteristics in a society in which they have achieved assimilation.*

---

[37] Herberg, *Protestant-Catholic-Jew*, pp. 30–31.

Section Four

RACIAL GROUPS: THE BLACK
AMERICAN FAMILY

The everyday division of racial categories—into black, yellow, red, and white peoples—fits quite well into the scholarly discussions of race in America, in which Negroes, Orientals, and Indians have typically been distinguished from white Americans.[38] While much that has been said about religious and ethnic groups applies to these so-called racial categories as well, there are also some points of divergence both in history and in current problems. Because of their numerical and structural importance in American society, this section will focus upon blacks, or Afro-Americans—those labeled "Negroes," until recently, in most investigations.

Seldom has there been a subject within social science literature into which more value judgments have been allowed to creep. From the turn of this century until the present, writers (both black and white) have had extreme difficulty in discussing the Afro-American without bias and prejudice, conscious and unconscious. The literature, while markedly improved by recent research, must still be handled with great caution. It seems to the present writer that it would be most valuable to begin by isolating the various areas of misconception and disagreement, first concerning history and then concerning the contemporary scene, and subsequently to introduce the research data which speak to those issues. We shall, therefore, divide our discussion of black families and their culture into historical issues and current issues.

History of the Afro-American

African history involves great kingships and a multitude of small societies. Yet the history of the *Afro-American* begins primarily in exploitation and cruelty. It begins in West Africa with the killing and capture of large numbers of men and women, the transporting of the captured to the New World, and their enslavement—usually as agricultural laborers—in a strange land. Their African heritage faded[39] during the period of indentured servanthood, especially under the influence of legalized and nonterminable slavery. Eventually slavery was superseded by their "emancipation" and by the weakening of the plantation system crucial to the existence of slavery.

---

[38] Though they are sometimes treated as a racial minority, Mexican Americans would be better dealt with as an ethnic group.

[39] The word *faded* is used advisedly at this point. Did the African heritage disappear entirely, or did certain seeds, such as the strong lineage, survive into the modern period? We shall return to this issue later.

The preceding paragraph is clearly not a full coverage of the 200–250 years it summarizes. However, we are concerned here with the effects of the occurrences of those years. What happened to the Afro-American during this period? We must answer by spelling out two versions of the story. One version is well exemplified by the concentration camp analogy so many commentators have adopted.[40] During World War II, some inmates of the Nazi concentration camps became childishly silly. Their relations with other inmates became unstable; they became pathological liars and dishonest in all their dealings. In effect, they regressed to childhood. Eventually, they identified with and imitated their captors, coming to view other inmates through Gestapo eyes and sometimes outdoing the Gestapo in cruelty to fellow prisoners.

What caused this type of behavior? The Gestapo used terror and torture, intimidation, isolation, and secrecy. Prisoners were rewarded for compliance with the Gestapo, and, above all, there was a "complete break with the outside world."[41] In a similar manner, says Stanley Elkins, the role of child was forced on the slaves. The master was the "father," who disciplined, taught respect, and held complete control over the life of the slave. The master was also the only person with whom identification might occur. Under these conditions, personal relations among the slaves, including those within the family, were extremely tenuous. But didn't the culture brought from Africa act as a stabilizing influence on relationships? The negative answer to this question has been arrived at by two different logical paths. Melville Herskovits' response is that the characteristics of the slave family—female dominance, common-law marriage, illegitimacy, and weak ties—can be traced back to the polygynous family of West Africa. In other words, the culture the blacks brought with them increased, rather than diminished, the instability of relationships during slavery. A more prevalent argument is that posed by E. Franklin Frazier: The culture brought from Africa had no stabilizing influence on relationships because that culture was virtually obliterated by experience in the New World. The "rare and isolated instances of survivals associated with the Negro family only indicate how completely the African social organization was wiped out by slavery."[42] The enslaved people were moved randomly from place to place, without any concern for tribal or national groupings. This, plus the conditions described by Elkins, served (over several generations) to destroy most vestiges of African culture.

---

[40] Stanley M. Elkins, *Slavery: A Problem in American Institutional and Intellectual Life* (New York: Grosset and Dunlap, 1963), was the first to present this.

[41] Elkins, *Slavery*, p. 104.

[42] For these two interpretations see Melville J. Herskovits, *The Myth of the Negro Past* (New York: Harper and Brothers, 1941); E. Franklin Frazier, *The Negro in the United States* (New York: Macmillan, 1957 ed.), pp. 11, 12.

Because internal stability had been provided (so the argument goes) by the white system and not by the slaves' own relationships, and because the slaves had previously had little or no freedom to govern their own destinies, the results of emancipation could only be disastrous.

> When the invading armies disrupted the plantation organization, thousands of Negroes were set adrift and began to wander footloose about the country. Not only were the sentimental and habitual ties between spouses severed but even Negro women often abandoned their children. Among the demoralized elements in the newly emancipated Negroes promiscuous sexual relationships and frequent changing of spouses became the rule.[43]

Such a description, without an offsetting account of the undemoralized elements, leaves the reader to infer that this pattern was typical. And Frazier's picture of postwar anarchy is echoed by Jessie Bernard, who writes that

> in 1865, desertions were innumerable. . . . When the Negroes were moving around to test their freedom, many of them seized the opportunity to desert their wives and children. . . . The young and strong deserted the aged, the feeble, the children, leaving them to shift for themselves.[44]

This is one view of the historical process: cultural obliteration, suppression, and order under slavery, and anarchy upon emancipation.

There is, however, a second possible perspective on the same era—one that may be pieced together with the help of a different analogy and a few alternative inferences. Helmut Schelsky writes at length, not about the concentration camp, but about the family in post–World War II Germany. He begins by tearing down a stereotype:

> In general, such times of disorder and distress are considered to be a cause for the disruption and weakening of the family; it is astonishing, therefore, that we must designate the effect of the difficult social experiences which I have mentioned as a *heightening of the stability of the German family.* With the collapse of political and economic order and in the face of the immediate peril to which almost everyone was subjected, marriage and the family were considered to be the natural point of stability and protection. . . . The family was often knitted together in the struggle for mere existence, where it was a matter of thriving or perishing, to such a degree that the personal tensions, the bored indifference of the usual marital "co-existence" gave way to a conscious and heightened sense of belonging together.[45]

---

[43] Frazier, *The Negro in the United States,* p. 313.
[44] Jessie Bernard, *Marriage and Family Among Negroes* (Englewood Cliffs, N.J.: Prentice-Hall, 1966), p. 110.
[45] Helmut Schelsky, "The Family in Germany," *Marriage and Family Living* 16 (1954), 331–32.

The family was felt by the German people to be the last element of stability in a disintegrating world. "Therefore," Schelsky asserts,

> the displaced farmer or the "declassed" official . . . lives with clear consciousness and decisiveness "only for the family," an expression which I heard often enough in the families I investigated.[46]

Solidarity between husbands and wives and between old and young is evidenced in the minimization of tensions and in the astonishingly slight amount of child neglect. When the rest of the society crumbled, the German people retreated into the family and lived for it. In addition, the balance of power and importance swung toward the female, causing most German families to take on an equalitarian character.

Before pursuing the possible use of Schelsky's account as an analogue to the postslavery family among Afro-Americans, let us back up a bit to the family in Africa. Did the social systems of West Africa, whence blacks were brought to America, act as a foundation for common-law marriages, weak relationships, and illegitimacy in the New World, as Herskovits claims? African history was one of family and lineage stability, but this stability, as well as African culture, was greatly shaken by the movement of Africans to America as slaves. What was not disrupted were the basic humanity and mutual concern, often expressed in extended kin ties, which were functions of that African heritage. Slavery was harsh and totalitarian, but it did not result in a continuous shuttling of blacks across the South. There was enough residential stability to permit the development of large-scale kin ties, even under slavery. Furthermore, with emancipation, not all blacks began to wander, footloose, on the countryside. In fact, the majority stayed close to where they had been as slaves, with the migrations to the great cities of the South and North beginning gradually over the next generation. Thus, with emancipation and the destruction of the southern way of life, large numbers of Afro-Americans retreated into their family and kin units, attempting to further survival and to find economic and social stability within them. Migrations, first urbanward and then northward, ordinarily involved family units—not footloose individuals. Whole kin groups often moved, one family at a time and over several decades, to a single location where economic opportunity was reported to be greater.

It should be added at this point that the present author feels that the issue of "cultural survivals" is not the key to the debate between the two analogies. How much obliteration of African culture took place is of historical interest in itself, and it is important today to U.S. blacks' search for

---

[46] Schelsky, "The Family in Germany," p. 332.

ethnic identity and cultural roots, as seen in Feature 2.[47] However, it is more important to the debate to reconstruct, through continuing historical research, the nineteenth century black family in the New World.

Which picture of Afro-American history is correct? Did the Afro-American succumb to the "concentration camp influence," with its dehumanization, weakening of peer relationships, and the opportunity it gave the "emancipated" to sever all ties and renounce all responsibility? Or did slavery result in a postdefeat world, in which the Afro-American drew upon a basic fund of humanity and upon mutual support—often within the family—in the struggle for stability and survival in a crumbling social system? An obvious possibility is that both analogies are partially correct: after emancipation, weak ties became weaker and strong ties became stronger. This, however,

-----

[47] Alex Haley's *Roots* (Garden City, N.Y.: Doubleday, 1974) describes one U.S. black's search for his identity and roots in Africa. An excerpt from the book and the account of how Haley came to write it may be found in *Reader's Digest* (May 1974), 73–84, from which Feature 2 has been taken; and Haley, "Researching the Unknown," *Writer's Yearbook '73*, 26–30, 106.

FEATURE 2

My earliest memory is of Grandma, Cousin Georgia, Aunt Plus, Aunt Liz, and Aunt Till talking on our front porch in Henning, Tenn. At dusk, these wrinkled, graying old ladies would sit in rocking chairs and talk, about slaves and massas and plantations—pieces and patches of family history, passed down across the generations by word of mouth. "Old-timey stuff," Mama would exclaim. She wanted no part of it.

The furthest-back person Grandma and the others ever mentioned was "the African." They would tell how he was brought here on a ship to a place called "Naplis" and sold as a slave in Virginia. There he mated with another slave, and had a little girl named Kizzy. ...When other slaves addressed him as Toby—the name given him by his massa— the African would strenuously reject it, insisting that his name was "Kin-tay."

Kin-tay often told Kizzy stories about himself. He said that he had been near his village in Africa, chopping wood to make a drum, when he had been set upon by four men, overwhelmed, and kidnaped into slavery. When Kizzy grew up and became a mother, she told her son these stories, and he in turn would tell *his* children. His granddaughter became my grandmother, and she pumped that saga into me as if it were plasma, until I knew by rote the story of the African, and the subsequent generational wending of our family through cotton and tobacco plantations into the Civil War and freedom. ...

Could this account possibly be documented for a book? During 1962, between other assignments, I began following the story's trail. ...

This book has taken me ten years and more. Why have I called it *Roots?* Because it not only tells the story of a family, my own, but also symbolizes the history of millions of American blacks of African descent. I intend my book to be a buoy for black self-esteem —and a reminder of the universal truth that we are all descendents of the same Creator.

Alex Haley, "My Search for Roots," *Reader's Digest* (May 1974), 73–78.

evades the issue of which pattern was dominant in the late 1800s. One piece of historical research which sheds some light on that issue is Paul Lammermeier's study of the urban black family in seven Ohio Valley cities from 1850 to 1880. Lammermeier found that 75 percent of black children fifteen years old or younger lived in two-parent families in the late nineteenth century, as compared with 66 percent in 1960. His conclusion is, very simply, that the urban black family during the nineteenth century was basically a male-headed, two-parent family that showed little evidence of the structural character which has been alleged to have characterized the slave family.[48] These findings may not, of course, be totally generalizable to the postslavery black family in the rural South, but they do raise questions about Frazier's view of the unattached, individualized urban migrant of the postslavery period.

It seems to this writer that the weakness of family ties under slavery has been overdrawn, and that after slavery the dominant pattern was family and kin solidarity as the emancipated blacks sought equilibrium, survival, and opportunity. It is likely, furthermore, that continuing historical research on the second half of the nineteenth century will corroborate this view. If the postwar Germany analogy is, in fact, the more accurate, how can one account for the predominance, in the historical literature, of descriptions of weak ties among the slaves? At least a part of the answer lies in the attempts of white scholars (and black scholars educated in a white society) to ease the guilt by minimizing the white race's inhumanity. That is, if slavery dehumanized the blacks and weakened their ties to one another, then the selling of slaves—the breaking up of family units—does not seem quite so inhumane. But if, in fact, the traffic in human chattel destroyed meaningful and supportive family ties, the crime becomes more appalling. In other words, because some white scholars wished to believe that black ties were weak, they wrote as if that had, in fact, been the case.

Of course, the particular conclusion the reader draws regarding the slavery and postslavery family among Afro-Americans is bound to be consistent with his conclusions concerning black families today. Keeping this in mind, let us seek to unravel the tangled strands of contemporary debate.

The Black American Family Today

Until the mid-1960s, there were two tendencies among students of the American family: one was for them to ignore the black family altogether; the other was for them to treat it as a social problem. The classic statement

---

[48] Paul J. Lammermeier, "The Urban Black Family of the Nineteenth Century: A Study of Black Family Structure in the Ohio Valley, 1850–1880," *Journal of Marriage and the Family* 35 (1973), 440–56.

of the latter approach is expressed by Frazier. "The mass migration of Negroes to the cities of the North resulted in considerable family disorganization." Life for urban Negroes, he feels, is casual, precarious, and fragmentary.

> It lacks continuity and its roots do not go deeper than the contingencies of daily living. . . . Without the direction provided by family traditions and the discipline of parents, large numbers of Negro children grow up without aims and ambitions.[49]

Frazier's characterization of the Negro family gained wide attention when it was repeated and programmed by Daniel P. Moynihan:

> The evidence—not final, but powerfully persuasive—is that the Negro family in the urban ghettoes is crumbling. . . . In a word, a national effort towards the problem of Negro Americans must be directed towards the question of family structure. The object should be to strengthen the Negro family so as to enable it to raise and support its members as do other families.[50]

Proponents of this view say that the black family is disintegrating, that it is disorganized, traditionless, free-floating, and matricentric. To them, the "free-floating" nature of rural southern and urban lower-class families means that sex relations are promiscuous, illegitimate births are prevalent, and marriage is not a part of the mores. As for the martricentric, or matriarchal, nature of the family, Moynihan claims that the Negro community has been forced into a pattern "which, because it is so out of line with the rest of the American society, seriously retards the progress of the group as a whole, and imposes a crushing burden on the Negro male and, in consequence, on a great many Negro women as well."[51] The household headed by a mother or grandmother is defined as a problem, since no adult male is present, and as problem-producing, since the absence of an adult male makes achievement by the younger generation even more problematic. As Moynihan puts it: "White children without fathers at least perceive all about them the pattern of men working. Negro children without fathers flounder—and fail."[52] One characterization thus becomes complete: Afro-Americans developed weak family ties during slavery; even these were loosened by emancipation. They then began the long process of trying to internalize the ways of the dominant society (including the concept of stable marriage), but the clustering together in urban ghettos and rural areas arrested the process. As a matter of fact, at present, acculturation appears to have become reversed, so that instability and weakness of relationships are once again becoming more prevalent.

---

[49] Frazier, *The Negro in the United States*, p. 636.
[50] Daniel P. Moynihan, *The Negro Family: The Case for National Action*, Department of Labor (1965), abstract and p. 47.
[51] Moynihan, *The Negro Family*, p. 29.
[52] Moynihan, *The Negro Family*, p. 35.

What has been the response to Moynihan's "tangle of pathology" characterization of the black family today? The first response to appear, especially in Andrew Billingsley's book *Black Families in White America*, was: it is not that disorganized, not that unstable, not that pathological. How can a people survive under oppression? One way is "to adapt the most basic of its institutions, the family, to meet the often conflicting demands placed on it."[53] Disagreeing directly with Moynihan and others, Billingsley states:

> We do not view the Negro family as a causal nexus in a "tangle of pathology" which feeds on itself. Rather, we view the Negro family in theoretical perspective as a subsystem of the larger society. It is, in our view, an absorbing, adaptive, and amazingly resilient mechanism for the socialization of its children and the civilization of its society.[54]

Is it disorganized and unstable? Frazier admitted that, while there is considerable family disorganization in the lower class, "there is a core of stable families even in this class."[55] To this, Billingsley adds that the large numbers of stable black working-class families never make the news and are seldom mentioned in social science reports. The majority of "poor Negroes live in nuclear families headed by men who work hard every day, and are still unable to earn enough to pull their families out of poverty."[56] It certainly cannot be surprising, says Bernard, to learn that lower-class black husbands "were rated least satisfactory in the role of provider. What is unexpected, in fact, is that relatively so few were. Only 10 percent of the wives felt that they were really missing out so far as level of living was concerned."[57] This fact, however, is surprising only if instability is expected or assumed.

Is the Afro-American family free-floating? Does it have weak ties and loose (by white middle-class standards) morality? Frazier admits that adequate information to answer these questions is lacking and that sexual promiscuity and weak marriage appear—from the data available—to be confined largely to the lower class. Billingsley, referring to illegitimacy, adds that white middle-class adoption processes are such that

> both women are protected from condemnation, for they both have "done the right thing." This contrasts sharply with the general efforts to expose to ridicule the Negro woman who has an illegitimate child and chooses to keep her own child, or must do so because of the policies of adoption agencies.[58]

---

[53] Andrew Billingsley, *Black Families in White America* (Englewood Cliffs, N.J.: Prentice-Hall, 1968), p. 21.

[54] Billingsley, *Black Families in White America*, p. 33.

[55] Frazier, *The Negro in the United States*, p. 324.

[56] Billingsley, *Black Families in White America*, pp. 137, 139.

[57] Bernard, *Marriage and Family Among Negroes*, p. 97.

[58] Frazier, *The Negro in the United States*, pp. 635, 319; Billingsley, *Black Families in White America*, pp. 162–63.

Finally, are black families matricentric? Frazier himself, from whom Moynihan drew heavily in preparing his report, finds in the 1940 census that only 21.7 percent of black families are headed by females.[59] Yet, when it comes to defining a "Negro problem," Frazier and his successors subtly allow this proportion to take on the character of typicality. There is a form of matrifocality that may be used to describe the black lower-class family, but it is hardly racially based and it must be distinguished from male absence. Lee Rainwater depicts this form of matrifocality as follows:

> Because of the high degree of conjugal role segregation, both white and Negro lower-class families tend to be matrifocal in comparison to middle-class families. They are matrifocal in the sense that the wife makes most of the decisions that keep the family going and has the greatest sense of responsibility to the family. In white as well as Negro lower-class families women tend to look to their female relatives for support and counsel, and to treat their husbands as essentially uninterested in the day-to-day problems of family living.[60]

Schelsky notes the conditions of social and economic disintegration which give rise to such a family style.

> The shifting of social functions and social balance in the family in favor of the wife is a phenomenon which is peculiar to industrial society in and of itself; the process, however, was vastly accelerated in Germany by the war and postwar events and, not only because women on their own part took over many more tasks and much more authority in the family and in public life, but also largely because the events themselves effected a lessening of the social self-consciousness of the husband.[61]

Thus, what Rainwater and Frazier say about black families (which is reinforced, to some extent, by Schelsky's account of postwar German families) is that they are primarily stable units, struggling together to survive in a white-dominated society. They are not typically weak or promiscuous in their relationships, but the way in which deviant behavior, such as illegitimacy, is treated accounts for some of the supposed difference between blacks and whites. Finally, they are characteristically matrifocal only in the sense that this is true of the lower-class model itself.

This response, then, is that black families are very much like white families, with the "pathology" view having arisen due to two factors: (1) the confusion of social class with race, and (2) the value orientations of researchers and writers. Much recent research has aimed at showing how wrong Moynihan was, how similar black and white families are. Jerold Heiss,

---

[59] Frazier, *The Negro in the United States*, p. 317.
[60] Lee Rainwater, "Crucible of Identity: The Negro Lower-Class Family," *Daedalus* (Winter 1966), p. 190.
[61] Schelsky, "The Family in Germany," p. 335.

for example, finds no evidence that parental marital instability among blacks is transmitted to their offspring, thus denying that such "pathology" is self-perpetuating.[62] Jacquelyne Jackson, looking at husband-wife roles and power among aging black couples, reports that males take a major role in decisions and that matriarchy is not prevalent among such couples in Durham, North Carolina.[63] Helena Lopata adds that, contrary to the assumption that older black widows live full and rich lives surrounded by kin, they are just as isolated as elderly white widows.[64] John Scanzoni, in an excellent study, finds great similarity between middle-class blacks in Indianapolis and their white counterparts.[65]

One of the problems with the characterizations "pathological" and "similar" is semantic and statistical. The use of such terms as *the majority, a large number, vast numbers,* and *a large portion* can be misleading when they are interpreted to mean *typically* or *in general.* Furthermore, not all black families follow the same pattern, nor are all black families simply a reflection in all particulars of white middle-class and lower-class models. Wherein do the differences among blacks lie, and what is the significance of those differences?

For Jessie Bernard, the debate regarding the nature of Afro-American society can be resolved by distinguishing members of two black cultures: the *acculturated* and the *externally adapted.* The former have internalized the moral norms of Western society; the latter are pleasure-loving and consumption-oriented. "The great chasm between the two Negro worlds is so great as to be, for all intents and purposes, all but unbridgeable, at least until now. Fear and hostility—even hatred and resentment—characterize the relations, or lack of relations, between them."[66] This great chasm of mutual rejection, drawn to some extent from Frazier's account in *Black Bourgeoisie,* can be used to explain the simultaneous increase in education and in illegitimacy, in achievement and in family instability. One set of phenomena are occurring among the acculturated and the other among the externally adapted, and there is little overlap.

This split has strong social class overtones: the acculturated are predominantly well off economically and socially, while the externally adapted are for the most part disadvantaged. There are, however, a few exceptions, such as the Black Muslims, who are economically disadvantaged but who

---

[62] Jerold Heiss, "On the Transmission of Marital Instability in Black Families," *American Sociological Review* 37 (1972), 82–92.

[63] Jacquelyne Johnson Jackson, "Marital Life Among Aging Blacks," *Family Life Coordinator* 21 (1972), 21–27.

[64] Helena Znaniecki Lopata, "Social Relations of Black and White Widowed Women in a Northern Metropolis," *American Journal of Sociology* 78 (1973), 1003–10.

[65] John Scanzoni, *The Black Family in Modern Society* (Boston: Allyn & Bacon, 1971).

[66] Bernard, *Marriage and Family Among Negroes,* pp. 33, 58.

have adopted the family values and moral codes of the middle-class model.[67]

The key to Bernard's conception is mutual rejection and separation—even combat—between these two cultural and social categories. Yet, within her own treatise, Bernard refers to research that calls into question this complete separation. Zena Smith Blau, for example, found that "fully 90 percent of the middle-class Negro women came from working-class backgrounds, in contrast to 35 percent in the white middle-class."[68] If there was mutual rejection between the two ways of life, how did these 90 percent become motivated to adopt the middle-class morality and success values? Billingsley claims that, not only is there not mutual rejection, but that, at present, there is an increasing sense of identity and peoplehood in the black communities of America. Those who have achieved middle-class positions are not severing their connections with the disadvantaged blacks, but are identifying with them. Here again there appears to be a great disagreement between writers: rejection, separation, and mutual hatred on the one hand; identification and a sense of peoplehood on the other.

In this case, it may not be necessary, as in the case of the historical models, to choose between Bernard's view and that of the "ethnic identification" proponents. Rather, it is at least possible that both are correct and that they describe a historical process. Perhaps when Frazier was describing the "black bourgeoisie," they were, in fact, trying very hard to be middle class and not "Negro"; while today these same professionals and white-collar workers are admitting their common Afro-American heritage with other blacks in this country. In other words, the 1960s may be seen as the decade when the "Negroes" became "Afro-Americans," when a minority began the process of becoming an *ethnic* minority. Billingsley himself notes that this change was occurring within his own lifetime. In the 1940s, he says, we were still ambivalent about our heritage. African students were treated with disdain, white students with adulation. Even after World War II, large numbers of blacks still felt a twinge of inferiority regarding their African heritage. "Yet the image is changing radically and rapidly."[69] The change is also reflected in research by Allen Williams, Nicholas Babchuk, and David Johnson, on participation in voluntary associations by Anglos, blacks, and Mexican Americans. These authors find such participation to be much higher among blacks than among either Anglos or Mexican Americans. "A possible key to this difference," they explain,

---

[67] Bernard, *Marriage and Family Among Negroes*, p. 46. On the family values of the Black Muslims, see Harry Edwards, "Black Muslim and Negro Christian Family Relationships," *Journal of Marriage and the Family* 30 (1968), 604–11.

[68] Zena Smith Blau, "Exposure to Child-Rearing Experts: A Structural Interpretation of Class-Color Difference," *American Journal of Sociology* 69 (1964), 605–7, quoted in Bernard, *Marriage and Family Among Negroes*, p. 45.

[69] Billingsley, *Black Families in White America*, p. 39.

may be a difference in awareness of minority status, i.e., a difference in the extent to which minority individuals perceive themselves and their group as objects of collective discrimination. In a manner similar to the development of class consciousness as a requisite for class action, some Black Americans seem to have gained a sense of ethnic community, Black consciousness, which has led to action-oriented social participation.[70]

They go on to state that, even as this rise in ethnic community consciousness occurred among blacks during the 1960s, so it may become increasingly evident in the '70s among Mexican Americans, American Indians, and U.S. residents from Cuba and Puerto Rico.[71]

Considerations of ethnic identity among blacks have led to a third position regarding the black family today. Tamara Hareven introduces the possibility of a third view as follows:

Research in progress on the Negro family structure promises to revise the breakdown stereotype initiated by Frazier and reinforced by Moynihan. Although attacking a theory, however, one can easily get trapped in its framework and spend too much energy in dispelling it.

It is not enough, says Hareven, to assert that black families are not disorganized, to talk of stable households and low illegitimacy rates. One should not ignore alternative analytic frameworks, such as varieties of family structure and the adaptability of alternative kin ties among urban blacks.[72]

This orientation, then, says that although the black family is not "just like the white," that does not mean it is "pathological." It means that there is cultural *uniqueness* and validity to the black model—a model which all members of this society must come to understand, and which, moreover, they can all learn from. Three important statements of this view of the black family have appeared during the 1970s. These are Robert Staples' decade review for the *Journal of Marriage and the Family*, Joyce Ladner's report on the black woman, entitled *Tomorrow's Tomorrow*, and Dmitri Shimkin, Gloria Louie, and Dennis Frate's ongoing research on the black extended family in Holmes County, Mississippi, and Chicago.[73]

---

[70] J. Allen Williams, Jr., Nicholas Babchuk, and David R. Johnson, "Voluntary Associations and Minority Status: A Comparative Analysis of Anglo, Black, and Mexican Americans," *American Sociological Review* 38 (1973), 644.

[71] Williams, Babchuk, and Johnson, "Voluntary Associations and Minority Status," p. 645.

[72] Tamara K. Hareven, "The History of the Family as an Interdisciplinary Field," in Rabb and Rotberg, *The Family in History*, p. 223.

[73] Robert Staples, "Toward a Sociology of the Black Family: A Theoretical and Methodological Assessment," *Journal of Marriage and the Family* 33 (1971), 119–38; Joyce A. Ladner, *Tomorrow's Tomorrow: The Black Woman* (Garden City, N.Y.: Doubleday, 1971); Dmitri B. Shimkin, Gloria J. Louie, and Dennis Frate, "The Black Extended Family: A Basic Rural Institution and a Mechanism of Urban Adaptation" (presented and discussed at the International Congress of Anthropological and Ethnological Sciences, Chicago, Illinois, September 1973).

Staples comments that Billingsley, though sympathetic, does not penetrate black families, but sees even their strengths through middle-class eyes. Instead, such divergences as the greater sexual permissiveness of black people should not be downplayed, but should be seen as reflecting the absence of a double standard of sexual conduct among blacks. Blacks can thus avoid the sex role conflicts and guilt which plague the white community. Therefore, sex relations both before and after marriage have "a much more positive meaning in the black community."[74] Among black women, he adds, children are a value in themselves, regardless of marriage. Along the same lines, Ladner asserts that a child has the right to exist, that motherhood is the fulfillment of womanhood, and thus that neither childhood nor motherhood should be degraded by artificial legal statuses. Blacks, she affirms, must "decolonize," that is, free themselves from white middle-class definitions of "the good" and "the right," since their own structures and values are good in themselves. A few additional examples may help to make her position clearer. Black women, she says, are strong but are not pathologically emasculating. Any emasculating of black men that has been done, has been done by white society. Black self-esteem is not low, but has been strengthened and clarified in the struggle for survival. Black marriage is not idealistic, or romanticized, but realistic—a stance which might help whites as well. Black women are now role models for many white women who are questioning the double sexual standard, traditional marriage, legal illegitimacy, and other norms whose violation in the black community has been defined as deviant by white middle-class morality.[75] So goes Ladner's often-compelling argument, which is based on interviews with teenage girls that she conducted as part of Rainwater's Pruitt-Igoe research team.

Thus far, the most convincing research acclaiming black cultural viability and uniqueness has been Shimkin, Louie, and Frate's continuing study of black extended families in Mississippi and Chicago. Black extended kin ties are not based on female dominance, and are important to both survival and social mobility. Black extended families may number one hundred or more individuals. Sometimes these individuals are clustered in one county; sometimes they are scattered from Mississippi to the great cities of the North. This picture of the black extended kin network, it should be added, has been corroborated in an entirely different research setting: a small Midwestern city. There William Hays and Charles Mindel have found more kin visiting and a higher value placed upon kin among twenty-five black couples than among a matched sample of whites.[76]

---

[74] Staples, "Toward a Sociology of the Black Family," p. 134.

[75] Ladner, *Tomorrow's Tomorrow.*

[76] William C. Hays and Charles H. Mindel, "Extended Kinship Relations in Black and White Families," *Journal of Marriage and the Family* 35 (1973), 51–57.

Blacks in such families and networks, Shimkin, Louie, and Frate feel, can be deservedly critical of the shortcomings of the white middle-class model and the dominant legal system.

> White people may feel keenly that marital instabilities and the acceptance of human frailties are signs of black failure. Black folks feel as keenly that the inadequacies of White care for "father and mother, brother and sister," White favoritism among children, and White indifference to the needs of distant kin are even more profound weaknesses.[77]

Thus, value ethnocentrism should be a two-way street, and, as the authors state in their introduction, it is time for cultural pluralism to be recognized by society's legal structures.

> The better recognition of Black family values, institutions, and customary law should serve as the basis of appropriate legislative actions, for example, in the rectification of currently biased laws on adoption and fosterage.[78]

Other authors have tried to account for the uniqueness of black culture, some by tracing African roots, some by noting the greater and more lasting prejudice and discrimination faced by blacks than by the European ethnic groups. But the basis for uniqueness is not the key issue confronting the spokesmen for this view of the black family. The key issue is: Is the unique black family culture a passing phase, or will it make a continuing contribution to the U.S. experience? That is, is ethnic minority status, and the resulting view of the black family as unique and good, merely a phase through which blacks must pass on the way to societal equality and success in middle-class terms, or is it a permanent part of the cultural pluralism of the United States? Shimkin clearly manifests the dilemma confronting those holding the "uniqueness" position:

> As more urbanized blacks ascend the ladder of success the tendency will of course be toward a more viable nuclear household. That appears to be a concomitant of much of modern urban life and is probably inevitable. But younger blacks, in particular, should always remember that what they are leaving is not something to be ashamed of. It is not something that is reflective of some deficiency in their culture. And it should not be disparaged.[79]

Is it true that, even for blacks, the process which has led to ethnic minority status will eventually lead to ethnic status? If so, this may mean that, as in the case of the ethnic groups discussed earlier, the problem

---

[77] Shimkin, Louie, and Frate, "The Black Extended Family," p. 184.
[78] Shimkin, Louie, and Frate, "The Black Extended Family," p. 11.
[79] Dmitri B. Shimkin, as quoted in Hamilton Bims, "The Black Family: A Proud Reappraisal," *Ebony* (March 1974), 125.

for the blacks will become one of keeping any of their unique culture intact in a society which—at least culturally—tends to "swallow up" its ethnic groups. Is "nuclearization" the inevitable price which the black family system will have to pay for self-esteem and success? Ladner would very likely say no, or at least that in the interim the larger society will learn much from the black experience and model. Only the future itself can answer these questions.

For the time being, our concern must be with the three current views of the black family: the Moynihanian *"pathology"* view and the views of its two sets of critics, those who say that the black family is *similar* to the white, or at least would not be very different if blacks were given a chance to assimilate economically, and those who say that the black family is *unique,* and should be recognized both legally and socially for its positive contributions.

Along with these orientations to the contemporary black family, several solutions to the problems of the black community have been proposed. One solution, which was based on a slight misrepresentation of the Moynihan report and drew a great deal of negative reaction, was that the strengthening of the black family should be the goal of government programs. If the family were stabilized, and the husband were a permanent member, then the tangle of pathology would begin to untangle. A stable family would mean more support for the achievements of offspring, and this would ultimately enable blacks to achieve social parity with whites. In short, this solution takes the onus off white society and its treatment of blacks, and places both problem and solution within the black community itself. Thus, it is not necessary to remake society's institutions, only to tinker with the lives of blacks in the United States. To this proposed solution, black leaders have responded that the problem to be solved by the white community is its own racism and prejudice. White leaders would do well to turn their attention and concern to the study, understanding, and resolution of prejudice and race hatred—emotions accompanied by debilitating and insidious effects on the prejudiced themselves.

By the same token, several solutions have been proposed by black leaders to their own problems. The three most prevalent might be labeled assimilation, separation, and power. The assimilative or incorporative approach is epitomized by the nonviolent civil rights movement and the writings of such men as Martin Luther King. Its goal is for the black man to be a part of the society and to share equally in its abundance; its means is to eliminate the racism and hatred of the whites through love and patient understanding. The desire for assimilation did not, of course, originate recently, but has been expressed by many black Americans for decades.

Some blacks, seeing the hope of assimilation go unrealized, have swung to the opposite pole. "Since they (the whites) reject us, we reject them." Here, in essence, you have the separatist movement so well illustrated by the Black Muslims. The group, no longer a "back to Africa" movement, has placed much of its emphasis upon having a separate area of the country (or several areas) in which the blacks may relocate themselves and run their own affairs.[80]

To many blacks today, both the assimilative and the separatist approaches sound too idealistic. The whites, they feel, are not really going to incorporate us, nor are they going to give us an area in which we can practice self-government. Therefore, for some, the solution is revolution. For others, it is black power, which takes several forms and has several goals. One of these goals is quasi-assimilative; a second is quasi-separatist. Both goals are well expressed in a programmatic statement by Billingsley. The Negro family is not going to be strengthened by direct government intervention, nor by income measures alone. The solution lies in more control by blacks over their own life conditions.

> We have been arguing that the best way to insure the viability of the Negro family life is to insure that the major institutions of the wider society are open and responsive to the Negro experience, and at the same time to insure that there are strong and viable institutions within the Negro community itself, controlled and managed by Negro people.[81]

Assimilation of people and cultural style into the larger society and, at the same time, greater control over their own communities: these are two goals of black power. The means to such goals are frequently debated. Can these goals be achieved by political participation and power, or must there be a more substantial revolution in the economic and political system?[82] Disagreements among black spokesmen, as well as slowness of change in the white community, keep this important issue unresolved.

The problem for blacks in the United States has differed greatly from that facing the Hutterites or that of the European ethnic groups. It has been a problem of *discrimination, misunderstanding, and nonacceptance* on the part of the dominant society. Is the black family and kinship system itself a pathological structure historically and currently, a misunderstood reflection of the dominant society and culture, or an unaccepted but unique solution to the problems thrust upon blacks in the United States? We shall begin our answer to this question by noting that Robert Staples, as Carl Broderick points out in an exchange of letters between them, equivocates

---

[80] *The Autobiography of Malcolm X* (New York: Grove Press, 1966 ed.).

[81] Billingsley, *Black Families in White America*, pp. 190–91.

[82] Stokely Carmichael and Charles V. Hamilton, *Black Power* (New York: Random House, 1967).

somewhat between the second and third views. He speaks of the unique and unappreciated black contribution, but elsewhere states that the black family is not "pathological," is less illegitimacy-prone, than the Census Bureau statistics would lead one to believe.[83] Broderick feels that Staples cannot have it both ways: either the middle-class view of illegitimacy is correct, and blacks should be seen as not all that different, or else the superiority of the black approach to illegitimacy should be stressed, and efforts should be made to build it into society's legal system.

It is at least possible, however, that Staples can have it both ways. To this writer the character of the black family seems very likely to lie somewhere between the *similarity* of the assimilationists and the *uniqueness* of the pluralists. Success will change many black families and their structure, perhaps toward the nuclear type, but that will not destroy the black cultural contribution—definable differences will remain. Nor will government programs provide the solution to such problems as the black family faces. Rather, the solution lies in continued intensification of black ethnic solidarity and the recognition that there will be little rapid or *voluntary* change in the white community. Precisely how the black family fits into this total scheme—as problem and resource—the reader must ultimately decide for himself. Help on that decision will continue to come from more and better research on the Afro-American family, based neither on biases nor on "preferred" types, but on empirical reality.

We have now completed a review of cross-cultural variations, the historical antecedents of the American family, the basic family types within the contemporary United States, and the theoretical and conceptual tools that are of value in understanding the family. At this point, our focus shifts to the family life cycle, beginning with socialization and continuing through mate selection to old age and family response to challenges. Throughout the subsequent chapters, the middle-class model "dominant" in the United States will be the prime object of analysis, although lower-class and other differing models will be brought in for comparison when they are significant.

---

[83] See Carlfred Broderick and Robert Staples' correspondence, in Carlfred B. Broderick, ed., *A Decade of Family Research and Action* (Minneapolis: National Council on Family Relations, 1971), pp. 161–62.

The Socialization Process

Socialization is the process by which the individual incorporates the attitudes and behaviors considered appropriate by any group or society. It involves self-concept (identity formation), which includes conscience development and the twin problems of identification and ego struggle—all of which are related to intrapersonal and interpersonal adjustment. There are differences in socialization, not only between societies, but also between the sexes and among the subcultural groups of a given society. The socialization process is the means whereby differences are perpetuated. Rapid social change and emphasis on peer expertise have resulted in the current phenomenon of "rearing by the book."

Every individual comes into the world with certain physical, emotional, and intellectual characteristics—a certain heredity. However, the infant has, at birth, the capacity to become a Chinese Communist, a Bushman, or an American—and what he does become depends greatly upon his socialization. This view, held by many social psychologists and anthropologists today, is well expressed by Margaret Mead:

> We are forced to conclude that human nature is almost unbelievably malleable, responding accurately and contrastingly to contrasting cultural conditions. The differences between individuals who are members of different cultures, like the differences between individuals within a culture, are almost entirely to be laid to differences in conditioning, especially during early childhood, and the form of this conditioning is culturally determined.[1]

Socialization (Mead's "conditioning") may be defined as *the process by which one learns or is taught how to behave in any group or society.* It is learning the culture, or ways, of a group; the process encompasses both the teachers and the learners, the socializing agents and the socialized.

---

[1] Margaret Mead, *Sex and Temperament* (New York: New American Library, Mentor Books, 1950 ed.), p. 191.

While the early years of childhood are stressed in much of the literature on socialization, the process actually continues throughout life, as a person changes roles and confronts new expectations.[2] During childhood, however, much of the individual's culture becomes fixed or internalized—as anyone who has moved from one society to another after childhood can attest.

Our biological inheritance *permits* and *requires* socialization, but also *limits* it.[3] No culture can demand that the individual run faster, lift more, or solve harder problems than is humanly possible. But within the bounds of these limitations, the potentialities are almost limitless. We tend to be unaware of much of our own socialization process, simply taking it for granted that our beliefs are "good" and that we know "the way" things should be done. Yet there are extreme differences between our "ways" and those of other cultures, involving even aspects of our attitudes and behavior that we may consider to be inherently "human." Economic competitiveness is not universal. Aggressive behavior may be rewarded in one cultural setting, passivity and amiability in another. Mead's summary of the differences between the Arapesh and Mungdugumor of New Guinea illustrates the variability in cultural styles:

> We found the Arapesh—both men and women—displaying a personality that, out of our historically limited preoccupations, we would call maternal in its parental aspects, and feminine in its sexual aspects. We found men, as well as women, trained to be cooperative, unaggressive, responsive to the needs and demands of others. We found no idea that sex was a powerful driving force either for men or for women. In marked contrast to these attitudes, we found among the Mungdugumor that both men and women developed as ruthless, aggressive, positively sexed individuals, with the maternal cherishing aspects of personality at a minimum. Both men and women approximated to a personality type that we in our culture would find only in an undisciplined and very violent male.[4]

The setting for such cultural differences may be diagramed as shown in Figure 5. Within the limits set by human endowment, each culture tends to reinforce certain attributes, while rejecting or punishing others. The result is that a particular type of personality comes to be dominant. Societies do differ, however, in the amount of variability (the size of the wedge-shaped section of Figure 5 they allow. Some, like the Mungdugumor, reward and value a very narrow range of personality types, so that only a small number of individuals diverge from the very specific cultural ideal. Such a society is called *homogeneous* with respect to its culture. Other

[2] For a good discussion of socialization after childhood, see Orville G. Brim, Jr., and Stanton Wheeler, *Socialization After Childhood: Two Essays* (New York: Wiley, 1966).

[3] On the first two, see Frederick Elkin, *The Child and Society* (New York: Random House, 1960), pp. 10–11.

[4] Mead, *Sex and Temperament*, p. 190.

Figure 5
Cultural Possibilities and Limitations

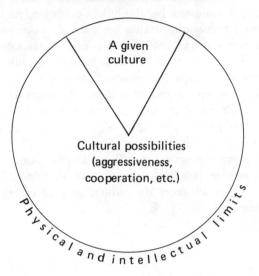

societies—the United States, for example—not only include several sub-cultural styles, but also reward a wider range of cultural possibilities, making these societies more *heterogeneous* in this respect. In addition, a given member of a heterogeneous society may be more strongly affected than a member of a homogeneous society by the pressures of conflicting cultural principles, such as expectations of cooperativeness and competitiveness, of honesty and success.[5] There are, then, differences between societies, both in the range of acceptable socialization patterns and in the range of alternatives offered the individual.

A particular pattern of socialization and culture also determines who will be the deviant in a society. Though it is impossible to know with certainty, Mead assumes—and other writers concur—that the range of hereditary types, or innate dispositions, is virtually the same from one society to another. Yet each culture tends to cultivate and value a specific portion of the range of possibilities. Thus, there may be a fundamental discrepancy between an individual's innate disposition and the kind of personality rewarded by the society into which he is born. Under these conditions, the socialization process may never bring that person to the point of conforming to society's expectations. Thus, in the past, the Cheyenne Indian boy who, by nature, was shy, fearful, and nonaggressive, and who never

[5] For a discussion of the range of cultural values in American society and of conflicts between those values, see Robin M. Williams, Jr., *American Society: A Sociological Interpretation* (New York: Knopf, 1960 ed.), chaps. 10–14.

overcame these tendencies, may never have reached the cultural ideal of courage and bravery. If he failed to "measure up" during puberty, when he was required to demonstrate his ability to be a brave, he may have been forced to become a transvestite, taking on both the appearance and social role of the Cheyenne woman.[6] The same boy might have been incorporated with relative ease into Arapesh culture. One reason for cultural deviance is, of course, that socialization is an imperfect process in two ways. First, as indicated by the Cheyenne example, it does not result in molding every individual to the cultural ideal; second, the individual is not *completely* socialized and, consequently, acts upon his society as well as being acted upon by its socializing agents.[7]

Without dwelling further upon the great diversities of socialization and cultural patterns in different societies, we shall now consider some general principles of socialization, after which we shall examine socialization in the United States.

Section One

SOME PRINCIPLES OF SOCIALIZATION

Socialization is the process by which the individual learns to control his biological drives, is taught what behavior is acceptable and what is unacceptable, and develops an identity, or self-concept. At least three relatively comprehensive theories have been advanced to explain various aspects of this process. These are psychoanalytic theory, learning theory, and role–symbolic interaction theory. Though the theories are sometimes viewed as contradictory, they are better seen as emphasizing different components of the human experience. Psychoanalytic theory stresses the importance of biological endowment and drives, as well as unconscious processes. Learning theory stresses responses to stimuli and mental or psychological processes. Role theory and symbolic interaction theory stress sociological processes or the importance of the socializing agents.[8] In this text we shall focus on role theory and symbolic interaction theory, though each of the three types will contribute to the discussion at certain points.

Socialization, we have said, involves self-concept or identity clarifi-

---

[6] On the Cheyenne, an excellent source is G. B. Grinnell, *The Cheyenne Indians: Their History and Ways of Life*, 2 vols. (New Haven, Conn.: Yale University Press, 1923).

[7] The latter point is well made in Dennis H. Wrong, "The Oversocialized Conception of Man in Modern Sociology," *American Sociological Review* 26 (1961), 183–93.

[8] For a brief discussion of the three theories, see Elkin, *The Child and Society*, pp. 18–44. For a lengthier discussion, see Morton Deutsch and Robert M. Krauss, *Theories in Social Psychology* (New York: Basic Books, 1965), chaps. 4–6.

cation.[9] Identity means a sense of the categories or groups to which one belongs and some conception of the kind of person he is. The child learns very early to relate himself to his environment. First, he cries or gurgles in response to a specific physical state. Soon he cries or yells to bring his parent, the "object" that has appeared in the past when he needed help. He learns what behavior is rewarded and what is not; by the repetition of rewarded behavior he begins to fix that action as part of his personality. (Of course, rewarded behavior must be defined by the goals of the individual. If the goal sought is simply the attention of the socializing agents, misbehavior may serve as well as acceptable behavior.)

The child also begins to do more than repeat rewarded and avoid unrewarded behavior. He makes the transition from the question "Am I a good boy?" to the internal feeling "I am a good boy." By noticing his parents' and others' general reaction to him, he begins to evaluate himself as a good boy, bad boy, smart boy, or nuisance. This is what Charles H. Cooley calls the *looking-glass self:* I see myself in the looking glass, or reflected by other people.[10] Many and repeated "reflections" begin to cohere and to become part of the self-concept, which is formed by extremely early experiences and reactions. It is relatively easy, for example, to see how a second (or later) child might develop a concept of himself as humorous or funny. As the second child makes his first, halting attempts to walk, to talk, or to eat, the older child may laugh. If this continues, and if the parents join in good-naturedly, the younger child may begin to view himself as a comic; this aspect of his self-concept may last for years—or a lifetime. R. D. Laing describes the process by which a child comes to define himself as naughty. The signals the child receives from significant others, Laing says, "do not tell him to be naughty; they define what he does *as* naughty. In this way, he learns that he *is* naughty, and *how* to be naughty in his particular family: it is a learned skill. Some children have a special aptitude for it."[11] Viktor Gecas has noted in a study of adolescent self-evaluation that if the child perceives his parents' behavior toward him as expressing a positive evaluation—for example, through love, concern, attention, support, and direction—he will evaluate himself positively.[12] Thus, one portion of self-concept formation is described by the notion of the looking-glasss self.

---

[9] An interesting approach to personality or self-concept formation that diverges from ours is Bingham Dai, "A Socio-Psychiatric Approach to Personality Organization," *American Sociological Review* 17 (1952), 44–49.

[10] Charles H. Cooley, *Human Nature and the Social Order* (New York: Scribner's, 1902), p. 184.

[11] R. D. Laing, *The Politics of the Family and Other Essays* (New York: Random House, 1971), p. 80.

[12] Viktor Gecas, "Parental Behavior and Dimensions of Adolescent Self-Evaluation," *Sociometry* 34 (1971), 481.

How able is the individual to perceive consciously the influence of his family on him? It might be well at this juncture to recall that most of this influence is not available to the individual for consideration and analysis. Laing describes the hiddenness of the family's configuration thus: "We are acting parts in a play that we have never read and never seen, whose plot we don't know, whose existence we can glimpse, but whose beginning and end are beyond our present imagination and conception." *"To be in the same family,"* Laing says, *"is to feel the same 'family' inside."*[13]

Conscience and Guilt

Part of one's self-concept is his *conscience,* involving the sense of right and wrong. As Freud and his followers noted, the individual learns to control his biological impulses, and to feel guilty when he fails to control them. At first, we have said, the child will ordinarily do "right" to avoid punishment; that is, he tries to do what he knows his parents will not punish. Later, he may feel good or bad, accordingly, when he does something that these significant other people would consider good or bad if they knew about it. He is thus reacting to what George Herbert Mead has called a *generalized other,* the internalized demands of the significant people in one's milieu.[14] Guilt is, therefore, the self-punishment that you administer when you do what might have been punished by others if they had seen you do it. By means of socialization, different consciences are taught to respond with guilt feelings to different behaviors. It is at this point that certain types of criminal behavior become understandable. The pickpocket who is the son of a professional pickpocket and part of a criminal subculture may feel little guilt about his behavior, only a concern not to be caught by the "bad guys," that is, the authorities. When one's socialization has not taught him that something is wrong, he may not feel guilty even though he is punished for it. On the other hand, when one has been taught that something is wrong, and is later told by others that it is not, he may agree that the arguments of the "others" are rational, but still find his emotions reacting with a sense of guilt to his newly acquired behavior. For example, the young person who has been raised in a conservative religious tradition that defines smoking, drinking, and dancing as sinful, may, when he arrives at college, be told that "everybody does it," and yet have great difficulty convincing himself that this type of behavior is acceptable. The individual with an underdeveloped conscience, who behaves according to the accepted patterns of his group and society only when others are around, is called a

---

[13] Laing, *The Politics of the Family and Other Essays,* pp. 87, 113.
[14] George H. Mead, *Mind, Self and Society* (Chicago: University of Chicago Press, 1934), pp. 154f.

psychopath.[15] Cultural and socialization differences play a big part in accounting for differences in conscience and guilt about specific acts, whether they be masturbating, head-hunting, or walking on the grave of one's ancestors.

This brings us to a general proposition regarding the relationship between cultural homogeneity or heterogeneity and conscience development: In the homogeneous society, the process of socialization may so uniformly reinforce the accepted definitions of right and wrong as to overdevelop the conscience of the members of that society. The result is that a serious breach of conduct may be followed by punishment or, if the individual is not caught, by such remorse and guilt as to lead, in the extreme instance, to suicide.[16] By contrast, the heterogeneous society may present the individual with so many conflicting conceptions of right and wrong as to either weaken his conscience and sense of guilt or to cause him to adopt the standards of whatever milieu he happens to be in—a sort of "conscience relativity."

Ego Struggle

Conceptions of right and wrong, and their internalization, are but one aspect of self-concept development. Two other important aspects of the process may be introduced as ego struggle and ego identification. *Ego struggle* is ✗ the attempt of the growing individual to discover and assert his uniqueness. Early in his life the infant does not distinguish between self and nonself. Yet he soon discovers his own boundaries and a sense of himself as separate from those about him. While the socializing agents impinge upon him in many ways during his early years, the child finds himself increasingly aware of and concerned about "I-ness" and "they-ness." Ambivalence toward and aggression against the socializing agents are likely by-products of this struggle; these attitudes tend to intensify as one moves from childhood into the teenage years. One reason for such ambivalence and struggle may be that one's innate disposition is somewhat at variance with his society's demands. Another is simply that he begins to evaluate those demands by means of his rational faculties. Thus, one of the most difficult parental tasks is to give the child a "proper" amount of freedom so that his sense of ego uniqueness can develop in a manner consistent with his capacities and with the demands of "life in society."

The fact that ego struggle is at least partially successful for many per-

---

[15] John Bowlby, *Child Care and the Growth of Love* (London: Penguin Books, 1953); Theodore R. Sarbin and Donald S. Jones, "Intrapersonal Factors in Delinquency: A Preliminary Report," *Nervous Child* 11 (1955), 23–27.
[16] Durkheim's brief discussion of fatalistic suicide might be interpreted to include such an instance of oppressive demands and a strong sense of guilt. See Emile Durkheim, *Suicide* (New York: Free Press, 1951), p. 276.

sons helps to account for the fact that cultural change does occur. Each new generation accepts, but also rethinks and alters, the behavioral norms and attitudes of the previous generation. This leads us to a second propositional distinction between the homogeneous and the heterogeneous society. The struggle, ambivalence, and rethinking are likely to be greater in the latter than in the former, since the individual in the heterogeneous society is exposed to divergent principles, to which he can compare those of his most immediate socializers. That is, ego struggle is more widespread and more intense in the heterogeneous than in the homogeneous society.

Identification

Opposite to ego struggle, but of equal importance in socialization, is the process of *identification*. How does the growing boy learn how he is supposed to behave as a male, a jobholder, a father, and a husband? He learns from significant other people, whom he sees playing these roles. Identification, according to Robert Winch, pertains to "the more or less lasting influence one person exerts on the behavior of another."[17] Identification is not a single variable in the type of relationship described; it involves personal or positional influence, or both. A "role model" is someone in a particular position, such as that of father or husband, from whom one learns how to behave when he assumes that same position. When I use my own father in this fashion, I can be said to have identified with him, or to have modeled my behavior as a father after him. But identification is broader than the concept of role model; it may also mean trying to be the kind of person we conceive someone else to be or striving toward some abstract characteristic he embodies. Thus, I may "identify" with my father's character or his success, while either rejecting or not even knowing the specifics of his role behavior. Identification, then, may be positional or personal.

Furthermore, identification may mean trying to emulate, to complement, or to negate the behavior of another. The child may try to be like his father, or he may try to be whatever he conceives his father not to be. In common parlance, however, the term *identification*, when unmodified, signifies positive identification, or trying to be like some other person. The complex of processes and meanings subsumed under the term *identification* is not unrelated to the concept of conscience development. Identification actually personalizes the question of where one learns standards of right and wrong, while also raising the question of the origin of other attitudes and aspects of behavior.

---

[17] Robert F. Winch, *Identification and Its Familial Determinants* (Indianapolis: Bobbs-Merrill, 1962), p. 142.

As a process, identification involves three steps, the first of which is (1) *awareness* of someone's modus operandi. The individual cannot identify with someone he knows nothing about. He may read about the way in which a certain contemporary, historical, or fictional person acts or performs his roles. More often, however, actually seeing a person in operation makes one aware of his characteristics. Furthermore, intensity and continuity of observation increase the likelihood of identification, making members of the same nuclear family a prime target for the process. After one becomes aware of the behavior of the role or character model, the next step in identification is (2) *evaluation*. It is at this point that the process may become either positive or negative. Though often unconscious, the reaction is: "This is the way (or not the way) to behave in the role of father," or "This is the way (or not the way) to react to the situation." Identification very often involves evaluations of a whole complex of behaviors by the same person; this is what is meant by "intensity."

The process of identification is not complete until the step of (3) *incorporation* is made. Incorporation often means "filing away for future reference" rather than immediate implementation. That is, the role of father may be modeled after one's own father, although it is not assumed for many years. Thus, the completed process might be illustrated as follows:

1. "I see how he plays the role of father."
2. "That is the proper way to play the role of father."
3. "When I become a father I shall play the role the way he does."

Who are likely objects of identification? Immediate possibilities, as indicated above, are one's parents and siblings. Works by Robert Winch, David Lynn, and Orville Brim have analyzed the intricate way in which the same-sex parent or an older sibling may influence the growing individual.[18] A proposition, modified slightly from one by Winch, is that, the more central the nuclear family is to the functioning of the society, the more likely it is that the individual will establish his major identifications within that unit. Conversely, the less central the nuclear family is to the functioning of the society, the more likely it is that the individual will establish his major identifications outside that unit.[19] Precisely how this proposition fits the historical facts regarding the family in the United States will be considered in Section Two.

---

[18] Winch, *Identification and Its Familial Determinants;* David B. Lynn, "The Process of Learning Parental and Sex-Role Identification," *Journal of Marriage and the Family* 28 (1966), especially 446–70; Orville G. Brim, Jr., "Family Structure and Sex-Role Learning by Children," *Sociometry* 21 (1958), 1–16.

[19] Robert F. Winch, *The Modern Family* (New York: Holt, Rinehart and Winston, 1963 ed.), p. 480.

Personality Integration

A further way to conceptualize the process of self-concept formation is in terms of the problem of personality integration. Each individual achieves two forms of integration, or adjustment, to a greater or lesser degree. The first is *intrapersonal,* or psychological, adjustment, which involves the reconciling of the individual's preferred self-concept, or how he wishes he were, with his actual self-concept, or the way he perceives himself to be. You may see yourself as a great lover and athlete, but you may be afraid of girls and unable to catch a ball. In such a case you must find some way of reconciling these, perhaps by lowering your goals, or by excelling as a musician or scientist. Without such a reconciliation, you may be headed for mental difficulties. Unfortunately, what Laing states concerning the family's hiddenness holds for the individual personality as well. That is, the individual cannot simply go to a blackboard and list his preferred and actual concepts and then proceed to make them agree. Neither may be immediately available to him for manipulation. A great part of psychotherapy is predicated upon the hypothesis that behavior is modified when one brings his preferred self-concept into line with the way he actually knows himself to be; this achievement requires that he uncover or become aware of both.

A second form of adjustment with regard to the self-concept is *interpersonal,* or social, adjustment. Each person must attempt to behave at least somewhat consistently with the expectations of others. That is, he must reconcile how he acts with how others think he ought to act. For example, a man may see himself as nonaggressive and friendly, and may live in accordance with this preferred self-concept, but his wife may chide him for lack of aggressiveness and for not getting ahead. Or, if he tries to keep peace in the family by aggressive behavior on the job, the result may be intrapersonal difficulties (for example, ulcers), due to the divergence between his preferred and his actual self-concepts. When one's preferred self-concept and other people's expectations are inconsistent, the conflict may be resolved by attaching greater importance to one or the other. You may have developed no clear or strong preferred self-concept, or part of this self-concept may be a concern to act in a way which is pleasing to others; in either case the demands of others will dominate. Or you may live according to your internalized principles and preferences, often based on strong ancestral role models, while ignoring the expectations of peers. Fortunate, it would seem, is the person for whom what he thinks he ought to be, what he perceives himself to be, and what others expect him to be all coincide.

In this discussion we have necessarily gone beyond the period of childhood in order to gain a broader perspective on the socialization process. With the tools and concepts developed above in mind, let us turn now to the specific historicocultural context with which we are most concerned: socialization in the United States.

SOCIALIZATION IN THE UNITED STATES

The Principles Applied

We must begin by bringing together two points that were made in distinguishing between homogeneous and heterogeneous. societies in general. First, the nuclear family of the modern industrial world places a great socializing burden upon parents. In an extended household, such as the joint family of India, there may be multiple adult role models with whom the growing child can identify. Among the Nayar, the biological father may have had no role in socialization whatsoever, the responsibility being borne by the women and certain aging males of the matrilineal kindred. It is not universally true, therefore, that one's parents are the prime significant others, *but it is true for the United States.* James Walters and Nick Stinnett state it thus:

> From the literature it would appear that in Western Society we think of the responsibility of rearing children as resting with their parents. The disadvantage of localizing this responsibility is that it places extensive responsibility on parents who may be inadequate.[20]

Parental cruciality in the United States must, however, be weighed off against a second conclusion concerning *heterogeneous* modern industrial society. Modernization, Darwin Thomas and Andrew Weigert find, leads to decreased conformity to *authoritative* significant others, in particular to parents and religious leaders. Conformity to nonauthoritative significant others, such as peer group members, does not show this relation to modernization.[21] Thus, we find that parents are the most influential significant others in industrial societies such as the United States, but that they have a more difficult time making their authority and influence "stick" than do the significant others—whoever they might be—in preindustrial societies.

How might these facts be related to the history of socialization in the United States? Colonial America, it may be recalled, was "nuclearized" but

---

[20] James Walters and Nick Stinnett, "Parent-Child Relationships: A Decade Review of Research," in Carlfred B. Broderick, ed., *A Decade Review of Research and Action* (Minneapolis: National Council on Family Relations, 1971), p. 130.

[21] Darwin L. Thomas and Andrew J. Weigert, "Socialization and Adolescent Conformity to Significant Others: A Cross-National Analysis," *American Sociological Review* 36 (1971), 843–44.

not "industrialized," and was less heterogeneous than the present-day United States. The nuclear family in colonial America had achieved a substantial degree of privacy with respect to its social network. Interrelations were fairly intense (in the sense in which that term was used above). That is, the child saw his parents at work, at play, at worship, under conditions of discipline, fun, and relaxation. The family was the hub of many societal functions; where this is so, we have postulated that positive identification within the family unit is extremely likely. Not only did the child see his parents carrying out the various aspects of their roles, but there were few alternative role models for him to emulate. Thus, even when the child had rankled under his own socialization, perhaps at the hands of a stern disciplinarian, he was likely to follow a similar pattern with his children later in life. Though he might have thought as he was being punished, "If I live through this I'll never treat my kids this way," when he became a father he did, in fact, behave as his father did, because that is "the way fathers are." Furthermore, the other models available to him, perhaps an uncle or an older sibling, were more likely to reinforce than to negate the model presented by the father.

What about a social setting in which nonfamilial socialization and divergent subcultural patterns vie with the family for influence in socialization, and in which the father plays his basic economic role outside the family? The proposition presented in the preceding section states that, the less central the nuclear family is to the functioning of the society, the more likely it is that the individual will establish his major identifications outside that unit. The pattern in the contemporary United States is not quite as simple as this proposition might indicate. The growing individual is most certainly confronted with multiple role model possibilities. He is unlikely to know precisely what his father does when he is away from home, but he may think he knows what the football coach or the movie actor does. That is, the son is aware of his father's home behavior, but not of his economic or extrahome role. On the other hand, daughters appear almost as likely to identify with their mothers today as in the colonial family. The intensity of their interaction—frequently greater than in the colonial family, due to the smaller size of families today—virtually offsets the influence of competing agents of socialization outside the home. Therefore, one major change from the colonial family to today's family is the weaker identification of sons with their fathers' role behaviors.

Even this difference must be qualified, however. The foregoing discussion has focused on positional identification, making the point that the range of possible role identifications between son and father is much more limited today, since many facets of the father's role are played away from the home. Forms of personal identification between a son and his father, however, are quite prevalent today. The son may identify with a general characteristic of his father, such as his success, or an aspect of his father's character, such as his honesty. Yet, on the whole, the proposition still holds: the modeling of day-to-day behavior after members of the nuclear family is somewhat less likely today than was the case in colonial times. In fact, precisely where the individual will find his role models, and whether or not they will reinforce one another, is problematic.[22]

This leads to an interesting point of speculation: If finding adequate sources of identification is currently more difficult than it was in the colonial family, can we conclude that ego struggle is, therefore, easier? Once again, the conclusion is not quite that simple. The colonial child, we have said, was given time free from supervision; in this way he resembled the Hutterite teenager with his cigarettes, movie magazines, and radio. Yet, in both of these instances, the intensity of the role models was such that the socializing agents were confident that the growing individual would internalize his group's standards and eventually cease to dabble in alternatives. In other words, the child might perceive himself as having substantial freedom, not realizing that the lack of clear-cut alternatives and the intensity of relations with significant others prevent ego struggle from ever really becoming an issue.

Ego struggle *is* an issue in the modern industrial world; but it is not necessarily an easy one. Parents are often quite successful in altering the child's unique development. They may, in some instances, dominate a child for the satisfaction of having someone to dominate. You may have seen cartoons in which the father, having taken a beating from his superiors at work, finds occasion to spank or scold his son upon arriving home. Or a parent may demand excessive achievement on the child's part in order to compensate for his own mediocre accomplishments, thus helping to solve his own (the parent's) identity problems. Ambitions that were thwarted in the father's youth, in athletics, for example, may be achieved through his offspring. Or— and this is a criticism often leveled at the middle-class mother—the parent may be so devoted to the child and so attentive to his every need as to overprotect him and thus thwart the development of his unique potentialities. Thus, it would be an oversimplification to say that ego struggle was the greater problem in the colonial family, and that in the present-day family identification is the greater problem. Due to a lack of awareness of adequate alternatives, ego struggle was not recognized as a problem in the colonial family. Nor is it true that parents today limit themselves to simply presenting alternatives and teaching their children how to think critically in order to make their own behavioral decisions. On the contrary, parents are still quite concerned to "orderly replace" their culture in their offspring, but the im-

---

[22] Portions of the preceding discussion are adapted from Winch's ideas in *Identification and Its Familial Determinants*. On measuring parental identification, see S. W. Gray and R. Klaus, "The Measurement of Parental Identification," *Genetic Psychology Monographs* 54 (1956), 87–114.

pinging of alternatives limits their ability to do so. The result is that identification is more problematic today than it was in the colonial family; ego struggle is more possible today, but is kept problematic by the conscious awareness of alternatives weighed against the indoctrinating efforts of parents and other socializing agents. Intrapersonal and interpersonal adjustment, when placed in a historical context, are quite closely related to the questions of identification and ego struggle just discussed. Both philosophical and empirical analyses have referred to a change in socialization emphasis over time toward more concern with interpersonal adjustment.[23] In colonial days, the behavioral standards of one's parents and other ancestral models were generally internalized and reinforced by one's experiences. When the individual did encounter divergent expectations, it was assumed that he would behave according to his internalized standards, that is, his preferred self-concept based on strong identifications. In contemporary society, however, parents have learned by their own experiences that, in order to be a successful member of society, one must be adaptable and flexible. In addition, most of the old behavioral absolutes have been called into question on what are assumed to be rational bases. Therefore, Daniel Miller and Guy Swanson feel that today's "bureaucratic-type" parents have as their major socializing principle teaching their child how to get along. The child

> must learn to produce a relationship that uses the symbols of genuine friendship as its currency without the actual commitment of the real thing. He must learn to be a "nice guy"—affable, unthreatening, responsible, competent, adaptive. It is this kind of skill in which the parents must train him.[24]

When it comes to a choice between following one's internalized standards and the demands of others, today's child is taught to follow the latter. This does not mean, as Melvin Kohn cautions, that socialization today undermines self-direction.[25] Rather, the interpretation must be phrased to indicate that the preferred self-concept itself includes as a major element getting along with people, fitting in, and cooperating. The individual in American society has changed, says David Riesman, from an inner-directed person, whose behavior is based on a preferred self-concept drawn from ancestral models, to an other-directed person, whose behavior is based on conforming to the expectations of his peers.[26] Riesman does not mean, as some have

---

[23] See, for example, Daniel Miller and Guy Swanson, *The Changing American Parent* (New York: Wiley, 1958); Frank Musgrove, *The Family, Education, and Society* (London: Routledge and Kegan Paul, 1966); David Riesman, Nathan Glazer, and Reuel Denney, *The Lonely Crowd* (New Haven, Conn.: Yale University Press, 1950).

[24] Miller and Swanson, *The Changing American Parent*, p. 203.

[25] Melvin L. Kohn, "Social Class and Parent-Child Relationships: An Interpretation," *American Journal of Sociology* 68 (1963), 476.

[26] Riesman, Glazer, and Denney, *The Lonely Crowd*.

concluded, that today people worry about what others think while formerly they did not. Instead, the issue is, Who are the others whose opinions and expectations influence us? In an earlier day the family and certain members of the ascending generation (often persons no longer alive) tended to dominate; today, as Thomas and Weigert have reported, authoritarian significant others, while still important, are less dominant models than was formerly the case. This, in turn, increases the influence of whatever group the individual is a part of at the moment.

Riesman's ideas are intuitively appealing but have been somewhat difficult to test empirically. Thus, our conclusions, while consistent with much historical information on American socialization, should be thought of as tentative. The data are too sparse and are drawn from too many sources to be considered final. In any case, the differences between inner- and other-directedness cannot be thought of in either-or terms, but only in terms of the degree of influence of parental-authoritarian models as compared to that of a large number of equalitarian significant and nonsignificant others.

Sex Differences in Socialization

Although definitions of masculinity and femininity have changed in certain particulars over the course of U.S. history, the patterns deemed "culturally appropriate" for boys and girls have generally included the following elements. Physically, males should be taller and more muscular, and should have facial and body hair. Females, in order to be "feminine," should have an attractive face and body, should be smaller, and should have little extraneous facial and body hair. Behaviorally, the Osofskys note, males should be verbally and physically aggressive, but should inhibit passivity, dependence, and conformity. Females should manifest the opposite pattern in the foregoing traits.[27]

These models, interestingly enough, are reinforced in the picture books which preschool children are expected to read. Lenore Weitzman reports that in these picture books boys are active and girls passive. Boys play and girls watch. Furthermore, the adult females are full-time wives and mothers, while the adult males are out in the world, actively involved. The storybook characters, then, whether children or adults, reinforce the traditional sex-role definitions of males as creative and curious and of females as neat and passive.[28]

Various writers and researchers have discussed the ways in which these sex-role definitions are actually implemented in socialization. Murray Straus,

[27] Joy D. Osofsky and Howard J. Osofsky, "Androgyny as a Life Style," *Family Life Coordinator* 21 (1972), 411–18.

[28] Lenore J. Weitzman, "Sex-Role Socialization in Picture Books for Preschool Children," *American Journal of Sociology* 77 (1972), 1125–50.

for example, notes that physical punishment is used much less frequently with girls than with boys. This, he says, links with the fact that the life conditions of girls involve "far less physical violence than is true of boys, while at the same time women have stronger internalized moral standards."[29] Matina Horner and Lois Hoffman have written separate accounts of the relation between socialization and achievement motives in women. Reviewing many studies, Horner concludes that in U.S. society femininity and competitive achievement continue to be viewed as desirable, but mutually exclusive, ends. As a result, the traditional feminine model still inhibits women from achieving.[30] Referring to socialization patterns, Hoffman offers an explanation for the inhibition of achievement in women:

> Since girls as compared to boys have less encouragement for independence, more parental protectiveness, less pressure for establishing an identity separate from the mother, and less mother-child conflict which highlights this separation, they engage in less independent exploration of their environments. As a result they develop neither adequate skills nor confidence but continue to be dependent upon others.[31]

---

[29] Murray A. Straus, "Some Social Antecedents of Physical Punishment: A Linkage Theory Interpretation," *Journal of Marriage and the Family* 33 (1971), 662.

[30] Matina S. Horner, "Toward an Understanding of Achievement-Related Conflicts in Women," *Journal of Social Issues* 28 (1972), 173.

[31] Lois Wladis Hoffman, "Early Childhood Experiences and Women's Achievement Motives," *Journal of Social Issues* 28 (1972), 129.

FEATURE 3

At the present time we are in a transitional stage, and women have devised four major ways of responding to the discrepancy between their life-styles as currently institutionalized and as they hope they will and can be. Some, probably the majority, *accept* the supportive role, partly because they do not know how to reject it or because they are afraid to reject it. Some *compromise* by accepting housekeeping as the primary female responsibility and at the same time pursuing careers on a part-time basis. Others *compensate* by giving the feminine role an aura, a mystique. These women emphasize femininity and its alleged qualities and claim that womanhood is actually superior to manhood. Finally, there are those women who totally *reject* second-class status and who are redefining themselves and their lives. Such women claim equal status with men. They are refusing the role of the "other." They are self-actuating women who are fulfilling their potentialities as human beings.

Gloria Steinem speculated on what the world would be like if the women's liberation movement were wholly successful. First of all, women would not want to turn the tables and oppress men. They would want an economic system that would provide equal opportunities and rewards to the sexes. They would try to discourage men's warlike and aggressive proclivities. They would be willing to share the problems of supporting families. In short, Steinem writes, "Men and women won't reverse roles; they will be free to choose according to individual talents and preferences." [*Liberation Now!* Dell, 1971, pp. 55–61.]

Furthermore, equality for women would mean the end to sexual hypocrisy. Men would no longer need to worry about whether women

All these writers would agree with Mead that such sex differences are not innate, but are a result of the differential socialization of boys and girls. Are these sex-role models healthy for personality development, or not? Much of the current discussion of socialization practices in the United States is related to this question. Rachel Inselberg and Lee Burke, for example, report that in kindergartens boys high in masculinity were more popular and had higher personality adjustment scores than boys who did not live up to the male sex-role stereotype.[32] To this kind of finding, Hoffman responds that female achievement performances, like female IQ scores, cluster closer to the mean and "do not show the extremes in either direction that male indices show." Could this mean, she wonders, that some boys are pushed prematurely into independence? could the high achievement needs of males also have an unhealthy base and result?[33] Weitzman, in concluding her article on sex roles in picture books, argues that rigid sex-role distinctions may actually be harmful to the normal personality development of the child.[34] Still others, such as the Osofskys and Lucile Duberman (Feature 3), have suggested that freedom from the traditional sex-role stereotypes, while obvi-

---

[32] Rachel M. Inselberg and Lee Burke, "Social and Psychological Correlates of Masculinity in Young Boys," *Merrill-Palmer Quarterly* 19 (1973), 41–47.

[33] Hoffman, "Early Childhood Experiences and Women's Achievement Motives," pp. 149–50.

[34] Weitzman, "Sex-Role Socialization in Picture Books for Preschool Children," pp. 1149–50.

---

find them attractive for themselves or for the security they offer. Nor will men be required any longer to live with domineering wives, emasculating women, overprotective mothers, or dependent child-women.

American children, too, would benefit. If parental responsibility were truly shared, children would have less "mothering" and more "fathering." Better still, they would have less interaction with either parent and more with peers in daycare centers. Women, contrary to popular sexist belief, are not interested in abolishing the family. Instead, they realize that equality with their men will strengthen the family ties because children will have the companionship of two parents who interact with them because they want to do so, not because one has no choice but to overinteract and the other has no choice but to underinteract.

Steinem believes that men's health is likely to improve when the stresses of masculinity are removed. There should be fewer heart attacks, fewer ulcers, and a lowered male suicide rate. Acceptance of women in the higher levels of the clergy might result in a radical redefinition of sin. There will be less sexism in literature, especially in children's books. Men and women will dress for comfort rather than to emphasize sexual characteristics. Feminine beauty will become less important, with the corollary that both men and women will be able to enjoy maturity without feeling inferior. In short, Steinem concludes, "If women's lib wins, perhaps we all do."

Lucile Duberman, *Gender and Sex in Society* (New York: Praeger Publishers, 1975), pp. 250–51.

ously beneficial to females, may prove beneficial to males as well.[35] Males might become less inhibited about entering into warm relationships and might be less competitive, or at least only as competitive as their particular personalities warranted. This discussion of the benefits of freedom from rigid sex-role modeling brings us to the verge of the entire feminist-humanist issue, the issue of women's *and* men's liberation, to which we shall return in Chapters 11 and 16. But for the time being, we close with Horner's reminder that the recent emphasis on freedom for women has not been effective, thus far, in removing the psychological barriers—caused by socialization—to the achievement of many otherwise motivated and able young women.[36] And such efforts on men's behalf, whether beneficial or not, have hardly begun.

Middle-Class and Lower-Class Styles of Socialization Compared

We have already noted the substantial differences in life-style between the affluent masses of American society—the middle class—and members of the lower class, who must strive to maintain an economic subsistence level. Mention was also made of the working class, that large aggregate of manual workers who enjoy stable employment and a standard of living that includes many of the luxuries that characterize the affluent. In this section we shall begin by comparing the middle and lower classes, but we shall subsequently bring in the working class.

Available evidence from studies conducted over a 40- to 45-year period indicates some of the more important differences between middle-class and both working- and lower-class socialization. (See Table 2.) Middle-class parents have consistently been found to be more emotionally warm and expressive toward their child, showing pleasure in him and generally bolstering his sense of self-esteem. Steven Tulkin and Bertram Cohler find that even in the first year of the child's life the attitudes of middle-class mothers reflect more moderate control of aggressive impulses, greater encouragement of reciprocity, greater acceptance of the emotional complexities of child-rearing situations, and greater satisfaction in perceiving and meeting the child's physical needs.[37] However, this distinction between the middle class and the working and lower classes is particularly acute in the case of fathers; Kohn has described the role of the middle-class father thus:

---

[35] Osofsky and Osofsky, "Androgyny as a Life Style," p. 414.

[36] Horner, "Toward an Understanding of Achievement-Related Conflicts in Women," pp. 173–74.

[37] Steven R. Tulkin and Bertram J. Cohler, "Childrearing Attitudes and Mother-Child Interaction in the First Year of Life," *Merrill-Palmer Quarterly* 19 (1973), 95–106.

Table 2
Some Differences Between Middle-Class and Working- and Lower-Class Socialization

Aspects of Socialization	Middle Class	Working and Lower Classes
Parental warmth and demonstration of affection	High	Low
Role of father	Supportive of child	Little role in socialization
Style of verbal communication	Reasoning and discussion	Much use of commands
Basis for discipline	Behavioral intent	Behavioral consequences
Use of physical punishment	Moderately low	High
Tolerance of children's impulses	High	Moderately low
Demand for responsible independence	High	Moderately low

SOURCES: Among the numerous sources are: Urie Bronfenbrenner, "Socialization and Social Class Through Time and Space," in Eleanor E. Maccoby, Theodore M. Newcomb, and Eugene L. Hartley, eds., *Readings in Social Psychology* (New York: Henry Holt, 1958), pp. 400–425; Melvin L. Kohn, "Social Class and Parent-Child Relationships: An Interpretation," *American Journal of Sociology* 68 (1963), 471–80; Grace F. Brody, "Socioeconomic Differences in Stated Maternal Child-Rearing Practices and in Observed Maternal Behavior," *Journal of Marriage and the Family* 30 (1968), 656–60; Arthur Besner, "Economic Deprivation and Family Patterns," in Lola M. Irelan, ed., *Low-Income Life Styles,* Department of Health, Education, and Welfare, Welfare Administration Publication No. 14 (1966), pp. 15–29; Bronfenbrenner, "The Changing American Child—A Speculative Analysis," *Journal of Social Issues* 17 (1961), 6–18; Maccoby and P. K. Gibbs, "Methods of Child-Rearing in Two Social Classes," in W. E. Martin and C. E. Stendler, eds., *Readings in Child Development* (New York: Harcourt, Brace, 1954), pp. 380–96; Kohn and Eleanor E. Carroll, "Social Class and the Allocation of Parental Responsibilities," *Sociometry* 23 (1960), 372–92; Catherine S. Chilman, "Child-Rearing and Family Relationships of the Very Poor," *Welfare in Review* (1965), pp. 9–19; James Walters and Nick Stinnett, "Parent-Child Relationships: A Decade Review of Research," in Carlfred B. Broderick, ed., *A Decade Review of Research and Action* (Minneapolis: National Council on Family Relations, 1971), pp. 99–140; Stanley B. Messer and Michael Lewis, "Social Class and Sex Differences in the Attachment and Play Behavior of the Year-Old Infant," *Merrill-Palmer Quarterly* 18 (1972), 295–306; Steven R. Tulkin and Bertram J. Cohler, "Childrearing Attitudes and Mother-Child Interaction in the First Year of Life," *Merrill-Palmer Quarterly* 19 (1973), 95–106. Additional references can be found in Chilman's article, Bronfenbrenner's paper in *Readings in Social Psychology,* and Walters and Stinnett's "Parent-Child Relationships."

> Middle-class mothers want their husbands to be supportive of the children (especially of sons), with their responsibility for imposing restraints being of decidedly secondary importance. . . . Most middle-class fathers agree with their wives and play a role close to what their wives would have them play.[38]

The lower-class husband, on the other hand, ordinarily plays a minor role in child rearing, and, as Lee Rainwater points out, "often his wife prefers it

---

[38] Kohn, "Social Class and Parent-Child Relationships," p. 479.

that way."[39] The support the middle-class father offers takes many forms: discussing events and goals, helping with homework, teaching skills, as well as complimenting and encouraging his child. There is, however, an apparent middle-class bias in the conclusions regarding warmth in the family. If, as some feel, the lower-class nuclear family is more embedded personnel-wise in its social network than is the middle-class family, then the lower-class child may not experience less emotional warmth; the sources of emotional warmth may simply be more dispersed, and may include a grandparent or an extrafamilial member of the social network.

In middle-class families, a great deal of emphasis is placed upon the development and use of verbal skills. Lower-class parents are less likely to live and work in the realm of ideas, or to give substantial attention to explanation, reasoning, and understanding of motives. This holds for interaction with children as well as between husband and wife. It takes not only inclination but *time* to reason and discuss; the middle-class tendency is reinforced by the greater likelihood that there will be a smaller number of children, giving parents more time to spend with each, and that the mother will be a full-time housewife. In the lower-class family, lack of both verbal skills and time combine to increase the use of commands and physical response. It should perhaps be noted here that success in U.S. society is related, not only to emphasis on verbal skills but also to the warm, accepting environment which is more characteristic of the middle class. Consensus existed in the studies reviewed by Walters and Stinnett that "academic achievement, leadership, and creative thinking of children was positively related to warm, accepting, understanding, and autonomy-granting parent-child relationships."[40]

A key area in which the foregoing difference appears is child discipline. In the first place, the basis for discipline in the middle class tends to hinge on the question of behavioral intent, while in the lower class it is predicated upon behavioral consequences. The middle-class parent is concerned with the motives of the child rather than with the negatively defined outcomes of specific behavior. By way of illustration, let us suppose that a six-year-old child turns over his glass of milk. An immediate attempt is made by the middle-class parent to assess his intent. Did he spill the milk because he was trying to cut up his own meat? If so, encourage him. Did he turn it over because he was angry at having beans for supper? Then he must be scolded or punished. The decision regarding behavioral intent must be made almost spontaneously; therefore, it is possible that the parent may make a mistaken assessment. The lower-class parent, when faced with the same situation, defines this behavior by the six-year-old as punishable, since it is disruptive of

---

[39] Lee Rainwater, *Family Design: Marital Sexuality, Family Size, and Contraception* (Chicago: Aldine, 1965), p. 60.

[40] Walters and Stinnett, "Parent-Child Relationships," in Broderick, *A Decade Review of Research and Action*, p. 120.

routine and damaging to furniture, as well as indicative of lack of control. A second difference in discipline concerns the use of physical punishment. Middle-class parents usually employ reasoning and shame, and sometimes a threat of love withdrawal, while lower-class parents are more likely to respond in a more physical manner.[41]

The last two differences in socialization to be discussed are middle-class parents' greater tolerance of children's impulses and spontaneous outbursts and their greater demand for responsible independence. Lower-class parents are likely to punish impulsive behavior when it occurs, but their style of socialization and discipline is not an effective deterrent and, in fact, may foster the behavior it aims to control. Thomas and Weigert substantiate this when they report finding "that support is significantly related to conformity to the expectations of authoritative others, while control has little effect."[42] Thus, it is not surprising to find Walters and Stinnett reporting that, while upper-middle-class mothers are confident of their child-rearing methods, lower-class mothers

> were the least confident of their methods, evidenced the least amount of responsibility for the behavior of their children, and while they saw their children as needing close parental control, felt that they were unable to influence behavior outcomes of their children.[43]

An important distinction is captured by the term *responsible independence*. By this is meant self-reliance, learning how to do things for yourself—but always within the bounds of the middle-class value system. The middle-class parent is excited when his child learns to tie his shoes at age four, to make his bed and put his clothes away, to set up a stand and sell lemonade. All these are signs of responsible or, to use Farber's term, "sponsored" independence. For the lower-class parent, a crucial element in socialization might be called freedom or "unsponsored independence."[44] Robert Sears et al. argued that earlier findings "of greater freedom of movement for the lower-class child were more properly interpreted not as 'permissiveness' but as 'a reflection of rejection, a pushing of the child out of the way.' "[45] To overstate it, the child is simply turned out with the expectation that he will re-

---

[41] This finding, reported in many earlier studies, is noted again by Walters and Stinnett, "Parent-Child Relationships," in Broderick, *A Decade Review of Research and Action*, p. 130. At least one study in the 1970s has found no difference between the use of physical punishment by working-class and middle-class parents, however. See Straus, "Some Social Antecedents of Physical Punishment," p. 622.

[42] Thomas and Weigert, "Socialization and Adolescent Conformity to Significant Others," p. 844.

[43] Walters and Stinnett, "Parent-Child Relationships," in Broderick, *A Decade Review of Research and Action*, p. 102.

[44] Bernard Farber, *Family: Organization and Interaction* (San Francisco: Chandler, 1964), pp. 367–78.

[45] Referred to in Urie Bronfenbrenner, "Socialization and Social Class Through Time and Space," in Eleanor E. Maccoby, Theodore M. Newcomb, and Eugene L. Hartley, eds., *Readings in Social Psychology* (New York: Henry Holt, 1958), p. 401.

turn home when he is hungry, sleepy, or injured. This approach on the part of lower-class parents, incidentally, is one of the historical connections between the modern subsistence-level urban family and the American subsistence farm of the past. In both instances, as noted in Chapter 6, when the child was not carrying out his family responsibilities, he was generally unsupervised. The major difference is in the proportion of free time available. Agrarian family economic endeavor and division of labor ordinarily left the growing individual with only a little time to himself. Urban lower-class life leaves the child with far less family responsibility and, thus, with much more time to spend in unsponsored independence, or staying out of the way.

How does the pattern of socialization in the working class (here defined as those families in which the husband is a stably employed manual worker with some skill) differ from the middle-class and lower-class models sketched above? At the outset, one must be aware of the inherent difficulties with the literature on working- and lower-class families, some of which we have already quoted. Certain studies have used the terms almost interchangeably, while others have used *working class* to designate both the working and lower classes. Nevertheless, the evidence, to the extent that it can be differentiated, points to the following distinctions. If middle-class socialization is best characterized by independence, interchange, and affection, and lower-class socialization by freedom and discipline, working-class socialization is oriented toward *respectability*—a concern with limits, neatness, and control. Consistently, Bronfenbrenner asserts, the working-class parent has "emphasized what are usually regarded as the traditional middle-class virtues of cleanliness, conformity, and control."[46] In addition, the mother, rather than desiring her working-class husband to stay out of the way or to be merely supportive, wishes him to help her with the directive function. This, however, he is generally unwilling to do. Kohn explains it thus:

> It is not that they (working-class fathers) see the constraining role as less important than do their wives, but that many of them see no reason why they should have to shoulder the responsibility. From their point of view, the important thing is that the child be taught what limits he must not transgress. It does not matter much who does the teaching, and since mother has primary responsibility for child care, the job should be hers.[47]

Although the differences between middle-class, lower-class, and working-class socialization appear to have remained over the 40- to 45-year period during which the studies have been carried out, the gap between middle- and working-class styles appears to be narrowing. To some extent, this may

---

[46] Bronfenbrenner, "Socialization and Social Class Through Time and Space," in Maccoby, Newcomb, and Hartley, *Readings in Social Psychology*, p. 423.
[47] Kohn, "Social Class and Parent-Child Relationships," p. 479.

be a function of the rise in the standard of living among the stable segments of the working class. Bronfenbrenner, however, feels that the narrowing is due to the fact that the working-class parent is making more use of middle-class techniques and sources of information, thus reducing the cultural differences between them.[48] These sources include child-care manuals, such as *Infant Care* and Benjamin Spock's *Baby and Child Care,* to which we shall refer below. Some have even coined the term *middle mass* to incorporate the skilled and stable segments of the working class and the less affluent segments of the middle class, for example, salesmen and clerks.[49] Yet Brody's and other studies in the late 1960s continued to produce sufficient differences to justify—at least temporarily—the retention of middle-class, working-class, and lower-class models.

A study by Arnold Green is an excellent point of departure for linking middle- and lower-class differences in socialization with the earlier discussions of identification and personality integration.[50] Middle-class parents ordinarily have more socioeconomic rewards to offer and grant more affectional rewards to their children than do lower-class parents. Since reward is related to identification, it follows that identification with parents is more likely in the middle-class family. There are, however, some peculiar problems of personality integration presented by the middle-class family setting. Remember that independence is demanded of the middle-class child, especially the male; that the child is in an affectionate family setting; and that punishment is characterized by shame and by the threat of love withdrawal. According to Green, if all of these elements are strong, this approach to socialization may confront the individual with the possibility of neurosis. Though he never defines it, the neurosis of which Green speaks is nothing more than an undercurrent of anxiety and nervous upset, resulting from a combination of a somewhat confused self-concept and the internalized threat of love withdrawal. In most cases of such neurosis, the individual continues to function in society, but is unduly worried about himself, his responsibilities and role, about others, or about the world in abstraction. How does this neurosis develop?

The child is taught and expected by his mother to be loving and responsive, and is thus bound to her by a close emotional tie. Yet punishment often centers in that very love relationship, so that the child in his early

---

[48] Bronfenbrenner, "Socialization and Social Class Through Time and Space," in Maccoby, Newcomb, and Hartley, *Readings in Social Psychology,* p. 420.

[49] On the middle-mass concept, see Bennett M. Berger, *Working-Class Suburb* (Berkeley and Los Angeles: University of California Press, 1960), p. 96; Richard F. Curtis, "Differential Association and the Stratification of the Urban Community," *Social Forces* 42 (1963), 72; Bert N. Adams and James E. Butler, "Occupational Status and Husband-Wife Social Participation," *Social Forces* 45 (1967), 503, 506–7.

[50] Arnold W. Green, "The Middle-Class Male Child and Neurosis," *American Sociological Review* 11 (1946), 31–41.

years is made to feel that being loved is dependent upon acting in a certain way—upon good or almost perfect behavior. Furthermore, in the case of the male child, both parents, but particularly the father, expect him to be aggressive and competitive outside the home, while his home environment stresses giving, consideration, and affection. Thus, the jelling of his self-concept, of what he is and wants to be, is made difficult. This is not to say that more than a small fraction of middle-class families produce neurotic offspring. The point is, however, that when middle-class socialization *does* cause a problem, intrapersonal maladjustment is the direction it is likely to take.

Included in Green's study was a brief comparison of middle-class socialization with socialization in the homes of recent Polish immigrants in the coal mining areas of Pennsylvania. Punishment in these homes was found by Green to be haphazard, overt, and spontaneous. Unsponsored freedom for the child was maximized, and neurosis, or conflict within the self, was averted. Though Green does not pursue the comparison, it would seem to follow that, in a situation of spontaneous and often antagonistic human relations, personality adjustment problems are more likely to be interpersonal than intrapersonal.

At least one study has verified the conclusion that problems in middle-class personality development tend to take the form of intrapersonal neuroses, while the more usual forms personality disorders take in the lower class are interpersonal neuroses and character disorders.[51] Elsewhere, however, both inter- and intrapersonal adjustment difficulties have been found to be more prevalent in the lower-class family. Yet, apart from consideration of differences between the middle class and the lower class, it does seem that when middle-class socialization causes the individual problems, they tend to be of an intrapersonal nature. The reader is left to pursue, on his own, considerations of schizophrenia, violence, and other forms of maladjustment suggested by the foregoing discussion.

Rearing by the Book

The orderly replacement of family culture from one generation to the next is most easily accomplished in a society that looks to ancestral models for authority, wisdom, and guidance. In the United States of the 1960s, however, Dr. Spock and *Parents' Magazine* have been extremely successful in "displacing grandmother as the authority on child development."[52] The result

---

[51] August B. Hollingshead, "Factors Associated with Prevalence of Mental Illness," in Maccoby, Newcomb, and Hartley, *Readings in Social Psychology*, pp. 425–36. See also Hollingshead and F. C. Redlich, *Social Class and Mental Illness* (New York: Wiley, 1958), for a fuller account.

[52] Winch, *The Modern Family*, p. 448.

of looking to our peers or contemporaries for guidance, as Martha Wolfenstein so beautifully demonstrates, is that, instead of receiving accumulated and relatively unchanging advice, the American parent tends to get advice that fluctuates with the latest fad. Wolfenstein shows how, in 1890, the dominant viewpoint was to indulge the child; by 1920, scheduling and a certain aloofness predominated; and, by 1945, indulgent mothering was once again recommended.[53] Are the fads bad for the offspring? An interesting insight can be gained into that question from a paper by Allen Williams, Frank Bean, and Russell Curtis on parental constraints. Neither permissiveness nor restrictiveness, the authors find, results in maladjusted offspring—unless either orientation becomes extreme. That is, the orientation does not seem to matter so much as that it be "in moderation."[54]

This swing of the pendulum is actually between two viewpoints regarding the nature and development of the child. These viewpoints are labeled the "traditional" and "developmental" by Evelyn Duvall.[55] The traditional view, which has some of its roots in Puritan ideology, reached its greatest strength during the Victorian era in Great Britain; this view sees the necessity of curbing the child's impulses. The child is less wise than his parents, so the reasonable form of socialization should stress nuclear family values, and obedience and reserve on the child's part. A typical reaction to the offspring who deviates from his family's expectations would be: "He is the black sheep *of the family.*" The developmental view, expounded by Freud, John B. Watson, John Dewey, and others, presents the idea that the child should be allowed to develop (his) own potentialities at his own speed and in his own way, thus maximizing creativity and uniqueness. The latter approach, of course, fits well this society's emphasis upon newness, creativity, change, and individualism. A typical reaction to an offspring's deviance is: "Where did we go wrong?" or "Where did we fail *him*?" In fact, the traditional and developmental emphases in socialization are closely related to personnel embeddedness in the nuclear family and individualism, respectively. It is not surprising that the overall long-range trend has been—although there have been fluctuations—toward the developmental, or individualistic, position.[56]

---

[53] Martha Wolfenstein, "Trends in Infant Care," *American Journal of Orthopsychiatry* 23 (1953), 120–30.

[54] J. Allen Williams, Jr., Frank D. Bean, and Russell L. Curtis, Jr., "The Impact of Parental Constraints on the Development of Behavior Disorders," *Social Forces* 49 (1970), 283–91.

[55] Evelyn M. Duvall, "Conceptions of Parenthood," *American Journal of Sociology* 52 (1946), 193–203.

[56] There is some question regarding the period since 1950. Wolfenstein and Winch feel that there has been some movement away from indulgence and permissiveness, and toward order and control. Michael Gordon, however, finds no such change in *Infant Care* or in Dr. Spock's manual, though he admits that it may have occurred in popular periodicals. Michael Gordon, "*Infant Care* Revisited," *Journal of Marriage and the Family* 30 (1968), 578–83.

It cannot, however, be concluded that individualism now predominates in U.S. society, but rather that the two views are currently vying for ascendancy.

In the next chapter we move to a consideration of the period of adolescence; our summary of socialization will appear at the close of that discussion.

Adolescence

Adolescence is a culture-bound and recent phenomenon upon which opinion is divided regarding both its significance and its age boundaries. Some of the ideal-typical views of the adolescent emphasize his growth, his desire for inclusion, his idealism, his honesty, his rebellion, his search for recognition, his irresponsibility, or his lack of certainty. Current attempts to ascertain the facts about adolescence in the United States focus on such aspects as the emancipation process, the notion of a "youth culture," and the generation gap. The college adolescent, due to his lengthy postponement of adult status, is of particular interest. The chapter closes with the author's reconciliation of the conflicting definitions of adolescence and a general summary of socialization in the United States.

An adolescent is an individual defined by his society as too old to be a child and too young to be an adult. The answer to the question "What is adolescence?" has been stated in physiological, emotional, intellectual, and cultural terms. To some, adolescence is fundamentally the period of *incipient physiological maturity*. Rapid growth, glandular activity, and surface bodily changes give the adolescent his unique character. For others, adolescence is primarily *emotional*. It is the period of emotional intensity, internal stress, and ambivalence during which former interpersonal commitments are tested. Still others see adolescence as basically *intellectual*, involving idealism and the questioning of the value systems and behavior of the older generation. This questioning makes it a period of uncertainty, since adolescents perceive the world's problems as insurmountable and the adult world as divided and unsure of itself. Finally, there are some who define adolescence *culturally*, as a period of fads and cultural limbo following physical maturation and preceding adult status. How do these four definitions fit the data on adolescence? The answer to this question must await the completion of our discussion.

Adolescence as a period of physical maturation has, of course, always existed; adolescence as defined in terms of emotions, intellect, and culture is felt by F. Musgrove and others to be a phenomenon of recent centuries.

"The adolescent as a distinct species," Musgrove asserts, "is the creation of modern social attitudes and institutions."[1]

"Verbal distinctions between childhood and youth, practically non-existent in the seventeenth century and still rare in the eighteenth, became much more common after 1800."[2] As recently as the early 1800s, the young, vigorous, expanding United States could give its young social tasks and roles. For, as Joseph Kett says, "in a stable agrarian society, the range of occupational and religious choices open to young people was so narrow as to preclude a period of doubt and indecision."[3] Now, however, the young are turned into adolescents by being "excluded from responsible participation in affairs, rewarded for dependency, penalized for inconvenient displays of initiative, and so rendered sufficiently irresponsible to confirm the prevailing teenager-stereotype."[4] They are made into ineffectual outsiders.

Not only is adolescence (according to the authors quoted above) a product of recent history, but (according to others, such as Margaret Mead) it is also culture-bound. The Samoan girl, says Mead, painlessly, quietly "slips from childhood into womanhood, loitering by the way, doing her share of the family work, but guarding herself against a reputation for too great proficiency which might lead to early marriage."[5] Instead of being the most stressful period in the Samoan girl's life, adolescence is perhaps the most pleasant time she will ever know. The patterns observed in both Samoa and Dobu suggest that "adolescence is not necessarily a period of stress and strain, that these familiar and unlovely symptoms flow from cultural anxieties."[6] That is, the problems by which we tend to define the period are aspects of American civilization, not of youth in general—and physiological changes alone cannot account for this variation.

But what of the adolescent period in the United States? what are its boundaries? Neither sociological nor physiological criteria are entirely unambiguous or satisfactory in defining its scope. The beginning of adolescence may, without great distortion, be considered synonymous with the onset of puberty. Yet one must decide which physiological changes to treat as most basic. While the appearance of pubic hair or the growth of the female's breasts might be used, a frequently employed index of the onset

---

[1] F. Musgrove, *Youth and the Social Order* (London: Routledge and Kegan Paul, 1964), p. 13.

[2] Joseph F. Kett, "Adolescence and Youth in Nineteenth-Century America," in Theodore K. Rabb and Robert I. Rotberg, eds., *The Family in History: Interdisciplinary Essays* (New York: Harper & Row, 1971), p. 98.

[3] Kett, "Adolescence and Youth in Nineteenth-Century America," in Rabb and Rotberg, *The Family in History*, p. 97.

[4] Musgrove, *Youth and the Social Order*, p. 16.

[5] Margaret Mead, "Adolescence in Primitive and in Modern Society," in Eleanor E. Maccoby, Theodore M. Newcomb, and Eugene L. Hartley, eds., *Readings in Social Psychology* (New York: Henry Holt, 1958), p. 343.

[6] Mead, "Adolescence in Primitive and in Modern Society," in Maccoby, Newcomb, and Hartley, *Readings in Social Psychology*, p. 347.

of puberty is first ejaculation by the male and first menses for the female. Even such an unambiguous criterion as the last, which ordinarily occurs about the twelfth year of life, has been found by Alfred Kinsey et al. to range from age nine to age twenty-five.[7] Furthermore, the age at first menses not only varies in a population, but it "has been getting earlier during the last hundred years by between three and four months per decade."[8]

Late adolescence might be considered to begin when the young person achieves his first adult status, such as being licensed to drive. But how does one determine when the entire adolescent period ends and adulthood begins? For certain high-status families in American society it might be the debut, coming anywhere between age seventeen and age twenty-two. For the masses, however, possible criteria might include graduation from high school, graduation from college, entering military service, beginning one's first full-time job, moving out of the parental home, and marriage. All these factors cannot coincide, and there is no ceremony marking the assumption of full adult status. Therefore, the passage from adolescence into adulthood is more a gradual occurrence than an abrupt or clearly demarcated transition. If two or three factors, such as college graduation, marriage, and the first full-time job, do coincide, the end of adolescence may be fairly clear-cut. Yet adolescence continues to be something of a vague concept in its empirical referent; perhaps the very ambiguity of its duration and nature increases the difficulties of the period.

Section One

THE ADOLESCENT AS AN IDEAL-TYPE

The early adolescent portion of the adolescent ideal-type is sometimes ignored, and is often tied together in people's minds with their view of the "late teenager." However, at least two strands of the adolescent stereotype come very much from the years right after puberty. One has to do with physical *growth*, with being typical, with not being too different. The early adolescent, then, because of the obvious physical changes taking place, is very much concerned with his body and its development. The early adolescent wants to be "on schedule": not too tall, and especially not too short. Thus, a focus of the connectedness of early adolescence is feeling a part of "the group," physically as well as otherwise.

This connectedness includes, besides growth, what Thomas Cottle calls

---

[7] Alfred C. Kinsey et al., *Sexual Behavior in the Human Female* (Philadelphia: Saunders, 1953), p. 123.

[8] Peter Laslett, "Age at Menarche in Europe Since the Eighteenth Century," in Rabb and Rotberg, *The Family in History*, p. 29.

integrity, or integration—being a part of things. "Exclusion and rejection are hardly bearable." Nor is it bearable to be deviant, either in one's physical characteristics or his social actions. For deviance threatens one's integrity, one's connectedness.[9] Chad Gordon calls this the need for acceptance, and couples with it a third important characterization of the typical early adolescent. He needs *achievement,* or a symbolically validated performance against a socially defined standard of excellence.[10] Achievement, Gordon adds, must be in those areas of life which do not negatively affect one's acceptance.

Most of the ideal-typical picture of the adolescent comes from the late adolescent period. The young person in American society has not yet assumed adult responsibilities; many adult observers believe that this fact makes it possible for him to do several things. First, as an outsider, the young person is typically perceived as playing the role of social critic. He desires honesty, yet finds many aspects of his complex society which are dishonest; as an idealist, he sees many inconsistencies in his society. The combination of idealism and honesty in the adolescent gives rise to a general despising of sham and pretense. In addition, he begins to move out from under the direct control of parents, teachers, and other authorities, but is not yet considered or allowed to be a responsible member of society. The need to rebel but to be supported, when coupled with irresponsibility, results in his being depressed by conformity, both in himself and in others. Finally, he seeks integrity (integration) and recognition, to be somebody among his peers. Thus, according to the adult world, the typical adolescent is bothered by sham and pretense, by conformity, and by lack of recognition.

J. D. Salinger's little novel *Catcher in the Rye* is a portrait of an adolescent who gets fed up with school and spends thirty-six hours at Christmastime wandering through the streets of New York City in search of something, namely, himself.[11] Though the novel is outdated in certain particulars, many young people can still identify quite readily with the strivings of Holden Caulfield, the late-teenage star of the story, for it is possible to see exemplified in some of his experiences the ideal-typical problems believed to beset the adolescent. First, Holden Caulfield liberally dispenses the term *phonies* to describe those given to sham or pretense. Most pointed in this regard is his depiction of Christmas at Radio City:

---

[9] See Thomas J. Cottle, "The Connections of Adolescence," *Daedalus* (Fall 1971), 1206, 1211, for much of this discussion.

[10] Chad Gordon, "Social Characteristics of Early Adolescence," *Daedalus* (Fall 1971), 944–45.

[11] J. D. Salinger, *The Catcher in the Rye* (Boston: Little, Brown, 1945).

All these angels start coming out of the boxes and everywhere, guys carrying crucifixes and stuff all over the place, and the whole bunch of them—thousands of them—singing "Come All Ye Faithful" like mad. Big deal. I can't see anything religious or pretty about a bunch of actors carrying crucifixes all over the stage. When they were finished and started going out the boxes again, you could tell they could hardly wait to get a cigarette or something.[12]

Sally Hayes kept saying how beautiful it all was, and

I said old Jesus probably would have puked if he could see it—all those fancy costumes and all. Sally said I was a sacrilegious atheist. I probably am. But the thing Jesus would've really liked would be the guy that plays the kettle drums in the orchestra.[13]

And Holden proceeds to describe the kettle drummer's sincerity and intensity.

Holden is depressed by authority and conformity, and often expresses this depression in the phrase "I could have puked." He tells of an old guy about fifty who came into his dormitory on Veterans Day and wanted to see if his initials were still in the bathroom door.

He kept talking to us the whole time, telling how the days he spent here were the happiest of his life, and giving us a lot of advice for the future and all. Boy, did he depress me! I don't mean he was a bad guy—he wasn't. But you don't have to be a bad guy to depress somebody—you can be a *good* guy and do it. All you have to do to depress somebody is give them a lot of phony advice while you're looking for your initials in some can door—that's all you have to do.[14]

In attempting to get out of the rut, Holden suggests to Sally Hayes that they get a car and go up to Massachusetts or Vermont and get a cabin and chop wood and live there. Sally replies, "You just can't *do* something like that."[15] With this he becomes depressed with Sally and soon leaves her behind.

Our "typical" adolescent appreciates sincerity, wants to escape from conformity and authority, and wants to be recognized. When his brother died, Holden smashed all the garage windows with his fist and could not attend the funeral because he was in the hospital himself. Cottle reports this need for recognition in the early adolescent as part of his need for

---

[12] Salinger, *The Catcher in the Rye*, p. 178.
[13] Salinger, *The Catcher in the Rye*, p. 178.
[14] Salinger, *The Catcher in the Rye*, p. 219.
[15] Salinger, *The Catcher in the Rye*, p. 171.

integrity, his need not to be left out. "There is envy," Cottle says, "of a person who travels with his parents or of someone who breaks his leg and gets to wear a cast on which people scrawl messages and signatures."[16] Once in a while Salinger allows his hero a moment of pleasure; it is almost always related to recognition and a certain amount of freedom from restraint. For example, Holden describes a "swell kid" in New York City as follows:

> He was walking in the street instead of on the sidewalk, but right next to the curb. He was singing and humming, and walking a straight line. He was just singing for the hell of it, you could tell. The cars zoomed by, brakes screeched all over the place, his parents paid no attention to him, and he kept on walking next to the curb and singing. . . . It made me feel better.[17]

Growth, integrity-recognition-achievement, honesty, rebellion, irresponsibility—these are some of the characteristics most often imputed to the young person in U.S. society. A further characteristic, appearing in the new novels and scholarly works on adolescence, is *uncertainty* and a turning inward. Cottle notes that, unlike their parents, who assume that things will eventually be "back to normal," today's adolescents have grown up amid uncertainty.

> One result of this constant stress on revelation is a recognition by young people . . . that in fact nothing seems to make sense, and that nothing connects. What had before seemed linear, logical, rational, and importantly predictable or calculable now seems irrational, absurd, nonsensical, and irreconcilable.[18]

The result is that the young person turns inward, or else he turns to a half-formed counterculture, wherein he hopes to allay his uncertainty, or at least to forget it momentarily.[19]

How close to reality is the ideal-typical picture of today's adolescent—with his concern for growth, achievement, and recognition balanced by integrity or connectedness, honesty, rebellion, irresponsibility, and uncertainty? Are some portions of this stereotype more accurate today than others? Let us begin to deal with these issues by examining the relations of adolescents with their parents and peers.

---

[16] Cottle, "The Connections of Adolescence," p. 1206.
[17] Salinger, *The Catcher in the Rye*, p. 150.
[18] Cottle, "The Connections of Adolescence," p. 1202.
[19] Lawrence Kohlberg and Carol Gilligan, "The Adolescent as a Philosopher: The Discovery of the Self in a Post-Conventional World," *Daedalus* (Fall 1971), 1081.

Section Two

ADOLESCENTS, PARENTS, AND PEERS

Adolescence as a process can be thought of as the movement from dependence upon and control by parents and other adults through a period of intensive peer group activity and influence and, finally, to the assumption of adult roles. Emancipation, youth culture, and the presumed generation gap are aspects of this process upon which much attention has been focused.

Emancipation

Douvan and Adelson's description of the emancipation process is an excellent introduction to our discussion.

> The direction of adolescent growth is clearly toward emancipation from the family. The period begins with the child almost entirely dependent on the family, needing its say-so for what he can and cannot do, still tied to his parents emotionally, still clinging to their ideas and ideals. It ends with the child reaching adulthood, freer to make up his mind about what he will and will not do, holding (if he so wishes) his own beliefs and values, and if need be looking elsewhere than the family for love and support.[20]

The end result is the autonomous or independent individual; a careful reading of the above quotation yields three types of autonomy. First, there is *emotional* autonomy, as the individual gives up ties to his family and looks elsewhere for love, support, confidence, and so on. Second, as the individual achieves freedom to decide what he will and will not do, he gains *behavioral* autonomy. Finally, the move from his parents' ideas and ideals toward his own beliefs and attitudes can be called *value* autonomy.[21]

Of course, not every individual moves through the emancipation process at the same speed or with the same degree of completeness in all three areas of autonomy. Bernard Farber draws a distinction between sponsored and unsponsored independence. The former characterizes the individual whose emotional and behavioral independence develop within the bounds of the parental value system; the latter characterizes the individual who, in the course of achieving independence, rejects many parental values and performs acts that meet with parental disapproval. In addition, there is the adolescent who, while making certain behavioral decisions for

---

[20] Elizabeth Douvan and Joseph Adelson, *The Adolescent Experience* (New York: Wiley, 1966), p. 125.
[21] Douvan and Adelson, *The Adolescent Experience*, p. 130.

himself, never really accomplishes either emotional or value autonomy. Thus, Farber's ideas and those of Douvan and Adelson might be related as in Table 3.[22]

Table 3
Levels of Independence in Relation to Different Aspects of Autonomy

Level of Independence	Rank in Various Aspects of Autonomy		
	Behavioral	Emotional	Value
Passive	Variable	Low	Low
Sponsored	High	High	Low
Unsponsored	High	High	High

Differences in level of independence are not distributed randomly within the American population, but are related to such factors as socio-economic class and the individual's sex. Middle-class socialization, with its emphasis on warmth and affection and its supportive tendencies, yields primarily adolescents characterized by sponsored independence—as indicated in Table 2. Lower-class socialization, however, is less warm and more concerned with control and direction, the result being that in order to achieve independence, the lower-class adolescent is more likely to have to resort to unsponsored acts.[23] This proposition is underscored indirectly by Charles Bowerman and Stephen Bahr, in their study of the relationship between the husband-wife power structure and the adolescent offspring's identification with his parents. Identification with parents is clearly higher when the parental power structure is viewed as equalitarian than when one parent is viewed as dominant.[24] And such equalitarianism, we may add, is more characteristic of the middle-class family than of the working- or lower-class family. It is noteworthy, however, that, regardless of social class, black females show greater attachment to their mothers and less to peers than do white females, according to a study by Michael Schwartz and Mary Baden.[25] (Schwartz and Baden do not find in either racial group a *great* separation between youth and adults.) There are, then, differences both by race and by class in the ties to parents which might give rise to sponsored independence.

---

[22] Farber's description of four independence levels, based on combinations of sponsored and unsponsored independence, differs from Table 3. For his divisions, see Bernard Farber, *Family: Organization and Interaction* (San Francisco: Chandler, 1964), pp. 376–77.

[23] See Farber, *Family: Organization and Interaction*, pp. 369–70.

[24] Charles E. Bowerman and Stephen J. Bahr, "Conjugal Power and Adolescent Identification with Parents," *Sociometry* 36 (1973), 366–77.

[25] Michael Schwartz and Mary Anna Baden, "Female Adolescent Self-Concept: An Examination of the Relative Influence of Peers and Adults," *Youth and Society* 5 (1973), 115–28.

Sex differences are equally noticeable in the literature on socialization. "In the sphere of emotional independence from the family, boys by and large outdistance girls."[26] College women, says Mirra Komarovsky, "are somewhat more attached to parents, less likely to make decisions contrary to the wishes of the parents, more frequently experience homesickness than is the case with the male undergraduates."[27] What these and other such references indicate is that, while the middle-class male is best characterized by sponsored independence, the middle-class female might be somewhat more inclined to remain passive, particularly in the area of emotional autonomy.

Another aspect of the emancipation process concerns confidence. Douvan and Adelson note that the adolescent boy who continues to rely on his parents for behavioral advice appears to be less confident than other boys. In a recent and as yet unpublished study of high school seniors, the author was able to trace the emancipation process from confident dependence on one's parents to confidence in one's own ability to cope with various situations. Some of these seniors seemed perfectly calm about the prospect of graduating and either going to college or to work; but upon further questioning it became apparent that their confidence was actually in their parents' ability to handle things and to cushion all shocks. At the other extreme were a substantial minority of seniors who indicated a basic *self-* confidence and a respect for their parents on a virtually adult-to-adult basis. By far the largest number were, however, in midstream, expressing some desire for parental guidance and some lack of confidence both in themselves and in their parents' ability to handle new situations for them. Thus, assurance, or confidence, appears to be curvilinear during the emancipation process, moving from that invested in parents, through a period of uncertainty, and to mature confidence in oneself and appreciation of parents (see Figure 6). It is also noteworthy that more females were still at stage one and more males had reached stage three in this high school sample, a finding that is consistent with the sex differences reported above.

Closely related to the issue of confidence is the adolescent's self-image. Roberta Simmons and Florence Rosenberg, in a study of almost 2,000 urban schoolchildren in grades three through twelve, have found that the greatest disturbance to the self-image of their sample occurred in the child's early adolescent years. Children in early adolescence, they found,

> exhibited heightened self-consciousness, greater instability of self-image, slightly lower global self-esteem, lower opinions of themselves with

---

[26] Douvan and Adelson, *The Adolescent Experience*, p. 149.
[27] Mirra Komarovsky, "Functional Analysis of Sex Roles," *American Sociological Review* 15 (1950), 513.

regard to the qualities they valued, and a reduced conviction that their parents, teachers, and peers of the same sex held favorable opinions of them.[28]

They conclude that, at least for their sample, the main reason why the major upheaval occurred at that age was environmental rather than maturational. The fact that the onset of puberty and the move to a larger, more distant, and more impersonal school had occurred simultaneously is felt by the authors to explain the disturbance to self-image. Thus, while their findings cannot be generalized to adolescents with differing school environments, the results do point up the influence of culture and environment in making adolescence the troubled period that it is.

Youth Culture

Another important aspect of emancipation, or the movement toward autonomy, involves the peer group, the adolescent's age companions. Much debate has centered on the question, Is there a distinctive youth culture or not? For years the developing child thinks that everyone is pretty much like his parents. Then, in the preteen years, he becomes aware of differences, but is likely to be convinced by his parents that their ways are

Figure 6
The Confidence of the Adolescent at Various Stages of the Emancipation Process

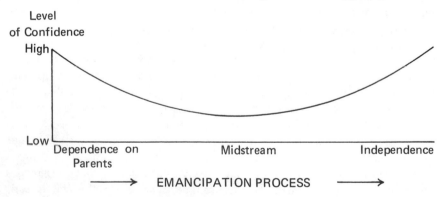

best. Now, in the adolescent years, he discovers that rational criteria for saying that his parents' ways are best do not always hold up. The peer group defines its own standards, apart from the values of any single set of parents. These standards include concern with cars, sports, social activities,

---

[28] Roberta G. Simmons and Florence Rosenberg, "Disturbance in the Self-Image at Adolescence," *American Sociological Review* 38 (1973), 564.

and popularity, and are often at odds with the values parents and school officials state they would like to see in young people. James Coleman, David Gottlieb and Charles Ramsey, and Gary Schwartz and Don Merten have written at length about these phenomena, which they call "youth culture."[29]

On the other side of the debate are those who argue that youth culture is a myth. Bennett Berger states that "there is absolutely no good body of data on adolescents, Coleman's included, which indicates the existence of a really deviant system of norms which govern adolescent life."[30] John Conger adds that the well-worn cliché that in adolescence the young person turns away from his parents and becomes a captive of his peers is false on two grounds. First, there is a considerable overlap between parental and peer values, and, second, neither parental nor peer influence is monolithic.[31] Those taking this side of the debate believe that youth culture is basically a sort of organized or patterned rebellion, the only genuine manifestations of which are fads that dabble in irrelevancies, with basic parental materialistic and goal-oriented patterns and values remaining intact.

As is the case in so many sociological debates, several authors have made great efforts to resolve the issue on some middle ground. Schwartz and Merten feel that the reality of a youth culture does not rest upon the repudiation or undermining of basic adult values. Rather, it is sufficient that youth experiment with and elaborate on "some of the partially unrealized or alternative possibilities in the adult moral order."[32] Gottlieb and Ramsey go even further in stating that the existence of a youth culture should not be predicated upon a conflict with adult values.

> For us, differences may be sufficient but they are not necessary in investigating adolescent behavior. In the case of the adolescent the question is not deviation from some universal norm but rather how involvement in and commitment to the peer group influence the behavior and beliefs of the participant. Once we can pinpoint areas of influence and how they operate we will be better able to evaluate the meaning of adolescent cultures.[33]

---

[29] See James S. Coleman, *The Adolescent Society* (New York: Free Press, 1961), p. 329; David Gottlieb and Charles Ramsey, *The American Adolescent* (Homewood, Ill.: Dorsey Press, 1964), p. 43; David Friesen, "Academic-Athletic-Popularity Syndrome in the Canadian High School Society (1967)," *Adolescence* 3 (1968), 50; Kenneth Keniston, *The Uncommitted* (New York: Dell, 1960).

[30] Bennett Berger, "Adolescence and Beyond," *Social Problems* 10 (1963), 395. See also Frederick Elkin and William A. Westley, "The Myth of the Adolescent Peer Culture," *American Sociological Review* 20 (1955), 680–84.

[31] John Janeway Conger, "A World They Never Knew: The Family and Social Change," *Daedalus* (Fall 1971), 1128.

[32] Gary Schwartz and Don Merten, "The Language of Adolescence: An Anthropological Approach to the Youth Culture," *American Journal of Sociology* 72 (1967), 460.

[33] Gottlieb and Ramsey, *The American Adolescent*, p. 33.

Although the present author would rather, for the sake of consistency, restrict use of the term *culture* to distinct differences in attitudes and values, let us for the moment accept Gottlieb and Ramsey's claim that the key is the extent to which the peer group defines its own standards. There are two reasons why the adolescent peer group *must* do this. First, society—meaning the adult world—does a poor job of defining roles for youth. The adolescent begins to drive at one age, to drink at another, and to vote at still another—and the ages differ from state to state. He is not yet wanted as an economic contributor, but his sex powers are developed and active. It is in the peer group that he must hammer out the relation between these factors. Thus, despite the fact that many parents and other adults are open to and desirous of intergenerational conversation, the young person is likely to feel that the adult world is responsible for his role dilemmas, and he is therefore unable to accept adult counseling in the solution of those dilemmas.

The second reason why the peer group must define its own standards is the social segregation of youth. Notice, in the following quotations, the use of terms that are virtually synonymous with the idea of segregation. "Youth," say Gottlieb and Ramsey, "are set apart. Only vaguely defined courses of action are recommended to them."[34] Musgrove says his data are consistent with those

American investigations which have shown adolescents belittled by their elders, regarded as a separate, inferior, and even threatening population, exposed to contradictory expectations and demands from the general body of adults, and consigned, as Hollingshead has said, to "an ill-defined no-man's land that lies between the protected dependency of childhood, where the parent is dominant, and the independent world of the adult, where the person is relatively free from parental controls."[35]

Historically, as in the case of the child, the treatment of the adolescent, not as an incipient adult, but as a distinct kind of person, is a fairly recent phenomenon. In industrial society the growing individual is no longer of much value in the family's division of labor and is not needed in economic production. He is, therefore, age-segregated in the school system and community and left to define his activity and value patterns within the peer group. These patterns, however, ordinarily reflect what youth perceive to be the most basic, if unverbalized, values of the adult world. Popularity and material goods, such as cars, may be central to adolescent society, but perhaps the reason for this is that they are seen by young people to be of great importance in the adult world.

[34] Gottlieb and Ramsey, *The American Adolescent*, p. 249.
[35] Musgrove, *Youth and the Social Order*, p. 105.

Adolescents, we have said, are segregated and allowed to define their own cultural forms within the peer group. As long as these activities take the form of recreation and study, and of inoffensive fads, they are condoned or at least permitted by the adult society. But when a few display an unwanted criticism of adult values, or when the fads are interpreted as symbolizing the questioning or rejection of society's dominant values, the result is suppression and the "belittling" of which Musgrove speaks.

The phrases *unwanted criticism* and *rejection of society's dominant values* prompt us to ask one further question about "youth culture." Is it necessary to restrict this designation to today's youth, to the fact of adolescence as a segregated and participant-run cultural system? Are there really no basic differences, only differences in the forms of expression, between what youth values and what is valued by their parents. Several authors have noted that a change in this regard has occurred just since the beginning of the 1960s. Parents, we noted earlier, can still remember a period of "normalcy"; in contrast, says Conger, "their children for the most part have no such frame of reference."[36] "The certainties I knew," adds Cottle, "seem to be disappearing, or at least they are not as apparent as before. Everything is doubted, including the narcissism which probably sustained and carried me and many of my generation."[37] Adult authority and institutions themselves seem, to many teenagers, to be fragmented and inconsistent. Furthermore, not only do they see the world they are moving toward as "in flux," but they view its "promise," that is, eventual incorporation into the adult economy, as insufficient to produce a sense of fulfillment. A part of this may be due to the affluence of their backgrounds; a part may stem from a general orientation toward resource exploitation and destruction. But a large part arises from the fact that opportunities are dwindling. The view of adolescence as a period of experimentation prior to "finding one's niche," says David Bakan, "must increasingly be viewed cynically if that niche in life is contingent upon an appropriate niche in the labor force."[38]

Not only has the economic "promise" become less certain, but the codification of a true "counterculture" has moved forward considerably during the 1960s and '70s. Self-revelation, through Eastern religions or drugs, and the search for intimacy and encounter, and the rejection of society's success values—these are facets of this older youth culture. It is a culture, claims Conger, that is seen by younger adolescents as in conflict with parent and adult goals for their loyalty and emulation.[39] What is new

---

[36] Conger, "A World They Never Knew," p. 1116.
[37] Cottle, "The Connections of Adolescence," p. 1216.
[38] David Bakan, "Adolescence in America: From Idea to Social Fact," *Daedalus* (Fall 1971), 991.
[39] Conger, "A World They Never Knew," p. 1110.

is not the questioning of the adult world or the idealistic desire to remake that world. Rather, according to Kohlberg and Gilligan and other writers, it is "a questioning culture providing half-answers to which adolescents are exposed prior to their own spontaneous questioning."[40]

What, then, are the significant conclusions that can be drawn regarding youth culture and society, and what are their implications? Adolescents in general reflect adult values, with an overlay of supposedly distinctive youthful interests. Irresponsibility is forced upon them by adults; as long as they stay out of the way and continue preparing for "legitimate" adult roles, they are tolerated. In other words, adolescents generally accept the dominant values and culture, but are not allowed into the dominant society in a responsible way. This, you may recall, is precisely the problem that has historically plagued racial minorities in the United States; the analogy between young people and blacks in the United States is most informative. The major difference is that adolescents are constantly being incorporated into the adult world and new youngsters are constantly entering the adolescent age group, while the racial minority is kept socially separate throughout the lifetime of the individual. Adolescents are, in short, more accurately described as a distinct society than as a distinct culture. This picture, however, is changing somewhat at present, in response to the fragmentation of the adult world and its goals, the lack of constancy in that world, and the increasing difficulty in simply finding one's economic niche. It is quite possible, moreover, that these developments will, over the coming years, produce an increasingly distinct youth culture.

Conflict with Parents and the Generation Gap

Until now, we have referred to the predominance of value similarity between adolescents and their parents, asserting that the crucial factor giving adolescence its character is the segregation of youth from adult society and concerns. There is a substantial body of literature on adolescence which stresses conflict between young people and their parents in the United States. Kingsley Davis begins by describing societal conditions under which parents and youth would not be in conflict. Stable rural society, with emancipation from parental authority marked by gradual and institutionalized steps, and with no great postponement of marriage and adulthood following puberty, is likely to be characterized by little parent-youth conflict. But American urban society, with its weak or unclear parental role models, much extrafamilial socialization, rapid change, postponed adulthood, and

---

[40] Kohlberg and Gilligan, "The Adolescent as a Philosopher," p. 1081.

individual choice of adult roles, is productive of intergenerational conflicts.[41]

One of these factors, rapid social and cultural change, means that within a generation, that is, twenty to twenty-five years, there is historically significant change. Clifford Kirkpatrick speaks of the breakdown of *one-way empathy* that results from the rapidity of change. By one-way empathy he means the ability of one party to put himself in the other's shoes, but not vice versa. The parent has already been an adolescent, but the adolescent has not yet been a parent. Yet, if the parent says, "I was once your age," the adolescent may respond or think to himself that things were different then. Conger states the breakdown of one-way empathy very clearly:

> To the extent that today's parents look only to their own experience as adolescents for expectations about their children's probable adolescent behavior, or for guidance in understanding their needs, outlooks, and goals, they are almost bound to encounter frustration, bewilderment, or disappointment.[42]

Youth today may feel that parents who danced the Charleston or fox-trot in their youth simply could not understand the problems and struggles of post-Beatles youth. Thus, one-way empathy breaks down in the response of the young person that his parents' experiences and ideas are outdated, that "things were different then."

Another source of parent-youth difficulties, Kirkpatrick claims, is the *clash of inferiority complexes.* Adolescents feel inferior because they lack experience and poise and because they know that they do. Overcompensation toward parents may mean that what is lacked in these respects is made up in defiance, aggressiveness, and pseudosophistication. On the other hand, parents often feel inferior because of an underlying impression that they really don't understand, because of a declining attractiveness and sex power in the face of youthful virility and attractiveness, and because of an awareness that in many cases they have achieved less than they had hoped. In addition, as we noted above, parental authority has been further eroded by the fact that the adolescent today may not see his parents as representing a unified adult society.[43] Age, then, even without true wisdom, may be glorified because age is what the parent has. The combination of enforced authority without wisdom and defiance without poise may result in a circular and escalating conflict between the generations.[44]

---

[41] Kingsley Davis, "The Sociology of Parent-Youth Conflict," *American Sociological Review* 5 (1940), 523–34.

[42] Conger, "A World They Never Knew," p. 1106.

[43] Conger, "A World They Never Knew," p. 1109.

[44] Clifford Kirkpatrick, *The Family: As Process and Institution* (New York: Ronald Press, 1963 ed.), pp. 266–67.

Conflict there is, but what is its focus? Is it the ideologies and values of the older generation? Schwartz and Merten say no. Open intergenerational conflict revolves, not so much around the values of the adult world, as around "the question of how much control adults rightfully can exercise over adolescents."[45] Since tolerance of adolescent deviance is limited at best, autonomy must be sought—as we said earlier—in minor acts of defiance toward adult authority.

The generation gap, according to these authors, is nothing more than the result of youthful rebellion against adult control. Yet it seems more complex than that. In the first place, there is no doubt that parents are attempting as much as ever before to implant their culture in their offspring. As Douvan and Adelson put it:

> The American parent does not separate himself enough from the child; instead he will want to live in the child, excessively, trying to re-realize, in the child's freshness, in the opportunity to make a new life, his own lost autonomies.[46]

Ironically, however, the frantic attempt to control the thinking and behavior of the young is accompanied by the parents' perception that they are actually losing control, that a major cultural as well as social gap separates them from their children. Part of this perception is based on the parents' own doubts about society's goals and values, which, however, they are unable to express actively because of their role commitments and life patterns of work, economic indebtedness, family, and leisure. Instead, such doubts are projected onto the uncommitted, the young, so that the adolescent fads are infused—from the adults' standpoint—with sinister and symbolic implications for society's values. In short, a portion of the generation gap is based on adult perception, doubt, and projection. That certain adults are aware of this is well illustrated in the following excerpt from a conference on the family held in the mid-1960s:

> Dr. Krech: "How much of the competition between the generations is in the mind of the perceiver?"
> Dr. Lee: "I would say this is its chief existence. . . ."
> Dr. Kirkendall: "I think that the extent to which this competition does exist may be a product in part of the extent to which parents and other adults feel it does."[47]

Projection and perception often result in what has been called the self-fulfilling prophecy. That is, if you talk and act as if something were true,

---

[45] Schwartz and Merten, "The Language of Adolescence," p. 459.
[46] Douvan and Adelson, *The Adolescent Experience*, p. 129.
[47] Seymour M. Farber, Piero Mustacchi, and Roger H. L. Wilson, eds., *Man and Civilization: The Family's Search for Survival* (New York: McGraw-Hill, 1965), p. 158.

the long-term result is likely to be the development of that very condition. The majority of youth do not desire an open break with their parents and other adults, but the combination of adult pressures for conformity, plus social segregation, plus pervasive adult concern about the value gap, tends to increase the very phenomena it seeks to control.

Besides adult perceptions and projections, there are aspects of adolescence in the contemporary United States which widen the gap. First, the mass media have made young people more aware than ever before of what is happening in the adult world from which they are systematically excluded. Second, as a result of events of the 1960s a vocal minority of adolescents took direct issue with the perceived inconsistencies in the society. Furthermore, the repressive response of adult "authorities" to such criticism and protest has served only to enlist the support—both tacit and overt—of formerly uninvolved youth.

At present, the vast majority of young people are still following the prescribed paths to societal position as defined by the dominant values of their society. The parent-youth conflict of which we speak is basically forced upon the adolescent if he is to gain behavioral autonomy instead of remaining passive. That sort of gap, as Allen Lambert points out, is a pervasive part of human history, the history of each new generation as it seeks to rework society's culture and to incorporate it.[48] However, what was once almost entirely an adult-imposed *social* gap appears to be changing gradually to include cultural elements as well. For some present-day adolescents, these cultural elements come from the counterculture of escape, intimacy, and self-revelation. For others, they include an even higher idealism and sense of social responsibility than that of adolescents in earlier years, causing these adolescents to put "economic gain" in a new perspective.[49] One way, perhaps, to summarize the current state of adolescence in the United States is to look briefly at the last stages of the emancipation process among those who postpone the traditional responsibilities of adulthood the longest: college students.

Section Three

THE COLLEGE ADOLESCENT

One of the basic factors in adolescence, to which we referred at the beginning of this chapter, is the postponement of adulthood. An aspect of postponement that is descriptive of the college student is deferred gratification.

[48] T. Allen Lambert, "Generations and Change: Toward a Theory of Generations as a Force in Historical Process," *Youth and Society* 4 (1972), 21–45.

[49] Sam Payne, David A. Summers, and Thomas R. Stewart, "Value Differences Across Three Generations," *Sociometry* 36 (1973), 20–30.

This means putting off desires, such as going to work and perhaps getting married, for the sake of greater fulfillment later on.[50] The college student defers adulthood and gets a college education, it is often said, in the hope that it will "pay off" or increase his life chances in the long run.

Clearly, adult middle-class society expects the dominant value orientation of the college population to be a form of sponsored independence. This is the orientation that sees education as utilitarian, with its major purpose being the obtaining of one's passport to society's affluence and goals. Social life, reasonably good grades, some influence on campus, kicks when they come—all these are means to such ends as a law career, a corporation slot, or finding a good husband. Why should you stay in school? why should you support the college of your choice? Because, said the TV commercial, the college graduate will make $150,000 more in his lifetime than the non–college graduate. This is the educational motivation fostered by the mass educational system and the adult world: the student is there, very simply, to get a degree. This motivation, when coupled with the increasing pressures of the job market, has resulted—in the 1970s—in a new seriousness and studiousness which the student hopes will aid him in the postgraduation competition for positions.

The same perspective on college students, which is based primarily on surface manifestations, concludes that there are two campus variants from the theme of sponsored independence: the activist and the retreatist. The former sees flaws and inconsistencies in the dominant culture and society and is seeking by various means to change them. The latter has truly "opted out" and is seeking fulfillment neither by a middle-class position nor by social reform, but by personal release and self-expression. According to this perspective, in the 1970s defeatism has resulted in a reduction in the number of activists and in an increase in the other two categories, especially in retreatists who have given up on changing society and are merely trying to "save" or remake themselves.

The sponsored, the activist, and the retreatist: such classification of college students is highly oversimplified despite its apparent usefulness to middle-class adults. It misses entirely the college students whom Kenneth Keniston calls the "apparently unalienated." These are the young people who go through college living by the rules—passing courses, buying new clothes, cheering at football games—but who, according to Keniston,

> show a lack of deep commitment to adult values and roles. . . . Rather, they view the adult world they expect to enter with a subtle distrust,

---

[50] For a good discussion of deferred gratification and achievement, see Murray A. Straus, "Deferred Gratification, Social Class, and the Achievement Syndrome," *American Sociological Review* 27 (1962), 326–35.

a lack of high expectations, hopes, or dreams, and an often unstated feeling that they will have to "settle" for less than they would hope for if they let themselves hope.[51]

On the surface they are living by middle-class society's goals and expectations; inside they are not really "sold" or committed. An increasing number of college students, many recent authors feel, should be classified as among these "surface committed." Kohlberg and Gilligan, for example, assert that "by the 1970's the extreme doubt and relativism which earlier characterized only a minority of college students appears both earlier and much more pervasively. It is now sometimes found toward the end of high school."[52]

Nor does the threefold classification clarify the situation of those who, according to Berger and others, look like deviants because they are caught up in the "fads which dabble in irrelevancies," but are inwardly committed to the middle-class goals of success, material possessions, and a respectable life pattern. These "outward deviants," who are not really seriously questioning or rejecting adult culture, but merely biding their time until they are allowed in, are the basis for Edgar Friedenberg's claim that adolescents are vanishing in the United States. They make it possible for many adults to "console" themselves with the observation concerning youthful activists that "in another ten years they will be using the same energy in selling encyclopedias." In other words, there are at least four definable types of college-age young people: (1) those internally and externally committed to middle-class values and norms; (2) Keniston's externally committed but internally questioning and uncommitted; (3) Berger's and Friedenberg's externally uncommitted but internally committed; and (4) those who are both internally and externally questioning the middle-class system. It is quite possible that today the second category predominates numerically, but the empirical classification of young people according to these types is of little consequence compared to the importance of understanding the significance of the categories themselves.[53]

Besides such categorizations, other aspects of the college student's outlook today are worth mentioning. In 1971, following up on a study done in 1958, Ted Goertzel administered a questionnaire on moral judgment and values to students at Oregon and Oregon State universities. His findings were that, overall, the severity of moral judgment—which had increased between 1929 and 1958—had declined by 1971. The "rip-off" received greater

---

[51] Keniston, *The Uncommitted*, p. 396.

[52] Kohlberg and Gilligan, "The Adolescent as a Philosopher," p. 1079.

[53] Another classification, developed by Martin Trow and Burton Clark in their essay "Determinants of College Student Sub-Culture," divides college students into vocational, nonconformist, academic, and collegiate. For a summary, see Gottlieb and Ramsey, *The American Adolescent*, p. 191.

support in 1971, as did concern for human life and the refusal to bear arms in an unjust war. In short, the "moral consciousness which emerges is more permissive in matters of personal morality which do not harm other individuals. It is less conforming to powerful institutions."[54] This is consistent with the cultural epoch in which these young people have grown up, and with a new combination of cynicism and idealism. In addition, George Levinger, David Senn, and Bruce Jorgensen observed, between 1959 and 1966, changes in the college population which are consistent both with Goertzel's findings and with observations made earlier in this chapter. According to Levinger and his colleagues, college students appeared to show an increasing emphasis on interpersonal warmth and a decreasing desire to be controlled by others.[55] Concern for people rather than for institutional rules and demands, then, seems to characterize the college populations of the '70s. These young people still despise sham and pretense, particularly in social relations, and still seek honesty and idealism—which they see as lacking in society's economic and other institutions—though the forms these attitudes take are new and in keeping with the historical events of the '60s and '70s.

Section Four

SOCIALIZATION AND ADOLESCENTS: SUMMARY AND CONCLUSIONS

We close the discussion of adolescence by returning to the question raised at the outset. How can the adolescent period in the United States best be characterized? Is it primarily the period of incipient physiological maturity, of emotional intensity and upheaval, of intellectual questioning, or of postponement-segregation-cultural limbo?

Since the first is a uniform human occurrence—while adolescence appears to be variable—physiological changes do not seem useful in defining the peculiar character of adolescence in U.S. society. In order to come to grips with the other three parts of the question, we must now recall the discussion of ego struggle and identification. It may be true that in colonial days identification was easy and ego struggle difficult; however, it must not be inferred from that statement that the opposite is the case today. Friedenberg, in The Vanishing Adolescent and other books, expresses his belief that the young person may be freer from parental domination than he was for-

---

[54] Ted Goertzel, "Changes in the Values of College Students, 1958–1971," Pacific Sociological Review 15 (1972), 235–44.
[55] George Levinger, David J. Senn, and Bruce W. Jorgensen, "Progress Toward Permanence in Courtship: A Test of the Kerckhoff-Davis Hypothesis," Sociometry 33 (1970), 427–43.

merly, but that the school system has taken over the chore of squelching deviance—and, with it, creativity. The creative person, says Friedenberg, often gets in trouble, while the person who cooperates, works hard, and plays the role of the good school "organization man" is rewarded.[56] Musgrove, while agreeing that the adolescent has trouble with ego struggle, sees the school as basically an extension of parental demands.[57] Thus, the young person may be freer from actual parental domination, but he is not freer from the extension of parental domination into the school system. Regardless of their differences concerning the relation between family and school, both authors suggest that the contemporary child is not presented with clear and intense role models and does not receive support, in his ego struggle, from the key socializing agents. He is thus prepared for life as a chameleon, an other-directed man, who can adapt to many social and organizational settings, but who has not gained a clear picture of the kind of person he is.

This is, of course, a somewhat overdrawn characterization of the pitfalls in American socialization. It does, however, suggest that the process can cause the individual trouble with both identification and ego struggle. Put simply, it is difficult for the individual to develop into a mature adult, with a clear self-concept.[58] A tentative answer to the definitional problem regarding adolescence would therefore be as follows. If we consider adolescence to be a period of intellectual questioning and idealism, then in our society there have been, until recently, only a few adolescents—only a few who ever overtly questioned the dominant pattern, even if they were not really committed to it. (We might, however, disagree on two counts with Friedenberg's assumption that they are "vanishing." First, there may never have been many young people who overtly questioned the dominant values during any earlier historical period. Second, the 1960s may have seen a substantial increase in their numbers.) Thus, the postponement of adult status following physiological maturity, when accompanied by social segregation and ill-defined cultural roles, is enough to cause the kind of emotional stress usually thought to characterize adolescence.[59] Postponement, we are saying,

---

[56] Edgar Friedenberg, *The Vanishing Adolescent* (New York: Dell, 1959).

[57] Frank Musgrove, *The Family, Education, and Society* (London: Routledge and Kegan Paul, 1966), p. 131.

[58] Of course, part of the reason for the self-concept problem, or "identity crisis," that is so much discussed today is simply an increased emphasis in twentieth century America upon introspection and self-awareness. That is, the crisis is at least partially a result of the continual posing of the question "Who am I?"

[59] For more on adolescence, see Glen Elder, "Adolescent Socialization and Development," in Edgar Borgatta and William W. Lambert, eds., *Handbook of Personality Theory and Research* (Chicago: Rand McNally, 1968), pp. 239–364. and the papers on youth in transition, in the proceedings of the American Orthopsychiatric Association, reported in the *American Journal of Orthopsychiatry* 39 (1969), 181–227, 306–19, as well as the issue of *Daedalus* (Fall 1971) referred to on numerous occasions in the preceding discussion.

is sufficient to define the adolescent period as it has been known for the past century in the United States. However, as noted above, serious questioning of the goals, economic values, and weak interpersonal commitments of adults may be an increasingly pervasive characteristic of U.S. adolescents.

How do the conclusions of Chapters 7 and 8 relate to the socialization continuum presented in Chapter 5? Orderly replacement of culture from parents to children is somewhat problematic, but not to the extent that socialization has been taken over by extrafamilial agencies. Rather, many of these agencies should be viewed as extensions of parental influence and others as in competition with parents. In either case, because parents are concerned about the possibility of losing control of their children's development, they try very hard to control their behavior and influence their values. Though socialization is an extremely complex and multifaceted process, we might summarize by reproducing the continuum and indicating approximately where the author feels socialization in the contemporary United States should be located (see Figure 7). The reader should, of course, feel free to relocate this complex of factors wherever he believes the facts would warrant.

Figure 7
The Approximate Location of Socialization in the Contemporary
United States on the Socialization Continuum

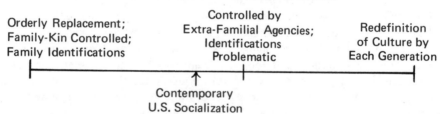

One further aspect of the young person's emancipation, or movement out of his family of orientation, involves heterosexual relations with peers. Therefore, in Chapters 9 and 10 we turn our attention to dating, love, and mate selection in the United States.

Dating, a twentieth century phenomenon on the American scene, has become so pervasive as to virtually embody the current mate selection processes of the United States. Besides serving the purposes of recreation and mate selection, dating functions for socialization, ego needs, and status achievement. Some of its more problematic aspects include parental intrusion, heterogeneous dating, emphasis on physical attractiveness, social awkwardness, superficiality, and insincerity. Due to behavioral and subsequent attitude changes, premarital sex, formerly prohibited, has been transformed into a cultural alternative in middle-class America, and is increasingly becoming a matter of nonmoral individual choice.

Premarital Relationships in the United States

Selecting a mate and establishing one's family of procreation is one of the crucial tasks of the emancipation process during adolescence. Historically, three clearly definable approaches to mate selection and the heterosexual contacts that precede it can be discerned; each of these approaches is closely linked to one of the types of personnel embeddedness. The first, *arranged marriage,* is found most frequently in those societies in which the individual and the nuclear family are embedded in the larger kinship group. In such societies marriages are arranged primarily for the purpose of fostering or strengthening the appropriate kin linkages and have definite economic overtones. Concern with domestic or individual happiness is strictly secondary.

The second and third approaches to mate selection are both based on individual choice, and are thus different in degree rather than in kind. Nevertheless, it is in this quantitative difference that dating as a basis for heterosexual relationships appears. *Restricted choice* occurs when the domestic unit is considered all-important, and when the preferences of the individuals involved are believed to be the most adequate basis for establishing a sound unit. However, historically such preferences have been restricted by several influences. One of these restrictive influences is the overt and expected intervention of parents in numerous ways, including the chaperoning of the heterosexual activity of teenagers. A second is the relative residential stability of the population, so that choice is made among persons with whom the individual has been acquainted most or all of his life. A third restriction is the length of time during which premarital relationships occur. The courtship period itself is quite brief, so that when a young person begins to court a member of the opposite sex, it is assumed that he has "serious intentions." Thus, restricted choice takes place under the considerable influence of significant others, often within the bounds of lengthy acquaintance, and usually within the scope of a few months or years.

Open choice, of which there is no pure example in the world at present, would best characterize a situation of complete family subservience to individual needs and desires. This is exemplified in Farber's ideal-typical model of universal and permanent availability. According to this idea, all members of the opposite sex are potentially available to me for mating, with no "artificial" restrictions. Furthermore, they are permanently available, so that if my first attempt to find a satisfying relationship fails, I am free to sever my ties and try again, for my individual needs and happiness are all-important.

The closest approximation to the open choice basis for mate selection is a result of historical developments within the United States. Prior to the twentieth century, most courtships resembled fairly closely the "restricted choice" alternative. Most young people lived at home until an early marriage. Though mate choice was individual, adult expectations were that heterosexual contacts would occur under the watchful eye of parents, and ruses were often used by the young to escape surveillance. Yet the seeds of change were present in the nineteenth century. Industrialization and mobility were increasing, and higher education, a development that postponed adulthood, was expanding. Particularly with the spread of coeducation during the first twenty years of this century, increasing numbers of young people spent several unmarried years living away from home and parental supervision. While coeducational colleges were expected to assume a position in loco parentis, college adolescents had much less difficulty than those living at home in arranging rendezvous free from adult supervision. During the early years of this century, then, the relations between the sexes prior to marriage began to become what Ira Reiss calls a participant-run system.[1]

Concurrent with the spread of coeducation in the United States, the growth of cities and advances in technology increased the number and types of places for urban entertainment, and improved the means for getting to them. Motion pictures, nightclubs, theaters, sporting events—these and other

---

[1] On the significance of the term *participant-run,* see Ira L. Reiss, *The Social Context of Premarital Sexual Permissiveness* (New York: Holt, Rinehart and Winston, 1967), pp. 165, 176, and passim.

places became increasingly available to the unchaperoned young couple, whose participation in such activities came to be known as "dating." At first, dating was considered a form of recreation which had little direct relation to courtship or mate selection. The same opportunities were available to high school–age people, but their young age plus the fact that they lived at home meant that it would be several more years before dating would be prevalent and acceptable at the high school level. Yet from this recent beginning under the influence of postponed adulthood, individual mobility, and urban entertainment, dating has come to be a ubiquitous and multipurpose aspect of premarital relationships in the United States. Let us, then, begin by examining its nature and functions.

Section One

THE NATURE AND FUNCTIONS OF DATING

The Dating Continuum

Geoffrey Gorer, an English anthropologist, describes American dating practices as a competitive game in which each side makes points; he concludes that "the ideal date is one in which both partners are so popular, so skilled, and so self-assured that the result is a draw."[2] One of the first sociological descriptions of dating produced in the United States, that of Willard Waller, is consistent both with Gorer's comments and with the early history of dating as a recreational pursuit. Waller's account of the "Rating and Dating Complex" was based on research done at Pennsylvania State College in the early 1930s.[3] Dating, says Waller, is a "dalliance" relationship, a recreational activity; the qualities rated highly in a date—campus leadership, money, a car, and good clothes—are not the same as the personality- and character-based qualities desired in a mate.

Since Waller's article appeared in 1937, his distinction between courtship and dating (the former serious and the latter not) has apparently become increasingly inappropriate. Instead, it seems justifiable to replace it with the concept of a *dating continuum* with various identifiable stages (casual dating, going steady, engagement) and with multiple purposes.

There are at least three reasons for this change in conceptualization. A first reason why the term *courtship,* as distinct from the term *dating,* is less appropriate is that young people themselves don't use it. The teenage male

---

[2] Geoffrey Gorer, *The American People: A Study in National Character* (New York: Norton, 1964 ed.), p. 114.
[3] Willard Waller, "The Rating and Dating Complex," *American Sociological Review* 2 (1937), 727–34.

does not tell his roommate or parents, "I'm going courting tonight," but rather, "I have a date," or "I'm going out tonight." The term *courtship* is rarely used in everyday speech, because it seems to have connotations of a bygone day.

Another reason why the term *dating* has incorporated the significance of the term *courtship* is the intensiveness and extensiveness of dating within the teenage population. Not only is dating no longer restricted to college students; it has spread back into the pre-high-school years. Samuel Lowrie, in 1950–51 studies involving over 2,800 midwestern high school and university students, found that dating experience had begun for the majority at age fourteen or fifteen. Lowrie's students were predominantly of middle-class origin; since 1950 others have reported the age at first date to be closer to thirteen for the majority of middle-class youngsters, and about fifteen for youngsters of the working and lower classes.[4] In a study of several hundred University of Wisconsin undergraduates carried out during 1966, this author found that *regular* dating, as distinct from the initial date, had begun at age fourteen for the majority of the girls and at fifteen for most of the boys. It seems likely, therefore, that Lowrie's 1950 research detected one point in the spread of dating, over four or five decades, from the college population back to the early teenage years. Dating, then, has become a primary activity for virtually all young people in the United States, covering for many of them a period of as long as ten years.

The third, and perhaps the most compelling, reason for abandoning Waller's distinction between recreational dating and serious courtship in favor of a dating continuum involves direct attempts to replicate Waller's research.[5] Robert Blood, for example, finds no sharp break between the characteristics desired in a casual date and those valued in a more serious relationship by University of Michigan students. As he puts it:

> The BMOC-fraternity-car-clothes-money complex has already been scrapped by Michigan girls in their casual dating preferences so that thinking of marriage requires no further significant changes in their orientation. Conversely, the personality-type items..., which were frequently chosen both as campus norms and as personal preferences in casual dating, continue to receive extensive support as qualifications for a potential marriage partner.[6]

---

[4] Samuel H. Lowrie, "Factors Involved in the Frequency of Dating," *Marriage and Family Living* 18 (1956), 46–51; Robert R. Bell and Jay B. Chaskes, "Premarital Sexual Experience Among Coeds, 1958 and 1968," *Journal of Marriage and the Family* 32 (1970), 81–84.

[5] For a list of the studies replicating Waller's work, see Ira L. Reiss, "Social Class and Campus Dating," *Social Problems* 13 (1965), 193–205.

[6] Robert O. Blood, "A Retest of Waller's Rating Complex," *Marriage and Family Living* 17 (1955), 41–47.

In a more recent study, Ira Reiss has noted that at a coeducational college in Virginia the competitive-materialistic values Waller described are present as a subdominant value-set—mainly within the Greek organizations. However, among the Greeks these same values appear to be related both to casual dating and to mate selection.[7]

In summary, then, the disuse of the term *courtship,* the ubiquity of dating, and the fact that dating appears to be motivated by serious as well as recreational purposes, make it reasonable to regard the dating continuum as the heart of the courtship system of the contemporary United States.

General Functions of Dating

Dating is more than a recreational outlet and the vehicle of mate selection in the United States. By drawing upon discussions by William Kephart, Robert Winch, and James Skipper and Gilbert Nass, it is possible to formulate a list of five complex functions that this system of heterosexual contacts performs for the individual in society.[8] (1) Dating is a form of *recreation.* "It provides entertainment for the individuals involved and is a source of immediate enjoyment."[9] (2) It is a form of *socialization.* It gives the individual an opportunity to learn about members of the opposite sex at close range, to develop techniques of interaction, to play roles, and to increasingly define his self-concept as he observes others' reactions to him as a person. (3) It meets *ego needs.* The young person—like all people—needs understanding, serious conversation, and to be considered important. A satisfactory dating experience may help him over the rocky period of independence struggle and postponement of adulthood which is called adolescence. (4) Dating functions as a means of *status placement.* This function is performed strictly by the family or kin unit in many societies, so that the unit into which an individual is born determines the category of persons into which he will marry as well as his adult status. In the United States, where personal choice is basic to mate selection, the dating system makes it possible for certain persons to be rated highly desirable and in this way to raise their status within the peer group. Thus, the dating system helps to control the operation of free choice by parceling out prospective

---

[7] Reiss, "Social Class and Campus Dating," pp. 194, 204.

[8] William M. Kephart, *The Family, Society, and the Individual* (Boston: Houghton Mifflin, 1961 ed.); Robert F. Winch, "The Functions of Dating in Middle-Class America," in Winch and Louis Wolf Goodman, eds., *Selected Studies in Marriage and the Family,* 3rd ed. (New York: Holt, Rinehart and Winston, 1968), pp. 505–7; and James K. Skipper and Gilbert Nass, "Dating Behavior: A Framework for Analysis and an Illustration," *Journal of Marriage and the Family* 28 (1966), 412–20.

[9] Skipper and Nass, "Dating Behavior," p. 412.

mates according to their status value. (5) Finally, of course, dating functions for the *selection of a marriage partner*. This, after all, is the end result of at least one dating relationship for the individual. Most young people do not begin each date by asking, "Would I want to marry this person?" Yet somewhere in the course of their dating experience this latent question is answered affirmatively. Mate selection is, therefore, both the cause and the final effect of the dating continuum.

Stages and Specific Functions of the Dating Continuum

The dating continuum may be thought of as a succession of gradual changes in seriousness, including such identifiable stages as random or casual dating, going steady, engagement, and marriage. In addition, some groups of young people recognize certain intermediate stages, such as "going steadily," a relationship not quite as exclusive as going steady, and "pinning," a serious step prior to engagement among some organized school groups.

The five general dating functions listed above are not *all* performed at *all* stages of *all* dating relationships. Recreation, and to a lesser extent socialization and status achievement, are the sole functions of many casual dating experiences. However, the meeting of ego needs and increasing seriousness may be concurrent aspects of a relationship as it becomes more intense and lasting. Interestingly, in a retrospective study of married student couples at Pennsylvania State University, Mary Hicks has found that these couples perceive going steady and engagement as having performed different functions for them. Going steady served for personality testing and exploration—what we have called ego needs and socialization. Informal engagement enabled them to plan for the future, while formal engagement served only the purpose of planning the wedding itself.[10] And, of course, the mate selection function can be considered synonymous with movement into the final stage of the dating continuum.

Besides the more general functions performed by dating, there are several functions, or purposes, that are more specific to a particular stage of the continuum. Of special interest in this regard is going steady, that stage which ordinarily embodies the transition from a recreational to a serious relationship. Research at the University of Wisconsin by Robert Herman and, later, by the present author has revealed several important motives for going steady.[11] Herman, who asked his students about their high

---

[10] Mary W. Hicks, "An Empirical Evaluation of Textbook Assumptions About Engagement," *Family Life Coordinator* 19 (1970), 57–63.
[11] Robert D. Herman, "The 'Going-Steady' Complex: A Re-examination," *Marriage and Family Living* 17 (1955), 36–40.

school experience, found that a frequent reason given for going steady was that "everyone's doing it"; that is, it is a high school fad. Many students, however, gave other reasons. Going steady guarantees one's participation in activities: it is good "date security." It also helps the young person to avoid the anxieties of competition for desirable dates. And, even on the high school level, it is a pledge of serious interest and intent to some—although the consummation in marriage may be understood to be many years in the future, and may never come to pass.

Looking at reasons for going steady among college students, the author found several of Herman's motives still present, but of lesser importance. Date security was still a secondary reason expressed by girls for going steady, and freedom from competition was a reason given by some boys, but seriousness and ego needs had become dominant. College students of both sexes expressed as the most basic reasons either love for their partner or the need to feel wanted and important. A minority (some 10 percent) of the male students also indicated that a reason for going steady is to guarantee a sexual outlet, a subject to which we shall return later in the chapter. In short, even a specific stage of the dating continuum, such as going steady, can have differing significance to different persons as well as to the same person at different ages.

Many high school students, even among the more popular in the school dating system, do not "go steady" today to the extent that young people did in the early 1960s. In fact, there has been a considerable move on the high school scene toward the "group date," in which a number of young people go out together without being paired off by sex. Later in the chapter we shall raise the issue of the group date again.

Thus far we have reviewed the general functions of dating, the stages of the dating continuum, and the functions of and reasons for going steady. Clyde McDaniel has attempted to synthesize several previous analyses of the dating process, giving particular emphasis to the changing role played by the female. Drawing upon Winch's work, McDaniel claims that the possible roles played by females during dating are assertive, receptive, or some combination of the two. Assertive daters are achievement-oriented, competitive, autonomous, dominant, and hostile. Receptive daters are deferential, succorous (desirous of help), prone to vicariousness (gaining pleasure from others' achievements), and anxious.

> Girls, in the early stage of courtship, are inexperienced and unsophisticated with regard to appropriate role behavior. They are assertive initially because they view their right to act as aggressors in social interaction as identical with boys' right to act as aggressors. In heterosexual interaction on dates, however, they are made aware of their inappro-

priate role behavior through negative reinforcement from boys. In this way, they learn that receptivity is more frequently approved than assertiveness.[12]

Waller's and Gorer's descriptions of dating as a competitive recreational activity seem to McDaniel to fit quite well the early stage of dating, in which there is assertiveness on the part of both couple members. However, socialization into "appropriate" roles occurs, and in the later or more serious stages the female plays a more acceptable receptive role.

McDaniel's interesting analysis does an injustice to previous research, especially Lowrie's and Waller's, because it tries to fit the differing views onto a single, nonhistorical continuum. However, it does raise certain intriguing questions. In closing, he reiterates his description of the "cycle wherein girls learn through trial and error to become receptive." It may not be overstating the case, McDaniel feels, to assert that "if they do not become receptive, they never get married."[13] One cannot help wondering whether McDaniel's closing assertion might not have been more correct in an earlier period of American history than it is today. In the colonial and Victorian eras of role separation and normative patriarchy, the female who could not learn to be receptive may have had great difficulty in finding a mate. Today, however, substantial change in the status of women and a blurring or loosening of role specifications make one question the extent to which female receptivity is a *necessary* condition for marriage. It is at least possible that the emphases of women's liberation, on freedom and equality, are hastening the day when women—premaritally as well as maritally—will no longer play a receptive role.

A second question raised by McDaniel's closing assertion concerns the relation between role playing and personality. To the extent that McDaniel is correct, it is quite possible that a female with an assertive personality will play a receptive role in dating in order to obtain a mate. What is the likely effect on the marriage when the wife's assertiveness is manifested subsequently? Will serious conflict occur? These are issues for further research, not idle speculation.

The process of love and breakup was investigated some years ago by Clifford Kirkpatrick and Theodore Caplow in a well-executed study involving 399 students at the University of Minnesota. They found that the early stages of a dating relationship tend to be controlled by the male, due to his role as initiator. At the more serious stages, however, it is generally the female who exercises greater control over the continuation or termination of the relationship. The period of heartache and adjustment following most

---

[12] Clyde O. McDaniel, "Dating Roles and Reasons for Dating," *Journal of Marriage and the Family* 31 (1969), 100.

[13] McDaniel, "Dating Roles and Reasons for Dating," p. 106.

breakups is extremely brief. Dating is described by the authors as a selective process through which the less stable and less compatible relationships are weeded out.[14] It is a total courtship continuum, but many relationships terminate at an early stage due to loss of interest, an alternative attraction, or some other reason. In the next chapter we shall examine at length the key factors in this weeding or filtering out process which leads to mate selection.

Two further comments regarding dating as a courtship continuum seem to be in order. First, personal choice of a mate is thought by many to be an extremely problematic basis for a stable marriage.[15] Yet it should be added that extended dating, or a lengthy dating experience, is conducive to the making of an adequate choice at a time when institutional or traditional controls are weak. Alan Bayer puts it this way: "It is the *length* of the dating experience prior to marriage which may have a crucial impact on the subsequent outcome."[16] Presumably, the more extensive one's contact with members of the opposite sex, the greater are his chances of making an intelligent choice of a mate. Second, discussion with students and academicians from Taiwan, India, and certain African nations has led this author to conclude that many persons in these countries consider dating to be an index of modernization. One reason is that dating represents freedom from adult control over mating and kinship, therefore symbolizing among the young leaders and potential leaders of these countries the rejection of traditional ways and entrance into the modern world. Thus dating is not unique to the family system of the United States, but has a symbolic value in other nations as well.

Section Two

PROBLEMATIC ASPECTS OF DATING

The reader may have surmised by this time that the present author regards dating as the courtship system par excellence. This conclusion, however, does not follow from the foregoing discussion of the nature and functions

---

[14] Clifford Kirkpatrick and Theodore Caplow, "Courtship in a Group of Minnesota Students," *American Journal of Sociology* 51 (1945), 114–25; and Kirkpatrick and Caplow, "Emotional Trends in the Courtship Experience of College Students as Expressed by Graphs, with Some Observations on Methodological Implications," *American Sociological Review* 10 (1945), 619–26.

[15] This statement itself is dependent upon the definition of the word *stable*. If stable simply means permanent, then the mode of choice is far less important than the strictness of the laws governing dissolution of the unit. If stable means satisfying or happy, individual choice is probably a better basis for stability than is arranged marriage, despite the fact that a loosening of the laws may allow more of the unsatisfactory units to dissolve.

[16] Alan E. Bayer, "Early Dating and Early Marriage," *Journal of Marriage and the Family* 30 (1968), 632.

of the dating system of the United States. It cannot be overemphasized that dating is a recent phenomenon. Five or six decades has been sufficient time to establish dating as the basis of the courtship process in the United States, but the specific norms governing that process continue to be in flux. With the fluidity of the cultural content of the adolescent period, and the fact that the dating system is, by and large, participant-run, each new generation redefines the dating codes or norms of the previous generation (and an adolescent generation is, of course, less than ten years long). Expectations and practices undergo constant reevaluation, and the following problems arise within the dating system.[17]

Parental Influence

Parents naturally take an interest in the dating behavior of their sons and daughters. In interviews with young people conducted more than thirty years ago, Alan Bates found that a high proportion of their parents had tried to influence their dating (see Table 4). In a later study, conducted in

Table 4
Percent of Parents Attempting to Influence the Dating Behavior of Their Sons and Daughters

	Fathers' Influence	Mothers' Influence
Sons	49.1	79.4
Daughters	68.7	97.1

SOURCE: Alan Bates, "Parental Roles in Courtship," *Social Forces* 20 (1942), 483–86.

the early 1950s, Marvin Sussman reported that parents in 81 percent of his middle-class New Haven sample "admitted they either persuaded or threatened their children with withdrawal of support during periods when they were courting persons of whom they disapproved."[18] There is no reason to assume that, in the time since Bates's and Sussman's studies, parental attempts at influence have declined appreciably. While most parents feel compelled to speak out on the subject, the reaction of young people to the intrusion varies from acceptance to resentment and conflict. This, then, is one aspect of current practices in which the choice falls short of being

---

[17] Much of the following discussion of problems in dating is adapted from Kephart, *The Family, Society, and the Individual*, pp. 293–300.

[18] Marvin B. Sussman, "Parental Participation in Mate Selection and Its Effect upon Family Continuity," *Social Forces* 32 (1953), 76–81.

"open," but is still a cross between restricted and open, between adult-influenced and youth- or participant-run.

It may be argued that since parental approval of the mate selected seems to be positively related to success in marriage for the offspring, such intrusion is therefore vindicated. Yet great parental insight is but one possible explanation for the relative success of parentally approved marriages. Another plausible explanation might be that when parents disapprove of a marriage, they tend to cause trouble for the young couple afterward, increasing the likelihood of its dissolution. Whichever interpretation one accepts, it must be concluded that, with a participant-run dating system and weak cultural supports for parental intrusion, parental approval will remain a problematic aspect of courtship in the United States.

Intergroup or Heterogeneous Dating

Dating somebody of a different background from one's own is a problem primarily in relation to the issue of parental intrusion, as well as that of kin and friends. If the young person were entirely free from group constraints, the difficulties posed by interclass, interreligious, and interracial dating would very likely be minimal. Either he would avoid such relationships because he had internalized the importance of the differences represented, or else he would engage in heterogeneous dating with no thought of the problems involved. (Note that we are speaking here of heterogeneous dating, not marriage.) Parents or other significant persons, in arguing against heterogeneous dating, may be motivated by a sincere belief that such relations are problem-producing if they culminate in marriage. Yet in this last phrase lies a part of the problem: while these "others" are focusing on the possibility of marriage, the young people involved may be seeking enjoyment and experience, with little or no thought of marriage. Thus, the fact that the dating continuum serves for both socialization and mate selection may become the basis for misunderstanding. A second issue in intergroup dating may be a basic value disagreement between the generations, or between persons in the same social network. Members of the older generation who consider group values to be very important may be considered by younger people to be snobbish and bigoted. Such differences, the young people may feel, "simply don't matter any more." Feature 4, on black-white dating in college, is interesting in this regard. The key point regarding group heterogeneity is what it signifies, that is, divergent values and norms; any trouble in intergroup dating is likely to be caused by disagreements concerning the importance of these divergences. This issue must be raised again when we discuss mate selection in Chapter 10.

Physical Attractiveness

One of the most problematic factors in dating concerns physical attractiveness. Elaine Walster et al. (who investigated a computer dance among University of Minnesota freshmen) and Glen Elder agree that sheer attractiveness is an overriding determinant of liking, and is particularly crucial in boys' reactions to girls.[19] This is the negative side of the status-placement function discussed above. While girls may be penalized more than boys, neither sex avoids the difficulties besetting the generally unattractive young person in a participant-run dating system. It is ironic that at a time in life when, perhaps, emotional security is needed most, the dating system is as

[19] Elaine Walster et al., "Importance of Physical Attractiveness in Dating Behavior," *Journal of Personality and Social Psychology* 4 (1966), 508–16; and Glen H. Elder, Jr., "Appearance and Education in Marriage Mobility," *American Sociological Review* 34 (1969), 519–33.

FEATURE 4

The barriers that once stopped black and white youngsters from socializing are coming down fast in many parts of the land. On weekends, mixed couples by the dozens stroll in Manhattan's Central Park, through Chicago's Old Town and Hyde Park areas, in San Francisco's North Beach. The strongest enclave for interracial dating is the school or college campus. . . .

Bill Alexander, 26, . . . notices an encouraging change in the attitudes of the community. "A couple of years back, I don't know if it took courage to walk about Philadelphia with a white girl, but you could sense the uneasiness. I don't feel that nervousness anymore."

Despite the increasing U.S. tolerance, the fact is that it is still far from easy for blacks to be seen with whites. . . .

Parental horror is another thing that mixed couples encounter. "Parents are a real hang-up about that part of my life," complains Candy Reuben, 21. . . . " 'We're just thinking about what's best for you,' they tell me." . . .

Black Power advocates are even more militantly opposed. . . .

In fact most interracial romances seem to be mostly exploratory; few so far have led to the altar. . . .

Says San Francisco Negro Drama Student Toni Johns, 20: "I feel proud that I can date white boys, that my companion can do it, that we have no hang-ups, that we have enough sense and our heads are in the right place." . . .

U.C.L.A. Co-ed Jacqueline Thomas, a Negro, appraises her experience more poignantly: "I've gone through the whole bit. There was a time when I was 'thinking white' like everyone else; then I went through a period of hating everybody. I've come to the conclusion that there are always a few people who understand you and know how you feel. When you find them, it doesn't matter what they are—red, black, white, or whatever—you've got to take a chance with those people."

"Black & White Dating," *Time* (July 19, 1968), 48–49.

likely to frustrate that need as to meet it. For every individual who achieves status in the peer group, another loses status because he lacks the qualities valued by the peer group—and one such quality is physical attractiveness. Under a system of arranged marriage, face and body are not quite so important, and equality of opportunity is at least theoretically easier to effect. The reader may have noticed that from time to time pictures of homely debutantes appear on the "society" page of the newspaper. Even in American society, lineage and economic value increase the chances of marriage for such individuals and help to balance the competition based upon looks. In general, however, physical attractiveness is a crucial element in the American courtship system.

Social Awkwardness

Social awkwardness and conversational inferiority are on the opposite side of the coin from socialization through dating. One learns by means of the dating experience, we said, how to interact with members of the opposite sex and how to play various roles. But if the participants run the system, as they do in the United States, a premium is placed upon social and conversational abilities at the outset; those deficient in these areas may have difficulty both in obtaining a date and in handling themselves once they have obtained one. Ideally, dating should afford opportunities for socialization, for developing social skills; it may, however, thwart the development of individuals who flounder in the attempt to make a good impression. This is a theme played upon in the mass media: glamour magazines and teen magazines are good examples. These publications demonstrate quite well how the dating system falls short of providing for the socialization function: one must practice elsewhere, the reader is told, in order to be a good conversationalist on the date. Dating may simply serve in many cases to accentuate tendencies already present for the smooth to become more so, and for the awkward to become less and less adept at handling social situations. With the high premium placed upon attractiveness and social facility by the dating system, it is not surprising that Richard Klemer finds a strong relationship between high self-esteem and a high frequency of dating among college women.[20] It could be that having high self-esteem makes one appealing as a date, or it could be that being asked frequently for dates raises one's self-esteem. But regardless of the causal connection, the relationship itself is significant.

---

[20] Richard H. Klemer, "Self-Esteem and College Dating Experiences as Factors in Mate Selection and Marital Happiness: A Longitudinal Study," *Journal of Marriage and the Family* 33 (1971), 183–87.

Superficiality

C. T. Husbands claims that a typical difference between dating in the United States and dating in Europe is that in the early stages of dating the U.S. teenager engages in "playing the field" or multiple dating, while in Europe the tendency is "to go out with one person of the opposite sex during any one period of time."[21] The result, he says, is that the major characteristic of U.S. dating relationships is their superficiality. Unlike those who see multiple dating as a learning experience, Husbands feels that it results in the playing out of the same role with one partner after another. The attempt to create a good impression keeps most relationships from ever reaching a deeper level, or from ever getting to a point at which conflict is possible, thus preventing "a valuable experience in socialization and personality development."[22] This superficiality may even carry over into marriage:

> If a couple does eventually marry, the residue of the lack of openness that characterized the initial stages of their relationship may produce particular tension once such premarital performance can no longer be sustained.[23]

Husbands admits that he is presenting an ideal-typical picture of the difference between European and U.S. dating. We may, therefore, admit that superficiality is a problem, without accepting the full impact of his conclusions. Quite possibly, as we noted earlier in reference to the paper by Mary Hicks, going steady and engagement enable couple members to plumb the emotional depths, even though they began several years earlier by playing the field. Furthermore, Robert Bell and Jay Chaskes have found evidence that Husbands' portrayal is perhaps not as accurate today as it once was. Though they found the age at first date to have been about the same in 1968 as it was in 1958, they discovered a significant difference in the number of individuals ever dated. In 1958, the mean number of individuals ever dated was 53, while in 1968 it was 25.[24] This may be an indication that playing the field is now less prevalent than it was in the mid-1950s. Thus, while superficiality is a problem in U.S. dating relationships, it should not be seen as all-encompassing. Nor, for that matter, can it be separated from the problem which we will take up next—insincerity.

---

[21] C. T. Husbands, "Some Social and Psychological Consequences of the American Dating System," *Adolescence* 5 (1970), 452.

[22] Husbands, "Some Social and Psychological Consequences of the American Dating System," p. 459.

[23] Husbands, "Some Social and Psychological Consequences of the American Dating System," p. 460.

[24] Bell and Chaskes, "Premarital Sexual Experience Among Coeds, 1958 and 1968," p. 82.

Insincerity

Insincerity grows out of the fact that dating functions for both enjoyment and mate selection. An obvious possibility is that one party has serious intentions while the other is simply seeking enjoyment; in such a case, the meeting of ego needs becomes highly problematic. This is where "the line" appears, as the less emotionally involved member of a couple tries to convince the more serious member that he cares more than he actually does. Skipper and Nass remind us that, in a dating situation characterized by differential interest, "the individual with the greater emotional commitment ... will have the least control over the relationship."[25] The fluid and multipurpose nature of the dating continuum mean that differences of motive and commitment are likely to be frequent in dating, thereby thwarting the individual's attempts to gain understanding and security from it.

Most of what has been said thus far regarding the nature, functions, and problems of the American dating system holds for young people at all levels of the socioeconomic ladder. Lower-class and middle-class courtship do, however, diverge at a few points. According to a national sample study analyzed by Alan Bayer, young people in lower-class families start dating later than do those in the middle class.[26] The dating activity of the former is governed by lesser financial resources and is oriented toward sex and marriage more immediately and directly than is that of the middle class. One reason for this is that only a small proportion of lower-class young people postpone marriage in order to attend college. Thus, the dating continuum of the lower class is foreshortened both by a later start and by a generally earlier age at marriage than is that of the middle class. In the chapter on marital dissolution we shall return to the issue of early marriage and its relation to marital permanence.

Dating serves as the courtship continuum of the contemporary United States. Yet the system is characterized by the convergence of familial and individualistic pressures: it is a participant-run system, but parents continue to influence the choice of mates; mate selection is open, but it is likely to be made within the bounds of certain social categories. The recency of dating, its multipurpose nature, and the fluid and sometimes contradictory character of the expectations it arouses make it a problem-producing experience for many young people. One issue in premarital relations, sexual intercourse, is treated as a problem by many commentators. We shall turn to that issue in Section Three.

---

[25] Skipper and Nass, "Dating Behavior," p. 413. Many years earlier this was labeled by Willard Waller as "the principle of least interest." See Waller, "The Rating and Dating Complex," p. 733.

[26] Bayer, "Early Dating and Early Marriage," pp. 628–32.

Section Three

PREMARITAL SEXUAL RELATIONS

Within the past generation the subject of human sexual relations has come to be considered a suitable topic for conversation and research in American society. The forerunners of current discussions of sex in the modern industrial world are ethnographic reports of anthropologists who studied a wide variety of preindustrial societies.[27] All societies, it seems, control sexual behavior in some manner; the two most universal forms of control appear to be the incest taboo and marriage. In addition, accounts of such practices as premarital sex, extramarital sex, masturbation, and homosexuality indicate that these activities may be encouraged, permitted, ignored, condemned, or suppressed, depending upon the society and its norms. Furthermore, there are variations in the degree of correspondence between verbalized norms and typical behavior.

Among the sex practices mentioned above, the one that has received most widespread cross-cultural acceptance is premarital intercourse. After analyzing a large sample of societies, George P. Murdock stated that "premarital license prevails in seventy percent of our cases. In the rest, the taboo falls primarily upon females and appears to be largely a precaution against child-bearing out of wedlock rather than a moral requirement."[28] The arrangements in the majority of societies that permit premarital sex include safeguards against exploitation of the female and equal and legitimate status for children born out of wedlock. In other words, where premarital sex is accepted as a part of a society's culture, few stressful and guilt-producing features are attached to it. The greater problems occur in those societies that officially prohibit premarital sex, since it is extremely difficult to enforce the prohibition and many societal leaders do not consider the prohibition important enough to enforce.

Sex outside of marriage, unlike sex before marriage, is *not* permitted by a majority of societies. Many factors concerning the stability and integration of societies and their family systems are related to the control of extramarital sex. We therefore introduce our discussion of premarital sex with the statement that the sex practices of a culture are usually consistent with its other characteristics. However, if a culture is changing rapidly, as that of the United States seems to be, a rethinking of previously accepted norms—

---

[27] The works of men like Bronislaw Malinowski were often read by the "civilized" but culture-bound public more for titillation than for information. Good examples of anthropological works dealing with sex are Malinowski, *Sex and Repression in Savage Society* (London: Routledge and Kegan Paul, 1927); and Malinowski, *The Sexual Life of Savages in Northwestern Melanesia* (New York: Liveright, 1929).

[28] George Peter Murdock, *Social Structure* (New York: Macmillan, 1949), p. 265.

including sexual norms—occurs, making it likely that there will be inconsistencies among the various aspects of the culture.

Extent and Significance of Premarital Sex in the United States

The massive research on sex in the United States carried out by Alfred Kinsey and his associates burst upon the public following World War II.[29] Because the research noted the prevalence of many types of sexual practices and the discrepancy between the expressed and behavioral morality of the middle classes, it was perceived as a threat by many persons. Researchers attacked its methodology, editorialists rejected its conclusions, and moral leaders accused its authors of undermining the moral fiber of the nation.[30] While the same criticisms would apply to much other sociological research, the significant fact is that the Kinsey studies were felt to deserve extensive critical attention. They were correctly viewed as heralding a new day of openness and frankness regarding sexual matters; the result has been a flood of studies examining sex, which continues unabated to the present.[31]

One focus of the Kinsey research—as well as of notable studies by Louis Terman, Winston Ehrmann, and Ira Reiss—is premarital sex relations. By drawing upon the findings of these and other authors and by tracing changes over time, it is possible to derive a fairly accurate estimate of the current prevalence of premarital sexual intercourse in the United States. Approximately 75 percent of the single male population engage in intercourse prior to marriage, while for females the figure is closer to 55 percent.

Granted, the male may have a more active biological drive for "sex where he finds it," and may feel freer due to the absence of pregnancy fears, but there is more to the sex difference than this. There is, first of all, evidence of a lingering double standard that considers premarital intercourse more reprehensible in a female than in a male. Reiss, for example, speaks of the millions of males who are engaged in reducing the number of virgins while at the same time holding a deep desire for a virgin mate. Second, a basic middle-class distinction between males and females has been, according to Ehrmann, that females base their indulgence in premarital intercourse on romanticism and males on eroticism. To elaborate, many a woman indicates that her premarital intercourse has been only with the man who later

[29] Alfred C. Kinsey et al., *Sexual Behavior in the Human Male* (Philadelphia: Saunders, 1948); and Kinsey et al., *Sexual Behavior in the Human Female* (Philadelphia: Saunders, 1953).

[30] See especially Jerome Himelhoch and Sylvia F. Fava, eds., *Sexual Behavior in American Society* (New York: Norton, 1955).

[31] For a review of studies before 1960, see Winston Ehrmann, *Premarital Dating Behavior* (New York: Holt, Rinehart and Winston, 1959), pp. 33–34. For later studies, see Reiss, *The Social Context of Premarital Sexual Permissiveness.*

became her husband. As a respectable girl, she seldom engages in sexual activities of the sort defined by the official morality as promiscuous or random; rather, her sexual expression is profoundly related to love and to a single partner. Premarital sex (when it occurs) is best viewed as an expression of love on the part of the middle-class female, and as an erotic release on the part of the male, who nevertheless desires a virgin bride. This serves to clarify Ehrmann's conclusion that, in the middle class, the degree of physical intimacy varies inversely with the intensity of affection among males, and directly with the intensity of affection among females.[32]

Ehrmann's results were based on research done in the late 1950s, and many questions are now being raised concerning the current validity of his conclusions. Erwin Smigel and Rita Seiden, writing on the "Decline and Fall of the Double Standard," claimed in the 1960s that "young men today are probably less promiscuous and more monogamous, and their relationships tend to be more stable. Both sexes are approaching a single standard based on sex with affection."[33] In other words, according to Smigel and Seiden, during the 1960s the inverse relation between affection and intercourse which Ehrmann found for middle-class males may have been changing toward a direct relation, so that, as seriousness of intent on the part of both the male and the female increases, so too does the probability that the couple will engage in premarital intercourse. But things have changed even since Smigel and Seiden wrote in 1968. Seriousness leading to intercourse is no longer an adequate, or even a prime, explanation for the diminishing hold of the double standard on middle-class young people. Bell and Chaskes, for example, find that in 1968, as compared to 1958, girls were more likely to report that they had first had intercourse while dating or going steady rather than during an engagement.[34] This weakening of the link between seriousness and intercourse on the part of college women is found attitudinally as well. Ira Robinson, Karl King, and Jack Balswick report a drastic change even between 1965 and 1970. In that five-year period the percentage of college females who felt that premarital intercourse was immoral dropped from 70 to 34.[35]

In the preceding paragraph the phrase *middle-class males and females* has been used several times. This is because the percentage approximations—75 and 55—are overall figures. For the lower classes the percentages are

---

[32] Ehrmann, *Premarital Dating Behavior*, p. 338.

[33] Erwin O. Smigel and Rita Seiden, "The Decline and Fall of the Double Standard," *The Annals* 376 (1968), 17. For an important normative interpretation, see Hallowell Pope and Dean D. Knudsen, "Premarital Sexual Norms, the Family, and Social Change," *Journal of Marriage and the Family* 27 (1965), 314–23.

[34] Bell and Chaskes, "Premarital Sexual Experience Among Coeds, 1958 and 1968," p. 83.

[35] Ira E. Robinson, Karl King, and Jack O. Balswick, "The Premarital Sexual Revolution Among College Females," *Family Life Coordinator* 21 (1972), 192.

Table 5
Percent of Males and Females (by Social Class) Engaging in Premarital Intercourse

Sex and Social Class	Percent Engaging in Premarital Intercourse
Middle-class males	60
Middle-class females	40
Lower-class males	85
Lower-class females	65

some 10 to 15 points higher for each sex; for the middle classes they are correspondingly lower. (See Table 5 for our estimates by sex and social class.)

It is important to note that the gap between middle-class and lower-class engagement in premarital intercourse has decreased considerably over the past few decades. This is one of the respects in which the U.S. middle class has moved increasingly toward a life-style which had characterized the manual classes for a considerable period of time. That life-style, called the "subculture of gratification" by Edward Shorter, stresses individual self-development and the gratifying of personal needs and is sufficiently tolerant of premarital intercourse to overcome the traditional verbalized and internalized norms against sex before marriage.[36]

The figures on premarital sex reported in the array of studies summarized by Table 5 may be somewhat misleading. Many of these studies are based on an unmarried population at a given point in time; that is, they are cross-sectional studies. When asked of unmarried persons, the question "Have you ever engaged in sexual intercourse?" must be interpreted: "Have you ever engaged in sexual intercourse up to now?" However, what the researcher ordinarily wants to know is how many persons engage in intercourse at any time prior to marriage. Thus, the most accurate studies of premarital sex must be confined to married persons, since only married persons are in a position to describe the entire dating or courtship period.

The foregoing criticism is particularly applicable to research on college populations. A study of college norms and behaviors, carried out by David Heise at the University of Wisconsin in 1966, involved approximately 800 undergraduates. Table 6 shows the percent of males and females stating that they had engaged in premarital intercourse, according to their year in college.[37] A simple statistical mistake, in summarizing the data of Table 6, would

---

[36] Edward Shorter, "Capitalism, Culture, and Sexuality: Some Competing Models," *Social Science Quarterly* 53 (1972), 338–56.

[37] The figures in this study are not to be interpreted as typical of *any* population, even that of undergraduates at the University of Wisconsin. They are presented to illustrate the difficulty in investigating cumulative phenomena by cross-sectional methods.

Table 6
Engagement in Premarital Intercourse by
800 University of Wisconsin Students,
by Sex and Year in College

Sex and Year in College	Percent Engaging in Premarital Intercourse
Males	
Freshmen	25
Sophomores	30
Juniors	60
Seniors	70
Females	
Freshmen	15
Sophomores	20
Juniors	30
Seniors	35

be to sum the totals for males and females and thus conclude that about 45 percent of the males and 24 percent of the females in this sample will have engaged in sex prior to marriage. This would, of course, be a serious underestimate, since such data must be handled cumulatively instead of by computing an average. The fact is that the correct figure for males in this sample is very likely 75–80 percent, while for females it is 40–45, for we may safely assume that even some of the seniors will engage in intercourse in the future, but before their marriage.

Having looked at the extent and significance of premarital intercourse by sex and social class, let us summarize briefly the current trends. Available data indicate, as was stated in Chapter 4, that one great period of increase in the incidence of premarital sex in the United States was the 1920s and that the other has been the period since 1965. The latter increase has been a primarily middle-class phenomenon. Even more important, attitudes and verbalized norms, which had been changing slowly for decades, are now rapidly approaching congruence with the individual choice–based practices. Has the birth control pill had much effect on the prevalence of premarital sex? Some feel that its effect has been negligible. Listen to Smigel and Seiden:

> We doubt that the pill has added materially to the increase in the numbers of young adults or adolescents who have had premarital sex. Effective techniques of birth control existed, and were used, before the pill. True, the pill makes birth control easier to manage (except for the memory requirement), but romantic love is still important; it makes taking the pill, when no definite partner is available, undesirable.

> What the pill does is to give sexual freedom to those who are having steady sexual relationships, for then the use of the pill adds to romantic love by making elaborate preparations unnecessary.[38]

Those who would use the pill to prevent a premarital pregnancy would have indulged in premarital intercourse even without it. What would have to happen to change behavior drastically would be, not just freedom from pregnancy fears, but a separation of sex from affection or "romantic love," as Smigel and Seiden put it. The female's reason, it is suggested, is either: "I am in love with him," in which case she is about as likely to engage in intercourse without the pill as with it, or else her reason is: "I was swept away by emotion and affection," an argument for spontaneity which is difficult to make convincing if she has been taking the pill for a week, or a month. Approaching the same issue from the perspective of premarital pregnancy and abortion, Phillips Cutright finds that formal barriers restricting access to the pill kept its effective use among sexually active unwed teenagers quite low as late as 1968. There is little evidence, he observes, that teenage girls of the late 1960s were much better protected against pregnancy than were teenage girls in 1940.[39]

Value Positions on Premarital Sex

Smigel and Seiden believe that "sex with affection" is coming to be the single standard of premarital sexual behavior. Yet the figures and data quoted throughout the preceding discussion would tend to belie any notion that premarital intercourse, even "with affection," is a "cultural universal." Some engage in premarital sex, others do not; both indulgence and abstinence may be based on a multiplicity of reasons. Disagreements rage in the adult population of the United States regarding the acceptability of premarital sex; the various current value positions are neatly summarized by Isadore Rubin, editor of a little magazine called *Sexology*. Rubin feels that there are six major competing value systems.[40] (1) *Traditional repressive asceticism* is a value still embodied in the official codes and laws of many states. Seven

---

[38] Smigel and Seiden, "The Decline and Fall of the Double Standard," p. 17.

[39] Phillips Cutright, "The Teenage Sexual Revolution and the Myth of an Abstinent Past," *Family Planning Perspectives* 4 (1972), 24–31.

[40] Isadore Rubin, "Transition in Sex Values—Implications for the Education of Adolescents," *Journal of Marriage and the Family* 27 (1965), 185–89. On many of these value positions, see "Premarital Sexual Behavior: A Symposium," *Marriage and Family Living* 24 (1962), 254–78, which includes the views of Lester Kirkendall, Thomas Poffenberger, Richard Klemer, Ira Reiss, Walter Stokes, and Blaine Porter. The symposium is reprinted in Edwin M. Schur, ed., *The Family and the Sexual Revolution* (Bloomington: Indiana University Press, 1965).

states have fines for premarital intercourse, ranging from $10 to $100; Oregon has a maximum penalty of $500 or five years in prison. Other states have sentences ranging from three months to three years. Though such laws are seldom enforced, the logic behind them is still asserted by many religious and other moral leaders in the United States. Sex is linked to procreation and is to be avoided outside of marriage; some spokesmen for this view feel that even within marriage sex should serve only the purpose of procreation. Sex behavior is handled in terms of absolutes—"thou shalt" or "thou shalt not." Both the study and the discussion of sex tend to be considerably restricted by this approach, since the rightness or wrongness of specific practices is not subject to debate.

(2) *Enlightened asceticism* is best exemplified in the views of David Mace. Mace sees asceticism or control in the sexual and other spheres of life as a necessary safeguard in American culture against the softness and weakness that result from overindulgence. He sees self-mastery as necessary to avoid individual weakness and national collapse. On these grounds he opposes a slackening of the sex codes. However, he takes neither a dogmatic nor a negative attitude toward premarital sex and is an ardent exponent of the open forum for studying and discussing the issue. In fact, his discussions of premarital sex with Walter Stokes and Albert Ellis are among the more valuable expositions on this issue—an issue that he feels requires debate in order to be understood, due to the contradictory nature of the present norms.[41]

(3) *Humanistic liberalism* is best exemplified in the ideas and works of Lester Kirkendall of Oregon State University. He, too, opposes inflexible absolutes, but he is above all concerned with interpersonal relations. Morality does not concern the omission or commission of certain acts, but, rather, the consequences of those acts for the relations between those who commit them. Kirkendall searches for a value system that will supply internalized controls for the individual at a time when, in his view, the older, institutional controls, such as religion, are breaking down. The "sex with affection" or "permissiveness with affection" position that Smigel and Seiden claim is dominant today is fairly close to the philosophy embodied in humanistic liberalism.[42]

(4) *Humanistic radicalism* likewise starts with concern for the human being, but states the need for major societal changes. Walter Stokes, a

---

[41] Tapes of these debates are available from the National Council on Family Relations, Minneapolis, Minnesota.

[42] The excellent research of Ira Reiss also concludes that sex with affection is probably the "most popular youth standard." See Reiss, *The Social Context of Premarital Sexual Permissiveness,* p. 174.

spokesman for this position, accepts Kirkendall's humanism, but proposes that society should make sexual freedom possible for young people. In order to do this, the official morality will have to rid itself of the cultural baggage that makes for guilt. Thus, Stokes envisions a cultural engineering project that may take generations. This project involves abandoning the Puritan heritage and approaching premarital sex as a natural act rather than as a moral issue.

(5) *The fun morality* has as its most consistent theoretical or academic spokesman Albert Ellis, and as one of its most effective practical advocates Hugh Hefner of *Playboy* magazine. Without compromise, Ellis upholds the view that sex is pleasurable and that the more such fun a human being has, the better and more psychologically sound a person he is likely to be. He believes that premarital intercourse should be encouraged for well-informed and well-adjusted persons. (Of course, Stokes might respond that there are not very many such people in American society at present.)

(6) *Sexual anarchy,* the sixth position, had as its philosopher the late French jurist René Guyon. Guyon attacked chastity, virginity, and monogamy, and called for the complete removal of all sex taboos and controls. In effect, he advocated complete or universal availability for sex. The only restriction would be against doing violence to or injuring one's fellow.

Unfortunately, neither Rubin nor anyone else has attempted to determine the distribution of these six value positions within the population. This author's estimate, based on evidence from Ira Reiss, Bell and Chaskes, and others, is that humanistic liberalism is the most prevalent empirically, followed by traditional asceticism, the fun morality, and enlightened asceticism, with sexual anarchy having a few advocates and with humanistic radicalism being more an action program than an empirically discernible type. The research of Bell and Chaskes indicates that the trend is toward an increase in the fun morality, with an equivalent lessening in traditional asceticism and perhaps in humanistic liberalism. The reader may, however, review the available evidence and draw his own conclusions regarding the empirical distribution of these value positions.

Premarital Sex as a Cultural Alternative

A cultural universal, as described in Chapter 6, is a belief, practice, or prohibition that is agreed upon (at least verbally) by virtually all the members of a given culture. In American society, two universals have traditionally and legally been monogamy and the prohibition of infanticide. Thus, you are not likely to find forums being held on the desirability or undesirability of infanticide. Instead, we speak absolutely about it and expect almost universal agreement. A cultural alternative, on the other hand, is a belief, practice, or prohibition on which opinion is divided in the various segments of society. Open give-and-take is expected when such an issue is broached. Within the official morality of American middle-class society, the prohibition of pre-marital sex was almost a cultural universal a century ago; today it is an alternative. Whereas at one time the inveighing of the religious leader against premarital sex aroused virtually unanimous verbal agreement, such a stand today would be met with open agreement by some, with doubt by others, and with laughter by still others. In fact, those who hold to the once quasi-universal position of premarital chastity often find themselves on the defensive in the face of the vociferous spokesmen for sexual liberalism. In any case, the "proper" view is no longer clear-cut, no longer prescribed in the dominant middle-class norms.

The changes that have increased the prevalence of premarital sex and made it a "legitimate" attitudinal alternative are defined by many writers as directionless and problem-producing. Without clear guidelines, the possi-bilities of exploitation, insecurity, or guilt are great. Peter Blau, for example, notes the female's sexual dilemma: she increases a man's love by granting favors, but if she dispenses them too readily she depreciates their value and their power to arouse an enduring attachment.[43] The problem of insincerity, referred to in the discussion of dating, is especially acute in the area of pre-marital sex. How can the female know *for sure* that the male's intentions are serious? The answer is simple: she can't. She can only take, or avoid taking, a calculated risk—without knowing whether either her indulgence or her abstinence will increase or decrease his interest. The pressure of sexual de-cisions on the young person is also heightened in situations in which peer-group and parental standards diverge, as they still tend to do.[44] Parental val-ues may cause the young person to feel guilty if he does engage in premarital sex, while a peer group may cause him to feel guilty if he doesn't.

The changes defined as problematic for the individual are seen by some writers, we have said, as anarchic and directionless within society. Vance Packard indicates this confusion or lack of direction in the title of his book *The Sexual Wilderness.* The changes, he feels, are currently "too chaotic and varied to describe yet as a revolution. A revolution implies a clear move-ment in an understood and generally supported direction."[45] While one could

---

[43] Peter M. Blau, *Exchange and Power in Social Life* (New York: Wiley, 1964), p. 80.

[44] On parental and peer influence, see Reiss, *The Social Context of Premarital Sexual Permissiveness,* pp. 162–75; Alfred M. Mirande, "Reference Group Theory and Adoles-cent Sexual Behavior," *Journal of Marriage and the Family* 30 (1968), 572–77; and James J. Teevan, Jr., "Reference Groups and Premarital Sexual Behavior," *Journal of Marriage and the Family* 34 (1972), 283–91.

[45] Vance Packard, *The Sexual Wilderness* (New York: McKay, 1968), p. 17.

argue with his conception of revolution, the important fact is that Packard finds no direction or trend in the changes in sex practices and attitudes—only chaos.

Another negative reaction to the changing expectations regarding premarital sexual activity, and one which has some merit, goes like this. Widespread discussion of the "sexual revolution" has made it seem to many young people that we have moved from one cultural universal to another, from abstinence to indulgence.[46] This has created expectations in many of them which they are incapable of achieving, and anxieties which they are incapable of allaying. Thus, the new indulgence norm, while just as much out of keeping with behavior as the old abstinence norm, has made many young people feel that they are "out of step," that they are not keeping up sexually with their peers. Two results of these expectations, though the causal connection may not be direct, are (1) an increase in rape, presumably attributable to those who believe they cannot get their "fair share" of sexual activity by appealing to the interest of the opposite sex; and (2) an increase in group dating, dating in which couples are not paired off, so that the sexual connotations of the one-to-one date may be avoided. Obviously, the implications of this assertion—that overly high premarital sexual expectations are related to both rape and group dating—require research attention. But they are worth thinking about.

Insincerity, chaos, too high expectations: unquestionably the changes we have been discussing have problematic aspects. There is, however, another way to interpret the changes that have made premarital intercourse a legitimate alternative to continence. The past century has seen a movement *away from two double standards* of the Victorian era. One of these demanded a higher level of morality for females than for males. The other involved a substantial discrepancy between verbal norms and behavior. It is easy to see the problems caused by today's competing value systems, but one can only imagine and infer from the literature of that era the difficulties caused by its two double standards. Restrictions, guilt, and lack of pleasure in sex for the female, resort to prostitutes for the male, and the results of hypocritical verbal norms may have made family and individual adjustment

---

[46] Jeffrey Hadden and Marie Borgatta show how it is possible to overstate the changes that have occurred, making it appear that premarital intercourse is now "normative." They put it thus: "In a college newspaper an editorial may assert that sex on the campus is so commonplace as to be a part of the mores. This kind of statement does not take into account the distinction between permissive patterns and normative patterns at another level. Persons are not prepared to ask the corollary question [concerning premarital sex as a new moral norm]: Is it immoral *not* to be involved in premarital sexual affairs?" (Italics added.) The fact that our answer to such a question is likely to be, "Of course not," indicates that premarital intercourse cannot be considered the "new norm." See Jeffrey K. Hadden and Marie L. Borgatta, eds., *Marriage and the Family* (Itasca, Ill.: Peacock, 1969), p. 219.

even more difficult than they are today. Though the process of change is still in midstream, its direction seems to be toward a reduction of the former confusions.

The last phrase is questionable if one assumes that the competing value systems are the end of the process. But they are not. They are, rather, a stage on the way *toward an individual-choice approach* to premarital sex. Indications supporting this conclusion can be traced historically as follows. In the post–World War II era of the Kinsey reports a new openness regarding sexual matters emerged. This was followed in the 1950s by a period of titillation and obsession with sex. Some deplored it, some embraced it, and many wanted advice—which their peers and societal experts were only too ready to give. During the early 1960s, one found in the United States the competing value systems described by Rubin. This is where the majority of middle-class adults still appear to be in the 1970s; that is, they are still debating the moral implications of premarital intercourse. Among young people, however, the beginnings of a further development can be discerned. There are signs that evangelism in support of some value stance and the seeking of advice have both begun to give way to a more laissez-faire attitude. Everyone should define his own morality or "do his own thing" in this area: whether he wants to indulge or abstain until marriage is his business. One recent study, for example, that of Robinson, King, and Balswick, reported that between 1965 and 1970 the percentages stating that "sexual behavior is a person's own business" rose from 85 to 96 for males and, more important, from 75 to 94 for females.[47] "Patient indifference" seems to be an increasing response of young people to the expert's presentation of the latest facts on premarital sex, replacing the old fascination and commitment regarding sexual matters. This conclusion, however, is based not so much on research as on the author's contact with young people during the 1960s and 1970s. The reader may still want to debate the question of just how far the adolescent peer group has progressed toward this sort of naturalism or individualistic morality in the area of premarital sex.

Though some would brand these developments as anarchy, it is unquestionable that individualism is more advanced in this area than in many others relating to our family system, in which domestic and individualist values are competing at present. The reason for this advanced individual freedom in premarital sex becomes apparent when we compare it with extramarital sex. Extramarital sex is seen as a threat to marital adjustment and thus to the nuclear family; the conflict of the value of domestic adjustment with the individual value of sexual freedom is decided at present in

---

[47] Robinson, King, and Balswick, "The Premarital Sexual Revolution Among College Females," p. 192.

favor of the former. By contrast, with pregnancy fears lessened, adults find it increasingly difficult to argue that premarital intercourse is detrimental to the stability of the family system.[48] Furthermore, that premarital sex is becoming an individual matter within the adolescent peer group is consistent with the combination of a participant-run dating system and emphasis upon individual adjustment in the family. Individual adjustment, a basic criterion of family success, has become central to premarital relationships as well. Thus, one's sexual adjustment prior to marriage competes with adherence to the traditional notion of sexual continence for the sake of a virgin bride and legitimate offspring.[49] Young people increasingly predicate their indulgence in or abstinence from premarital sex upon whether or not it is perceived as making for good personal adjustment—a sense of well-being.

In the lower class, many of the changes we have been discussing have simply not occurred. Premarital intercourse has been widespread in the lower class for centuries, and is still more widespread there than in the middle class. An important difference, however, is that premarital intercourse in the lower class has been primarily a matter of exploitation by the male and defenselessness or ignorance on the part of the female. The distinction between this approach and that of the middle class, with its adjustment basis and its concern for female as well as male enjoyment, is embodied in Reiss's description of "respectable" permissiveness in the middle class. This new type of permissiveness places a high value on intellectual autonomy and, while it may be defined as deviant behavior by parents, it is not viewed as such by the young people themselves.[50]

In summary, neither intercourse nor sexual continence can be considered normative in adolescent society. Rather, the norm shows signs of becoming individual choice, without either the Freudian fascination or the moral overtones that still preoccupy the adult generation. Individualism in this area is likely to be defined as anarchy rather than as freedom by that large number of persons who prefer well-defined guidelines (traditions) to

---

[48] In their 1965 article, Pope and Knudsen argue that premarital sexual norms are and will continue to be "connected with maintenance of family lines and position" unless "social arrangements that allow separation of premarital coitus from unwed parenthood are also adopted." See Pope and Knudsen, "Premarital Sexual Norms, the Family, and Social Change," p. 322. This author would argue that much of that separation has, in fact, been accomplished.

[49] "The arrangement," which has become prevalent enough among college student couples to receive attention from the press, is one illustration of concern with sexual adjustment. The arrangement is a situation in which an unmarried young man and woman live together as if they were married, in order to discover, if possible, whether or not they are suited for each other sexually and otherwise, without the responsibilities and legal entanglements of marriage. This approach differs from the historical radical and bohemian rejection of marriage and the nuclear family in that the majority of the participants indicate their expectation of marriage and a home in the not-too-distant future. We shall mention the arrangement again in Chapter 16.

[50] Reiss, *The Social Context of Premarital Sexual Permissiveness*, p. 178.

the necessity of making an individual evaluation and choice. But, whether the changes in premarital sexual attitudes and behavior are defined as anarchic, directionless, and problem-producing or as freeing, confusion-reducing, and adjustment-based continues to be primarily a matter of the value position of the observer.

Section Four

CONCLUSIONS

Dating is the focus of the participant-run courtship system of the United States, having become the basis of a continuum that ranges from casual heterosexual relationships to mate selection. Of recent origin, dating includes aspects in which individual and nuclear family values reinforce one another, for example, the view that personal choice is the most adequate basis for a happy or adjusted marriage. It also includes aspects in which individual and nuclear family values are in conflict, examples being parental intrusion and the strictures against heterogeneous dating. Dating has become institutionalized as the courtship system, but the norms governing behavior within the system are fluid and often problem-producing for the individual.

Premarital sex is an element of heterosexual activity which is more widespread in the lower class than in the middle class, though that difference is lessening. In the middle class there are currently several competing value approaches to premarital sex, with humanistic liberalism, or "sex with affection," apparently predominating empirically. However, there are signs that premarital intercourse is becoming increasingly a matter of individual choice among middle-class young people, neither commanding the undue attention nor possessing the moral overtones that it still does among middle-class adults. One reason for this is that the phenomenon poses so little threat to the family system. As William O'Neill indicates: "Conservatives continue to be unhappy about the rise of promiscuity and, of course, they resist it when they can. But it proved to be something they could live with."[51] Whether these developments are viewed positively or negatively is as likely to be based on the biases of the writer as on empirical evidence that they are either good or bad for the individual himself.

The result of the dating continuum is still marriage for most persons, and much research has been done to determine the factors which govern the choice of a mate. In Chapter 10 we examine those factors.

---

[51] William L. O'Neill, *Divorce in the Progressive Era* (New Haven, Conn.: Yale University Press, 1967), p. 141.

Love and Mate Selection in the United States

The societies of the Western world, unlike many other societies, have institutionalized romantic love as the basis for mate selection. Love does not, however, occur in vacuo. Among the conditions that may serve to limit love and mate selection are: the incest taboo, propinquity, and various subsocietal categories, such as race and religion. Factors that have been treated by different authors as enhancing love and increasing the likelihood of marriage are: common interests, shared values, complementary needs, empathy, and parental image. Yet mate selection is too complex to be reduced to a set of single factors; understanding is improved when selection is treated as a process. An important example of nonuniversal availability in American mate selection is racial intermarriage; a consideration of this issue closes the chapter.

Love, Kin Group, and Mate Selection

Love is an innate disposition, a complex emotion, which—like humor, anger, hate, fear, and jealousy—is a universal potentiality in human beings.[1] As universal potentialities, emotions that manifest themselves behaviorally may pose a threat to the structures and solidarities of societies. The behavioral manifestation of anger may be injury or murder, and, while societies permit anger, they take drastic measures against injury and murder in an attempt to control the disruptive aspects of the emotion. Fear—when expressed in either immobility or flight—can dissolve social solidarity. Therefore, a society must devise means to control fear; for example, magic may be used to allay anxiety and increase courage. The emotional attraction of one person for another, which we call love, has as its behavioral manifestation sexual relations. However, sexual relations are defined in human societies as integrally related to procreation and mating. Thus it is that three strong controls have been placed upon love in order to avoid or channel its behavioral manifesta-

---

[1] William J. Goode draws this conclusion in his article "The Theoretical Importance of Love," *American Sociological Review* 24 (1959), 38–47. A good compilation of views on attraction and love is found in Bernard I. Murstein, ed., *Theories of Attraction and Love* (New York: Springer, 1971).

tion. The most universal of these controls involves the *incest taboo,* which is based, as we said in Chapter 2, on the great potentiality for the development of love among immediate kin and on the equally great desire in most human societies for mating to occur exogamously with respect to this category of kin. The second control, which is stringently imposed when sexual relations are defined as strictly a matter of procreation, concerns the *prohibition of homosexuality,* since the sexual expression of emotional attachment between two members of the same sex cannot result in procreation.[2] Of primary interest in the present chapter is the third control, that over *choice of a marriage partner.* This is more variable than the first two; it also differs from incest and homosexuality prohibitions in the extent to which it controls not only the sexual manifestation of love, but the development of the emotion as well.

Why should a society attempt to control the nonincestuous development of love between members of the opposite sex? The most obvious answer, if the above argument is correct, must be that the members of that society are convinced that giving love free reign would be detrimental to structures and solidarities. By the expression *giving love free reign,* we mean allowing heterosexual love to be the only basis for mating and procreation. Thus, a further question arises: In what kind of society would social structures and solidarities be threatened if love were permitted to operate as the sole basis for mate selection? This would obviously be detrimental in a society whose basic functions are performed and controlled by kin groups. If economic productivity, political authority, inheritance, residential location, and religious symbols are controlled by the lineage or kin group, it is imperative that the marriage linkages of its offspring be arranged, or at least limited. Individuals and nuclear families are embedded in the kin group, which controls mate choice in order to guarantee the appropriate continuation of solidarities and functions. The "free reign" of romantic love is minimized by such mechanisms as child marriage, stringent definition of eligibles, and isolation from potential mates.[3]

Romantic love is not unique to the Western world. Given the opportunity, it can "break out" in any society. Variation from one society to another in the prevalence and desirability of love is thus not a matter of emotional capabilities, but of definition and control. Love is an inadequate basis for mating and sex relations in the kin-centered society, and is therefore

---

[2] One side effect of improved birth control methods, with the resultant increase in the separation of sexual relations from procreation, has been to reopen the question of the legitimacy of homosexuality. Though homosexuality is not likely to become an accepted part of the societal mores, there has been more debate on the practice in recent years than in earlier years, and the debate has been more intense in the United States than in many other societies.

[3] Goode, "The Theoretical Importance of Love," pp. 43–44.

defined negatively and controlled by the kin group. A love relationship may develop between mates, but this is not the basis for, nor even a necessary concomitant of, their marriage. "Kinfolk or immediate family," says Goode,

> can disregard the question of who marries whom, only if a marriage is not seen as a link between kin lines, only if no property, power, lineage honor, totemic relationships, and the like are believed to flow from the kin lines through the spouses to their offspring. Universally, however, these are believed to follow kin lines.[4]

The logical alternative to kin control of mating would be found in a society in which kin lines are totally unimportant and solidarities and functions are individual-based, with the domestic unit—if it exists—serving individual needs. In such a society, which can be observed nowhere in the empirical world, entirely free choice could be permitted; this choice would in all likelihood be based strictly upon emotional attraction. Such a scheme is related to Farber's "universal availability" conceptualization.

Between the two polar alternatives described above, that is, complete kin control and completely free choice, can be found several degrees of restriction upon love and mating. In the colonial American family, for example—in which the nuclear family dominated many functions and vied with the kin group for solidarity—choice was individual, but was greatly restricted by nuclear family and kin influences. In the contemporary U.S. family, in which individual values and functions compete with both nuclear family and kin solidarity, mate selection is, by choice, based on love; but family and kin still use various methods, often successful, to influence the process.

Love is, therefore, an emotional potential that is controlled to varying degrees by different societies. The amount of control varies directly with the degree to which institutional functions and personnel are embedded within the kin group. In modern American society, love has been institutionalized as the basis for personal choice of a mate, but even in this society diverse means are employed by family and kin to restrict the opportunity for love to develop.

Normatively, then, an American will cite love as the reason for his marriage. Love may cause marriage, but (1) what is love? (2) what causes it? and (3) how is it controlled in American society? The first question has seldom been answered directly. A novelist may view love viscerally and sexually, giving descriptions of the attraction one human being holds for another. A poet may ennoble love through the use of adjectives and hyperbole, as he "counts the ways" in which he is drawn to his beloved. The sociologist

---

[4] Goode, "The Theoretical Importance of Love," p. 43.

Robert Winch reduces love to a twofold definition, more causal than descriptive, which sees love as resulting from the person's (1) having certain attributes highly prized by me, and (2) meeting specific personal or psychological needs which I have.[5] Goode is perhaps most realistic when, having attempted a definition of his own, he admits that verbal definitions of the emotion called love "are notoriously open to attack."[6] It is better perhaps to refer to the experience without attempting an inclusive and conclusive definition, such as one might give for fear or anger, and to assume that most readers are sufficiently familiar with the phenomenon to provide their own intuitive perception of its meaning. Thus, we shall move on to a consideration of controls upon and causes of love in the United States, an approach that will very likely lead us closer to an understanding of love than would expending further effort in trying to define it.

Section One

NEGATIVE FACTORS IN MATE SELECTION

The negative or limiting factors in mate selection are those concerned with the question, Whom *won't* you marry? These factors include not only kin and family controls or restrictions, but any other conditions that limit the field of eligible persons. Though the direction of change in American society may be toward an increase in universal availability, the contemporary family system is still far from embodying that principle. There is considerable personal choice in the selection of a mate, but there are also factors that operate to limit that choice. In this section we shall take up three of the more important factors.

Incest Taboos

Since the prohibition against marrying close kin has already been discussed at length, it will only be referred to here. In the United States, as in the great majority of societies, this taboo involves parents and siblings, as well as other close kin of the ascending generation, such as aunts, uncles, and grandparents. First cousins are also ordinarily excluded from marriage, though examples of cousin marriage are reported from time to time. No distinction is made between parallel cousins and cross-cousins in terms of eligibility for marriage.

---

[5] Robert F. Winch, *Mate-Selection: A Study of Complementary Needs* (New York: Harper and Brothers, 1958).
[6] Goode, "The Theoretical Importance of Love," p. 41.

Propinquity

One seldom marries a person he has not seen, met, and interacted with; and one is more likely to interact with a person located nearby than with a person located at a distance. These self-evident facts introduce a second limiting condition upon mate selection—propinquity, or proximity. This obvious factor in mate selection was first described in detail by James H. S. Bossard in 1932. After investigating 5,000 marriages in Philadelphia, Bossard discovered that one-third of the couples applying for marriage licenses lived within five city blocks of each other, and that more than half lived twenty or fewer blocks apart.[7]

Subsequently, other researchers reported the same results: the closer to each other two persons live, the more likely they are to get married. Many writers interpreted the findings as another manifestation of homogamy. That is, people of the same social and cultural group tend to live close together. Thus, they interact more frequently, and, therefore, they marry each other. In 1958, Alvin Katz and Reuben Hill reviewed and summarized the research on propinquity by means of three propositions.[8] (1) *Marriage is normative*, or follows subcultural lines. This, of course, embodies the homogamy interpretation of many previous writers. (2) Within the normative field of eligibles, *the probability of marriage varies directly with the probability of interaction*. Many of us have heard stories about couples who correspond by letter for years and marry at their first meeting. These are the exceptions which prove the rule that the possibility of frequent interaction is the logical precondition for dating and marriage. (3) *The probability of interaction is lessened by intervening opportunities for interaction*. This might be called the density factor; it becomes apparent when we compare the likelihood that two persons on adjoining farms one-half mile apart will interact and become well-acquainted with the likelihood that two residents of dormitories or apartment buildings one-half mile apart will become acquainted.

The locational character of any given individual's life may not be stable. He may move from place to place, thus complicating the operation of propinquity. Thus, for example, we can say that a student at the University of Pennsylvania is more likely to marry a coed at the University of Pennsylvania than a coed at the University of Florida, unless he resided near the Florida coed at an earlier stage of their lives. This does not void the effect of propinquity, but merely complicates it.

A final factor which complicates the operation of propinquity in mate

---

[7] James H. S. Bossard, "Residential Propinquity as a Factor in Mate Selection," *American Journal of Sociology* 38 (1932), 219–24.

[8] Alvin M. Katz and Reuben Hill, "Residential Propinquity and Marital Selection: A Review of Theory, Method, and Fact," *Marriage and Family Living* 20 (1958), 27–35.

selection can be inferred from Wesley Burr's discussion of kin contacts. Ease of interaction—which, after all, is a necessary condition for marriage—is a function of proximity + resources.[9] Resources can bring you into proximity with many you would not otherwise meet, and interaction is easier once you are there.

The operation of incest taboos and propinquity as limiting or negative factors in mate selection is so obvious as to require only brief attention. Of more interest is the influence of the "background categories," and to that influence we turn next. .

Homogamy in Mate Selection

The third and final negative, or limiting, factor in American mate selection is in reality a complex of social structural categories. When availability allows, the person chosen as a mate is ordinarily from the same general social background as oneself. If, for example, one is a WASP (white Anglo-Saxon Protestant), the chances are pretty good that he will marry another WASP. Four categories within U.S. society have received substantial research attention with respect to their limitation upon mate selection. These are race, religion, ethnic or nationality group, and social class. One further terminological clarification is in order. Homogamy and heterogamy—the marriage of people who are alike and the marriage of people who are different—are simply opposite sides of the same coin. The same holds for endogamy and intermarriage—marriage within one's group and marriage outside one's group. These terms are used almost interchangeably in the literature; their relationship can be seen in the fact that if the rate of religious endogamy is 90 percent, then the rate of religious intermarriage is 10 percent. For the most part, we will use *homogamy* and *intermarriage,* the two terms most prevalent in the literature.

Studies of *racial* homogamy, or marriage within the same racial group, have generally divided the population into white and black and—if included in the sample—Native American, Chicano, and Oriental. The norms restricting racial intermarriage are extremely stringent; this issue will be dealt with at length in the last section of the chapter. Most investigations of *religious* intermarriage have been based on the threefold division into Protestants, Catholics, and Jews, although a few have further subdivided Protestants into the largest denominational groupings, such as Presbyterians, Methodists, Baptists, Lutherans, and Episcopalians, and Jews into Orthodox, Conservative, and Reformed. *Ethnic* or nationality categories are difficult to distinguish definitively from both racial and religious categories. Chicanos, for example,

---

[9] Wesley R. Burr, *Theory Construction and the Sociology of the Family* (New York: Wiley-Interscience, 1973), p. 150.

are actually an ethnic group, but are often treated as a racial category. Also, the members of many nationality groups are almost all of the same religion; for example, the vast majority of Italians are Roman Catholics, while Scandinavians are largely Lutheran. The United States comprises numerous ethnic groups, including the Irish, Spanish, Italians, Japanese, Chinese, Filipinos, Hungarians, Norwegians, Germans, Poles, and English. In some studies of ethnic homogamy, such national aggregates have been combined into more inclusive groupings, such as southeastern European, northwestern European, and so on. It is apparent that the possibilities of confusion, both within the ethnic category and between the ethnic category and race or religion, are substantial; studies of ethnic homogamy must, therefore, be interpreted cautiously. *Social class,* or status grouping, is the only one of the four structural designations that the individual himself is unlikely to make. The individual may say: "I am a white Irish Catholic," but he is unlikely to add: "I am upper middle class," or "I am working class." Thus, while an observer will recognize that there are actual differences in education, income, and occupation within U.S. society, and that these differences have behavioral manifestations, it may be argued that social class designations are artifacts of the investigator. Some studies of social class homogamy have divided the population into only two categories, middle class and working class, or—according to occupation—white collar and blue collar. Others have dichotomized each of these categories into upper and lower, while still others have used as many as six or seven class divisions. Of course, the rate of intermarriage reported is bound to fluctuate as a result of the number of categories employed. Since social class divisions are made by observers using various indicators, and not by the population itself,[10] it might be well to indicate the possible interpretations of social class homogamy which seem viable. According to Bruce Eckland, *class endogamy,* the term he uses for homogamy, may be explained by: (1) similar values, which reflect within-class cultural similarity; (2) residential segregation along class lines (noted in the discussion of propinquity); (3) the close relation between class and ethnicity-race; (4) family pressure to marry one's "own kind"; (5) educational advantages or disadvantages that cause class differences to persist. These five explanations show once again the interrelations between the four categories used in homogamy studies. Therefore, keeping in mind the cautions concerning interrelationships among categories and the arbitrary nature of the number of subdivisions within each of them, let us turn to the research on homogamy rates.

The general tendency in American society is for homogeneity between

---

[10] Many studies conducted since World War II show that people do have a general notion of the meaning of the terms *upper class, middle class, working class,* and *lower class.* This is partially a consequence of the constant use of these terms by sociologists since the early 1930s.

mates (according to the four categories) to persist. Eckland summarizes the rates of homogamy (drawn from numerous studies) as follows: "Most studies in the United States report a very high rate, over 99 percent, for racial homogamy, an overall rate perhaps as high as 90 percent for religious homogamy, and moderately high rates, 50 percent to 80 percent for class homogamy."[11] The 90 percent rate of religious homogamy is based primarily on studies that divide the population into only three religious categories—Protestant, Catholic, and Jewish.[12] When a further breakdown of Protestant and Jewish groups is employed, the rate becomes 75 percent marrying within their own denomination or religious subdivision. This finding causes both Andrew Greeley and Ruth Cavan to conclude that the United States is still very much a denominational society.[13] Also, Eckland's 80 percent figure for class homogamy is based on studies that dichotomize the population into middle and working class, while his 50 percent limit is drawn from studies employing six or seven divisions. Finally, Eckland does not deal with ethnic homogamy, but if six to ten of the most populous nationality groupings are considered, the homogamy rate is fairly close to that for religion when the same number of categories is used. Thus, racial homogamy is most nearly complete at present; the rate of social class homogamy is the lowest; the rates for the other two social categories are about equal and are dependent to a large extent on how many subdivisions are utilized.

When we turn from the consideration of comparative rates to trends in the rates, we find that social class intermarriage rates are hardly changing at all, that intermarriage between ethnic categories has increased gradually, that religious intermarriage increased considerably between the 1940s and the 1960s, then leveled off, and that racial intermarriage is increasing slightly, though more between certain racial categories than others. A key reason for the increase in religious intermarriage was the decreasing salience of the religious subdivisions in American life; as the importance of such differences diminished, emphasis upon homogamy according to religion also diminished. This trend was much more noticeable when the three general religious categories—Protestants, Catholics, and Jews—were subdivided than when only intermarriages among the three were considered. The increase in religious intermarriage was a gradual, but perceptible, process in the twentieth century United States up until very recently. A key cause of the decrease in

---

[11] Bruce K. Eckland, "Theories of Mate Selection," *Eugenics Quarterly* 15 (1968), 79.

[12] August B. Hollingshead, "Cultural Factors in the Selection of Marriage Mates," *American Sociological Review* 15 (1950), 622. This article is a good example of a study based on the trichotomization of religious bodies into Protestant, Catholic, and Jewish.

[13] Andrew M. Greeley, "Religious Intermarriage in a Denominational Society," *American Journal of Sociology* 75 (1970), 949–52; and Ruth Shonle Cavan, "Jewish Student Attitudes Toward Interreligious and Intra-Jewish Marriage," *American Journal of Sociology* 76 (1971), 1064–71.

ethnic group solidarity was the cessation of large-scale immigration during the 1920s, resulting in the "Americanization" of the immigrants and their offspring.[14] Black-white intermarriage, as we shall note in the closing section of this chapter, has been very slow to increase, but the same cannot be said for intermarriage between Japanese-Americans and whites. A weakening of Japanese-American cultural distinctiveness, and the desire on the part of Japanese-American females to escape the traditional submissive sex role, may have been factors contributing to the rise in outmarriage from 30 percent in the 1950s to 50 percent by 1970.[15] In general, says Lawrence Guillot in Feature 5, the fences around intermarriage are being knocked down.

The influence of social categories upon mate selection in the United States can be recapitulated by reviewing the significance of four terms: consciousness, availability, visibility, and salience. The question, "What social categories do you belong to?" is not always, and perhaps *not* even usually, verbalized or *consciously applied* to one's dating partners. Yet limitation does occur, if not as a conscious process, then as a result of feeling more "at home" with a partner of similar background or as a result of the residential segregation imposed by parents' choice of location. The mention of residential segregation leads to the second issue in homogamy, that of *availability*. August Hollingshead's and John Thomas' articles on homogamy illustrate the importance of this factor. Hollingshead found that in New Haven only 6.2 percent of the Catholic marriages were with non-Catholics, while Thomas reported that in the state of Connecticut as a whole 40.2 percent of Catholics who married, married persons of other religious faiths.[16] This

---

[14] This is reported in Will Herberg, *Protestant-Catholic-Jew* (Garden City, N.Y.: Doubleday, 1955).

[15] John N. Tinker, "Intermarriage and Ethnic Boundaries: The Japanese-American Case," *Journal of Social Issues* 29 (1973), 49–66; and Akemi Kikumura and Harry H. L. Kitano, "Interracial Marriage: A Picture of the Japanese-Americans," *Journal of Social Issues* 29 (1973), 67–81. The reader may wish to reexamine the author's interpretation of trends by reviewing the following studies of homogamy and intermarriage, in addition to those referred to above: T. C. Hunt, "Occupational Status and Marriage Selection," *American Sociological Review* 5 (1940), 495–504; Ernest W. Burgess and Paul Wallin, "Homogamy in Social Characteristics," *American Journal of Sociology* 49 (1943), 117–24; Richard Centers, "Marital Selection and Occupational Strata," *American Journal of Sociology* 54 (1949), 530–35; Simon Dinitz, Franklin Banks, and Benjamin Pasamanick, "Mate Selection and Social Class: Changes During the Past Quarter Century," *Marriage and Family Living* 22 (1960), 348–51; Harvey J. Locke, Georges Sabagh, and Mary Margaret Thomes, "Inter-faith Marriages," *Social Problems* 4 (1957), 329–33; David M. Heer, "The Trend of Interfaith Marriages in Canada: 1922–1957," *American Sociological Review* 27 (1962), 245–50; Lee G. Burchinal and Loren E. Chancellor, "Ages at Marriage, Occupations of Grooms, and Interreligious Marriage Rates," *Social Forces* 40 (1962), 348–54; Burchinal and Chancellor, "Survival Rates Among Religiously Homogamous and Interreligious Marriages," *Social Forces* 41 (1963), 353–62; and Glenn M. Vernon, "Bias in Professional Publications Concerning Interfaith Marriages," *Religious Education* 55 (1960), 261–64. Several studies on racial intermarriage are listed in notes 54f.

[16] Hollingshead, "Cultural Factors in the Selection of Marriage Mates," p. 622; and John L. Thomas, "The Factor of Religion in the Selection of Marriage Mates," *American Sociological Review* 16 (1951), 487–92.

divergence, Thomas feels, is to be explained principally by availability. That is, the Catholic who grows up in a predominantly Protestant community is much more likely to marry a Protestant than is the Catholic who grows up in a ghettolike Catholic neighborhood in a city such as New Haven. Thus, the nonavailability of persons of one's own background is a key factor in various sorts of intermarriage (and is related to the propinquity factor discussed earlier).

A third influence upon the operation of background categories in limiting mate selection is *visibility*. Recognition of the influence of the visibility factor makes it easy to see why religious intermarriage is more frequent than racial intermarriage. However, even more important is the fourth and final influence upon homogamy—*salience*. Two persons of different races who say, "Sure we are of different races, but what difference does it make?" may very well get married. But an interracial couple who say, "We are strongly attracted, but, conditions being what they are, our racial difference would be bound to cause our children and us lots of heartaches," are demonstrating that their racial difference is salient to them. The salience or nonsalience of each of the four social categories could be illustrated in a similar way by asking: "Does their background heterogeneity matter to the couple, or doesn't it?" If it matters, it may not stand in the way of dating for enjoyment or experience, but it may very well stop them from marrying. Burr makes it

FEATURE 5

In one sense every wedding is an intermarriage because it joins persons with some differences. Our society has a segregating character because some marriages are threatening—to personal values, group identity or group survival. Interestingly, we have culturally focussed most of our attention on nationality, race and religion and almost none on other marital factors like class, physical constitution, regional background or politics. . . .

The rate of interracial marriages, which is probably of most interest today, is the least frequent, but occurring two and a half times more frequently now than in 1930. Also evident is the increasing ineffectiveness of restrictions on any of these categories of marriages by either the state or the churches. What little is known about what happens afterward indicates that most of the warnings and diatribes predicting certain dire consequences for intermarriages have been badly overstated.

Growing mass participation in middle class culture seems to be shaping the trends more than anything else. In plastic, semiliberated middle America, ethnic, religious and to a lesser extent racial differences are minimized and obscured. When Joe and Sue have the cars, the same kind of clothes, the same schools, and feel closer to each other's world than to the world of their parents, most of the fences around "intermarriages" are knocked down.

Lawrence Guillot, "Every Wedding Is an Intermarriage," *Kansas City Times*, June 17, 1972, 16C, a review of Milton L. Barron's *The Blending American*.

very plain that salience acts to temper the influence of the background categories upon mate selection.[17] We might diagram the role of salience as follows:

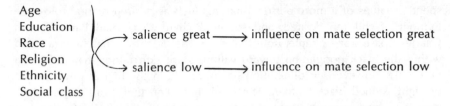

Age
Education
Race
Religion
Ethnicity
Social class

salience great ⟶ influence on mate selection great

salience low ⟶ influence on mate selection low

Farber makes a very good point when he says that "intermarriage is occurring not only because of a breakdown in parental control over mate selection, but also because the traditional social categories for inmarriage are themselves becoming vague and diffuse."[18] This decrease in salience is particularly noticeable in college populations, but does not hold for racial barriers to the extent that it does for the other three social categories.[19] The question of salience or nonsalience is really one of values, of what matters to the individual. An individual who values highly a particular aspect of his background or a particular characteristic of his group is unlikely to compromise it for the sake of marriage. When viewed in a broader perspective, however, the notion of values introduces us to the positive factors in mate selection. Thus, at this point let us examine the factors that determine the answer to the question, "Among the eligibles, which one will you pick?"

Section Two

POSITIVE FACTORS IN MATE SELECTION

Values in Mate Selection

After incest taboos, the necessity of propinquity, and the pressure of social group ties have narrowed the field of eligibles, the young person finds that other factors affect his dating and mate selection. A question that is likely to arise as one becomes more seriously inclined toward a dating partner might

---

[17] Burr, *Theory Construction and the Sociology of the Family*, p. 87.
[18] Bernard Farber, *Family: Organization and Interaction* (San Francisco: Chandler, 1964), p. 152.
[19] On this, see Gerald R. Leslie and Arthur H. Richardson, "Family Versus Campus Influences in Relation to Mate Selection," *Social Problems* 4 (1956), 117–21; and Albert I. Gordon, *Intermarriage: Interfaith, Interracial, Interethnic* (Boston: Beacon Press, 1964), p. 38. The strictness of racial endogamy norms in U.S. society will be considered at length in Section Five of this chapter.

be expressed thus: "Do we see eye to eye on the things that matter to me?" Salience and similarity, or mutual nonsalience (a matter's being considered as unimportant by both members of the couple), are important not only with respect to religious, racial, ethnic and status distinctions, but also with respect to values of a more personal nature, such as desired marital roles, the number of children desired, and so on. Richard Udry, Karl Bauman, and Charles Chase, for example, note that since the '50s there has been a trend within the black population toward valuing dark skin rather than light skin in a male. However, no diminution has occurred in the higher valuation set on light-skinned black women. The result has been that more darker black men have been marrying lighter black women—a direct effect of values on mate selection.[20] Yet, it must be admitted that there is marked disagreement concerning the importance of values as possible selective factors. Robert Coombs, in an article entitled "A Value Theory of Mate Selection," suggests that most other theories can be incorporated into and explained by a value theory that includes background factors, propinquity, and personal values.[21] Eckland reviews the mate selection theories and qualifies the influence of values on mate selection. "Apparently," he says, "our *perception* that other persons share with us the same or similar value orientations and beliefs facilitates considerably our attraction to them." (Italics added.) This idea that perception of consensus is more crucial than actual consensus is consistent with many social psychological studies of friendship attraction.[22] However, Eloise Snyder's study of 561 students of primarily rural background beclouds the issue by asserting that similarity of attitudes among marital pairs appears to be "the result of the adjustive interaction shared by the couple and not necessarily an affinity present at the outset of the relationship."[23] In other words, attraction may be the basis for increased perception of value consensus or even for an actual increase in consensus, or consensus may produce attraction.

Thus, values may have some influence upon mate selection which is separate from that based on salient social categories, but the extent of this positive influence is impossible to ascertain from most of the available studies.

---

[20] J. Richard Udry, Karl E. Bauman, and Charles Chase, "Skin Color, Status, and Mate Selection," *American Journal of Sociology* 76 (1971), 722–33.

[21] Robert H. Coombs, "A Value Theory of Mate Selection," *The Family Life Coordinator* 10 (1961), 51–54.

[22] Eckland, "Theories of Mate Selection," p. 80. On perceived similarity, see Anthony J. Smith, "Similarity of Values and Its Relation to Acceptance and the Projection of Similarity," *Journal of Psychology* 43 (1957), 251–60; Joseph A. Precker, "Values as a Factor in the Selection of Associates," *Dissertation Abstracts* 12 (1952), 107; and Carl W. Backman and Paul F. Secord, "Liking, Selective Interaction, and Misperception in Congruent Interpersonal Relations," *Sociometry* 25 (1962), 321–35.

[23] Eloise C. Snyder, "Attitudes: A Study of Homogamy and Marital Selectivity," *Journal of Marriage and the Family* 26 (1964), 336.

Common Interests

Occasionally one hears that two musicians are marrying in order to make beautiful music together forever. George Bernard Shaw portrays his acquaintances the Webbs thus: "two typewriters beating as one." One or a few common interests may be the major motivating force behind a marriage, but such cases are exceptional enough to be newsworthy. Unquestionably, common interests, or activities enjoyed together, form one foundation for a durable dating relationship; this relationship, in turn, is the typical prelude to marriage in U.S. society. Yet, a direct link between such interests and the ultimate choice of a mate is doubtful in most cases. Related research by Purnell Benson has shown that certain kinds of common interests may be detrimental to a satisfactory engagement or marriage, and that there is little or no relation between the *number* of common interests and adjustment in either engagement or marriage. Common familistic interests, such as home, children, and religion, are characteristic of well-adjusted engaged persons, while individualistic and pleasure-seeking interests, such as success, drinking, money, travel, commercial entertainments, and companionship as a means to avoid loneliness, are more prevalent among poorly adjusted engaged couples.[24]

If Benson's findings are slightly reinterpreted, the interests related to good adjustment can be seen to be values of the sort discussed in the previous section, while the pleasure-seeking interests are the enjoyments and activities that are the major focus of the term *common interests*. Does this, then, mean that common activity interests, though important in the early stages of a relationship, come to be detrimental as the relationship becomes more serious? Is the long-term result of activity interests either an unhappy engagement or an unhappy marriage? It seems that a better interpretation of Benson's results would be as follows: Common activity interests may be an excellent beginning point for a premarital relationship. However, if that relationship reaches the engagement stage with the couple still having nothing more in common than the activities and personal pleasures that originally brought them together, then the engagement is precarious. In the absence of a deeper and more serious value consensus, common activities form a superficial and inadequate basis for a stable engagement and marriage— unless an activity has been transformed into a basic value or goal, as in the cases of the Webbs and the musicians. The "superficial" activity-based engagement or marriage exemplifies Husbands' criticism of U.S. dating and mate selection in general, and may illustrate Charles Bolton's concept of escalated

---

[24] Purnell Benson, "The Interests of Happily Married Couples," *Marriage and Family Living* 14 (1952), 276–80; and Benson, "The Common Interest Myth in Marriage," *Social Problems* 3 (1955), 27–34.

commitment, in which a couple has been impelled toward marriage by various "pushes," including pressure from significant others.[25]

Benson's research, the reader may have noticed, does *not* say that persons do not marry on the basis of pleasure-seeking interests, but rather that this is an inadequate basis for a *satisfactory* marriage. To the present author it seems that any increased societal tendency to define marriage as a *voidable* relationship might be accompanied by an increased tendency to marry for reasons of enjoyment, without any deeper value commitments. Farber speaks of the movement in American society toward *permanent* availability, so that if a marriage does not work out the couple are free to break ties and try again. If this movement has progressed since Benson wrote in the early 1950s, common activity interests may actually be more prevalent as a basis for mate selection at the present time. A couple may feel that common interests and enjoyment are sufficient to justify a marriage, whether or not they are an adequate basis for its permanence. This, however, is an interpretation that can be held only tentatively, pending further research on activity interests and mate selection.

Complementary Needs

"Birds of a feather flock together." "Opposites attract." For centuries the concepts embodied in these two aphorisms have existed side by side in the chronicles of human thought. Both concepts have likewise made their way into the scholarship pertaining to mate selection in American society. The concept embodied in the first aphorism is inherent in the previously discussed tendency toward categorical homogamy, while the concept embodied in the second is the essence of Robert Winch's argument that love, and therefore mate selection, is attributable to need complementarity. The reader will recall that Winch's definition of love included attraction to another who shows promise of meeting one's psychological needs. He explicates this idea throughout his book *Mate-Selection*, detailing at length that the way needs are gratified is by finding a partner whose personality characteristics are the opposite of, but complementary to, one's own.[26] If you are basically a submissive person, you will seek as a mate someone who will dominate you. If you are a "nurturant" person (need to have things done for you), the mate you choose will be a succorant, or receptive, person (that is, someone who is gratified by doing things for others). Winch's intensive study of 25 married student couples at Northwestern University revealed the presence of these and other complementary need patterns, which Winch assumed to have been

---

[25] C. T. Husbands, "Some Social and Psychological Consequences of the American Dating System," *Adolescence* 5 (1970), 452; Charles D. Bolton, "Mate Selection as the Development of a Relationship," *Marriage and Family Living* 23 (1961), 234–40.

[26] Winch, *Mate-Selection*.

a key factor in their selection of each other as mates. What is attractive about this theory is its fascinating simplicity and its intuitive reasonableness. The problem it presents is the inconclusive nature of the evidence. Winch and his students Thomas and Virginia Ktsanes are among the few who have been able to compile any evidence that complementary psychological undercurrents are operative in the mate selection process.[27] On the other hand, research by Schellenberg and Bee, Bowerman and Day, and Murstein discloses a random relation between complementarity and mate selection.[28] That is, for every couple characterized by a particular form of complementarity, another couple can be found whose members share the same general personality traits. In a study of 47 married and 50 engaged couples, J. Richard Udry noted a tendency to project one's own traits onto the partner. Furthermore, he found no evidence of general complementarity in mate selection, though some asymmetrical specific complementarity was discovered.[29] Winch's traits are too broad, Udry feels, to be useful as predictors of mate choice. In a study of Kent State students B. A. Seyfried and Clyde Hendrick, likewise, found the support for the complementary needs hypothesis to be quite weak. Rather, subjects seemed attracted on the basis of need similarity. Seyfried and Hendrick note, however, that their subjects may be responding to similarity of attitudes rather than similarity of more basic "need states." Perhaps, they conclude, complementary attraction may actually be based on certain types of roles or role playing rather than on deeper personality needs (recall McDaniel's distinction between playing a "receptive" role and having an internalized receptiveness in one's personality).[30] One further study has made an interesting attempt to get at complementarity in heterosexual relations. Augustus Napier reports a tendency to marry someone whose parents play their roles in a fashion opposite to one's own. However, he finds that the

---

[27] Robert F. Winch, "The Theory of Complementary Needs in Mate Selection: Final Results on the Test of the General Hypothesis," *American Sociological Review* 20 (1955), 552–55; Winch and Thomas and Virginia Ktsanes, "Empirical Elaboration of the Theory of Complementary Needs in Mate-Selection," *Journal of Abnormal and Social Psychology* 51 (1955), 508–14; Winch, Ktsanes, and Ktsanes, "The Theory of Complementary Needs in Mate-Selection: An Analytic and Descriptive Study," *American Sociological Review* 19 (1954), 241–49; Thomas Ktsanes, "Mate Selection on the Basis of Personality Type: A Study Utilizing an Empirical Typology of Personality," *American Sociological Review* 20 (1955), 547–51; and Horace Gray, "Psychological Types in Married People," *Journal of Social Psychology* 29 (1949), 189–200.

[28] Charles E. Bowerman and Barbara R. Day, "A Test of the Theory of Complementary Needs as Applied to Couples During Courtship," *American Sociological Review* 21 (1956), 602–5; James A. Schellenberg and Lawrence S. Bee, "A Re-examination of the Theory of Complementary Needs in Mate Selection," *Marriage and Family Living* 22 (1960), 227–32; and Bernard I. Murstein, "The Complementary Needs Hypothesis in Newlyweds and Middle-Aged Married Couples," *Journal of Abnormal and Social Psychology* 63 (1961), 194–97.

[29] J. Richard Udry, "Complementarity in Mate Selection: A Perceptual Approach," *Marriage and Family Living* 25 (1963), 281–89.

[30] B. A. Seyfried and Clyde Hendrick, "Need Similarity and Complementarity in Interpersonal Attraction," *Sociometry* 36 (1973), 207–20; and Clyde O. McDaniel, "Dating Roles and Reasons for Dating," *Journal of Marriage and the Family* 31 (1969), 100.

couple themselves are characterized by a complex mix of similarity and complementarity.[31] As he puts it: "You are like me, you remind me of myself, but you are also strange and different."

Winch, it should be noted, has never said that complementarity is the only factor governing mate selection in the United States. Rather, he feels, it operates to weed out the bad bets after homogeneity considerations have already greatly limited the field of eligibles. In his latest article on the subject, he suggests that complementarity should perhaps be supplemented by the concept of role compatibility.[32] Thus, despite our attempts to isolate and examine individually the factors in mate selection, Winch, Napier, and other recent authors will not let us ignore the interrelations and complexities. These interrelations will be the topic of a later section of this chapter, after several additional positive factors have been introduced.

Other Psychological Factors in Mate Selection

Various researchers have proposed several other psychological factors to account for mate selection, but the evidence for the influence of these factors is meager. Ernest Burgess and Paul Wallin, and Anselm Strauss, writing prior to the appearance of Winch's complementary needs theory and using data on a well-educated sample of 373 engaged or recently married persons, found that *personality needs* influence mate choice. Burgess and Wallin claim that "a high proportion of persons fail to find the satisfaction of their chief personality needs in their relation with their mates. Yet the fulfillment of personality needs appears to be of primary importance in mate selection."[33] In other words, the individual has needs and he finds the mate who he feels will come closest to meeting them. However, the mate is unlikely to be able to meet all of his needs, or, for that matter, to satisfy any of them completely. What sorts of needs are Burgess and Wallin talking about? Strauss gives some hints in the following observations:

> The person had as a child emotional experiences which have developed in her the need for recognition, approval, gentle consideration, emotional support, and the like. These psychological necessities, whether consciously or unwittingly sought, quite understandably enter into the girl's anticipations of married life and more or less determine her ideal.[34]

---

[31] Augustus Y. Napier, "The Marriage of Families: Cross-Generational Complementarity," *Family Process* 9 (1971), 373–95.

[32] Robert F. Winch, "Another Look at the Theory of Complementary Needs in Mate Selection," *Journal of Marriage and the Family* 29 (1967), 756–62.

[33] Ernest W. Burgess and Paul Wallin, *Engagement and Marriage* (Philadelphia: Lippincott, 1953), p. 202.

[34] Anselm Strauss, "The Ideal and the Chosen Mate," *American Journal of Sociology* 52 (1946), 207.

Little evidence has been compiled since the Strauss–Burgess-Wallin research that would indicate more precisely the manner in which these needs operate in mate selection. Perhaps they operate as Winch claims: one searches out as a mate a person who is perceived as able to meet one's needs because that person's needs and personality are opposite and complementary. Strauss does hint that this notion is also related to some sort of ideal mate that the individual seeks. His own needs help to structure the ideal, and that ideal may in turn influence his mate choice. Most persons, or so the argument goes, develop some conception of the kind of person they want as a mate and carry it with them throughout their dating experience. This *ideal mate concept* may include physical characteristics, personality characteristics, cultural traits, or some combination of all three. However, the problem raised by the ideal mate concept as a positive factor in mate selection is very similar to that raised by the values concept. Udry writes:

> What is the significance of ideal mate conceptions for mate selection? From this study, it appears that the ideal mate is not an actual basis of mate selection. . . . mates are selected on some other basis without regard to pre-existing ideal mate images. Furthermore, the ideal mate images are not attributed to selected persons, but probably change in response to new relationships into which the person enters. Ideal mate images can therefore be seen as resultants—reflecting need structures, changing in response to changing interpersonal relationships, responding to experiences with particular people—rather than determinants of heterosexual selections.[35]

As we noted above, Strauss believes that the ideal mate image influenced the mate choice of at least some of his sample; he also thinks that this image might have served to exclude certain categories of persons from consideration. In other words, he feels that the ideal acts as a limiting factor for many persons, and as a selective factor for some. Yet we are again confronted with overlapping concepts: Strauss finds that for many persons the ideal includes the qualities that we discussed earlier under the heading of "homogamy." The concept of the ideal mate, like the concept of values, can be interpreted broadly enough to incorporate most of the other factors. However, if homogamy is omitted from the ideal mate concept, we are forced to agree with Udry's assessment that the ideal mate image is not a selective factor in mate selection—at least until further evidence is provided.

A third possible psychological or personality factor in mate selection, which has been linked by Strauss and others with the ideal mate image, is *parental image*. A narrow application of this factor is indicated in the words

---

[35] J. Richard Udry, "The Influence of the Ideal Mate Image on Mate Selection and Mate Perception," *Journal of Marriage and the Family* 27 (1965), 477–82.

of the song: "I want a girl just like the girl that married dear old Dad." However, Burgess and Wallin find several patterns of attraction other than that based on the similarity of one's chosen mate to the opposite-sex parent. These include attraction to a person who: is similar to the same-sex parent, is the opposite of one or the other parent, combines characteristics of both parents, or has the traits of a surrogate parent.[36] Napier adds that it is insufficient to see one's partner as simply an "oedipal" choice, or as a "reasonable facsimile" of one's opposite-sex parent. The new mate, says Napier, is a rebellion against, a fulfillment of, and a repetition of that parent. But he also represents other members of the individual's family of origin.[37] In light of this multiplicity of possibilities and the ordinarily post hoc nature of the linkages, Eckland's conclusion should not be too surprising. He maintains that though it "would seem reasonable to expect parent images to either encourage or discourage a person marrying someone like his parent, no clear evidence has been produced to support the hypothesis."[38]

Some time ago Clifford Kirkpatrick and Charles Hobart studied 306 couples at Indiana University.[39] These couples included 62 who were "favorite dates," 66 who were going steady, 75 who were engaged, and 103 who were married. The authors' major concerns were to trace disagreements and *empathic ability* (or the ability to predict the action, thoughts, and feelings of one's partner accurately, that is, to put oneself in his shoes). They found that empathic ability was much greater among couples who were going steady than among those in the favorite date category. Similarly, the ability was greater in married couples than in engaged couples. Yet, since this was not a longitudinal study, following the same couples through all four stages, these differences had to be interpreted cautiously. Is it length of association that increases empathic ability, or is it selectivity, with the nonempathic couples weeding themselves out at certain points? According to the authors, the latter explanation is more satisfactory than the former, since *within* each of the four categories there was no correlation between length of dating and empathy score. Kirkpatrick and Hobart conclude that when a couple define their relationship as "steady" or "married," they decide that it is time to find out more about each other, thereby increasing empathic ability. Of course, with increased empathy, one may either like or dislike what he dis-

---

[36] Burgess and Wallin, *Engagement and Marriage*, p. 197.

[37] Napier, "The Marriage of Families," p. 387.

[38] Eckland, "Theories of Mate Selection." As in the case of common interests, there are data showing that if the spouse resembles one's ideal and one's opposite-sex parent, marital adjustment is better. This, however, cannot be used as evidence for mate choice, only for later satisfaction. See Eleanor Braun Luckey, "Perceptual Congruence of Self and Family Concepts as Related to Marital Interaction," *Sociometry* 24 (1961), 234–50.

[39] Clifford Kirkpatrick and Charles Hobart, "Disagreement, Disagreement Estimate, and Non-Empathic Imputations for Intimacy Groups Varying from Favorite Date to Married," *American Sociological Review* 19 (1954), 10–19.

covers about his partner, so that empathy may act either to perpetuate or to terminate the relationship. Can this factor, therefore, be considered a positive factor in mate selection? Only if it is combined with values and interests to constitute an "understanding-agreement" factor—another interrelation among factors!

What conclusions can be drawn regarding personality needs, ideal mate image, parent image, and empathy as factors in mate selection? With the present state of research, empathy appears to be the psychological factor most closely correlated with mate selection. However, one difficulty with the other psychological factors is simply the need for better measuring instruments and more data. Another difficulty appears to lie in the attempt to treat these and other positive and negative factors as if they were static, rather than in process. A third difficulty lies in the complex relationships among the various factors that we have isolated analytically and discussed individually. Let us take up these last two difficulties.

Section Three

MATE SELECTION AS PROCESS

Winch never claimed, we have said, that complementary needs are the only factor in mate selection, but rather that they act as a final filter, weeding out the bad bets and aiding the individual in his choice. The notion of a filtering process leads us to the consideration of an extremely provocative article of Alan Kerckhoff and Keith Davis. Stated summarily, the authors' claim is that mate selection is not a matter of either homogamy or heterogamy, that is, of marrying likes in background or unlikes in needs. Instead, all these factors—background group memberships, values and interests, and complementary needs—may in fact operate at various stages of a courtship, from its inception to marriage.[40] Thus, if these factors are salient, the individual will limit his dating experience at the outset to persons of roughly the same social background as himself. Race, religion, and social class have already limited his choices when he begins dating, though this limitation may be unconscious or may be determined by residential location and other parental influences.

The early stages of dating involve doing enjoyable things together. Many relationships never survive this period, since the enjoyment simply wears off. But those relationships that do survive the idealized and companionship stage are affected by a third factor. This is the complementarity

---

[40] Alan Kerckhoff and Keith E. Davis, "Value Consensus and Need Complementarity in Mate Selection," *American Sociological Review* 27 (1962), 295–303.

with which Winch was most concerned. Over time, a much more realistic appraisal of the good and bad points in the dating partner (increased empathic ability) develops, and, according to Kerckhoff and Davis, a much more personality-based bond appears. When this complementary psychological bond appears, the likelihood of marriage is much greater. In short, the filtering process begins with homogeneous limitation, moves through enjoyment, idealization, and a search for commonness, and ends with a complementary bond that leads to marriage. And, of course, many relationships weed themselves out along the way.

Though this summary of Kerckhoff and Davis' filtering process is somewhat oversimplified and pat, it does cover the essential elements. One problem in the empirical process, which Kerckhoff and Davis point out, is that in the sequence of a particular dating relationship the first two factors may be reversed. An individual may be dating several persons whose company he enjoys, and may not narrow the field of eligibles on the basis of race or social class until he finds himself becoming increasingly serious about one of them. And, as hinted above, if a couple marry because they enjoy each other, they may later discover basic value and category incompatibilities—too late to weed out the relationship without a divorce.

An attempt to test Kerckhoff and Davis' filtering process theory has been made by George Levinger, David Senn, and Bruce Jorgensen at the Universities of Massachusetts and Colorado. Using a sample of couples who were going steady, they administered Kerckhoff and Davis' instruments twice, six months apart. They failed to confirm the theory, and concluded that objectively derived indices of couple progress may be less useful than the perceptions and predictions of the couple members themselves.[41] It is, however, quite possible that six months in the lives of "going steady" couples is simply too short a time span to isolate the effects of Kerckhoff and Davis' filtering factors. Perhaps the majority have passed the simple enjoyment stage and have not yet reached the stage of "need fulfillment." Suffice it to say that further testing of the filtering process theory is needed before it can be rejected.

Levinger, Senn, and Jorgensen do, however, propose some interesting alternative ways of viewing the process of relationship intensification. One process, they say, entails encounter, disclosure, and discovery of coorientation. A second is the development of the relationship per se.[42] These two

---

[41] George Levinger, David J. Senn, and Bruce W. Jorgensen, "Progress Toward Permanence in Courtship: A Test of the Kerckhoff-Davis Hypothesis," *Sociometry* 33 (1970), 427–43.

[42] Levinger, Senn, and Jorgensen, "Progress Toward Permanence in Courtship," pp. 441–42.

processes have been discussed at greater length by other writers, though in slightly different terms. We shall begin with Bernard Murstein's view of person perception and courtship progress. In Murstein's stimulus-value-role theory of courtship, the couple are at first stimulated by each other's attractiveness; they then compare values and either continue the relationship on the basis of similarity or discontinue it; finally, they either play more intense roles appropriately, or the relationship dies. Thus, mutual gratification goes through the stages of stimulus $\rightarrow$ value $\rightarrow$ role compatibility $=$ marriage. Furthermore, empathic ability, or the ability to predict the other person's view of himself, becomes increasingly important to the continuance of the relationship, though empathy on the woman's part seems more important than empathy on the man's part.[43] Thus, understanding each other and playing roles appropriate to each other's wishes are both involved in the deepening of a courtship relation.

The second approach proposed by Levinger, Senn, and Jorgensen— focusing on the relationship per se—was applied by Charles Bolton some years earlier, but his findings have often been neglected. Based on intensive research with twenty married couples, Bolton's study departs radically from the numerous attempts to isolate and determine specific factors in mate selection. Mate selection, he feels, has unfortunately been treated as a decision or a single operation instead of as a developmental process. He feels that mate selection should perhaps be viewed as "a process in which the *transactions between individuals* in certain societal contexts are determinants of turning points and commitments out of which marriage emerges."[44] Marriage is problematic in the sense that both homogamy and heterogamy are inadequate explanations for mate selection; the interactions and changes in commitments during a developing relationship must be taken seriously. Information is thus needed, not only on the initial situation and characteristics of the couple, but also on what transpires subsequently.

Marriage is not merely a function of the needs, values, and backgrounds that a couple bring to the relationship. The process of increasing commitment develops a momentum of its own, and is carried forward by a series of *escalators*, factors that "push" the couple toward marriage. Among these escalators is (1) *value-activity* involvement, which is based on both a patterning of time spent together and an increasing congruence of values and

---

[43] Bernard I. Murstein, "Person Perception and Courtship Progress Among Premarital Couples," *Journal of Marriage and the Family* 34 (1972), 621–26; Murstein, "Empirical Tests of Role, Complementary Needs, and Homogamy Theories of Marital Choice," *Journal of Marriage and the Family* 29 (1967), 689–96; and Murstein, "Stimulus-Value-Role: A Theory of Marital Choice," *Journal of Marriage and the Family* 32 (1970), 465–81.

[44] Charles D. Bolton, "Mate Selection as the Development of a Relationship," *Marriage and Family Living* 23 (1961), 235.

goals, as Snyder pointed out. A second escalator is (2) *commitment,* the formal and public redefinition that occurs as a couple moves through the stages of seriousness toward marriage. A good example of a commitment escalator is the engagement announcement, which helps to propel a couple into marriage. Closely related to the commitment escalator is the (3) *"habitualized"* escalator, which causes the individual to avoid the grief reaction and psychological upheaval that would accompany the dissolution of an intensifying relationship. A fourth escalator is based on (4) *identity* needs, which develop as the individual defines himself as "Jane's fiancé," or "Tom's steady." The dating and mate selection process is related to the young person's search for identity and recognition, and the dating partner offers a means of asserting one's identity. Relinquishing this identity can be a painful process. (5) The *image* of the partner serves to perpetuate the relationship, as the romanticized conception of the partner and self-esteem, based on one's ability to "pick 'em," combine to intensify involvement. Two escalators not discussed by Bolton concern the influence of others on the relationship. In a study of University of Georgia students Robert Lewis found that being labeled as a couple by friends and family was correlated with a pair's increasing commitment to each other. Furthermore, getting such recognition and support from one's family appears more vital to relationship intensification than does getting it from one's peers.[45] The other escalator, referred to in an article by R. G. Ryder, J. S. Kafka, and D. H. Olson, is the contending third party influence. Third parties tend to have a shifting influence, depending upon the stage of the courtship process. At an early stage, their intrusion may drive a couple apart, while at a later stage, taken in conjunction with the identity and image needs referred to above, the intrusion of third parties may draw the couple together and move them rapidly toward marriage.[46]

Bolton himself indicates other escalators and other ways in which escalators operate to propel a relationship toward marriage. His major point, however, is that the transactions that take place within a relationship itself are generally overlooked in favor of the traditional factors used to account for mate selection. This picture is changing, as Lewis, Ryder, Murstein, and others investigate the process of relationship intensification, apart from the psychological and social background characteristics of the persons involved. It is, furthermore, difficult to argue with Bolton's assertion that attempts to understand mate selection in the United States by simply isolating and specifying individual factors have been inadequate.

---

[45] Robert A. Lewis, "Social Reaction and Formation of Dyads: An Interactionist Approach to Mate Selection," *Sociometry* 36 (1973), 409–18.

[46] R. G. Ryder, J. S. Kafka, and D. H. Olson, "Separating and Joining Influences in Courtship and Early Marriage," *American Journal of Orthopsychiatry* 41 (1971), 450–64.

Section Four

CRITIQUE AND TENTATIVE CONCLUSIONS

Throughout our discussion of some ten factors in mate selection, the issues of convolution and combination have arisen time and again. One author will define values broadly enough to include the effect of propinquity, background categories, and common interests. Another's definition of value will encompass personality needs, homogamy desires, and parental image within the "ideal mate" conception. Winch, while stressing complementary needs, acknowledges the fact that notions of homogamy and role compatibility must be added to the explanation of mate selection.[47] Kirkpatrick and Hobart, and Murstein, find that empathy and agreement, taken together, yield substantial insight into male selection. Kerckhoff and Davis suggest that homogamy, values and interests, and complementary needs work processually to filter out the bad bets. Finally, Bolton, Lewis, and Ryder caution us that homogamy and heterogamy considerations must be augmented by the consideration of process itself. A relationship, as it progresses, acquires qualities that may serve to perpetuate it despite discoveries by the couple that their values differ, that they meet each other's needs imperfectly, and so on.

All these observations make it impossible to accept one explanation based on a single factor, and reject the others. Rather, some sort of intuitive interpretation, supported by a knowledge of history, is about as far as the current state of research will carry us. Farber has tried such a historical weighting of factors, while commenting on Kerckhoff and Davis' filtering process. The idea of the companionship family, says Farber, is that individuals seek personal happiness, adjustment, and freedom within the family setting. This is the type of family toward which the United States is moving. Now, Farber adds, in a society in which the trend is also toward permanent availability (so that if things don't work out the couple may divorce and try again), one mate selection factor-complex stands out. Mutual enjoyment and general goal similarity take precedence in the selection process over both background homogamy and complementarity. If, he says, the most salient aspect of marriage were its permanence, we would be much more careful than we are to filter out background factors and to determine deeper psychological compatibility. Complementarity may be needed and desired under institutionalized conditions, or under conditions of permanent

---

[47] On the notion of role compatibility as a factor in mate selection, see Murstein, "Empirical Tests of Role, Complementary Needs, and Homogamy Theories of Marital Choice."

mating; however, under conditions of availability, interests and congeniality of goals appear to override both complementarity and categorical distinctions in the U.S. selection process. Permanent availability, therefore, implies that the basic interests of the individual may change, as may his goals, in the course of his lifetime; since these interests and goals were the prime bases for the marriage, it may be voided by such changes. Farber feels that what may happen is that a marriage already consummated on the basis of interests and certain shared goals may be severely tested if social categories and needs are found to be incompatible.

Here, then, is one attempt to compare the importance of several mate selection factors. This author cannot, however, accept Farber's interpretation in its entirety. For one thing, while the movement toward universal and permanent availability is apparent, it does not seem to have progressed quite as far as Farber assumes it has. Within the racial categories, the three general religious divisions, and the major social classes, homogamy is still the rule. Furthermore, propinquity both reinforces homogamy and further limits the field of eligibles, though the mobility of the individual complicates its operation. It is unquestionable that the incest taboo, homogamy considerations (when they are salient), and propinquity act to greatly limit the number of possible mates available to the individual. But *limitation* is only part of the mate selection process: there are "pulls," or *selective* factors, and, as Bolton reminds us, "pushes," or *intensification* and processual factors. Among the selective factors, the most fruitful seem to be common interests, perceived value consensus (which includes the idea of goals referred to by Farber), and empathy. The couple in the United States who find that they can predict each other's behavior and responses, who enjoy each other's company, and who at least assume that they agree on certain important goals and attitudes, are very likely to get married.

It would be most convenient if limitations plus interests, empathy, and values accounted for all of the variability in mate choices, but this is simply not so. Many people marry to escape an unhappy home, or because of a premarital pregnancy; in such cases the importance of background homogamy, value consensus, and empathy may be minimal. Also, in American society, people expect to be married by a certain age. If the "right one" has not come along by the time the individual reaches his mid-twenties, he may stop waiting for the right one and choose someone who merely shows an interest. For, as Gudmund Hernes points out, as one gets older and more of one's cohort are married, there is increasing pressure to get married but the possibility of doing so decreases, due to the reduced number of "eligibles."[48] In addition, any given relationship may, over time, develop

---

[48] Gudmund Hernes, "The Process of Entry into First Marriage," *American Sociological Review* 37 (1972), 182. An excellent discussion of age at marriage is found in Glen H.

pressures for continuation and intensification, as Bolton noted. These pushes toward marriage cannot be accounted for by what the two individuals bring into the dating process with them; they are processual elements of the developing relationship. Finally, love—which is, after all, what we are trying to explain—is not uniformly intense from one marriage to the next. William Kephart, in a study of more than one thousand college students, found that some females were open to the possibility of marrying a person who had qualities they desired in a mate, but with whom they were not in love.[49] Nor, for that matter, does the intensity of love appear to be closely related to the satisfactoriness of a marriage.[50]

To say that the task of understanding mate selection is incomplete would be an understatement. A beginning has been made, but three major problems remain. First, the need for *further research* is obvious. Perhaps, with sufficient research, certain psychological needs, along with the limiting conditions and the empathy-agreement variables that are already somewhat substantiated, will be found to be clear predictors of mate selection. Second, *specification* may be valuable. More sophisticated research may lead us to agree with Kephart that sex-specific theories are needed, rather than an overarching framework. That is, we may find that the determinants of mate choice are not exactly the same for males as for females. Or it may be that different explanations are needed for mate selection among (with respect to age) early marriers, "normal" marriers, and late marriers. Perhaps the "pushes" into marriage are greater among both early and late marriers, while homogamy, empathy, and value-interest agreement can apply fairly well to those who marry between ages twenty and twenty-five in the United States. The third problem may not be solved by research alone. How can the *pushes* toward marriage be incorporated into the explanation? Bolton has convinced us of the necessity of doing so, and others are now generating the required methodological tools. Even if such tools are developed, it may still be necessary to admit the presence of fortuitous, or *chance*, factors that cannot be rationally handled. These problems will not, of course, keep writers from trying to explain "who marries whom and why" in the United States. This author's reading of the data places mate selection in the contemporary United States as shown in Figure 8, in which we utilize

---

Elder, Jr., "Role Orientations, Marital Age, and Life Patterns in Adulthood," *Merrill-Palmer Quarterly* 18 (1972), 3–24.

[49] William Kephart, "Some Correlates of Romantic Love," *Journal of Marriage and the Family* 29 (1967), 470–74.

[50] William Kephart, "The 'Dysfunctional' Theory of Romantic Love: A Research Report," *Journal of Comparative Family Studies* 1 (1971), 26–36. Other recent sources on romantic love include the following: Charles B. Spaulding, "The Romantic Love Complex in American Culture," *Sociology and Social Research* 55 (1970), 82–100; David H. Knox, Jr., "Attitude Toward Love of High School Seniors," *Adolescence* 5 (1970), 89–100; and Knox, "Conceptions of Love at Three Developmental Levels," *Family Coordinator* 19 (1970), 151–57.

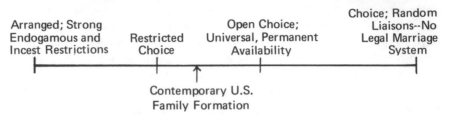

Figure 8
The Author's View of Mate Selection or Family Formation in the Contemporary United States in Relation to the Family Formation Continuum

the family formation continuum proposed in Chapter 5. As always, our interpretation is tentative and subject to the reader's reinterpretation and relocation.

One aspect of mate selection on which the evidence is clear is the continuing, though lessening, tendency for marriage to occur between persons of a generally similar social background. Prime among homogamous considerations is race; a discussion of black-white intermarriage closes this chapter.

Section Five

RACIAL HOMOGAMY: A CASE IN NONUNIVERSAL AVAILABILITY[51]

For most white persons in the United States, the field of eligibles simply does not include members of the black race; conversely, the field of eligibles for most black persons does not include whites. While the issue of racial homogamy includes Orientals and others, the following discussion concentrates on the norms, laws, and motives (and their respective behavioral manifestations) governing intermarriage between whites and blacks in the United States.

Norms Governing Black-White Intermarriage

The question of norms, or expectations, regarding marriage by race has focused historically in the antiamalgamation doctrine, which says that the various races were meant to be separate. Gunnar Myrdal's classic study in the mid-1940s, published as *An American Dilemma*, makes clear what Americans,

[51] The author is indebted to H. Kent Geiger for several of the ideas in the following section.

both white and black, believe regarding racial intermarriage.[52] For many years white Americans argued more strongly and publicly against black-white intermarriage than did blacks. They based themselves on notions of the inherent inferiority of black people, frequently bolstered by religious pronouncements concerning the curse of Canaan (translated by some ministers as a curse on black people). The lower one's social class position, the greater his *expressed* opposition to intermarriage was likely to be. Educated whites also demonstrated substantial prejudice, but were better able to hide it. In some cases, because these whites felt less threatened by intermarriage, they were able to talk a more liberal line.

Whites have justified the position they assign to blacks with the argument: "They are doing the best they can." If black persons or families escape from the bottom they can be treated as exceptions to the basic inferiority of their race. Some white people refer to the inferior position that black people have been assigned in this society as a rationalization for their strong feelings against marriage with blacks. In short, many whites have considered blacks inferior and thus not suitable as mates.

Since the time of Myrdal's study, there has been a needed increase in racial pride among blacks (especially among black leaders). Along with this development has come an argument against marriage with whites. This argument is based on the ground that blacks need to recognize their own identity and heritage and, in some cases, on the ground that whites are inherently degenerate.[53] The result is that today there are conspicuous pressures toward homogamy, among both whites and blacks, as well as opposing pressures toward intermarriage from liberal elements of the population trying to manifest their lack of concern for the racial barrier. Which pressures are greater? Perhaps by the close of this discussion we can decide.

A second major question regarding the norms is: Where will change occur in interracial matters? This, says Myrdal, depends on the "rank order of discrimination" (see Figure 9).[54] Listed at the top are those areas in which, according to Myrdal, whites are most desirous of remaining separate from blacks, while the areas listed at the bottom are the ones in which blacks are most anxious to effect changes. Though it is possible to argue that there has been some rearranging of priorities since Myrdal wrote, the important point is that the likely direction of change is approximately from bottom to top, with intermarriage being one of the last areas of desegregation and equality accepted into the norms of both races.

---

[52] Gunnar Myrdal, *An American Dilemma* (New York: Harper and Brothers, 1944).

[53] Many of the authors referred to in Chapter 6 note this increase in racial pride and solidarity.

[54] Myrdal, *An American Dilemma*, pp. 60–61.

Figure 9

Myrdal's Rank Order of Discrimination of Whites Against Blacks

RANK ORDER OF DISCRIMINATION	Black Desire for Change	White Desire for Perpetuation
Intermarriage and sex with white women		
Close interpersonal relations and behavioral cues		
Use of public facilities	↑	
Political involvement: voting, office holding, etc.		
Law, police, and court treatment		↓
Economics: credit, jobs, etc.		

Intermarriage Laws

Recent changes in antimiscegenation laws—laws forbidding racial inter-marriage—in the United States have been tremendous. As late as 1960, 29 states, mostly southern and western, still had such laws. In 1964 there were only 19 such states; in 1966, 17; and in 1967, 16. In 1967, antimiscegenation laws were declared unconstitutional by the Supreme Court. Will this decision have any direct effect upon intermarriage rates? Though it is too early to tell, the answer seems to be: probably not in and of itself—at least as long as the norms against intermarriage remain strong.

Black-White Intermarriage: How Many and Who?

A New York attorney recently claimed that there are 1,000,000 racially inter-married persons in the United States, of whom 810,000 are either passing or don't even know that they are intermarried. The idea that they "don't even know" signifies that the person may have a black ancestor somewhere in his past, which raises the question of whether or not a marriage is a racial intermarriage if none of the phenotypic manifestations are discernible. The notion that someone has one-fourth or one-sixteenth colored blood, and therefore his marriage is interracial if he marries a white person, is simply not scientifically defensible. It is much more appropriate to discuss rates of intermarriage in terms of their overt numbers, rather than to be concerned with those who are passing or "don't know."

We do not have national data on the frequency of racial intermarriage. Figures are available for New York State and Boston for the early years of this century, and for California, Hawaii, Michigan, and Nebraska during the 1950s and 1960s. "For the period 1916 through 1937, Negro-white marriages in New York State exclusive of New York City varied from 1.7 to 4.8 percent of all marriages involving Negroes."[55] The equivalent percentages for whites would, of course, be even lower. In Boston, the period of maximum

---

[55] Ruth Shonle Cavan, *The American Family* (New York: Crowell, 1969 ed.), pp. 204–5.

racial intermarriage appears to have been 1850–1900. From the 1900–1904 period to the 1914–18 period, the racial intermarriage rate declined from 14 to 5 per 100 marriages involving blacks.[56] Since that time, the rate of intermarriage in Boston has averaged 3.9 per 100 black marriages and 0.12 per 100 white marriages, with a slight, but perceptible, decline up until World War II.[57] The decline in intermarriages in Boston after the turn of the century was almost entirely due to a decline in marriages involving black grooms and white brides.

Figures for Boston and New York State stop at about 1938, forcing us to look elsewhere for more recent trends. David Heer, studying 1950–60 data for four states, concludes that at least for California, Michigan, Hawaii, and Nebraska there are current indications of an upward trend in interracial marriage.[58] Thus, by piecing together the earlier and later data, though they are from different locations, we may tentatively conclude that the rate of black-white intermarriage has been curvilinear, declining from the late 1800s to about 1940, and rising gradually since that time. Thomas Monahan, for example, reports that the rate of intermarriage of Kansas blacks rose from 1 percent in 1947 to 7 percent in 1969. However, even in Hawaii, the state with the highest present intermarriage rate, the average rate for whites between 1956 and 1964 was only 24 in 10,000, or 0.24 percent.[59] To say that the rate is rising is *not*, therefore, to say that large numbers of blacks and whites are now intermarrying in the United States.

The second aspect of black and white behavior with respect to intermarriage concerns not *how many*, but *who*. Who are the intermarriers? Among whites, racial intermarriage seems to have involved widowed or divorced persons more often than persons who never married; older persons more often than younger persons (perhaps a function of their reduced field of eligibles); urban people rather than rural people; native-born white women and foreign-born white men more often than their opposites; and lower-class white women more often than working- or middle-class white women. As for blacks who intermarry, St. Clair Drake and Horace Cayton listed the following as the types of Chicago blacks who intermarry with whites: intellectuals and bohemians, who are not responsive to social restrictions; members of cults that include disregard of racial differences as part of their social philosophy; and lower-class blacks, without pride of race.[60]

---

[56] David M. Heer, "Negro-White Marriage in the United States," *Journal of Marriage and the Family* 28 (1966), 267.

[57] Cavan, *The American Family*, 204–5.

[58] Heer, "Negro-White Marriage in the United States," p. 266.

[59] Thomas P. Monahan, "Interracial Marriage and Divorce in Kansas and the Question of Instability of Mixed Marriages," *Journal of Comparative Family Studies* 2 (1972), 107–20; and Heer, "Negro-White Marriage in the United States," p. 264.

[60] St. Clair Drake and Horace Cayton, *Black Metropolis* (New York: Harcourt, Brace, 1945), pp. 137–39.

Kingsley Davis had stated a few years earlier that intermarriage more often than not includes a high-status black man and a low-status white woman—though this assertion has since been questioned, as we shall see below.

Intermarriage by sex may be between a white female and a black male, or a black female and a white male. The rank order of discrimination, including as it does the high value whites place on "protecting our women," might lead the reader to expect that racial intermarriage would more often involve a white man and a black woman. However, black men and white women are by far the more frequent marital partners, some 80 percent of interracial marriages being of this type. In view of Myrdal's "rank order," how can this be explained? According to Kingsley Davis, there may be two possible explanations. First is the *attractiveness-accessibility* hypothesis. Since sexual exploitation of black females by white males has been quite possible historically in the United States, marriage was not necessary between them for the male to express such an interest. If, however, a black male is attracted to a white female, the stringency of the norms has been such that he has been forced to legitimate that interest by marriage. That is, the very weakness of the controls governing the exploitation of black females by white males has made it less necessary for the males to marry in order to pursue their interest in black females.

A second hypothesis, based on the notion that the marriage of high-status black males and low-status white females is more frequent than any other combination, is the *economic penalty* hypothesis. Given the current discriminatory and prejudicial aspects of U.S. society (this hypothesis goes), the economic-occupational penalty is great for the white male with a black wife. Yet the black male with a white wife is penalized hardly at all, and may even be helped by his wife's race. The difficulty with this second explanation is that recent data have not shown any great discrepancy between the social status of the white and black partners to an intermarriage. Todd Pavela's exploratory study in Indiana includes this conclusion: "It would appear that such intermarriage now occurs between persons who are, by and large, economically, educationally, and culturally equal and who have a strong emotional attachment, be it rationalization or real."[61] Jessie Bernard likewise notes that, in general, "racial intermarriages as of 1960 tended to be as homogamous educationally as marriages between Negro men and women. The wives of Negro men—whether white or Negro—tended to average more schooling than their husbands, reflecting the generally lower

---

[61] Todd Pavela, "An Exploratory Study of Negro-White Intermarriage in Indiana," *Journal of Marriage and the Family* 26 (1964), 211.

[62] Jessie Bernard, "Note on Educational Homogamy in Negro-White and White-Negro Marriages, 1960," *Journal of Marriage and the Family* 28 (1966), 274–76.

level of schooling of Negro men."[62] Thus, Davis' accessibility hypothesis seems to be more useful today than the hypothesis based on economic penalties, though, of course, the latter may have been more applicable when the two hypotheses were first propounded.

Do black-white marriages have as many "strikes against them" as their critics would like us to believe? Thomas Monahan reports that racially mixed marriages have a divorce rate of 45 in 100, while the divorce rate of racially homogamous couples is only 27 per 100.[63] Here, the interpretation is up to the reader. The difference is substantial, but is it sufficient to discourage any who would intermarry? It is quite possible to infer that, with all the social pressures against interracial couples, their rate of divorce is actually surprisingly low.

Motives for Racial Intermarriage in the United States

What are the motives behind racial intermarriage in the United States, when the norms of both races are so strongly against it? Though seeking motives can sometimes be a fruitless exercise in intuition, several motives that have been suggested recently might be of interest to the reader. One is *repudiation*. Cavan sums up this viewpoint well when she asserts that an interracial marriage "indicates either that the person has not been thoroughly integrated into his social group or has withdrawn from it for some reason. His needs are not met there; he seeks elsewhere for contacts, friendship, and marriage."[64] He may feel like a misfit, he may have been rejected, and he is manifesting a mutual rejection by overstepping the bounds of one of his group's strongest norms.

A second motive, akin to and perhaps a part of the first, is *identity* reinforcement. Earlier in the chapter we noted how the individual may establish his identity through his choice of a mate. If a part of an individual's identity is a liberal life approach and a concern to deal with people on a personal rather than a categorical basis, he may seek to demonstrate this identity by means of an interracial marriage. It would seem to the present author, nevertheless, that this motive would in all likelihood be coupled with one of the others, rather than be the sole factor in an interracial marriage.

Psychoanalytically oriented writers have suggested *oedipal fear* as a third motive for racial intermarriage. Racial intermarriage, or marriage across any major social barrier, is a result, they say, of the person's strong attraction

---

[63] Monahan, "Interracial Marriage and Divorce in Kansas and the Question of Instability of Mixed Marriages."

[64] Cavan, *The American Family*, p. 206.

to his opposite-sex parent; his heterogamy, or intermarriage, reinforces the incest taboo, subtly convincing him that he is not in reality trying to marry his own parent. This idea is as difficult to test as it is intriguing.

The fourth motive for racial intermarriage, alluded to earlier in the chapter, is that racial categories are simply *not salient,* or don't matter, to the individual.[65] It seems doubtful to the present author, however, that nonsalience is currently the basis for many black-white intermarriages in the United States, since race is made salient by societal structures and attitudes in so many ways that it can only rarely be shrugged off as inconsequential. An increase in nonsalience, however, would be a significant move toward universal availability in this area of mate selection. Whether or not Supreme Court decisions and a liberalization of attitudes will have this effect in the near future is conjectural, though it is possible that the small increase in racial intermarriage rates since World War II is accounted for by such so-called nonsalient unions. Yet a lot of societal restructuring appears to be necessary before racial intermarriage can become prevalent, and before such marriages can be a matter of nonsalience, instead of a reaction to something in the individual's life history. At present, the pressures toward racial homogamy still seem to outweigh the opposing pressures toward nonsalience and universal availability.

---

[65] On this, see Frank Musgrove, *The Family, Education, and Society* (London: Routledge and Kegan Paul, 1966), pp. 67–68.

Marriage is a mixture of change and pattern. In the early years of marriage the habit patterns of a couple mesh and their role choices become fixed routines. However, these routines are not completely fixed because abrupt and gradual transitions constantly result in the necessity for new adjustments and roles. Childbirth, task accomplishment, the departure of offspring, retirement, and death are examples of abrupt transitions; while gradual transitions are exemplified by deferred gratification, goal failure, the effects of deterioration, and behavioral intensification. Little research on marriage has been done from a processual perspective, though marital satisfaction has been found to decrease over the first twenty years of marriage and then to increase. A second valuable perspective on marriage is that which views it as consisting of role choices, patterns, and conflicts. In the course of U.S. history, the role patterns of husbands and wives at first became increasingly defined as economic and domestic, respectively. While these roles still dominate, the roles of marital partners are being based increasingly on choice rather than on tradition or prescription. The issues involved in husband-father and wife-mother role choices and behavior comprise the closing sections of Chapter 11.

Marriage: Processes and Roles

Section One

MARRIAGE AS A PROCESS

A young man and woman have dated, have narrowed the field of potential mates through various conscious and unconscious means, and have finally ceremonialized their relationship in marriage. The early months of marriage are likely to be characterized by a sense of euphoria, or general emotional well-being, and also by experimentation and pattern development. Eventually, however, the euphoric solidarity peculiar to the newly married begins to recede, and the husband and wife find themselves faced with daily adjustment to each other. In view of the separate habit systems they brought into the marriage, they must begin to adjust to the fact that they are now a dyad—a marriage—and experimentation and routinization become predominant. "The social form created by marriage must find its way," remarks Willard Waller, "by a rather tentative process, making many false starts but attaining at last a tolerable living pattern. . . . Some patterns will be highly successful; these will tend to stabilize in the form of powerful habits."[1] Involved in the formation of joint habits is, among other things, the interchange of tastes and of likes and dislikes.

Not all marital patterns are successful; conflict also emerges. It may appear due to a basic, but heretofore undiscovered, value disagreement—perhaps over politics, or over leisure pursuits, or over the activities which should characterize the wife and woman or the husband and man. Oftentimes, however, the conflict revolves around some seemingly inconsequential aspect of the everyday behavior brought by a couple member into the marriage. It might be a disagreement over the preparation of foods or the time for meals; it might concern bedtime routine, or even something as simple as toothbrushing. Whatever their bases, such conflicts as occur may produce a blockage of communication or, if accommodations and adjustments are made, may produce a new form of solidarity. Strictly speaking, then, "engagement or no engagement, every new marriage is an undefined situation, just as every new status involves undefined elements for the neophyte."[2] Yet, during the early months, routines *do* develop, and the marriage itself becomes a problem, or a mutual meeting of internal situations and a joint facing of the external world, or some combination of problem and solution.

Routines and patterns develop, but they never become completely fixed. This is because transitions, some abrupt and some gradual, are constantly altering former patterns. The *abrupt transitions,* which have received considerable research attention, include the marriage ceremony, parenthood, occupational change, task accomplishment, the departure of children, residential movement, retirement, and death. These are transitions that affect the individual's personality integration and energy management either positively or negatively, and that demand new roles and adjustments for the nuclear family unit. Preparation for such transitions can never be complete. The pregnancy period, for example, may give a couple time to discuss parental roles and the readjustment of household routines, but it can never truly prepare the husband and wife for the transition to parenthood. In

---

[1] Willard Waller and Reuben Hill, *The Family: A Dynamic Interpretation* (New York: Holt, Rinehart and Winston, 1951), p. 254. On the honeymoon, see Rhona Rapoport and Robert Rapoport, "New Light on the Honeymoon," *Human Relations* 17 (1964), 33–56.

[2] Waller and Hill, *The Family,* p. 254.

fact, becoming a mother appears to require an even greater role transition —from wife to wife and mother—than that from single to married.[3] Nevertheless, each new role created by an abrupt transition can be anticipated and planned for to some extent. This planning, or role learning in advance, is called "anticipatory socialization," and Wesley Burr proposes the following relation between anticipatory socialization and ease of transition:

> The amount of anticipatory socialization influences the ease of transitions into roles and this is a positive, ... curvilinear relationship in which the influence decreases as the independent variable increases.[4]

Thus, for example, presocialization for marriage can be made either by observing one's own parents, or by intense interaction with members of the opposite sex.

However, anticipatory socialization can take one only so far when the transition involves either the arrival or the departure of children. Thus, another question to ask about a couple's response to abrupt transitions concerns task accomplishment, or how capable the couple members are of accomplishing the necessary adaptations. "The lack of prior models is stressful," the Rapoports state, "but it also provides new opportunities for creativity." The "new patterns are crystallized within a few weeks after the critical transition period of intensive involvements."[5] Whether or not the couple members can accomplish the tasks required by the transition is a matter of coping ability, or the ability to adjust, as well as a matter of the clarity of role models. If, for example, upon becoming a mother, the young female has a clear picture of the way in which new mothers operate, and if that picture is applicable to her times and not to some earlier and different era, this model can help her to accomplish the required tasks. If, however, she either lacks a clear model or the model she has is no longer applicable, then coping ability is at a premium. It seems likely, therefore, that coping ability is more important today than it would have been in a traditional family setting, since even those young mothers who have a distinct picture of how their mothers behaved are apt to feel that cultural change has largely nullified the applicability of the model.

Fully as important to understanding the family as the abrupt transitions are the *gradual transitions,* those changes that cannot be fixed at a given

---

[3] Alice S. Rossi, "Transition to Parenthood," *Journal of Marriage and the Family* 30 (1968), 27; Robert O. Blood, Jr., and Donald M. Wolfe, *Husbands and Wives* (New York: Free Press, 1960), p. 43; and Mirra Komarovsky, *Blue-Collar Marriage* (New York: Random House, Vintage Books, 1967), p. 31.

[4] Wesley R. Burr, *Theory Construction and the Sociology of the Family* (New York: Wiley, 1973), p. 125.

[5] Robert Rapoport and Rhona Rapoport, "Work and Family in Contemporary Society," *American Sociological Review* 30 (1965), 388, 389.

point in time, but nevertheless influence both the individual's personality and his family life. Few writers have attempted to deal with such changes; Bernice Neugarten's research is probably the most insightful and useful, though it takes an individual rather than a family perspective.[6] She notes at the outset that, except for Erik Erikson's eight stages of ego development, dynamic theories of personality have generally assumed "that the personality is stabilized, if not fixed, by the time early adulthood is reached."[7] To Neugarten and her associates, personality is a moving complexity of intrapsychic and socioadaptive elements. In their volume *Personality in Middle and Late Life,* they summarize the results of several exploratory studies of personality processes. The studies were carried out as part of the Kansas City Studies of Adult Life, based on probability samples of Kansas City residents between the ages of forty and ninety, the total pool consisting of 701 men and women.

The intrapsychic aspects of personality include perceptions, impulses, and mental abilities, and their operation is related to the aging process in terms of continuity, simplification, and deterioration. According to Neugarten, "personalities maintain their characteristic patterns of organization as individuals move from middle into old age."[8] Responses to various stimuli in old age can, therefore, be traced to earlier tendencies within the personality, and continuity observed. The sources of change are twofold: simplification and deterioration. The energy supply decreases, cognitive or thinking processes become impaired, and impulse control becomes somewhat erratic; all these forms of deterioration increase the individual's tendencies to become inwardly oriented or preoccupied with self. Along with the increased interiority that accompanies the various forms of deterioration, Neugarten asserts,

> there seems to go a certain reduction in the complexity of the personality. With the shrinkage in psychological life space and with decreased ego energy, an increasing dedication to a central core of values and to a set of habit patterns and a sloughing off of earlier cathexes which lose saliency for the individual seem to occur. It is probably this quality which has led to frequent observations, on the one hand, that behavior in a normal old person is more consistent and more predictable than in a younger one—that, as individuals age, they become increasingly *like themselves*—and, on the other hand, that the personality structure stands more clearly revealed in an older than in a younger person.[9] (Italics added.)

---

[6] Bernice Neugarten, *Personality in Middle and Late Life* (New York: Atherton, 1964).
[7] Neugarten, *Personality in Middle and Late Life,* p. xvi.
[8] Neugarten, *Personality in Middle and Late Life,* p. 187.
[9] Neugarten, *Personality in Middle and Late Life,* p. 198.

Simplification of personality, we might add, is a lifelong facet of intrapersonal adjustment. The adolescent seeks for identity by experimentation with various types of behavior and attitudes, as he struggles to make sense of his impulses and of the conflicting norms being presented to him by others. When the adolescent becomes a young adult, these behaviors and attitudes do not automatically become fixed—whether by marriage, occupational experience, or parenthood. Rather, experimentation continues. Specific responses do, however, begin to be rank-ordered in their salience to him; simplification involves the reinforcement of the most rewarding responses and a growing tendency to ignore alternative possibilities.

The socioadaptive aspects of personality consist of the individual's ways of relating to the external environment, including the interpersonal elements we discussed in Chapter 7. Though affected by simplification and deterioration processes, these aspects are influenced more by work status, health, financial resources, and marital status than by chronological age. Continuity in this area of personality may mean that the individual continues to demonstrate socioadaptive abilities in social interaction and role performance for years after intrapsychic deterioration has begun. Or socioadaptive adjustment may be altered by what Neugarten calls "accumulation." As a result, says Neugarten,

> of the life history with its accumulating record of adaptations to both biological and social events, there is a continually changing basis within the individual for perceiving and responding to new events in the outer world.[10]

The aging individual may, as we have said, continue to adapt to social demands after intrapsychic deterioration is well under way. Or, on the other hand, various setbacks in the external world may impair his socioadaptivity even before the deterioration based on age has become noticeable. The intrapsychic and the socioadaptive aspects of the personality are related, but they also operate separately, with the former being much more closely and directly related to chronological age than are the latter.

Neugarten and her research associates are concerned primarily with individual personality processes during adult life, not with family experience. Nevertheless, their insights are extremely useful in understanding the gradual transitions that influence the relations between husbands and wives. The following illustrations show how these insights may be applied to marriage.

The young couple may start their life together looking forward to success and achievement on the part of the husband. As their experience ac-

---

[10] Neugarten, *Personality in Middle and Late Life*, p. 194.

cumulates and success continues to recede, they may come to realize that their goals have not been, and may never be, reached. Sometimes at age forty, but more often gradually, the husband admits to himself that he has not accomplished and cannot expect to accomplish what he set out to do. This realization may be accompanied by his awareness of his diminishing energy. A realistic husband may be able to lower his sights without severe ego difficulties. More often, however, his response will be discouragement or anticipatory disengagement. The discouragement of the husband in middle age may demand succor from the wife, but the couple's previous marital experience may not have prepared her to provide it. By anticipatory disengagement we mean that the husband gradually begins to look forward to the time when he can stop striving and can shed his occupational role. (For those working-class persons who find little meaning in their jobs, anticipatory disengagement may be an aspect of their entire working life, so that there is no attitudinal discontinuity at retirement.) Thus, admission of failure to achieve one's goals may be accompanied by changes in socioadaptive personality, and may demand a personality reorientation on the wife's part which she is unable to accomplish.

Our second illustration is a problem in deterioration that has ramifications for husband-wife relations. Deterioration in appearance is one form of deterioration not discussed directly by Neugarten. In a society in which a crucial element in the traditional marriage is the physical attraction of the male to the female, the gradual lessening of the wife's beauty, due to both childbearing and the direct influence of time, may have serious implications for her personality as well as for the marriage. Unquestionably, the husband and wife whose accumulated experiences and habit patterns have provided alternative bases of solidarity are best prepared to maintain both intra- and interpersonal continuity as physical decline progresses. In some instances, however, the wife becomes oriented to the past or to a fantasy regarding her current beauty, while the husband begins to look elsewhere for new attractions. Changing orientations that result from diminishing physical attractiveness may, therefore, affect both personality adjustment and marriage.

A final illustration of a gradual transition involves two possibilities: intensification or simplification. The husband and wife who in the early years of marriage show slightly divergent tendencies in a given area—the handling of money, for example—may over time either intensify or simplify their interaction patterns in that area. Thus the husband may want to lay money away for a "rainy day"—a possible emergency—while the wife may have been brought up to believe that money is to be spent. In an area of disagreement such as this, simplification occurs if, for example, the husband and wife decide not to discuss the issue and arrange some method of avoiding conflict, such as allowing the wife a certain amount of money for household expenses, or having her handle the family budgeting. A possibility other than blocking off the troublesome area and simplifying the pattern is intensification of the situation. Intensification is a result of the interplay between accumulation of experiences and simplification, and in the example we are considering may happen as follows. At first, both husband and wife are characterized by subordinate as well as dominant tendencies in their attitude to money. Thus, there are times when he desires to spend and she wants to save for the future. However, frequent conflicts over their dominant tendencies drive them toward opposite poles. These accumulated conflicts result in the simplification of orientations toward this specific issue: he responds increasingly with criticism and anger to her expenditure patterns, while she becomes increasingly bitter about his inability to use money enjoyably. A tendency that had resulted in periodic disagreement has become, over time, a constant and painful antagonism. The same sort of intensification may occur with respect to similarities, as well as differences, with the result that in some areas married persons may become more and more alike and agreeable as they move through life together.

Marriage as a process consists of abrupt and gradual transitions and the effect of these transitions on the course of personality development, interpersonal accommodations, and role alterations. It is in the varying abilities of couples to readjust, and in such processes as anticipatory socialization, task accomplishment, the accumulation of experience, deterioration, and simplification that we are apt to find much of the explanation for marriage outcomes. Unfortunately, little research employing a processual perspective on marriage has as yet been published.[11] The major exception to this dearth of processual research is the investigation of changing marital satisfaction over the course of marriage. The classic investigation of such change is Peter Pineo's twenty-year follow-up on the couples studied by Burgess and Wallin. These couples were first studied during engagement, and again after four to five years of marriage. Pineo investigated their marital satisfaction after they had been married twenty years. He concluded that there had been a general decline in marital satisfaction and adjustments over those twenty years—a result he called "disenchantment."[12] A study by Wesley Burr reported a slightly different result. Among his couples, satisfaction actually began to rise during the children's teenage years, and continued to do so

---

[11] In addition to the work done by Neugarten and her research associates, work is now being done by John Clausen, Glen Elder, and a few others utilizing a processual and age-oriented perspective on the Oakland Growth Study. We shall return to Neugarten's perspective once again in Chapter 14—on aging.

[12] Peter C. Pineo, "Disenchantment in the Later Years of Marriage," *Marriage and Family Living* 23 (1961), 3–11.

until the husband's retirement. Similar results were reported by Karen Renne, who found that couples currently raising children were more dissatisfied with their marriages than those who either had never had children or whose children had left home.[13] A study reporting that retirement is the happiest period of married couples' lives was conducted by Nick Stinnett, Linda Carter, and James Montgomery, who investigated 408 couples between 60 and 89 years of age.[14] And, finally, a study by Boyd Rollins and Harold Feldman confirmed Pineo's and Stinnett's studies. These researchers found marital satisfaction to be high at the childbearing and early child-rearing stages, low during the period when the children are leaving home, and growing through retirement—with a brief decline just prior to the husband's retirement.[15]

These various studies present a fairly clear *curvilinear* picture of marital satisfaction over time. This satisfaction is highest right after marriage, soon stabilizes at a high level, and stays high through the birth of the children. Then it begins to decline. There is a difference of opinion in the literature as to whether marital satisfaction is lowest when the children are preteenagers or during the "launching" years. However, there is general agreement that it rises after the launching years, so that if both couple members survive into old age their marital satisfaction will again be at a high level. It is this author's impression that further research will most likely find Pineo and Rollins and Feldman to be generally correct: the child launching period is the most difficult for a marriage. This, however, may vary according to such factors as number of children and social class.[16]

As we turn now to view marital roles, interactions, and adjustments statically, it will be good to keep in mind that marriage is actually always in flux, always changing. The shifts in marital satisfaction are related to specific events and changes of the sort that we will be discussing. Transitions and personality alterations require constant redefinition of a marriage; in the redefinition process lies the basis for both the excitement and the difficulties inherent in modern marriage.

---

[13] Wesley R. Burr, "Satisfaction with Various Aspects of Marriage over the Life Cycle: A Random Middle Class Sample," *Journal of Marriage and the Family* 32 (1970), 29–37; Karen Renne, "Correlates of Dissatisfaction in Marriage," *Journal of Marriage and the Family* 32 (1970), 54–67.

[14] Nick Stinnett, Linda M. Carter, and James E. Montgomery, "Older Persons' Perceptions of Their Marriages," *Journal of Marriage and the Family* 34 (1972), 665–70.

[15] Boyd C. Rollins and Harold Feldman, "Marital Satisfaction over the Family Life Cycle," *Journal of Marriage and the Family* 32 (1970), 20–28.

[16] Burr, "Satisfaction with Various Aspects of Marriage over the Life Cycle," studied a middle-class sample. It is at least possible that middle-class couples have more to look forward to after launching than do working- or lower-class couples, thus making the launching period less traumatic for them. This, however, deserves research attention rather than speculation. For other sources on marital satisfaction over the life cycle, see Mary W. Hicks and Marilyn Platt, "Marital Happiness and Stability: A Review of the Research in the Sixties," in Carlfred B. Broderick, ed., *A Decade Review of Research and Action* (Minneapolis: National Council on Family Relations, 1971), pp. 70–72.

Section Two

MARRIAGE AS CHANGING ROLES

A couple get married and immediately set about discovering their own and each other's views on how they should behave as husband and wife. The patterns that develop—out of the interplay between expectations, experimentation, and personality—become their particular definitions of husband and wife *roles*. A role consists, therefore, of one's characteristic behavior in a particular position, such as that of husband, clerk, father, or citizen. This section deals with the question of how the roles of husband-father and wife-mother have changed during the history of the U.S. family, the three foci being role differentiation, role blurring, and role choice and conflict—in that order.

Role Differentiation

An important source of change in the family, introduced in Chapter 5, is the increasing functional differentiation of modern industrial society, so that economic, political, religious, educational, and other institutional functions are less and less embedded within either the nuclear family or the kin group. Talcott Parsons describes the process of differentiation thus:

> Differentiation refers to the process by which simple structures are divided into functionally differing components, these components becoming relatively independent of one another, and then recombined into more complex structures in which the functions of the differentiated units are complementary. A key example in the development of industrial society everywhere is the differentiation . . . of the unit of economic production from the kinship household.[17]

The key word in Parsons' definition is *independent*. Parsons' example concerns the way in which the economic-productive role has been removed from the family setting in the modern industrial community.

Parsons' conception of differentiation as it pertains to the family was influenced greatly by his collaboration with Robert Bales, a social psychologist interested in small groups. Bales, in earlier research, had noted that in any small, task-oriented group there tends to evolve a task or *instrumental* leader, whose job it is to lead the way in solving the problem at hand, and a social-emotional or *expressive* leader, who acts to maintain morale and control conflict. By reducing strain, the expressive leader makes a positive

---

[17] Talcott Parsons, "Youth in the Context of American Society," *Daedalus* (Winter 1962), 103.

contribution to the group's perpetuation and thus to its ability to accomplish its task. The same person, the "great man," may play both the task and social-emotional leadership roles, but more often they are played by two different persons.

Utilizing this perspective drawn from small group research, Parsons' co-worker Morris Zelditch discovered in cross-cultural research that the same differentiation of leadership roles occurs within the nuclear family. In the majority of societies, the husband plays the role of instrumental leader, governing the family's economic division of labor, while the wife plays that of the expressive leader.[18]

From this starting point, Parsons feels he can answer those who complain that the husband has lost power in the family to the wife. In his view what has really happened is that as a result of the removal of the economic producing function from the home to an outside setting, plus the increase in the importance of happiness and emotional satisfactions to family solidarity, the husband plays his major role in the outside world, while the wife's role of social-emotional leadership has become central to the family unit per se. Thus, the husband's role has not lost its importance, but it is now being performed in an extrafamilial milieu. The husband has not lost authority; rather, the kind of authority he formerly held within the family cannot now be appropriately exercised because the family no longer engages as a unit in the kind of economic activities over which men exercise authority. The husband formerly ran the economic machinery of the family; the wife continues to run the social-emotional machinery of the family. (See Figure 10 for a diagrammatic representation.)[19]

These same facts, that is, the differentiation of the husband's economic role from the home, can be interpreted in a different, and perhaps more convincing, fashion as follows. The removal of the economic-productive function from the home, combined with the male's retention of that function, gives the male greater control than ever before over the family unit. As industrialization increases, the position of women declines, for they become increasingly dependent upon male economic provision, and are increasingly captives of the domestic scene.[20] Thus, what Randall Collins calls the private household of the market economy becomes increasingly male dominated,

---

[18] Morris Zelditch, Jr., "Role Differentiation in the Nuclear Family: A Comparative Study," in Talcott Parsons and Robert F. Bales, eds., *Family, Socialization, and Interaction Process* (Glencoe, Ill.: Free Press, 1955), pp. 307–42.

[19] For a good discussion of this subject, see Hyman Rodman, "Talcott Parsons' View of the Changing American Family," in Rodman, ed., *Marriage, Family, and Society: A Reader* (New York: Random House, 1965), pp. 273–74.

[20] For this view of women's status, see the references in Arlie Russell Hochschild, "A Review of Sex Role Research," *American Journal of Sociology* 78 (1973), 1011–25.

Figure 10
Diagram of Parsons' View of the Differentiation of Economic Production from the Family Unit as a Result of the Industrial Revolution

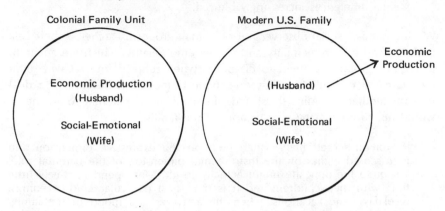

with the female having to use her sexuality to bargain for income favors.[21] It is no accident, therefore, that studies of achievement in the industrial United States have ordinarily used male respondents, while studies of the family have actually been studies of women. For as a result of the industrialization and the differentiation of society the dominant male role is, more than ever before, one of provision-independence-achievement, and the dominant female role one of consumption-dependence-domesticity.

Has the male, then, lost or gained authority in the home? The *nuclearization* of the family gave him increased direct control over the family, while *industrialization* increased his economic veto power—though it lessened the amount of time he would actually spend in "administering" the family unit, a point which leads us to the issue of role blurring.

Role Blurring

The concept of increasing role differentiation, resulting in the removal of the husband's dominant life role from the family setting, is employed by Parsons, Zelditch, Smelser, and others to account for many characteristics of the industrial family. However, another strand of literature—some of it popular, some based upon research—stresses, not differentiation, but the *blurring* of men's and women's roles and behaviors. In several publications Charles Winick has expressed the conviction that

---

[21] Randall Collins, "A Conflict Theory of Sexual Stratification," *Social Problems* **19** (1971), 3–21.

the most significant and visible aspect of the contemporary American sexual scene is the tremendous decline, since World War II, in sexual dimorphism. Sex roles have become substantially neutered and environmental differences increasingly blurred.[22]

Writing not as a social observer but as a small group researcher, Robert Leik finds that male instrumentality and female emotionality, which are apparent in random groupings, "tend to disappear when subjects interact with their own families. Particularly is this true for instrumentality, because of a dual role for mothers."[23] Alice Rossi adds, in speaking of parental roles, that it would not surprise many investigators of the family

> if women scored higher than men on the expressive dimension and men scored higher on the instrumental dimension of the parental role. Yet quite the opposite might actually result. Men spend relatively little time with their children, and it is time of a particular kind: evenings, weekdays, and vacations, when the activities and mood of the family are heavily on the expressive side. Women carry the major burden of the instrumental dimension of parenting.[24]

Zelditch himself points out that "the American middle-class family approaches most clearly to equal allocation (or 'no allocation') of instrumental and expressive activities."[25]

One way in which the historical process of role blurring is described is by the terms *conventional* and *companionate* roles, also called traditional and equalitarian roles.[26] Conventional, or traditional, roles find the husband dominant and the wife subordinate, with the roles of males and females within the home predetermined by tradition. Companionate, or equalitarian, roles involve similarity, choice, and equality—all of which, when compared with the traditional-conventional roles of the colonial and Victorian past, can be considered to exemplify role blurring.

Are the notions of role differentiation and role blurring in conflict, or

---

[22] Charles Winick, "The Beige Epoch: Depolarization of Sex Roles in America," *The Annals* 376 (1968), 18; see also Winick, *The New People: Desexualization in American Life* (New York: Pegasus, 1968).

[23] Robert K. Leik, "Instrumentality and Emotionality in Family Interaction," *Sociometry* 26 (1963), 144.

[24] Rossi, "Transition to Parenthood," p. 39.

[25] Zelditch, "Role Differentiation in the Nuclear Family," in Parsons and Bales, *Family, Socialization, and Interaction Process,* p. 338. Popular references on role blurring include the following: Bruno Bettelheim, "Fathers Shouldn't Be Mothers!" *This Week Magazine,* April 20, 1958; Dorothy Barclay, "Trousered Mothers and Dishwashing Dads," *New York Times Magazine,* April 28, 1957; and Mike Wallace and John A. Schindler, "Are the Two Sexes Merging?" *New York Post,* October 17, 1957.

[26] Annabelle Bender Motz, "Conceptions of Marital Roles by Status Groups," *Marriage and Family Living* 12 (1950), 136, 162; and Ernest W. Burgess, Harvey J. Locke, and Mary Margaret Thomes, *The Family,* 3rd ed. (New York: Litton Educational Publishing, 1963), pp. 3–4.

do they describe divergent aspects of reality? This question can best be answered by beginning with two varying orientations to the study of the family —those of Talcott Parsons and Ernest Burgess. When Parsons writes about the family, he is concerned about the relation of part to whole, of the family to the larger society and its institutions. He therefore describes role differentiation and specialization as a society-wide process that includes as one of its features the removal of the husband's economic-productive role from the home. Burgess, on the other hand, is chiefly interested in what goes on within the family unit itself, in the "unity of interacting personalities" which we call "family." From this perspective it is possible to agree with Parsons that differentiation is important and still to focus on the question: "But how do husbands and wives act *when they are at home*?" Though this is a somewhat oversimplified reconciliation of the "differentiation" and "blurring" viewpoints, it does demonstrate that these two perfectly valid, though interrelated, questions can be asked about the modern family: (1) What effect does increased societal differentiation and the removal of the economic-productive function from the home have on the family? (2) How do husbands and wives act in relation to each other and their children?

The reason our reconciliation of the "differentiation" and "blurring" viewpoints is oversimplified is that some of those who have spoken of "role blurring" think they are talking about the relation of the family to the larger society. Women can work if they want to, this argument goes, and men can be expressive at home; decisions can be made together; and all this means that Parsons' view of industrial differentiation and the family no longer holds, that women have greater societal opportunities than ever before.

To this view Elizabeth Janeway has responded very pointedly as follows:

> *Nothing much has happened.* Man's world, woman's place remain, and our society continues to ascribe different psychological attributes to each sex, and to assign different duties and ways of living to men and women because it is assumed that they have differing capabilities, moral, social, and intellectual as well as physical.[27]

How much women's liberation has occurred? Very little, Janeway feels. The change that has occurred has been a change from an openly recognized and accepted sex differentiation, expressed legally and in other ways, to a covert differentiation which Harriet Holter calls quasi-egalitarianism.[28] This quasi-, or better pseudo-, egalitarianism functions in several ways. First, women dominate institutions which have low status in modern society, one example being

---

[27] Elizabeth Janeway, *Man's World Woman's Place: A Study in Social Mythology* (New York: Dell, Delta Books, 1971), pp. 8–9.

[28] Harriet Holter, "Sex Roles and Social Change," *Acta Sociologica* 14 (1971), 2–12.

grade school teaching. Second, women have greater influence in the home itself, but at a time when the home is under attack. Third, and most important, men and women have, not companionate roles, but what Margaret Poloma and Neal Garland call "neo-traditional" roles. This means that, although the husband and wife can both work if they wish, the husband's work comes first, both in terms of the amount earned and in influence on the residential movement of the family. The wife can work, but only if she is capable of "holding two jobs," that of housewife as well as her paid position.[29] Furthermore, socialization still raises the sexes to be different, so that the "neo-traditional" woman must continue to be "feminine." Thus, this position argues that, while many legal barriers to social equality have been removed, most of the sexual role blurring has remained verbal, and has not as yet pervaded either the role behaviors or the personalities of the U.S. population. The major obstacle to further change, Poloma and Garland feel, is the nuclear family itself.[30]

Role Choice and Conflict

One result of the neo-traditionalization of family roles has been that the role definitions for spouses and parents are not entirely determined by tradition. Because they are given such alternatives as whether or not the wife will work, or how the husband will play the father role, it is incumbent upon couple members not only to think out and make choices regarding their own roles, but to discover their spouses' role definitions as well.

Several studies have shown the intricacies involved in role choice and agreement, and the problems caused by disagreement. Some years ago Robert Ort looked at roles and role conflicts in relation to marital happiness. First, he found a low probability that the spouse of a person who rates himself or herself as happily married will rate himself or herself as equally happy. There is, then, a low correlation between the perceived happiness of husbands and wives. Second, according to Ort, happiness appears to be a function of how well one couple member plays the role or roles that he expects or desires for himself, and of how well one spouse plays the role or roles desired for him/her by the other spouse.[31] The question that arises from these two findings is whether or not the low correlation between the happiness of husbands

---

[29] Margaret M. Poloma and T. Neal Garland, "The Married Professional Woman: A Study in the Tolerance of Domestication," *Journal of Marriage and the Family* 33 (1971), 535.

[30] Poloma and Garland, "The Married Professional Woman," p. 539.

[31] Robert S. Ort, "A Study of Role-Conflicts as Related to Happiness in Marriage," *Journal of Abnormal and Social Psychology* 45 (1950), 691–99.

and wives stems from the difficulty marriage partners have in playing out their desired roles at the same time.

But role conflict between couple members is most likely to occur when they have internalized different sex role conceptions, for example, husband-traditional and wife–neo-traditional or –equalitarian, and when the family system is under great pressure to de-differentiate roles. Yet, as William Knox and Harriet Kupferer report, conflict is much less likely when the husband has internalized a "companionate" and the wife a "conventional" conception than when the husband seeks a conventional and the wife a companionate role. This, of course, is because in the latter case the wife is seeking something the husband is loath to relinquish, while in the former case the husband is willing to concede something the wife does not demand.[32]

Role desires, for oneself and one's spouse, thus appear to be one of the crucial aspects of marriage which demand adjustment and communication on the part of the couple members. Robert Stuckert and Eleanore Luckey, in separate researches, add that it is particularly important that the wife perceive her husband's role expectations for himself correctly, and that she agree with them.[33] This, also, is expectable, since the wife must do more of the adjusting in marriage than her husband, and it is another indication of the lesser role choice available to U.S. females. Role choice, therefore, makes disagreement and conflict a possibility; and conflict may, in turn, disrupt the marriage itself. Yet, while role consensus is important to happiness, conflict or disagreement does not inevitably lead to marital dissolution. Inaccurate perception of role expectations and disagreement based on accurate perception do not necessarily result in dissatisfaction with the marriage if these problems are accepted as typical of marriages in general.[34] "Sure we have our disagreements," this view says, "but so does everyone else we know." Burgess and Locke present a second caution regarding the direct influence of role conflict upon a marriage: "Even if a mate does not live up to the expectations of the other or up to his conception of his role in marriage, the marriage may survive because of the expectations of one or both of the permanent nature of marriage."[35]

It must be concluded that role choice is at least a problematic aspect

---

[32] William E. Knox and Harriet J. Kupferer, "A Discontinuity in the Socialization of Males in the United States," *Merrill-Palmer Quarterly* 17 (1971), 251–61.

[33] Robert P. Stuckert, "Role Perception and Marital Satisfaction—A Configurational Approach," *Marriage and Family Living* 25 (1963), 415–19; Eleanore B. Luckey, "Marital Satisfaction and Its Association with Congruence of Perception," *Marriage and Family Living* 22 (1960), 49–54; Luckey, "Marital Satisfaction and Congruent Self-Spouse Concepts," *Social Forces* 39 (1960), 153–57.

[34] Stuckert, "Role Perception and Marital Satisfaction," p. 418.

[35] Burgess, Locke, and Thomes, *The Family*, p. 204. Copyright © 1963, by Litton Educational Publishing; reprinted by permission of Van Nostrand Reinhold Company.

of modern marriage, since it may lead to communication, adjustment, and primariness, or to conflict and dissolution. Let us at this point, then, review the kinds of role choices confronting males and females in the U.S. family.

Section Three

HUSBAND-FATHER ROLE CHOICES

The constant outpouring of words about the American woman in recent years, says Myron Brenton in his book *The American Male,* "has made it seem as though the male either had no problems or didn't count enough to have them aired."[36] The American male does, however, confront several issues that demand resolution. First, he must reconcile his sedentary role with the traditional image of the male as subduer of nature. Second, he must determine—with the removal of his economic role from the home—how much of his time and energy he will invest in the extrafamilial world and how much he will reserve for his family. Finally, he must reconcile the prevailing democratic ideology with the lingering image of the male as patriarch, as the authority over his wife and children. Let us look briefly at each of these issues.

The "Feminization" of Occupations

The shift of the husband's economic role out of the home, and the increasing importance to the family of the wife's social-emotional role, are not felt by Robert Winch to be a sufficient explanation for the push toward androgyny,* or at least role blurring, in U.S. society. Winch observes that, cross-culturally, the family systems in which the husband is most apt to be the dominant figure are those in which the importance of human strength and endurance, in which males ordinarily excel, are central to the economic institution.[37] That is, if family economic maintenance is based on the physical strength of the male, he tends to have the key role in the family.

In modern industrial society technological advances have reduced the contribution of human strength to societal maintenance to a small proportion of what it has been cross-culturally and historically. Viewed in these terms, technology has resulted, in a sense, in the "feminization" of the occupational structure—not just in its removal from the home. This statement should not be construed to mean that the market no longer favors the male. What it does mean is that there is a great incongruity between the "feminization" of the occupational-economic structure and the male dominance of that struc-

---

[36] Myron Brenton, *The American Male* (New York: Coward-McCann, 1966), p. 13. Copyright © 1966 by Myron Brenton; reprinted by permission of Coward-McCann, Inc.

[37] Robert F. Winch, *The Modern Family* (New York: Holt, Rinehart and Winston, 1963 ed.), pp. 399–400.

ture which followed the industrial revolution. This makes it much more difficult for employers to hire and to determine salary on the basis of male superiority in handling a particular job. Perception by the male of his occupational "replaceability" by the female may be a severe jolt to his self-concept. This particular problem would seem to be most acute at the lower-middle-class level, where sales and clerical personnel may be more painfully aware of their replaceability than are either professionals or manual workers. The male self-concept based on mastery, competition, nonemotionalism, and strength is the focal point of the "men's liberation movement." This movement, described in Feature 6, seeks to free the male from the traditional masculine definition, so that he may be more completely human.

Home Versus Community

In an era of institutional nonembeddedness, the male is confronted with a completely new decision: "How much of myself shall I invest in my occupation and community, and how much in my family?" Not only does he have

---

FEATURE 6

Warren Farrell, a young egghead with a nifty black beard, intends to liberate the men of America.

He expects the Men's Liberation Movement he heads will make life happier for men, women, and children.

. . . Farrell said the problems of masculinity include pressures on a boy to recall with joy his first touch of Playboy magazine, his first Little League exposure. Also: such masculine pressures as—boys never cry, boys always are strong, boys and-or men must always be problem solvers. . . .

Farrell said a society that makes "success objects" out of men keeps the men in the rat race. This success object—win the game, bring home the bacon—role is just as unfair to men as is the sex object role thrust on women. . . .

NOW's Masculine Mystique task force focuses on those problems of masculinity which simultaneously hurt both women and men.

Consider:

√ The expectation for a man to dominate in conversations prevents a man from listening while it discourages a woman's full participation.

√ The pressure of society which dictates a dependent role for a woman pressures a man into being the problem solver. The pressure for her to be sexually indirect forces him to put his ego on the line by taking the initiative.

Farrell said:

"The task force's belief that the problems of masculinity start in many of the same areas in which the discrimination against women occurs, has led to its encouragement of research and actions in the areas considered in the past only concerns of women's lib.

These areas include advertising, labor, reproduction, among others. . . .

Patricia McCormick, "Men's Liberation Movement Fights Male Mystique," *Wisconsin State Journal*, June 17, 1974.

few guidelines to follow in making the choice, but wives disagree greatly in their expectations for their husbands in this area. One of the popular newspaper columnists opened the issue to a public forum after publishing a letter from a wife who complained bitterly that her husband expended all his energy at work and had none left for her or the children. The results were most instructive. A large number of wives agreed entirely with this complaint, expressing the wish that their husbands would spend a little less time and energy trying to "get ahead," and a little more in meeting their wives' and children's needs. Yet an equally large number argued vehemently that they would rather be married to a successful husband who provided well for his wife and children than to a family man with little ambition.

Since guidelines are virtually nonexistent, husbands must work out in terms of personality traits and in interaction with their wives precisely how they shall divide their time and energy resources. Most men can keep busy with their occupations and community affairs as much of the time as they are willing to give. Thus, those who *want* to escape the home are likely to employ the ready-made excuse of extrafamilial demands.[38]

Husband and Father

Not unrelated to the foregoing issue is the question of how the male will perform as husband and father. Does he try to be patriarch, making the key decisions himself and restricting his wife to housewifery and motherhood? Does he reject "women's work" around the house? does he do it grudgingly or willingly? As Brenton notes, it is not doing what was formerly women's work that causes him trouble; it is worrying about doing it because of the vestiges of patriarchal values.[39] It is not the decline in parental and male authority that is a problem; the problem is the couple's disagreement over their respective roles or the husband's excessive concern about the position he has presumably lost. Leonard Benson, in his excellent summarization of *Fatherhood*, puts this issue very well:

> A man wields power in the contemporary household only if he has the personal characteristics to pull it off or because of a unique pattern of domestic relationships, not because society backs him up with strong support.[40]

---

[38] For additional ideas regarding the relationship between work and the family, see Rapoport and Rapoport, "Work and Family in Contemporary Society."

[39] Brenton, *The American Male.* pp. 28–29. On the decline in male authority, see J. M. Mogey, "A Century of Declining Paternal Authority," *Marriage and Family Living* 19 (1957), 234–39; Knox and Kupferer, "A Discontinuity in the Socialization of Males in the United States," pp. 260–61.

[40] Leonard Benson, *Fatherhood: A Sociological Perspective* (New York: Random House, 1968), pp. 99–100; on this see Morris Freilich, "The Natural Triad in Kinship and Complex Systems," *American Sociological Review* 29 (1964), 529–40.

Perhaps the most open issue confronting the male in the home is the definition of the father role. When the father headed the family's economic division of labor in an agrarian society, his responsibilities were clear. But in the modern industrial world what should a father be? Should he be the *adviser and grand inquisitor*—the final authority and high court of appeals? This approach is caricatured in the description of the mother who, having taken all the misbehavior she can stand from her children, finally announces, "Just wait 'til your father gets home." Father is thus expected to walk in the door and spank or scold the child for actions he did not even witness. Such a role is acceptable to some fathers because it convinces them that they have not yielded their position as patriarch, despite the fact that they are not at home much of the time.

Should the father be the *everyday Santa Claus,* who wouldn't dare come home from a business trip without "something for the kids"? This pattern is caricatured in the father whose return home is greeted, not by, "We're glad you're home, Dad," but by, "What did you bring us, Dad?" It is a viable approach for many fathers who invest neither time nor energy in their offspring, but who do have money.

Finally, should the father try to be the *buddy and pal,* who can't really appreciate his children until they are big enough to catch a ball, or to enjoy camping? This is caricatured in the cartoon that depicts the teenage son's response when his aging and paunchy father enters the room clad in his baseball uniform: "Gee, Dad, I want a Father, not a pal!" There are advice-givers and critics to match each of these role choices; Brenton depicts the dilemma as follows:

> If he concentrates on being a pal to his son, he's evading his role as authority figure. If he has a nurturant bent, some of the psychiatrists call him a motherly father. If he doesn't do any nurturing to speak of, he's accused of distancing himself from his children. If he's the sole disciplinarian, he takes on, in his youngsters' eyes, the image of an ogre. If he doesn't discipline them sufficiently, he's a weak father. If he's well off and gives his children all the material advantages he didn't have, he's spoiling them, leaving them unprepared for life's hard knocks. If he's well off but doesn't spoil them the way other fathers in the community do their boys and girls, he gains the reputation of a latter-day Scrooge.... And, repeatedly, the accusing voices tell him that he has given up his rightful place as head of the family, as guide and mentor to his children.[41]

Obviously, for most fathers, the performance of the father role includes some combination of the possibilities, often with one tending to be dominant. Sociological research has done little to determine the empirical distribution

---

[41] Brenton, *The American Male,* p. 135.

of "fathering" styles, though it is reasonable to assume that the "inquisitor" or authority approach might be more a working- or lower-class orientation, and the "Santa Claus" approach a primarily middle-class orientation. Nor, for that matter, has sociological research indicated much concerning the effects of different approaches to the father and husband roles on marital adjustment and child development.[42] Wesley Becker did report, however, that if the father's relationship to his children was loving, democratic, and emotionally mature, the mother rated them better adjusted, outgoing, and not as demanding.[43] The crucial issue, however, is that the norms and guidelines are so ill-defined that the husband is compelled to determine his role specifications in accordance with his personality and his wife's expectations.

Section Four

WIFE-MOTHER ROLE CHOICES

About the year 1950 a movie was made which strikingly illustrated the "woman's dilemma." The heroine of *The Red Shoes*, unable to choose between her love for her husband and her career as a ballerina, resolves her problem by suicide. In real life, most women choose less dramatic compromises. Nevertheless (as we noted in Chapter 4), the change in the status of women—legal, political, economic, and educational—has presented them with broader, though still limited, role choices. No longer is a woman bound by a single option, that of housewife and mother. Though societal values still stress her role within the home, the interplay between mass education for women, the possibility of economic independence, and depreciation of the housewife's role, combined with the expectation that the woman will assume that role, have intensified the problematic aspects of her role choices.

Much of the literature on the contemporary female poses the issue dichotomously, as one strictly between working and staying home. Popular books such as Betty Friedan's *The Feminine Mystique* and Phyllis McGinley's *Sixpence in Her Shoe* do not necessarily clarify the choice; in fact, they may make it more difficult by overstating the advantages of one or the other alternative.[44] Furthermore, to pose the so-called woman's dilemma as simply

---

[42] On conjugal role relationships, see Lee Rainwater, *Family Design: Marital Sexuality, Family Size, and Contraception* (Chicago: Aldine, 1965), pp. 28–60. On family patterns and their effect on offspring, see J. W. Getzels and P. Jackson, *Creativity and Intelligence* (New York: Wiley, 1962).

[43] Wesley C. Becker, "The Relationship of Factors in Parental Ratings of Self and Each Other to the Behavior of Kindergarten Children as Rated by Mothers, Fathers, and Teachers," *Journal of Consulting Psychology* 24 (1960), 507–27.

[44] For a review of the debate on women's roles, see Hilda Sidney Krech, "Housewife and Woman? The Best of Both Worlds?" in Seymour M. Farber, Piero Mustacchi, and Roger H. L. Wilson, eds., *Man and Civilization: The Family's Search for Survival* (New York:

involving the choice of whether to be a housewife or a housewife and job-holder is to pose it strictly in terms of the traditional–neo-traditional debate outlined above. At present, however, the issue is becoming more complex. Elizabeth Havens, for example, has reported that unmarried status among females is directly related to income when other variables, such as amount of education, are controlled for.[45] That is, the woman who has success aspirations is more likely to achieve them if she remains single. Approaching the drawbacks of domestic life from another angle, Walter Gove and Jeanette Tudor have noted that the rate of mental illness is higher among married women than among any other category of women. This is not, however, due just to feminine socialization, to playing the role of woman in U.S. society, but is due to playing the *married* woman or wife role. The restrictiveness of that role, its frustrations and lack of visible rewards, and the limitations within which women's choices operate today, make it more apt to produce mental illness than the role of husband.[46] A third expansion of the traditional–neo-traditional debate concerns the supposed joys of pregnancy and childbearing. Warren Hern has argued that it is erroneous to assume that pregnancy is a normal and desirable state. A more accurate view, he feels, would be that human pregnancy is an episodic, moderately extended chronic condition with a definable morbidity and mortality risk to which females are uniquely though not uniformly susceptible.[47] The fact that many young women have altered their views of pregnancy and child rearing in the direction suggested by Hern has drastically reduced the birthrate since 1967, and has been consistent with demands for population control and more liberal abortion laws.

Marriage is incompatible with societal success, the role of wife is productive of frustration and even mental illness, and pregnancy and childbearing are not normal but are temporary upsets in human life—these and other arguments have begun to alter the focus of the "woman's dilemma." Now it is not merely a question of family and work or just family, but of marriage or nonmarriage and of childbearing or no childbearing. For many women, however, the neo-traditional question is still uppermost. Gilda Epstein and Arline Bronzaft, for example, found that 48 percent of girls entering college in 1970

McGraw-Hill, 1965, pp. 136–52. See also Betty Friedan, *The Feminine Mystique* (New York: Dell, 1963); Phyllis McGinley, *Sixpence in Her Shoe* (New York: Macmillan, 1964); Simone de Beauvoir, *The Second Sex* (New York: Bantam Books, 1961); Ferdinand Lundberg and Marynia Farnham, *Modern Women: The Lost Sex* (New York: Harper & Row, 1947); and Kate Millett, *Sexual Politics* (Garden City, N.Y.: Doubleday, 1970).

[45] Elizabeth M. Havens, "Women, Work, and Wedlock: A Note on Female Marital Patterns in the United States," *American Journal of Sociology* 78 (1973), 975–81.

[46] Walter R. Gove and Jeanette F. Tudor, "Adult Sex Roles and Mental Illness," *American Journal of Sociology* 78 (1973), 814–16, 831.

[47] Warren M. Hern, "Is Pregnancy Really Normal?" *Family Planning Perspectives* 3 (1971), 10.

expected to be married career women with children fifteen years later, while 28 percent expected to be housewives with children. No one expected to be a housewife without children, and a very small percentage looked forward to becoming single career women or married career women without children.[48] In addition, the neo-traditional orientation is increasing empirically, as the number of working women with children continues to rise (see Feature 7). Let us, therefore, look in some detail at the working wife and her more traditional counterpart.[49]

Working Wives: Role Consensus, Motives, and Social Class

In the twentieth century industrial society, women have increasingly gained the right to enter the labor market on their own, to obtain jobs and promotions independently. In 1890, when the labor force of the United States was one-sixth female, few women worked for reasons other than economic necessity. Today, however, when women comprise about one-third of the labor force, many work because they want to, either to raise the family's standard of living or because work gives them a creative outlet.[50] At one time, it was assumed that if the wife worked, the result would necessarily be a poorer marital adjustment between herself and her husband. Were this view correct, it would still be incumbent upon those who hold it to answer the following question: Does the marriage become maladjusted because the woman works or does the woman work because her marriage is maladjusted?[51] Yet even this statement of the dilemma, Lois Hoffman feels, is un-

---

[48] Gilda F. Epstein and Arline L. Bronzaft, "Female Freshmen View Their Roles as Women," *Journal of Marriage and the Family* 34 (1972), 671–72.

[49] For some of the sociological literature on working wives, see F. Ivan Nye and Lois Wladis Hoffman, *The Employed Mother in America* (Chicago: Rand McNally, 1963 ed.).

[50] William J. Goode, *World Revolution and Family Patterns* (New York: Free Press, 1963), p. 61, quotes these figures on women's employment.

[51] This same issue is raised by Leland J. Axelson, "The Marital Adjustment and Marital Role Definitions of Husbands of Working and Non-Working Wives," *Marriage and Family Living* 25 (1963), 195; and F. Ivan Nye, "Marital Interaction," in Nye and Hoffman, *The Employed Mother in America*, p. 272.

FEATURE 7

The number of working mothers with children in this country is soaring. More than 57 percent of all women with children aged 6 to 17 worked during 1972. Some of the pressures bringing mothers to the labor market are divorce, falling birth rates, boredom and simple economic necessity, the last the most important and frequent pressure.

As an increasing number of American mothers seek and obtain employment, the need for increased and improved child day-care centers grows more acute.

Lloyd Shearer, "Intelligence Report," *Parade: Wisconsin State Journal*, June 30, 1974.

satisfactory. The dichotomy between working and nonworking is too grossly stated; it needs to be broken down and examined in terms of certain test variables. Following her advice, we shall examine the marital adjustment of working and nonworking wives, using the following variables: (1) role consensus, or how the wife and husband feel about her particular role choice; (2) motives, or why the wife is doing what she is doing; and (3) social class differences in marital adjustment according to the work status of the wife. In each case we shall attempt to discern from the literature what effect the "test variable" has upon the wife's and the husband's marital adjustment.

What roles do college men expect their wives-to-be to play? In an interesting response to that question, Mirra Komarovsky found that 24 percent intended to marry a woman who would find sufficient satisfaction in remaining at home. Another 16 percent said they would be willing to have their wives work, but hedged their approval with qualifications that no woman could meet. A neo-traditionalist response was given by 48 percent, who said that their wives could work, then stop working for childbearing, and eventually return to work. Only 7 percent indicated a willingness to modify their own roles significantly to facilitate their future wives' careers.[52] The men in this sample showed great ambivalence toward both the housewife and the career roles for their wives, deprecating the former and feeling threatened by the latter. This ambivalence, Komarovsky is convinced, is bound to exacerbate the role conflicts in the wives.[53]

When the wife's desires for herself and the husband's expectations for her are combined logically, four possibilities emerge. First, she works because both she and her husband agree that she should. Second, she stays home because both she and her husband think she should. Third, she works despite the fact that her husband thinks she should be at home. Finally, though least likely in view of Komarovsky's findings, she doesn't work, although her husband thinks she should. In general, either of the first two alternatives is considerably more satisfactory than the third and fourth. Does working, therefore, have a detrimental effect upon marital adjustment which is independent of role consensus? The crucial test of this question is in the comparison of the first two types, in which role consensus is controlled. Ivan Nye's answer is yes: when only those husbands who approve of what their wife is doing are compared, those whose wives are not working manifest a better marital adjustment.[54] One reason is that, even if the husband expresses a willingness to have his wife work, he may still define

---

[52] Mirra Komarovsky, "Cultural Contradictions and Sex Roles: The Masculine Case," *American Journal of Sociology* 78 (1973), 873–84.

[53] Komarovsky, "Cultural Contradictions and Sex Roles," p. 883.

[54] Nye, "Marital Interaction," in Nye and Hoffman, *The Employed Mother in America,* p. 279. See also Artie Gianopoulos and Howard E. Mitchell, "Marital Disagreement in Working Wife Marriages as a Function of Husband's Attitude Toward Wife's Employment," *Marriage and Family Living* 19 (1957), 373–78.

this as threatening or as undermining his dominant role as economic provider. Furthermore, he may be willing to have her work, as long as he does not have to contribute equally to running the household. That is, if she will work sixteen hours a day, half on the job and half at home, that would be fine with him. But the effect of such an uneven burden upon the marriage can only be negative.

Omitting role consensus from consideration, Susan Orden and Norman Bradburn, in a study of 1,651 married persons, conclude that the wife who works by choice tends to have the best marital adjustment, followed first by the wife who stays home and then by the wife who works out of necessity.[55] Catherine Arnott and Vern Bengtsen find that educated women who work feel that the homemaker role has brought them neither the status nor the recognition they deserve.[56] Their motive for working, then, is to be doing something approximately commensurate with their training and abilities. Although these findings are interesting in themselves, they do not deal with the issue of husband-wife consensus, or with questions involving general orientation and perception. In their study of twenty-five working-wife and twenty-five non-working-wife families in Champaign, Illinois, Jeanne Hafstrom and Marilyn Dunsing find that of the ten wives who say they are working out of necessity, seven indicate that they would continue working even if it were not necessary. The fact that a wife works, according to Hilda Krech, still has negative connotations regardless of her motivations:

> In the eyes of many people, saying that a woman *must* work for financial gain casts a reflection on her husband. The question is raised: "Can't he support her?" Ironically, reflections are also cast on the woman who has chosen to work. The question is raised: "Does she really love her children?"[57]

What, then, does it actually mean for a wife to be "working out of necessity"? The important fact, it would seem, is that she *perceives* working to be a necessity rather than a choice. If she perceives and defines it as a necessity, all the negative intimations that her working still arouses regarding her and her husband are heightened, and her marital adjustment suffers.

Yet why consider motives separately at all? Krech, for example, points out that "making a sharp distinction between women who must work and those who have decided to work leaves out of account the powerful but

---

[55] Susan R. Orden and Norman M. Bradburn, "Working Wives and Marriage Happiness," *American Journal of Sociology* 74 (1969), 407.

[56] Catherine Arnott and Vern L. Bengtsen, "Only a Homemaker: Distributive Justice and Role Choice Among Married Women," *Sociology and Social Research* 54 (1970), 495–507.

[57] Krech, "Housewife and Woman?" in Farber, Mustacchi, and Wilson, *Man and Civilization*, pp. 146–47.

often ignored phenomenon of 'mixed motivations.' "[58] Furthermore, to say that one is working "out of necessity" is actually to describe a particular instance of role dissensus: she prefers to stay home but is forced to work. For, as Hafstrom and Dunsing report, if many who say they are working out of necessity would work anyway, what is the significance of necessity?[59] In short, then, much of the discussion of motivation, in terms of its influence upon adjustment, can be subsumed (with one extension) under the four-fold typology presented above: the wife stays home or works because she and her husband agree that she should. In such instances adjustment is satisfactory. The wife stays home although her husband wishes she would work. This is perhaps the least frequent option empirically, but it could result in marital maladjustment. Finally—and this is the extension—the wife works, but either her husband wants her to stay home or else *she wishes she could stay home*, the result being a substantial likelihood of marital mal-adjustment.[60]

The several studies of working wives which take *social class* level into consideration tend to agree with Nye that "any net *adverse* effect of employment on marital adjustment is less in the higher socioeconomic families than in the lower."[61] Why this should be so is clarified by Orden and Bradburn and by Mirra Komarovsky's study *Blue-Collar Marriage*. The former authors report that "the proportion of employed women who are in the labor market by choice increases with education from 34 percent among those with an eighth-grade education or less to 77 percent among college graduates."[62] Komarovsky, noting that wives work for different reasons, adds that working-class husbands seem a bit more ambivalent than do middle-class husbands. The former tend to hold the traditional ideology that woman's place is in the home, though they appreciate the higher standard of living that the wife's income provides.[63]

Thus, the greater marital problems caused when the wife in the lower-status family works are a direct function of the fourth alternative presented above. That is, more low-status wives work out of necessity, wishing they could stay home (or at least that they had the option of doing so), and

---

[58] Krech, "Housewife and Woman?" in Farber, Mustacchi, and Wilson, *Man and Civilization.*

[59] Jeanne L. Hafstrom and Marilyn M. Dunsing, "A Comparison of Economic Choices in One-Earner and Two-Earner Families," *Journal of Marriage and the Family* 27 (1965), 409.

[60] A more complex model of the wife's task performance, including whether she works or not, is presented in Burr, *Theory Construction and the Sociology of the Family*, p. 255.

[61] Nye, "Marital Interaction," in Nye and Hoffman, *The Employed Mother in America*, p. 280.

[62] Orden and Bradburn, "Working Wives and Marriage Happiness," p. 398.

[63] Komarovsky, *Blue-Collar Marriage*, p. 65.

more low-status wives work whose husbands would prefer, on traditional ideological grounds, that they stay home. It is in the middle-class family that the combination of an equalitarian ideology and choice increases the likelihood that husband and wife can reach a consensus regarding her role choices based on preference.

However, three major problems confront the highly trained married female today. She may have reached a consensus with her husband, but it may still be difficult for her to pursue a career, rather than to simply "hold a job." Her first problem is getting started: there are still many more clerical and sales openings for women than openings in the professions and management. Her second problem is that even if she gets started on a career, she may do so at a lower salary level and with less possibility of promotion than a male with equal training.[64] Her third problem is that most males are willing to accept neo-traditional roles, but no more. That is, they are willing to let their wives work, but do not want them to be overly committed to their work. Thus, in a sample of couples where the wife was a teacher the highest marital adjustment scores were reported when both couple members were satisfied with their jobs and the husband was high and the wife low on job satisfaction and salience.[65] Even with consensus, then, the husband does not want his wife's work to "get in the way" of other things. In terms of role consensus, regardless of social class, U.S. couples are still a long way from the goals of either women's or men's liberation.

Wife's Work Status and Child Adjustment

In general, the mother who is working for self-fulfillment or to raise an already adequate standard of living while the couple is young enough to enjoy it[66] (and whose husband wholeheartedly agrees with her choice) is neither inherently worse nor inherently better for the children than the non-working mother.[67] In fact, Carmi Schooler reports that when background and family structural variables are controlled, the only variation that emerges is

---

[64] Good sources on the problems confronting the professionally trained woman are: Carolyn Cummings Perrucci, "Minority Status and the Pursuit of Professional Careers: Women in Science and Engineering," *Social Forces* 49 (1970), 245–59; and Cynthia Epstein, "Encountering the Male Establishment: Sex-Status Limits on Women's Careers in the Professions," *American Journal of Sociology* 75 (1970), 965–82.

[65] Carl A. Ridley, "Exploring the Impact of Work Satisfaction and Involvement on Marital Interaction When Both Partners Are Employed," *Journal of Marriage and the Family* 35 (1973), 229–37.

[66] This is noted in Hafstrom and Dunsing, "A Comparison of Economic Choices in One-Earner and Two-Earner Families," p. 409.

[67] Marian Radke Yarrow et al., "Child Rearing in Families of Working and Non-Working Mothers," *Sociometry* 25 (1962), 122–40.

that the offspring of working mothers are more receptive to innovation than are those of nonworking mothers.[68] In terms of satisfaction, control, and other aspects of child rearing, the worst adjustment is found among those nonworking mothers who prefer to work (perhaps as an escape from their deficiencies as mothers).

But do the children not feel deprived when their mother works? Yarrow et al. indicate that working mothers may actually spend more time with their children doing what the *children* enjoy than do nonworking mothers. They may even show more love toward their children, either because they are happier working and miss their children, or perhaps because they feel a certain amount of guilt at working in the face of the lingering conventional ideology.[69] Once again, a mother's relations to her children, as well as the children's adjustment, are determined not so much by the fact that the mother works as by attitudinal dimensions.

Two qualifications upon the foregoing generalization can be found in articles by Lois Hoffman and Aase Skard. Part-time employed mothers seem to have better-adjusted children than do mothers employed full-time. Perhaps the reason for this is that the mother feels less guilt; but the most direct advantage of part-time over full-time employment is that the former is less likely to communicate to the children that the father is a failure, or is not the primary breadwinner.[70] In addition, no matter how much the mother works, it is best if her hours are relatively regular and if she works from the early months after the child's birth or else waits until he starts school. In other words, the child's feelings of maternal (that is, parental) deprivation, which are of great concern to those who argue against the mother's working, are most apt to appear if the mother starts to work while the child is between ages two and five. And, of course, adequate help in the form of daytime care is necessary for the child's adjustment to remain satisfactory.[71] Given the qualifications regarding part- versus full-time employment, regularity and permanence, and adequate help, Skard is able to summarize the effect of the mother's employment upon the child as follows: "Children develop best and most harmoniously when the mother herself is happy and gay. Whether she has work outside the home or not seems rather unimportant from the child's viewpoint."[72]

---

[68] Carmi Schooler, "Childhood Family Structure and Adult Characteristics," *Sociometry* 35 (1972), 255–69.

[69] Yarrow et al., "Child Rearing in Families of Working and Non-Working Mothers."

[70] Lois Wladis Hoffman, "Effects on Children: Summary and Discussion," in Nye and Hoffman, *The Employed Mother in America*, p. 197.

[71] Aase Gruda Skard, "Maternal Deprivation: The Research and Its Implications," *Journal of Marriage and the Family* 27 (1965), 333–43.

[72] Skard, "Maternal Deprivation," p. 343.

Conclusion

"To work or not to work" is obviously an oversimplified depiction of the home versus community choice confronting the contemporary female. Many nonworking women spend as much time in various volunteer community activities as they would on a job. These, too, can be a source of strain or a source of pride for their families, depending upon their orientations. Moreover, as we indicated in the early part of this chapter, adjustments do not remain unchanged. Many husbands, for example, who agree with their wives' role choices eventually find themselves annoyed by the amount of time that their talented and busy wives spend in various sorts of community activities. Couple members cannot decide such matters prior to marriage, or even when role decisions are first made; therefore, a concomitant of role choice in the contemporary U.S. family is the necessity of continuing communication.

By this point it should be apparent that family adjustments are determined, not by the structural arrangements themselves, such as the wife's working or not working, but by the attitudinal and expectational components of role choices.

> "Fräulein Spöckenkieker is a divorced woman, so I have heard," said Frau Rittersdorf. "She is, I am given to understand, a woman of business—a lingerie business of sorts, she has three shops and has kept her maiden name in all circumstances. No wonder she no longer has a husband. It may also account for her manners, or lack of them."
>
> "I wished to continue with my teaching after marriage," said Frau Hutten, with wifely pride, "but my husband would not hear of it for a moment. 'The husband supports the family,' he told me, 'and the wife makes a happy home for them both. That is her sacred mission,' he said, 'and she must be prevented at all costs from abandoning it.' And so it was. From that day to this, I have done only housework, except to act as secretary to my husband."
>
> Frau Schmitt blushed. "I taught for years," she said, "in the same school with my husband, who was in poor health, almost an invalid, after the war. He could not carry a full professorship; it was important for him not to be too heavily burdened. We had no children, what else should I have been doing? There was not enough to do in our simple little house to keep me occupied. No, I was glad to help my husband. And we had a happy home as well." Her tone was gently defensive and self-satisfied.[73]

Thus does Katherine Anne Porter portray the subtle dominance of traditional roles among the available options. Family maladjustment, we have found, is

---

[73] Katherine Anne Porter, *Ship of Fools* (Boston: Little, Brown, 1945), pp. 155–56. Copyright 1945, 1946, 1947, 1950 © 1956, 1958, 1959, 1962 by Katherine Anne Porter; reprinted by permission of Atlantic-Little, Brown.

most likely if there is no choice available at all, or if the husband and wife have differing expectations, or if the choice is interpreted as disparaging one or more members of the family (such as the husband in his role as bread-winner). And all these bases for family maladjustment, we should repeat, still leave the contemporary family a long way from the goals of the liber-ation movements: from freedom for the man to stay at home and not feel "disparaged," from freedom for the woman to reject marriage or childbear-ing altogether, from freedom for a couple to share in a truly equal way the drudgery that is housework.

In discussing the general issues regarding marital roles in the contem-porary United States, we have passed over the more specific interactional and adjustment problems that must be faced by the married couple. How do they make day-to-day decisions? Who does what in the household? What about the economic and sexual adjustments of husbands and wives? These and other such issues are the subject matter of Chapter 12.

Marriage:
Interactions
and Adjustments

Many interactions of husbands and wives that occur in the course of performing their roles involve the making of day-to-day decisions and the carrying out of tasks in the household division of labor. Expectations concerning decision-making have become increasingly equalitarian, though differences between expectations and actuality become apparent when middle-class and lower-class couples are compared. The apportionment of household tasks, while no longer central to economic productivity or carefully delineated by sex, is still a central concern of married couples. Two areas of marital adjustment—finances and sex—are assumed by many observers to hold a uniquely important place within U.S. marriage; we explore some reasons for this assumption. Discussion of three issues—marital predicaments, communication, and the desirability of choice—is used to summarize Chapters 11 and 12.

Roles and transitions are the central axes of marriage; around them revolve the daily decisions, the household tasks, and the financial and sexual adjustments that give each marriage its particular character. This chapter concerns the day-to-day interactions and adjustments of modern marriage, with some assessment of the ways in which these aspects of marriage have changed since colonial days. We begin with decision-making and the division of labor.

Section One

HUSBAND-WIFE INTERACTION: RUNNING THE HOUSEHOLD

Studying Power and Decision-Making

No area of family study is at the same time more intriguing and more fraught with problems than that of power and decision-making—the determination of family outcomes. The problems in this area are the usual twofold bane of social science: *conceptualization* and *measurement*. David Olson and Carolyn Rabunsky put it thus: "Although theorists and researchers have shown considerable interest in this concept, it is still lacking in conceptual clarity and valid operational measures."[1]

What is wrong with the concepts used in the study of family power? "Most investigators," says Constantina Safilios-Rothschild, "have used interchangeably the terms 'family power' or 'power structure' and the terms 'decision making,' 'family authority' and 'influence.' "[2] Use of the same term with different meanings and of different terms with the same meaning by writers in this area has made the comparison of their results extremely difficult. As for measurement, Safilios-Rothschild notes that most studies of power have been based solely on the responses of wives, and Olson and Rabunsky note that responses do differ, depending upon whether the respondent is a father, a mother, or a child. Equally troublesome is the fact that different research methodologies—surveys, laboratory experiments, observation in the home—produce somewhat different pictures of "who has the power."[3] These authors assert, therefore, that what is needed are studies using multiple measuring techniques, so that the biases of the various approaches can be more adequately determined.

But what can be done to clarify the concepts? Some have suggested that the concept *power* be dropped entirely, while others, such as Robert Ryder, feel that it should be used in a strictly interpersonal sense. A has power over B, says Ryder, only (1) if A can lead B to act in keeping with A's intentions, or (2) if A can get B to do something B does not want to do.[4] Power, then, is the overarching interpersonal concept, and can be treated as the sum total of the relations between authority, influence, and decision-making. *Authority* is the most easily accessible concept, since it is based on who *ought* to determine outcomes. Much of the information gained from questionnaires pertains to people's ideological views of the way things should work.

Outcomes, however, are not always consistent with authority relations, and the difference between authority and outcome is accounted for by *influence*. Influence may be based on very personal attributes, or on acceptance of authority, and may, therefore, either reinforce or undermine the "authority structure." *Decision-making* is the actual event-point in the interplay between influence, authority, and outcome. Yet decision-making is

[1] David H. Olson and Carolyn M. Rabunsky, "Validity of Four Measures of Family Power," *Journal of Marriage and the Family* 34 (1972), 232.

[2] Constantina Safilios-Rothschild, "The Study of Family Power Structure: A Review 1960–1969," *Journal of Marriage and the Family* 32 (1970), 539.

[3] Olson and Rabunsky, "Validity of Four Measures of Family Power"; Safilios-Rothschild, "The Study of Family Power Structure."

[4] Robert G. Ryder, "What Is Power?: Definitional Considerations and Some Research Implications," *Science and Psychoanalysis* 20 (1972), 40.

synonymous neither with doing nor with power. The key issue here is the relation between delegating, deciding, and doing. It is obvious that the one who dominates a particular decision may not, in fact, be the one who implements it, that is, actually does the task. Furthermore, it is even possible for the decision to be made by one member of a couple because the other member has delegated the decision-making function, or is simply uninterested. This, then, greatly complicates the relationship between decision-making and power, since a decision may be a result of struggle, delegation, or default. In the first case, one can say that the decision-maker has the power; in the latter two cases, greater power appears to lie with the non-decision-maker.

Let us not belabor these difficulties any longer. Suffice it to say that this writer does not consider the ambiguities and difficulties in the study of family (or better, marital)[5] power to be insurmountable. The foregoing clarifications should help to resolve them and may be useful in presenting the results of the studies already available.

Power and Decision-Making in the U.S. Family

"No change in the American family," say Robert Blood and Donald Wolfe, "is mentioned more often than the shift from one-sided male authority to the sharing of power by husband and wife."[6] The point is not that the wife had no influence over what went on within the colonial family, though she frequently did have to resort to subtle means in order to get her way. Rather, the ideology of the colonial family was that the husband had the authority, and the ideology of the modern family is becoming more equalitarian.[7] Does this change mean that Blood and Wolfe are correct? Not necessarily. It could mean that the husband's lessened authority has been compensated for by a rise in his influence, so that his determination of the family's direction is as great or greater than ever before. This is Dair Gillespie's conclusion. Women today, Gillespie concludes, are at a great power disadvantage. Men can keep their wives, or women in general, from doing things. Wives take on their husbands' social rank. Women are socialized to play inferior, deferential, receptive social roles. Wives still lack legal power, in terms of such things as the names they bear and control over financial resources. Husbands still dominate in determining whom the couple will

---

[5] Safilios-Rothschild, "The Study of Family Power Structure," p. 549, notes that studies of "family power" have almost universally ignored family members other than the husband and wife, and are thus actually studies of marital, not family, power.

[6] Robert O. Blood, Jr., and Donald M. Wolfe, *Husbands and Wives* (New York: Free Press, 1960), p. 11.

[7] Herman Lantz et al., "Pre-Industrial Patterns in the Colonial Family in America: A Content Analysis of Colonial Magazines," *American Sociological Review* 33 (1968), 419.

associate with. In some families the husband still uses physical coercion. Wives only get power when their husbands default, that is, manifest weakness of some sort.[8] It is possible to respond that Gillespie is to some extent debating a "straw man," that those being refuted never said that U.S. marriages were now equalitarian, only that they were moving away from institutionalized patriarchy toward equalitarianism. Yet Gillespie's evidence is compelling: while wives may make many decisions and carry out many household tasks, power is still predominantly in the hands of their husbands.

Power and decision-making in the U.S. family are affected by many factors. Several authors, including William Kenkel and Fred Strodtbeck, have noted the distinction between perceived and actual decision-making patterns within the home.[9] Both husbands and wives tend to perceive the husband as having the dominant role, with the wife's opinion solicited but the final decision being his. Yet, observation of numerous married couples showed that well over half of them were actually equalitarian in their decision-making, coming to decisions together. Other research has found a correlation between social class position and the perceived and actual authority of the male. William Goode describes these tensions thus:

> Lower-class men concede fewer rights *ideologically* than their women in fact *obtain,* and the more educated men are likely to concede *more* rights ideologically than they in fact grant. One partial resolution of the latter tension is to be found in the frequent assertion from families of professional men that they should not make demands which would interfere with his *work:* He takes precedence as *professional, not* as family head or male; nevertheless, the precedence is his. By contrast, lower-class men demand deference as *men,* as heads of families.[10]

On the one hand, the lower-class male claims authority on the basis of traditional or ideological patriarchy (he is "supposed" to be the boss), whereas in actual decision-making the lower-class wife wields substantial authority. A part of the husband's lesser role in decision-making may, of course, be accounted for by delegation. That is, lower-class husbands may feel that there are many family matters which they do not want to decide *or* act upon. On the other hand, Goode is saying, the middle-class or educated

---

[8] Dair L. Gillespie, "Who Has the Power? The Marital Struggle," *Journal of Marriage and the Family* 33 (1971), 445–58.

[9] William F. Kenkel and Dean K. Hoffman, "Real and Conceived Roles in Family Decision-Making," *Marriage and Family Living* 18 (1956), 308–14; Kenkel, "Observational Studies of Husband-Wife Interaction in Family Decision-Making," in Marvin B. Sussman, ed., *Sourcebook in Marriage and the Family* (Boston: Houghton Mifflin, 1963 ed.), pp. 144–56; and Fred L. Strodtbeck, "Husband-Wife Interaction over Revealed Differences," *American Sociological Review* 16 (1951), 468–73.

[10] William J. Goode, *World Revolution and Family Patterns* (New York: Free Press, 1963), pp. 21–22. See also Lee Rainwater, *Family Design: Marital Sexuality, Family Size, and Contraception* (Chicago: Aldine, 1965), p. 54.

male ordinarily expresses the *norm* of equalitarianism, but in authority situations he manages to have more power anyway. Consistent with this is Kerckhoff and Bean's finding that high- and middle-status couples are in full agreement that the husbands are behaviorally, but not ideologically, more dominant than their wives.[11] At least a partial explanation for the divergence between both perceptions and expectations and actuality is found in Blood and Wolfe's "resource" theory. Blood and Wolfe argue that higher-status husbands have more resources at their disposal—financial and intellectual—than do lower-status husbands. Middle-class wives, even if they do work, still contribute a smaller proportion of the total family income. Thus, the higher the family's social and economic position, the greater is the husband's bargaining position, despite the fact that higher-status families have moved further away from traditional patriarchal ideology toward equalitarian expectations.[12]

A second factor that complicates the simple change from patriarchal to equalitarian marriage concerns areas of influence. William Dyer and Dick Urban report that in a predominantly middle-class sample, decision-making has been virtually institutionalized as equalitarian, except in the area of finances, where the wives prefer mutual decisions, whereas the husbands would rather divide up the various consumption areas and decide unilaterally.[13] Blood and Wolfe divide the decision-making areas into eight categories: husband's occupation, car, insurance, vacation, housing, whether or not the wife should work, choice of a doctor, and food budget. They find that high-status husbands do not exercise authority equally in all eight areas. Rather, they

> make more decisions in only three areas: whether to buy life insurance, what house or apartment to get, and especially whether the wife should go to work or quit work. Actually what happens is not that more high-status husbands make these decisions unilaterally, but that fewer wives do. In other words, high-status husbands take a more active part rather than the wife making the decisions by herself.[14]

Why do high-status husbands take a greater part in these three areas specifically? The reason, Blood and Wolfe feel, is related to the issue of surplus income. Both insurance and housing are likely to be more important and

---

[11] Alan C. Kerckhoff and Frank D. Bean, "Social Status and Interpersonal Patterns Among Married Couples," *Social Forces* 49 (1970), 264–71.

[12] Blood and Wolfe, *Husbands and Wives*. A variation on the resource theory, David Heer's exchange theory, is discussed in David M. Heer, "The Measurement and Bases of Family Power: An Overview," *Marriage and Family Living* 25 (1963), 133–39, and "Rejoinder," pp. 475–78.

[13] William G. Dyer and Dick Urban, "The Institutionalization of Equalitarian Family Norms," *Marriage and Family Living* 20 (1958), 58.

[14] Blood and Wolfe, *Husbands and Wives*, p. 33.

costly to middle-class families than to families at the lower end of the socio-economic continuum. Furthermore, if the wife works, it is not out of economic necessity, but to supplement the standard of living, and the middle-class husband therefore plays a greater role in deciding whether or not she should work.

A third study dealing with areas of influence is based on a sample of skilled workers and college professors in a southern city. Combining specific decisions into four areas—child care, purchases and living standards, recreation, and role attitudes—Russell Middleton and Snell Putney find a general tendency toward equalitarianism; that is, toward an equal role in decision-making, not toward equal power in Gillespie's terms. The working wife, however, plays a somewhat greater role in financial decisions—decisions regarding purchases and living standards—than does the nonworking wife, but a lesser role in the other three areas.[15] In a study of 89 matched pairs of working and nonworking wives, Lois Hoffman adds that the working wife makes fewer decisions about routine household matters than does the nonworking wife, and that the husband of the working wife makes more.[16] These findings are consistent with the economic contribution made by the working wife and the smaller amount of time she spends in the home.

What is the *total* effect of the wife's working or not working upon husband-wife power relations? On this point, the various studies are in disagreement. Blood and Wolfe observe, as had authors of earlier studies, that not only does the working wife have substantially more power than the nonworking wife at all status levels, but that the "more years the wife has worked since marriage, the more power she has." In opposition to this is Middleton and Putney's conclusion, which they admit contradicts the findings of previous studies, that families in which the wife works are significantly *more* patriarchal in decisions than are those in which the wife does not work. Perhaps Hoffman is most accurate when she reports that in toto there is "no difference in husband-wife power between working and nonworking women in the matched sample."[17] Such a conclusion is warranted, at least until further evidence appears.

Husband-wife power relations do not remain static over the family's life

---

[15] Russell Middleton and Snell Putney, "Dominance in Decisions in the Family: Race and Class Differences," *American Journal of Sociology* 65 (1960), 605–9.

[16] Lois Wladis Hoffman, "Parental Power Relations and the Division of Household Tasks," in F. Ivan Nye and Lois Hoffman, eds., *The Employed Mother in America* (Chicago: Rand McNally, 1963 ed.), pp. 229–30.

[17] Blood and Wolfe, *Husbands and Wives*, pp. 40–41; Middleton and Putney, "Dominance in Decisions in the Family"; and Hoffman, "Parental Power Relations and the Division of Household Tasks," in Nye and Hoffman, *The Employed Mother in America*. Wesley R. Burr, *Theory Construction and the Sociology of the Family* (New York: Wiley, 1973), p. 197, agrees with Blood and Wolfe that working does increase the wife's overall power.

cycle. One interesting study, by Robert Lewis, reports that the wife's role in decision-making reaches its zenith during the children's teenage years, and is at its lowest ebb after child launching and before the husband's retirement. This, of course, is consistent with the fact that the domestic role is crucial during the teenage years, while the husband's breadwinning role is dominant after the child-rearing role has been completed. It is, however, equally noteworthy that after launching wives want to make more decisions than they made during the preschool years, but would prefer to make *fewer* decisions than they made during the teenage years. A more equalitarian role in decisions, therefore, seems to be what they seek.[18] These are decisions, we must keep in mind, concerning the household, not the "world at large."

To summarize the issue of decision-making and power, we must repeat that much still remains to be done to clarify the concepts used and to adequately measure what happens. However, from available studies we have concluded that, despite the fact that in the middle classes companionate or equalitarian ideologies are expressed increasingly, husbands continue to dominate. In the middle class, resources, skill, and deference enable them to do so; in the lower class they dominate—when possible—by delegating tasks and decisions to the wife. Extensions of our discussion have included consideration of the family life cycle, areas of influence, and women's roles, plus the fact that the manner in which a couple perceive themselves to make decisions and the manner in which they actually do so are frequently two very different things. Some groups, however, such as the individualistic Texans of whom Strodtbeck wrote, make a conscious or rational effort to be equalitarian in family affairs.[19] Such conscious equalitarianism is at present more characteristic of the middle class than of the working and lower classes.

The Sexual Division of Labor

Once decisions are made regarding child care, financial expenditures, or other family matters, they must be implemented. Someone must *do* the various household tasks, handle day-to-day financial matters, and take care of the children. Traditionally, the man's work involved running the family's productive machinery and supervising its economic division of labor, while the woman's work was to handle the day-to-day tasks of cooking, sewing, and caring for the children. With the removal of the economic-productive function from the home, the husband-father was confronted with two alternatives: he could leave the running of the household to the wife and restrict

---

[18] Robert A. Lewis, "Satisfaction with Conjugal Power over the Family Life Cycle" (paper delivered at the National Council on Family Relations meetings, Portland, Oregon, October 31, 1972).

[19] Strodtbeck, "Husband-Wife Interaction over Revealed Differences."

himself to making a living, or he could take a hand in the heavier, dirtier household tasks and play a supportive role in child rearing in the realization that his would be a helping role in the household. In the United States, the former pattern has been most characteristic of lower-class families, while the latter has been a predominantly middle-class pattern.

The best single study showing social class differences in the distribution of household tasks was carried out by Marvin Olsen in Omaha, Nebraska. The sample included 391 housewives, who were asked "who does what" in the home, with the following major findings.[20] The amount of household responsibility assumed by the husband increases as status increases up through the upper-middle-class, or business and professional, families. In the wealthy, or upper-class, families, help is hired to do many of the tasks that husbands perform in the middle class. The responsibilities that middle-class husbands assume at home are for those tasks ordinarily believed to be men's work. There is joking and practical concern about the middle-class husband in an apron, but he is much more likely to lend a hand in painting, putting up screens or storm windows, shoveling snow, cleaning out the garage, assembling a swing set, helping with lawn and garden care, and so on. In the middle class, budgeting, supervising children's schoolwork, and planning vacations are joint tasks, while these tasks are avoided by working- and lower-class husbands to a marked degree. Blood and Wolfe's description of the division of labor in middle-class families agrees substantially with that of Olsen. Husbands predominate in household repairs, snow shoveling, and lawn mowing. Wives handle meal preparation, housecleaning, and dishwashing. Neither spouse predominates in buying groceries or paying bills, with the latter function being the most evenly divided.[21] Thus, while decision-making is ideologically equalitarian, the division of labor still tends to be somewhat specialized by sex in the middle-class family. The role of the middle-class husband in household tasks, like that of the working wife in the occupational sphere, is considered to be a subordinate and helping role, rather than a role based on equality of responsibility and privilege.[22]

As reported in Chapter 7, the middle-class wife generally wants her husband to be supportive of their children, especially of sons, and the husband is ordinarily satisfied to play such a role. Working- and lower-class mothers, in contrast, tend to want their husbands to be directive, setting limits and structuring their children's lives, but the husbands are often unwilling to play

---

[20] Marvin E. Olsen, "Distribution of Family Responsibilities and Social Stratification," *Marriage and Family Living* 22 (1960), 60–65.

[21] Blood and Wolfe, *Husbands and Wives*, p. 50.

[22] Dyer and Urban, "The Institutionalization of Equalitarian Family Norms"; and Ruth E. Hartley, "Some Implications of Current Changes in Sex-Role Patterns," *Merrill-Palmer Quarterly* 6 (1959–1960), 153–64.

such a role, feeling that their wives can do this as well as they can.[23] The net consequence is less differentiation between the child-rearing roles of husbands and wives in the middle class than in the working and lower classes, with a more intensive involvement of middle-class wives than husbands. The lower-class father is likely to play a minor or sporadic role, with the working-class father somewhere between the other two in child-rearing involvement.

At this point, much of what he have learned about marital roles and interactions from Knox and Kupferer, Blood and Wolfe, Olsen, Kohn, and other researchers can be brought together. Middle-class husbands and wives may or may not both work, but in either case the husband tends to dominate, though the couple may consciously strive for equalitarianism in decision-making. Compared to the working- and lower-class husband, the middle-class husband takes a greater hand in household tasks and child rearing. Thus, despite the quasi-companionate nature of the home, the middle-class husband as a "good provider" is accorded considerable status and authority by his family. The lower-class father, on the other hand, plays a minor role in child-rearing and household tasks; he thus perceives himself to be running the family, having delegated responsibility in these areas to his wife. But, because he has fewer resources at his disposal (and for other reasons as well), he finds it difficult to actually assert *consistent* and *acceptable* authority within the home. Some of the comparatively more frequent marital difficulties found in lower-class—and, to some extent, working-class—homes may be due to this differential between the husband's expected and actual roles.

Section Two

FINANCIAL AND SEXUAL ADJUSTMENTS IN MARRIAGE

We have discussed husbands' and wives' role choices and commented briefly upon decision-making, household tasks, and socialization. Two further aspects of husband-wife relations deserve attention: financial and sexual adjustments. Lee Rainwater comments concerning the black lower-class family that the "precipitating causes of marital disruption seem to fall mainly into economic or sexual categories."[24] One gets the distinct impression from many popular marriage manuals that this is not a peculiarly lower-class phenomenon, but that about half of all marital difficulties are traceable to finan-

[23] Melvin L. Kohn, "Social Class and Parent-Child Relationships: An Interpretation," *American Journal of Sociology* 68 (1963), 476.

[24] Lee Rainwater, "Crucible of Identity: The Negro Lower-Class Family," *Daedalus* (Winter 1966), 192.

cial disagreements and the rest to sexual maladjustment. While this may be an overstatement, it does indicate that a couple who have determined their major roles and the decision-making and household division of labor, have by no means solved all their problems.

Financial Adjustment

Of eight possible areas of husband-wife disagreement—children, recreation, personality, in-laws, roles, values, sex, and money—*money* causes the greatest number of problems, according to Blood and Wolfe's study.[25] Finances are, of course, crucial in the lower-class family with limited resources. In some instances the U.S. welfare system has made it necessary for the husband to absent himself from the home so that the wife and children may obtain a steady income from welfare. Or the financial burden of the lower-class family may be aggravated by the husband who dissipates on drink what surplus funds he has. Such examples are not, however, meant to convey the impression that financial adjustment is strictly a low-status problem. It involves the day-to-day explicit and implicit budgeting of family expenditures as they relate to general norms or expectations regarding how any family should live and what they should have. As Jeffrey Hadden and Marie Borgatta point out, "Failure to handle this problem may spell disaster for young families," not just in the lower class but in any portion of the society.[26]

Differing orientations toward money, typified by the husband who hoards and the wife who spends, may derive from the very same economic conditions, such as an economic depression. But why should financial orientations, and the disagreements that arise from divergences in outlook, be as problem-producing as Blood and Wolfe, Rainwater, and others find them to be? At least three factors make money a greater problem in U.S. society than it might otherwise be. First, money and *economic values* are at the heart of the American value system. The standard of living and "things" are crucial elements in the American definition of personal happiness, and personal happiness is, in turn, a focal concern of marriage.[27] The reader may wish to argue that monetary and material values *should not* be central, but it is difficult to contend convincingly that they *are not*. Second, *deferred gratification*, or putting off immediate desires for goals perceived to be of greater value in the future, *can continue for only so long.* In the lower-class

---

[25] Blood and Wolfe, *Husbands and Wives*, p. 192.

[26] Jeffrey K. Hadden and Marie L. Borgatta, "The Economics of Family Living," in Hadden and Borgatta, eds., *Marriage and the Family* (Itasca, Ill.: Peacock, 1969), p. 449.

[27] On economics in the value system of the United States, see Shepard B. Clough, *Basic Values of Western Civilization* (New York: Columbia University Press, 1960), p. 15; and Robin M. Williams, Jr., *American Society: A Sociological Interpretation* (New York: Knopf, 1960 ed.), chaps. 10–14.

family, the personal frustrations that may result from being unable to get ahead in a society that values affluence may be vented against the marital partner. In the middle-class family, a more likely occurrence is that the wife simply runs out of "deferments" before her husband does. She begins, often gradually, to want things now, while he is still establishing his career. And, of course, the economic system is consciously geared to the fostering of such "wants" in individuals and families. This particular manifestation of the problem, that is, the wife "wanting things" while the husband is still establishing himself, is, of course, a result of the conventional present-day marriage, with the husband as provider and the wife as chief consumer or spender. There are numerous other ways in which the frustration or deferment of material gratifications may result in marital difficulties. The third factor that increases the probability of conflict regarding finances in the U.S. family is that *it is extremely difficult to talk about and reconcile differences in financial attitudes prior to marriage.* Dating couples may discuss their financial orientations, but even if they do, it is difficult to foresee how they might react ten years later to the added pressure of an occupation, a home, children, inflation or recession, and perhaps aging parents. This is, then, one of those issues in marriage which require continuing communication on the part of the spouses if an adequate adjustment is to be maintained.

Sexual Adjustment

The understanding of sexual adjustment as an issue in contemporary marriage is facilitated by historical comparison. The biggest change has to do with the term itself: *sexual adjustment.* Not too many years ago—and, in many lower-class families, even today—the husband sought sexual gratification, and the wife was expected to provide it. Accompanying this asymmetry was an inhibition and feeling of sinfulness that *increasingly* pervaded U.S. and British society during the nineteenth century. These historical factors, asymmetry and guilt, form the backdrop against which today's sexual adjustments in marriage must be understood.

Beginning with the Kinsey reports of the late 1940s and early 1950s and continuing into the 1960s, researchers have found a relationship between sexual adjustment and total marital adjustment.[28] In Bruce Thomason's study

---

[28] Alfred C. Kinsey et al., *Sexual Behavior in the Human Male* (Philadelphia: Saunders, 1948); Kinsey et al., *Sexual Behavior in the Human Female* (Philadelphia: Saunders, 1953); Bruce Thomason, "Marital Sexual Behavior and Total Marital Adjustment: A Research Report," in J. Himelhoch and Sylvia F. Fava, eds., *Sexual Behavior in American Society* (New York: Norton, 1955), pp. 153–63; and Robert A. Dentler and Peter Pineo, "Sexual Adjustment, Marital Adjustment and Personal Growth of Husbands: A Panel Analysis," *Marriage and Family Living* 22 (1960), 45–48.

of young well-educated couples, for example, mutuality of orgasm was related to marital adjustment. In addition, Thomason reported that both sexual and marital adjustment tended to be better if the spouse was perceived to be sexually attractive, if sexual intercourse was by mutual desire, and if mates were willing and able to have intercourse as often as they wished.[29] Such results, when coupled with the influence of Freud and the Kinsey reports, caused some to overcompensate for earlier inhibitions by seeing sexual adjustment as the central fact of marriage, rather than as but one element among others. However, the overemphasis on sex cannot be totally accounted for by sex research and discussion. Elizabeth Janeway examines two historical factors which have combined to make sex a more important part of our lives: one is the lessening of ties to nonfamilial individuals; the other is the nonstimulating and artificial nature of the material environment.

> Our high valuation of sex today is greatly influenced by this physical background: in a world where other bodily satisfactions have lost their sharpness, it remains. But there is a social reason too. The narrowing of the world of physical satisfaction as modern man withdraws from his contact with nature has been paralleled by another phenomenon: . . . the dwindling in the variety and extent of personal relationships and social bonds. . . . The sexual connection, that is, is emphasized by the loss of other social ties just as sexual experience is emphasized by the dwindling of other bodily pleasures.[30]

An immediate problem presented by the conclusions of Kinsey, Thomason, and other researchers is that even when a correlation is found, as between sexual and overall adjustment, one must be cautious about arguing that sexual adjustment is causative. An equally plausible conclusion would be that marital maladjustment results in an unsatisfactory sexual experience, including the inability of the wife to achieve orgasm. Moreover, later researchers have called the correlation itself into question. Mirra Komarovsky finds that the relation between sexual adjustment and total marital adjustment is low in working-class couples. Many unhappy women have a satisfactory sex life; nevertheless, she finds that, as the wife's educational level increases, so does the relation between sexual and other adjustments.[31] John Cuber and Peggy Harroff's study of the marriages of professional and managerial men offers insights into the sexual adjustments of the highly

---

[29] Thomason, "Marital Sexual Behavior and Total Marital Adjustment."

[30] Elizabeth Janeway, *Man's World Woman's Place* (New York: Dell, Delta Books, 1971), pp. 266–67.

[31] Mirra Komarovsky, *Blue-Collar Marriage* (New York: Random House, Vintage Books, 1967), p. 111.

educated. Their study, which included 235 men and 202 women of the upper middle class, indicated that

> many remain clearly ascetic where sex is concerned. Others are clearly asexual. For still others, sex is overlaid with such strong hostility that an *anti*sexual orientation is clear. In sum, we found substantial numbers of men and women who in their present circumstances couldn't care less about anything than they do about sex.[32]

For some of Komarovsky's working-class couples, then, sex was still so segregated from the rest of marriage as to make the correlation between sex and marital adjustment negligible. For some of Cuber and Harroff's middle-class couples, sex had simply become a matter of mutual nonsalience, with the marriage left to revolve around other aspects of their busy lives. Can the sexually exploitative or asexual marriage be truly well adjusted? Perhaps it is only the expectations and overcompensations born of the post-Victorian era which cause us to consider this impossible.

But what of these expectations? The fact that wives as well as husbands are increasingly expected and expecting to find gratification in the sex act is at the heart of the problem of sexual adjustment today. "The contemporary male," says Myron Brenton,

> faces sexual responsibilities far exceeding those of men in earlier times. He must gratify himself *and* his sexual partner. He has to make sure he's a better lover—or at least no worse—than other men. He has to cope with the sexually liberated woman, something that can require a considerable amount of coping.[33]

As a result, some men tend to question their masculinity, or their ability to "satisfy" the female. In addition, the discovery of the clitoral orgasm has freed the female to seek her sexual gratification as aggressively as the male seeks his, thereby freeing the female sexually from dependence upon the male penis. Such freedom and ideals, says Susan Lydon, have made the bed a "competitive arena, where men and women measure themselves against these mythical rivals, while simultaneously trying to live up to the ecstasies promised them by the marriage manuals and the fantasies of the media."[34] The media do indeed play upon the theme of satisfying one's sex partner, while the manuals, as may be seen in Feature 8, are hardly likely to add to the self-assurance of the sexually insecure.

---

[32] John F. Cuber and Peggy B. Harroff, *The Significant Americans* (New York: Appleton-Century-Crofts, 1965), p. 172.

[33] Myron Brenton, *The American Male* (New York: Coward-McCann, 1966), p. 29. Copyright © 1966 by Myron Brenton; reprinted by permission of Coward-McCann, Inc.

[34] Susan Lydon, "The Politics of Orgasm," in Robert R. Bell and Michael Gordon, eds., *The Social Dimension of Human Sexuality* (Boston: Little, Brown, 1972), p. 170.

If "I wonder whether I can satisfy her" expresses the male's fear of the emancipated female, "Why don't I enjoy this as much as I should?" is her frequent response. The problem is likely to be that she is still sexually inhibited by her socialization, yet in marriage she is expected—and expects herself—to be able to gain personal satisfaction from giving herself to a man. Even premarital sex, as long as it includes lingering overtones of guilt, will do little to prepare the female for sexual responsiveness in marriage. Thus, the combination of overtones of guilt, plus overemphasis on the importance of sex, plus new expectations of mutuality, serves to intensify the problem of sexual adjustment in the contemporary U.S. family, and will continue to do so until the attitudinal and behavioral inconsistencies are reconciled.

FEATURE 8

. . . The recent manuals push hard to be encouraging, and they do squash some mossy myths, such as the notion that only simultaneous orgasms are acceptable. But you still suspect that they may merely increase the tensions which the authors aim to dissolve. . . .

Most of these guides, which are intended as a gateway to freedom, actually suggest a new conformity—or even tyranny—in that you *ought* to have multiple orgasms at this moment, or at that one. But what if you don't? Meanwhile, the manuals may make one partner much more demanding—and he or she could be outraged if the other doesn't collaborate correctly. Despite the authors' steady protestations, many manuals can sound like rulebooks, and they may be promoting certain styles of sex life which some people just can't manage. For example, the Sensuous Woman says that anal sex is "an optional." However, on the next page, she starts lecturing like a strict governess: "For rectal intercourse (you're not going to chicken out at this point, are you?) the most comfortable position is. . . ." Her message throughout is "be a good sport"—and cooperate

with "his pet practice," unless you simply detest it. . . .

Meanwhile, one figure who punctually reappears in the new sex books—fiction or nonfiction—is a fantasy of the liberated woman. Independent, often uninterested in marriage, she may even have a career. She'll gladly hit the hay with any man and will teach him things as yet undreamed of—while showing him that he's possessed of a potential genius which has never been unleashed before. . . .

You don't expect the prose of Pater from these volumes. But since most of them were written with a buzzsaw, the sadistic passages can be disturbing. (Most of these dwell on the familiar insistence that the protesting partner "really likes" the act that he or she is strenuously resisting.) But some manuals which claim to be enlivening are really quite numbing—perhaps because there's so much emphasis on all the things which can go wrong. Thus, they might be almost paralyzing for beginners.

Nora Sayre, "Ahh!," *New York Times Book Review,* February 11, 1973, 3, 12, 14.

Section Three

A SUMMARY OF MARRIAGE:
PREDICAMENTS, COMMUNICATION,
AND CHOICE

By now it should be evident that there are some crucial adjustments and choices confronting the married couple in a day when the nuclear family is but slightly embedded in the kin network and when the other institutions operate, for the most part, apart from the family unit. Today's neo-traditional U.S. couples are still ordinarily persons who *believe* their commitment at marriage to be for life. Yet, because of the loss of many cultural supports for the permanence of the individual unit, the nuclear family has fewer resources at its disposal which differentiate it from the short-term relationship and which insure permanence. Some of the issues confronting married couples today are well summarized in four predicaments that we shall paraphrase from Bernard Farber.[35]

Marital Predicaments

Each of the four predicaments, or issues, that married couples must resolve can be derived from one or more portions of the two preceding chapters. The first concerns *instrumental and social-emotional roles* in marriage. Women's roles, decision-making, the family division of labor—these are all aspects of role differentiation or role similarity. Blood and Wolfe find that joint decision-making, confiding in each other, and having mutual friends are all related to the wife's satisfaction with her marriage, but that the husband's performing household tasks is not. At home, the wife plays both an instrumental and a social-emotional role and the husband is also apt to play a social-emotional role. The husband, however, still dominates in the instrumental or productive sphere of economics.

The last sentence indicates that, while role choices are available to husbands and wives, these choices are still governed to a considerable extent by the traditional ideology. Societal role blurring has not yet proceeded to the point that the husband who prefers to do so can stay home and take care of the children while the wife pursues a career and provides for the family's financial needs. This is not yet considered a viable option, although Warren Farrell and many others would argue that it should be legitimated as as cultural alternative. At present, the alternatives along the instrumental–social-emotional dimension tend to be variations on the theme of hus-

---

[35] Bernard Farber, *Family: Organization and Interaction* (San Francisco: Chandler, 1964), pp. 285–332.

band dominance in the economic-occupational-financial (instrumental) area and wife dominance in the home-children-kin (social-emotional) area.[36]

A second predicament, closely related to the first, concerns *internal versus external commitment,* or involvement in family versus involvement in community. How much of themselves should the husband and wife invest in the family and how much in the extrafamilial environment? Farber notes that in a society in which the norms reinforce orderly replacement of family culture, the male can give himself to his work with little worry that his family will disintegrate for lack of his attention. However, if the family subsists on the personal involvement of its members, the father who is devoted entirely to his occupation may, in fact, be a disintegrative element. Familism, or the investment of self in the family, is a likely aspect of both husbands' and wives' roles if the satisfactions expected from the family are to materialize.

Yet the "family versus community" orientation only becomes a predicament when the community does not support, or is in competition with, family values. In the mass media, including motion pictures and literature, and certain forms of recreation, there is tension—if not antagonism—between family and community values. Certain industries, however, have begun at least superficially to stress husband-wife togetherness and the socializing of their employees as family units. These companies are not fostering happy marriages as ends in themselves, but because they regard the happily married man as a more efficient worker. Furthermore, many businesses and advertisers stress the home because families are the central units of economic consumption. Yet, despite the fact that elements of the community support family values—for whatever reason—the predicament of how much time and energy should be invested in the family and how much outside the family must still be resolved by each married couple.

Short-term gratification versus long-term planning within the family is the crux of the third predicament.[37] Short-term, or short-run, gratification is epitomized (or perhaps overstated) in the words of a song that was popular some years back: "We'll sing in the sunlight, we'll laugh every day . . . and be on our way." If a couple's solidarity is based on common interests, immediate physical gratification, or an ideal image of the kind of person the spouse is or is going to be, then a change in roles or interests may void

---

[36] Some have argued that there is in fact a more insidious form of discrimination against women today than ever before, in that we speak of equality between the sexes at a time when women's empirical position in the society is becoming increasingly worse. On this, see Dean D. Knudsen, "The Declining Status of Women: Popular Myths and the Failure of Functionalist Thought," *Social Forces* 48 (1969), 183–93.

[37] Farber, *Family: Organization and Interaction,* talks of "role versus career orientation" at this point. However, given the other common uses of the terms *role* and *career,* we have decided to refer to "short-term" and "long-term" planning and gratification.

the relationship. Long-term, or long-run, planning demands that the couple regard their relationship as relatively stable and orderly. Farber, however, feels that the tendency today is toward more short-run gratification in marriage and regards this tendency as consistent with the movement of U.S. society toward *permanent* availability, that is, the voidable relationship. Yet, it should be added that as long as deferred gratification and long-term planning remain strong in families, the pendulum cannot be said to have swung all the way to permanent availability.

The fourth predicament is an issue with which we have been concerned throughout the volume: *individualism versus familism.* The issue here, which is closely linked to the third predicament, is whether the adjustment and happiness of the individual are primary, or whether they are subordinated to the needs of the family. Farber, who labels this issue "parent versus children orientation," states that there is a tradition, especially among wives, of subordinating personal needs to those of the children. Once again, any tendency of the spouses toward gratifying their own needs first, especially when this tendency is coupled with a short-term orientation, is linked with movement away from orderly replacement—since the parents are less concerned about the consequences of their behavior for their children—and toward permanent availability. Not only do such parents fail to put socialization before personal gratification, but they are less likely to keep the family unit intact for the children's sake. One purpose of singling out these four predicaments is to remind the reader just how far the U.S. family still is from permanent availability or serial monogamy. In fact, many attributes of the truly equalitarian or companionate marriage—including familism, long-term orientation, and freedom to choose marital roles—may help to stabilize family life and culture. Much of the stabilizing efficacy of such factors, however, seems to be a function of communication between husbands and wives.

Communication in Marriage

Throughout Chapters 11 and 12 we have hinted that many interactional and adjustment problems of modern marriage can be resolved only if couples will keep open the communication channels between them. Nearly twenty years ago Harvey Locke, Georges Sabagh, and Mary Margaret Thomes reported that primary communication, or communication "which is intimate, free-flowing, and unrestricted," is correlated positively with marital adjustment.[38] More recently Norman Goodman and Richard Ofshe con-

---

[38] Harvey J. Locke, Georges Sabagh, and Mary Margaret Thomes, "Correlates of Primary Communication and Empathy," *Research Studies of the State College of Washington* 24 (1956), 116–24.

firmed this contention that communication and understanding are central to marriage.[39]

Yet it would be an oversimplification to assert that open communication necessarily contributes to a happy marriage. Beverly Cutler and William Dyer, for example, note that among newly married couples

> nearly half of the non-adjustive responses for both husbands and wives came as a result of an open sharing of the feelings about the violation of expectations. Contrary to what might be expected, an open talking about the violation of expectations does not always lead to an adjustment.[40]

Likewise, Komarovsky reports that among her working-class couples the correlation between self-disclosure and marital happiness is far from perfect. Some husbands don't want to be told too much; others are happy precisely because they have some privacy. The better educated tend to communicate more, and in general the wives are less satisfied than the husbands with what they believe to be too little communication.[41]

Communication, therefore, can be problem-producing rather than integrative if it exceeds the amount desired by the husband or if conflict is defined as aberrant behavior or as a sign of the incipient breakup of a marriage. Communication often leads to conflict and, unfortunately, many married couples are afraid of conflict—having been socialized to the value of cooperation and "getting along," and thus being unable to cope with open conflict.[42] Many couples would rather seal off an area of life, such as finances, and avoid discussing it than take the chance that disagreement will lead to marital disruption.

In summary, then, communication may help to resolve interactional and adjustment problems in marriage, but not if conflict is defined in strictly negative terms. It seems a bit ironic that the individuals who are most likely to communicate openly, that is, middle-class persons, are also more likely to define conflict as a purely negative or disintegrative phenomenon.

Summary and the Value of Choice

Differences between the traditional and the neo-traditional family types may be cataloged in ideal-typical terms, and the reader should recall that

---

[39] Norman Goodman and Richard Ofshe, "Empathy, Communication Efficiency, and Marital Status," *Journal of Marriage and the Family* 30 (1968), 597–603.

[40] Beverly R. Cutler and William G. Dyer, "Initial Adjustment Processes in Young Married Couples," *Social Forces* 44 (1965), 201.

[41] Komarovsky, *Blue-Collar Marriage*, pp. 142f; on the uncommunicative husband, see Jack O. Balswick and Charles W. Peek, "The Inexpressive Male: A Tragedy of American Society," *The Family Coordinator* 20 (1971), 363–68.

[42] On this issue, see Gibson Winter, *Love and Conflict* (Garden City, N.Y.: Doubleday, 1958).

Table 7
A Summary of Traditional and Equalitarian Roles of Husbands and Wives

Type of Marriage	Husband	Wife
Traditional (Conventional)	Legal authority and disciplinarian at home Breadwinner Economic coordinator and decision-maker	Homemaker and child-rearer Normatively subordinate in virtually every area of marriage
Neo-traditional (Companionate)	Subordinate role in socializing and home tasks Breadwinner Equalitarian decision-making	Works if she wants to, or does volunteer service Shares overtly in decision-making Dominates homemaking and child rearing

U.S. families are fairly well divided between the two types, with the traditional model still dominant among the working and lower classes. (See Table 7.) How do these types look when they are placed upon the marital role continuum of Chapter 5? (See Figure 11.) Unquestionably, the middle-class family is closer to the "choice-blurred-equalitarian" end of the continuum than is either the working- or lower-class family. Yet a large minority of middle-class marriages are still quite traditional, and neo-traditional marriages cannot be considered entirely open and choice-based as long as the traditional ideology defines certain options as deviant and unacceptable—an example being the aforementioned husband-homemaker–wife-breadwinner choice.

Our final comment concerns the vocabulary employed to describe the equalitarian marriage—both in the popular press and in the sociological literature. We have, throughout Chapters 11 and 12, used the language of the literature at our disposal: *predicaments, dilemmas, ambiguities, problems, ill-defined.* These terms that relate to choice are loaded with negative

Figure 11
The Author's View of Marital Roles in the Contemporary United States in Relation to the Marital Role Continuum

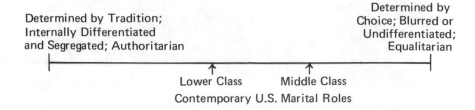

Determined by Tradition;
Internally Differentiated
and Segregated; Authoritarian

Determined by
Choice; Blurred or
Undifferentiated;
Equalitarian

Lower Class   Middle Class
Contemporary U.S. Marital Roles

connotations. However, the same historical changes that have given rise to ambiguity could be described in terms of freedom, emancipation, and opportunity—but seldom are. As Erich Fromm has pointed out, the human being prefers tradition over choice, predetermination over ambiguity—and sociologists and magazine writers are no exception.[43] Furthermore, when the sociologist or magazine writer is male, or has been trained in a male-dominated society, the pattern he considers desirable would obviously include male control. Perhaps Charles Winick is correct; too much uncertainty is unhealthy.[44] On the other hand, it is at least possible that once the contemporary family has escaped its midstream position, abandoning the lingering elements of a traditional patriarchy, the freedom to choose for oneself may result in a heightened fulfillment and development of the unique potentialities of each person and marriage.[45] Listen to the Handlins:

> Freedom carries with it obligations—for decisions, for choices and for unexpected experiences. It threatens routine and order, breeds change, conflict, and insecurity. Yet some men and women seek it in preference to the comfort of unvarying habit, to the certainty of infallible authority, to the peace of a rigid system which admits no questions and holds each individual in place.[46]

Regardless of whether one sees increasing freedom as opportunity or problem, he should be cognizant of the subtle value implications of the terms being used to describe the now and future role choices of males and females.

---

[43] See Erich Fromm, *Escape From Freedom* (New York: Rinehart, 1941).

[44] Charles Winick, "The Beige Epoch: Depolarization of Sex Roles in America," *The Annals* 376 (1968), 24.

[45] A more positive view is stated by Goode, *World Revolution and Family Patterns*, p. 57; and Robert and Rhona Rapoport, "Work and Family in Contemporary Society," *American Sociological Review* 30 (1965), 394. Likewise, Dennis H. Wrong, "The 'Break-Up' of the American Family," *Commentary* 9 (1950), 380, speaks of changes in the family as increasing the freedom of the individual rather than breaking up the family.

[46] Oscar Handlin and Mary F. Handlin, *Facing Life: Youth and the Family in American History* (Boston: Little, Brown, 1971), p. v.

Kinship Relations

Kinship units in certain societies, such as the Papago, serve economic, political, religious, and other institutional functions. Additional functions performed by the larger kin units in some societies include: property-holding and inheritance, housing, need-obligation, and affective or emotional ties. There is, however, no simple, linear removal of these functions as one moves from Durkheim's "mechanically solidary" society to the "organically solidary" modern industrial state. Yet, compared to the Papago, the kinship units of the United States are less central to the society's operation, fulfilling a primary affective function, and a secondary need-obligation function, and performing idiosyncratically in the areas of inheritance and housing. In this chapter we consider the meanings of "distance" with respect to kin, the significance of kin terms, and the kinsman as a person. The last portion of the chapter is given to a characterization of relations between the following kin: parents and adult offspring, adult siblings, secondary kin, and in-laws.

The maturing individual in modern industrial society ordinarily lives with his parents, brothers, and sisters. He is also likely to be acquainted with aunts, uncles, cousins, and grandparents, with whom he does not live but whom he nevertheless considers important because of their status as kinfolk or relatives. Upon reaching adulthood and marrying, he does not terminate his relationship with his family of orientation, that is, parents and siblings, but they, too, become a part of his kin network—his "kin of orientation." It is this network, involving parents and adult offspring, siblings, grandparents, aunts, and uncles, as well as in-laws, that concerns us in the present chapter. The very fact that kin outside the individual's nuclear family have been virtually ignored since the early chapters of this volume should indicate to the reader something of the author's perspective on the importance of kin in the United States. But in order to understand U.S. kinship we shall once again resort to cross-cultural and historical comparison.

Section One

KIN FUNCTIONS IN CROSS-CULTURAL PERSPECTIVE

In such societies as the Papago of Arizona and northern Mexico, institutions and personnel alike are embedded within the larger kin unit, so that most of the activities and interactions that occur are predicated upon kin ties of one sort or another. David Schneider characterizes as follows the difference between kinship in such societies and kinship in modern, Western societies:

> The kinship systems of modern, western societies are relatively differentiated as compared with the kinship systems found in many primitive and peasant societies. By "differentiated" I mean simply that kinship is clearly and sharply distinguished from all other kinds of social institutions and relationships. In many primitive and peasant societies a large number of kinds of institutions are organized and built as *parts of the kinship system itself*. Thus the major social units of the society may be kin groups—lineages perhaps. These same kin groups may be property-owning units, the political units, the religious units, and so on. Thus, whatever a man does in such a society he does *as a kinsman of one kind or another*.[1] (Italics added.)

The institutionally embedded Papago, for example, have no political institutions beyond the village council, which consists of the elders in the various family units. These same elders perform the major religious rituals on behalf of their kin. Even the economic division of labor is coterminous with the kin networks, there being no separate market functionaries.

One major variation described in Chapter 4 is that between institutional embeddedness within the kin network and institutional embeddedness within the nuclear family. It was noted that the classical Chinese society differed from Papago society in being characterized by a small number of powerful, institutionally embedded and personnel-embedded patrilineages over against the state, but that the majority of nonaffluent kin networks were functionally separated into nuclear families. The description of colonial America showed the major institutional functions somewhat embedded in nuclear families, but not in kin networks. Finally, a crucial change that took place between colonial times and the present was seen to be the increasing differentiation of institutional functions from the nuclear family—the larger kin group having already lost most of its institutional significance by the colonial period. There are, however, other functions that the kin groups have performed in

---

[1] David M. Schneider, *American Kinship: A Cultural Account* (Englewood Cliffs, N.J.: Prentice-Hall, 1968), p. v.

some societies, whose change cannot be traced in a linear fashion. These functions include: (1) property-holding and inheritance; (2) housing and the maintenance of residential proximity; (3) obligation, or helping in time of need; and (4) affection, emotional ties, or primary relationships.[2] The first of these, *inheritance,* is clearly a kin function in societies with corporate lineages. But in both the small band, such as characterizes the Andaman Islanders, and in colonial America, the property-holding unit through which inheritance is controlled is the nuclear family represented by its male head, whose socially determined prerogative may be to pass the inheritance to one offspring or to divide it among them all.[3] Thus, one change that has taken place since colonial times is that the wife can hold property separate from that of her husband, and can distribute it to her offspring separately if she so desires. Furthermore, there are not only differences *between* societies in the stress on inheritance and the control of property, but also differences by status *within* societies. In U.S. society, Bernard Farber has noted, high status groups have much to gain by working out mutually beneficial marriage alliances, and by stressing not only the economic family estate but what he calls the "symbolic family estate." Inheritance, then, includes both property and "name," or a significant ancestry, and these forms of inheritance serve to separate or differentiate those of higher status from the rest of society.[4]

The *housing–residential proximity* function, which is in reality two functions, is most difficult to place on a change continuum. For one thing, household sharing may assume various forms. In one society the form may be the "longhouse," in which the men live apart from the women and children. In another it may be a joint family of brothers and their wives and children. In a third aged parents may live with one of their married offspring. Furthermore, although the norms of certain societies include household sharing, residence may actually be proximate rather than shared —with the kin group functioning as a unit. Finally, housing may be temporarily shared with kin in virtually any society, including the contemporary United States.[5] Thus, if the issue is simply kin proximity, one might argue that there is a progressive change toward greater dispersion from the small,

[2] Bert N. Adams, "Kinship Systems and Adaptation to Modernization," *Studies in Comparative International Development,* vol. 4 (1968–1969), p. 55.

[3] A. R. Radcliffe-Brown, *The Andaman Islanders* (Cambridge: Cambridge University Press, 1922); on this, see Meyer F. Nimkoff and Russell Middleton, "Types of Family and Types of Economy," *American Journal of Sociology* 66 (1960), 215–25.

[4] Bernard Farber, *Kinship and Class: A Midwestern Study* (New York: Basic Books, 1971), pp. 6, 115.

[5] An interesting discussion of the "branch family" is found in James S. Brown, Harry K. Schwarzweller, and Joseph J. Mangalam, "Kentucky Mountain Migration and the Stem-Family: An American Variation on a Theme by Le Play," *Rural Sociology* 28 (1963), 48–69.

undifferentiated society to the modern industrial society.[6] But, if the issue is stated as the provision by kin of housing for one another, this is about as likely in rural-to-urban migrant groups in the United States as it is in the Hindu joint family of India. The difference is that, in the former case, the relative with whom one *should* share his residence is not specified, and permanent sharing is not expected.

The *obligatory* function, based on the expectation that one will help kin under certain circumstances, varies greatly. In one society, the strongest obligation may be to the mother's brother; in another, to the grandfather; and in still another, to one's own parents. Also, the obligations range from warrior allegiance and a proper burial to financial assistance or simply keeping in touch. The strongest sense of obligation in contemporary U.S. kinship seems to be between aging parents and their adult offspring, but even this is mitigated by the equally powerful societal value of nuclear family independence and self-sufficiency.

Unlike the U.S. upper class, in which the inheritance-differentiating function is still strong, the working and lower classes are characterized by proximity and strong obligation. "Domestic aspects of kinship," says Farber, "are those which emerge in the course of living together. . . . The domestic level predominates in the lower class and represents the use of kindred as an aggregate by a population at the mercy of economic uncertainties."[7]

The final function, providing affectional or *emotional ties* for the individual, operates as a matter of choice in most kinship systems. Though each society has an expectation that certain kin will provide such ties, the actual strength of affectional relationships is extremely varied. In societies in which institutions are embedded in the kin network, so that one kin line has jural and economic power over the individual, his closest ties are often with members of the other line. For example, in some patrilineal societies, the individual's closest feelings are toward members of his mother's kin group.[8] Perhaps the most outstanding examples in U.S. kinship of the blocking of affect by functional ties are those instances when sons and their father work in the same business, and, as a result, seek emotional gratifications elsewhere among their kin.[9]

To conclude this section, then, one can say that the greatest single difference in kinship between, say, the Papago and the contemporary United

---

[6] Even this has been questioned in A. O. Haller, "The Urban Family," *American Journal of Sociology* 66 (1961), 621–22.

[7] Farber, *Kinship and Class*, pp. 114–15.

[8] Examples of close affectional ties to noncorporate kin are found in William J. Goode, *World Revolution and Family Patterns* (New York: Free Press, 1963).

[9] Bert N. Adams, *Kinship in an Urban Setting* (Chicago: Markham, 1968), p. 132.

States is the removal of institutional functions so that the kin network qua kin network seldom performs economic-productive, political, religious, or educational functions. Apart from that change, however, it is difficult to summarize briefly the changes in the specific functions performed by kin in different societies. It is best perhaps to stop with the assertion that, in the contemporary United States, kin perform a general affective function, a particular obligatory function, and operate differentially by class in the areas of inheritance and housing. Yet, this type of summarization only hints at many crucial issues that must be confronted before kinship in the United States can be adequately characterized. Some of these issues in kinship analysis are presented in Section Two.

Section Two

SOME ISSUES IN KINSHIP ANALYSIS

Of the many issues regarding kinship which could be reviewed in a book on the family, we have chosen five which seem most essential to understanding kin relations in the United States. These include the general issue of the significance of *kin terms,* the idea of the *kinsman as a person,* the meanings of kin *"distance,"* and the specific issues of kin *unimportance* and nuclear family *isolation* in urban-industrial society.

Kin Terms

For many years, the significance of kin terms has been debated in the literature on kinship. Do the terms used—such as *mother's brother, parallel cousin,* or *aunt*—have direct behavioral connotations, so that the compilation and comparison of terminological systems can be used to symbolize the kinship systems of different societies? Or are the terms psychologically grounded cultural constructs only indirectly related, at best, to behavioral patterns? Or are the terms anachronistic survivals only partially correlated with actual kinship norms, behaviors, and roles in a given society? Lewis Henry Morgan, says Robin Fox, "saw in the study of terminology the royal road to the understanding of kinship systems." Fred Eggan states bluntly that "the verbal behavior symbolizes the socially defined relationships." Radcliffe-Brown shows that Choctaw and Omaha kin terms are as reasonable for their kinship systems as are our terms for our system. Likewise, Rodger Davies points out that the kin-based Syrian Arabs employ terms that distinguish among five generations.[10] This stress on the sociological significance

---

[10] Robin Fox, *Kinship and Marriage* (Baltimore: Penguin Books, 1967), p. 240; Fred Eggan, *Social Organization of the Western Pueblos* (Chicago: University of Chicago Press,

of terminology is epitomized in George P. Murdock's book *Social Structure*, in which various types of kinship systems are classified and distinguished from one another primarily on the basis of terms.[11]

On the other side of the question are such scholars as A. L. Kroeber, who claims that kinship terms reflect psychology, not sociology. In fact, says Kroeber, kinship systems are "linguistic patterns of logic, and their uncritical and unrestrained use as if they were uncontaminated reflectors of past or present institutions" is unsound and dangerous.[12] And, as Robin Fox notes, Bronislaw Malinowski had little use for the study of kin terms, arguing that the study of norms and actual relationships would be more productive.[13]

While the debate has not been completely resolved, it seems that Robin Fox's conclusion is valid. Kinship systems, he says, are many-sided, and terminology may not reflect every side. What a system of terms may tell us

> is *how the people themselves* see their world of kin. Who do they distinguish from whom and on what basis? It is often the case that they regard a certain distinction as crucial which has no meaning for us in terms of *our* analysis of the system of groups, alliances, etc.[14] (Italics in original.)

There is, then, a correlation between terminology and behavior, but it is simply not perfect.

A part of the discussion of kin terms has concerned the European–U.S. system and its peculiarities. Fox, for example, points out that in this system "the terms for members of the nuclear family (father, mother, son, daughter, brother, sister) are *not used for anyone outside the family*. This is very different" from the terminological systems of societies in which the nuclear family receives little or no stress.[15] Among the Papago, for example, "all cousins of every degree, on both sides, are called brothers and sisters," although the Papago can, if need be, use words that mean a "near brother" (his own) and a "far brother" (a cousin).[16] Thus, the European-American terminological system (which Murdock classifies with the "Eskimo") manifests both the bilateral nature of our kin relations—that is, our normatively

---

1950), p. 295; A. R. Radcliffe-Brown, "The Study of Kinship Systems," *Journal of the Royal Antropological Institute* 71 (1941), 3f; and Rodger P. Davies, "Syrian Arabic Kinship Terms," *Southwestern Journal of Anthropology* 5 (1949), 249.

[11] George P. Murdock, *Social Structure* (New York: Macmillan, 1949).

[12] Alfred L. Kroeber, *The Nature of Culture* (Chicago: University of Chicago Press, 1952), pp. 172, 181.

[13] See Fox, *Kinship and Marriage*, p. 240, on this.

[14] Fox, *Kinship and Marriage*, p. 243.

[15] Fox, *Kinship and Marriage*, p. 258.

[16] Ruth M. Underhill, "The Papago Family," in Meyer F. Nimkoff, ed., *Comparative Family Systems* (Boston: Houghton Mifflin, 1965), p. 150.

equal relation to both mother's and father's kin—and the special importance attached to members of the nuclear family.

The above-mentioned studies are concerned with comparative differences in kin terms. A few authors have tried to determine the significance of American kin terms. David Schneider and George Homans assert that one of the more fundamental and interesting characteristics of American terminology is the wide variety of alternatives for the same individual.

> Mother may be called "mother," "mom," "ma," "mummy," "mama," by her first name, nickname, diminutive, "old woman," and a variety of other less commonly used designations.
>   Father may be called "father," "pop," "pa," "dad," "daddy," by his first name, diminutive, "old man," "boss," and a variety of less commonly used designations. Uncles may be addressed or referred to as uncle-plus-first name, first name alone, or uncle alone. Similarly for aunts.[17]

Schneider and Homans then proceed to report the relationship between terms and behavior. Among their findings are the following: (1) On the assumption that parental terms can be ranged on a continuum from most formal, *father* and *mother,* to least formal, first name only, there is a tendency for both sexes to become relatively more formal with their same-sex parent. (2) Use of the terms *father* and *mother* for one's parents symbolizes a more formal and less close relationship with them. (3) Females use a wider variety of terms for their parents than do males for theirs. (4) The tendency is "for more first-name-alone designations to be applied to aunts and uncles on the mother's side than on the father's." (5) Males are more likely than females to address aunts and uncles by first name alone. In cases of either strong positive or strong negative sentiment the formal terms *aunt* and *uncle* are dropped and first name only is used.[18]

Since Schneider and Homans' article appeared, attempts at replication have been made by Lionel Lewis and by Warren Hagstrom and Jeffrey Hadden.[19] These later investigations—which, like Schneider and Homans' study, have employed accidental or nonrandom samples—have verified only findings (3), (4), and (5). Hagstrom and Hadden interpret these findings to mean

---

[17] David M. Schneider and George C. Homans, "Kinship Terminology and the American Kinship System," *American Anthropologist* 57 (1955), 1195.

[18] Schneider and Homans, "Kinship Terminology and the American Kinship System."

[19] Lionel S. Lewis, "Kinship Terminology for the American Parent," *American Anthropologist* 65 (1963), 649–52; and Warren O. Hagstrom and Jeffrey K. Hadden, "Sentiment and Kinship Terminology in American Society," *Journal of Marriage and the Family* 27 (1965), 324–32.

that females are generally more involved in kinship and that people tend to be somewhat closer to maternal kin. Hagstrom and Hadden also found that, with the exception of females and their fathers' siblings, aunt and uncle terminology and sentiment is unilinear rather than curvilinear; that is, the closer the individual feels to his aunt or uncle the more likely he is to use first name only.[20]

That there may be more than one kinship system in the United States is made clear by Farber in his reconciliation of the views of Ward Goodenough and David Schneider on terminology. Goodenough, after working with a New England sample, reported that affines (kin-by-marriage) as well as blood kin are considered to be relatives. However, first cousins "have no ascribed lifelong obligations other than a show of cordiality."[21] Schneider, on the other hand, having investigated kin terms in the Midwest, concluded that kinship is primarily a matter of blood ties. Thus, the first cousin is in the inner circle of kin, while affines are not truly kin at all.[22] Moreover, he finds that terminological distinctions exist which express the structural distinctions he is reporting.

Farber's response is that they are both right. There is the old New England kinship system, with its emphasis upon marriage as linking two kin groups, and there is the midwestern type, with its emphasis upon blood kin. He goes on to conclude that in present-day U.S. society the former is more prevalent in higher-status groups, the latter in lower-status groups. Suppose, then, one felt close to his parents-in-law. This would probably be expressed at the higher statuses, says Farber, by the use of the terms *mother* and *father,* and at the lower statuses by the use of their first names—to indicate that they are friends, not kin. Farber further generalizes this distinction to speak to the issue raised by Hagstrom and Hadden: in high-status families affection is generally expressed by using the appropriate kin term; in low-status families, by using first names.[23]

In addition to cross-cultural comparisons and analysis of the significance of kin terms in the United States, the study of kin terms is concerned with the naming of children. In a sample of 384 primarily middle-class women in the Chicago area, Alice Rossi noted that between 1920 and 1950 there was a tendency away from naming offspring for mother's mother and father's father and toward naming them for mother's father and especially father's

---

[20] Hagstrom and Hadden, "Sentiment and Kinship Terminology in American Society."

[21] Ward H. Goodenough, "Yankee Kinship Terminology: A Problem in Componential Analysis," *American Anthropologist* 67 (1965), 281.

[22] David M. Schneider, "American Kin Terms for Kinsmen: A Critique of Goodenough's Componential Analysis of Yankee Kinship Terminology," *American Anthropologist* 67 (1965), 292–94.

[23] Farber, *Kinship and Class,* pp. 44–52.

mother.[24] This, she feels, may indicate a greater equalitarianism within the family and the lessening role segregation between males and females and between maternal and paternal kin.

Rossi's article has, of course, only scratched the surface of what might be discovered from a study of names and naming. In fact, there is much left to be done in the analysis of kinship terms in a single society such as the United States. Farber's discoveries are a step in the right direction.

The Kinsman as a Person

The kinship network does not consist of terminological distinctions, or of roles and functions, but of people. These people have various personalities, behave in various ways, and view their social worlds from various perspectives. The kinship component of a relationship gives it an enduring quality, as distinct from the contingent solidarity of friendship; but, within this difference, the unique character of a kin relationship results from the involvement of kinsmen with one another. There are, as Schneider points out, "Famous Relatives" who hold a particularly honored place among their kin.[25] Whether dead or alive, they are referred to with pride. Or a cousin with whom one enjoys doing things may be described as "more a friend than a relative," the implication of the expression being that the term *cousin* ordinarily connotes little affection or interaction, while this particular cousin is of greater significance than that. On the other side of this coin are the friends one refers to as "Uncle Roald" and "Aunt Maureen," though they are actually not relatives at all. The kin terms indicate a relationship that is based on more than the fleeting interests and activities of the typical friendship, and is enduring and intimate to a degree usually present in relationships with certain kin.[26]

It is very likely that the fuzziness of kinship designations in the United States, and the flexibility with which kin ties are interpreted by specific people, are related to the great emphasis that is placed on personal achievement rather than on ascription. This emphasis is related both to the restricted terminological system referred to above and to the great variability in the actual relations between people holding the same structural positions within the kinship system, such as mother-son or uncle-niece. This variability is made clearer by examining the three meanings of "distance" in kinship, especially as these pertain to U.S. kin relations.

---

[24] Alice S. Rossi, "Naming Children in Middle Class Families," *American Sociological Review* 30 (1965), 512.

[25] Schneider, *American Kinship*, p. 67.

[26] Bert N. Adams, "Interaction Theory and the Social Network," *Sociometry* 30 (1967), 75–76.

Kin "Distance"

Distance, says David Schneider, means three things in U.S. kinship.[27] First, it signifies *genealogical* distance, so that we may speak of a second cousin as being a more distant kinsman than an uncle. Some have tried to delineate the various circles of relatives in American society according to genealogical distance. Thus, the inner circle of relatives includes only those from Ego's family of orientation, that is, his parents and children, brothers and sisters. The outer circle of relatives includes those from Ego's parents' family of orientation, including aunts, uncles, and grandparents. Finally, beyond this outer circle are cousins, great aunts, and so on.[28] In analyses of this kind, only Goodenough has fixed the position of affinal relatives, such as in-laws or aunts and uncles by marriage.

The terms *closeness* and *distance* immediately elicit a second interpretation that Schneider calls *socioemotional* distance. Feelings toward kin may or may not be governed by genealogical distance. Thus, Lee Robins and Miroda Tomanec report the following findings regarding affective closeness or distance: "Grandparents were closer to Ego than aunts and uncles, who were in turn closer than cousins. . . . Within kinship roles, maternal relatives were found to be closer than paternal relatives, female relatives closer than male relatives."[29] This type of distance or closeness is governed as much by the interactions and experiences shared or not shared with certain relatives as by genealogical distance.

This matter of "sharing or not sharing" takes us to the third type of distance that pertains to kinship: *physical* or residential distance. Intense interaction clearly requires proximity, and proximity in U.S. society is broadly related to genealogical closeness. However, the association between the three types of closeness or distance is far from perfect. Elizabeth Bott, for example, notes that proximity is a quasi-necessary, but not sufficient, condition for intimacy or socioemotional closeness. Parents, on the one hand, are considered intimate relatives even when not physically accessible.[30] Aunts, uncles, and cousins, on the other hand, may be quite proximate, yet not be objects of great affection or frequent interaction. Schneider puts the same point thus: "A person who is genealogically close may be physically

---

[27] Schneider, *American Kinship*, p. 73.

[28] Lee N. Robins and Miroda Tomanec, "Closeness to Blood Relatives Outside the Immediate Family," *Marriage and Family Living* 24 (1962), 340–46; Talcott Parsons, "The Kinship System of the Contemporary United States," *American Anthropologist* 45 (1943), 22–38; Goodenough, "Yankee Kinship Terminology"; and Allan D. Coult and Robert W. Habenstein, "Closeness to Non-Primary Relatives in the American Kinship System," *Journal of Comparative Family Studies* 2 (1972), 15–32.

[29] Robins and Tomanec, "Closeness to Blood Relatives Outside the Immediate Family," pp. 342–43.

[30] Elizabeth Bott, *Family and Social Network* (London: Tavistock, 1957), p. 129.

distant and neutral on the socioemotional dimension. Or a person may be close socioemotionally and physically but distant genealogically."[31] The same functional character of U.S. kinship which gives rise to a terminological system stressing the nuclear family and which allows for fuzzy boundaries and idiosyncratic personal relationships within the kin network also makes for a relatively low correlation between the three types of closeness or distance in U.S. kinship. But what, precisely, is the "functional" character of U.S. kinship? Although this subject was roughly summarized in Section One, let us return to this important question.

Unimportance, Isolation, and Consistency

More than thirty years ago, Talcott Parsons wrote an article on kinship in the United States in which he made three major points. First, compared to kinship in many other societies, kinship in the United States is relatively unimportant to the ongoing of the society. With the parceling out of institutional functions to other settings—institutional differentiation—the kinship network has little role to play in societal maintenance, particularly compared to the role it played in the past (which it still plays in other cultures). Second, the normal household unit is the nuclear, conjugal family, living "in a home segregated from those of both pairs of parents (if living) and . . . economically independent of both. In a very large proportion of cases the geographical separation is considerable."[32] Third, this isolated, open, bilateral kinship system with nuclear household units is most functional for, or best suited to, the U.S. occupational system and urban living. It makes residential mobility in pursuit of occupational opportunities much easier than if one's corporate kin group have to be carried along on each move.

From this article, which echoes the sentiments of Louis Wirth and others regarding contemporary urban life,[33] three conclusions could be drawn: (1) Compared to other times and places, U.S. kinship is functionally unimportant. (2) The nuclear family is generally isolated from kin, economically and otherwise. (3) This system fits well with the other characteristics of U.S. society. However, the article and its conclusions have been a favorite target of kinship researchers since the 1950s. Among other things, these researchers have discovered that adult offspring are more likely to live close to their parents and other kin than "considerably separated" from them. Noting that Parsons was writing about the middle class, specifically excluding farmers,

[31] Schneider, *American Kinship*, p. 73.

[32] Parsons, "The Kinship System of the Contemporary United States," p. 27.

[33] See especially Louis Wirth, "Urbanism as a Way of Life," *American Journal of Sociology* 44 (1938), 1–24.

matrifocal lower-class families, and the upper class, Marvin Sussman and Paul Reiss find that even among middle-class families the separation from kin is not likely to be great.[34]

Even more important, researchers have noted that the kin network does "function" in several ways: providing affectional ties, help when needed, and even supports for or deterrents to residential mobility.[35] The functionality of the kin network, demonstrated in study after study, leads Marvin Sussman to conclude that

> the evidence on the viability of an existing kinship structure carrying on extensive activities among kin is so convincing that we find it unnecessary to continue further descriptive work in order to establish the existence of the kin network in modern urban society.[36]

Some lower-class individuals and families may be isolated, and some highly residentially and socially mobile middle-class families may pay little attention to kin. However, as Farber has indicated, the pattern is for working-class people to have a cluster of kin close at hand, and for high-status individuals to be very much concerned about their kin links—the symbolic family estate.[37] It is worth noting at this point that at present both the domestic and the symbolic estate function can be found among the black population of the United States. As reported in Chapter 6, Dmitri Shimkin, Gloria Louie, and Dennis Frate are currently analyzing the way in which the domestic, that is, the obligatory and residential, functions are being performed by kin among both the poor black population of rural Mississippi and the upwardly mobile blacks of Chicago.[38] In addition, one aspect of the increasing ethnic solidarity of the black community is what Alex Haley calls the search

[34] Marvin B. Sussman, "The Isolated Nuclear Family: Fact or Fiction?" *Social Problems* 6 (1959), 333–40; and Paul J. Reiss, "The Extended Kinship System: Correlates of and Attitudes on Frequency of Interaction," *Marriage and Family Living* 24 (1962), 333–39.

[35] Eugene Litwak, "The Use of Extended Family Groups in the Achievement of Social Goals," *Social Problems* 7 (1959–60), 177–87; Marvin B. Sussman and Lee Burchinal, "Kin Family Network: Unheralded Structure in Current Conceptualizations of Family Functioning," *Marriage and Family Living* 24 (1962), 231–40; Hope Jensen Leichter and William E. Mitchell, *Kinship and Casework* (New York: Russell Sage Foundation, 1967); Robert F. Winch, Scott Greer, and Rae Lesser Blumberg, "Ethnicity and Extended Familism in an Upper-Middle-Class Suburb," *American Sociological Review* 32 (1967), 272; and Sussman, "Relationships of Adult Children with Their Parents in the United States," in Ethel Shanas and Gordon F. Streib, eds., *Social Structure and the Family: Generational Relations* (Englewood Cliffs, N.J.: Prentice-Hall, 1965), p. 73.

[36] Sussman, "Relationships of Adult Children with Their Parents in the United States," p. 63.

[37] Farber, *Kinship and Class*, pp. 97–118.

[38] Dmitri B. Shimkin, Gloria J. Louie, and Dennis Frate, "The Black Extended Family: A Basic Rural Institution and a Mechanism of Urban Adaptation" (presented and discussed at the International Congress of Anthropological and Ethnological Sciences, Chicago, Illinois, September 1973).

for "roots." In Farber's terms, these roots are the black individual's symbolic family estate.

Therefore, although Parsons claimed that kinship is relatively unimportant in U.S. society, and that this is consistent with the economic-industrial structure of this society, his critics have rightly responded: "Yes, but nuclear families are not isolated, kin networks do function, and many of their functions are perfectly consistent with the economic structure of the society."[39] Parsons himself has sought more recently to reemphasize his comparative perspective, while at the same time acknowledging the findings of his critics. The view of the "isolated nuclear family" and that of its critics, Parsons claims,

> are not contradictory but complementary. The concept of isolation applies in the first instance to kinship structure as seen in the perspective of anthropological studies in that field. In this context our system represents an extreme type, which is well described by that term. It does not, however, follow that all relations to kin outside the nuclear family are broken. Indeed, the very psychological importance for the individual of the nuclear family in which he was born and brought up would make any such conception impossible.[40]

Thus, it may be concluded that neither institutions nor personnel are as embedded in the kin networks of the United States as they have been in many other societies. This is not to say, however, that kinship performs no functions in the United States. Nor is it to say that its performance of certain functions is inconsistent with the achievement-based institutions of that society. Nor, finally, is it to say that the absence of personnel embeddedness in a household and solidarity sense means that kin are isolated from one another, either interactionally or emotionally. It does mean that the volitional element, the flexibility and variety that come with choice, is heightened in American kinship. It also means that generalizations about kin are risky, and that when they are based simply on "the kin network" they are clearly overgeneralizations. One must, instead, speak of the relations between specific categories of kin—parents and offspring, siblings, in-laws, and so on—as we shall do in Section Three.

---

[39] Where kinship and economics are in conflict is ordinarily where kinship and the economic-productive function are linked directly. Yet even this does not automatically cause trouble. See Leichter and Mitchell, *Kinship and Casework*, pp. 138, 145; and Adams, *Kinship in an Urban Setting*, p. 132.

[40] Talcott Parsons, "The Normal American Family," in Seymour M. Farber, Piero Mustacchi, and Roger H. L. Wilson, eds., *Man and Civilization: The Family's Search for Survival* (New York: McGraw-Hill, 1965), p. 35.

Section Three

CATEGORIES OF U.S. KIN AND THEIR CHARACTERISTICS

Kin might be subdivided into a large number of categories, including cousins, grandparents, grandchildren, mothers-in-law, and many others. For the purposes of the present summary, however, four divisions seem sufficient. These are: parents and their adult offspring, siblings, secondary kin (that is, all blood kin and their affines outside the nuclear family of orientation), and in-laws.

Parents and Adult Offspring

This author wrote in 1970 that "the relations between young adults and their aging parents are ordinarily the closest kin tie attitudinally and residentially."[41] The relations between parents and their adult offspring can be characterized by the phrase *positive concern*. This positive, or active, concern is manifested in several ways. First, there is extremely frequent contact between these intergenerational kin. When they live close to one another, weekly or more frequent interaction is the rule. But even when parents and their offspring are separated by a considerable geographic distance, communication by mail or telephone tends to be at least monthly. Substantial mutual aid is a second manifestation of positive concern. Immediately after the marriage of the young adult, aid tends to flow primarily from the parents—in the form of loans or cash, large gifts for the new household, and, if the parents are proximate, babysitting and other services when children are born. Later, as the parents age and become infirm, the direction of aid begins to reverse, so that the middle-aged adult cares for his own offspring and helps his aging parents as long as they live.[42]

A third manifestation of the positive concern between adult offspring and their parents is a social psychological bond that includes a strong affectional tie and a secondary obligatory element—with the latter subsuming both the general duty to keep in frequent touch and the specific obligation to help out in time of need. The obligatory element, which is quite evident in parent-offspring relations, does not seem to stand in the way of affectional

[41] Bert N. Adams, "Isolation, Function, and Beyond: American Kinship in the 1960's," in Carlfred B. Broderick. ed., *A Decade of Family Research and Action* (Minneapolis: National Council on Family Relations, 1971), p. 177.
[42] Reuben Hill, "Decision Making and the Family Life Cycle," in Shanas and Streib, *Social Structure and the Family*, p. 125.

closeness, or to be dysfunctional, except when it becomes the primary factor in continued contact. An example of such a situation is the young adult male who has few interests in common with his widowed mother, but who feels obliged to help her tangibly or in other ways.[43] Yet, for the most part, frequent contact, mutual aid, affectional closeness, and a feeling of obligation result in a close relationship between parents and their adult offspring. Even in the middle class these kin do not fit the residential pattern of "considerable separation," which Parsons claimed was true of kin in general.

Of the four possible parent-offspring relationships—mother-daughter, mother-son, father-daughter, and father-son—the closest, both affectionally and interactionally, tends to be that between mother and daughter. This is true regardless of the socioeconomic, or social class, positions of the two. A partial explanation for this closeness is the female role convergence of which Peter Willmott and Michael Young speak.[44] If we can assume that the major life role of most women is wife-mother, while that of most men is occupational, then we can say that mothers and daughters are more likely to play the same major roles in adulthood than are fathers and sons, mothers and sons, or fathers and daughters. In this author's Greensboro study, many young females explained their positive feelings toward their mothers with some version of the following: "Now I know what my parents went through in raising me." The words *realize, know, appreciate,* and *understand* appear over and over in the female responses. Thus, when role convergence is coupled with the generally greater social-emotional involvement of females with all sorts of kin, you have the basis for an extremely close relationship between adult daughters and their mothers. Yet, all four parent-offspring relationships tend to be closer than relationships between any other two relatives in U.S. kin networks. Most of the exceptions to this are found among siblings, to whom we now turn.

Adult Sibling Relations

The terms that seem to summarize best the relations between adult siblings are *interest* and *comparison/identification. Interest* simply means a general feeling that one should keep up with his siblings, keep posted on their activities, but that except in extreme circumstances there is no need for contact to be as frequent or mutual aid to be as great as is that with parents. In fact, apart from the exchange of babysitting between proximate sisters, the sharing of financial or other forms of aid between siblings is likely to

---

[43] Bert N. Adams, "The Middle-Class Adult and His Widowed or Still-Married Mother," *Social Problems* 16 (1968), 50–59.

[44] Peter Willmott and Michael Young, *Family and Class in a London Suburb* (London: Routledge and Kegan Paul, 1960), p. 84.

become a bone of contention or even a basis for alienation. Interest, then, is just that: the individual is "interested" in how his brothers and sisters are getting along.

The notion of sibling rivalry has been a topic of discussion for some time in the socialization literature. It must now be added that when brothers and sisters leave home such rivalry does not end, but is transformed into *comparison* or *identification*. In a success- and achievement-oriented society, with substantial emphasis on individualism within the family, brothers and sisters are the comparative reference group par excellence. That is, the question "How am I doing?" can well be answered by noting how one's achievements compare with those of his siblings. Siblings, unlike friends, are "givens" in the individual's social network. He cannot (as he can with friends) drop them if he becomes dissatisfied with them. And when the kin of orientation (adult offspring and their parents) get together, conversation is likely to turn—sometimes subtly, sometimes openly—to how well George is doing in his business, or to what a good marriage Susan made. Therefore, there may be considerable emotional alienation between brothers whose occupations diverge greatly in prestige. In the other sibling combinations, a prestige divergence generally results in a one-way, or unreciprocated, identification. That is, the lower-status sibling expresses affection for and wants to be like the higher-status sibling, but his feelings are not reciprocated. This, then, is one point at which the economic success values of the society impinge upon and help to determine the social psychology of kin involvement. It is noteworthy, however, that such variations in feeling are not very evident in the area of interaction. Females especially seem to have little control over the frequency of their contact with siblings, and are thus unable—due to obligation—to bring that frequency into line with their feelings. This is, of course, another indication of the greater obligatory burden that females bear in kinship relations.[45]

Some pairs of brothers or sisters evolve activity patterns that make them extremely close friends in adulthood. "Best friend" status for a sibling is, however, the exception rather than the rule. Yet, activity-based relationships are even less prevalent between secondary kin, such as cousins.

Secondary Kinship

Secondary kin are all those relatives who were not at some time in the past a part of Ego's family of orientation: aunts, uncles, cousins, grandparents, and so on. The best terms to use in describing the contacts between such kin in U.S. society are *circumstantial* and *incidental*. Allan Coult and Robert Ha-

---

[45] See Adams, *Kinship in an Urban Setting*, pp. 93–132, for more on adult sibling relations.

benstein find that most of the respondents in their Kansas City study consider three or fewer "non-primary" (that is, secondary) relatives to be "close or important enough to mention, in spite of the fact," they say, "that we did not indicate *any* degree of closeness or importance was necessary in order for a relative to be mentioned."[46] The fact is, such relations seldom involve frequent contact, common interests, mutual aid, or strong affectional and obligatory concern. Yearly contact—the Christmas card, for example, or perhaps a kin reunion at holidays or during a vacation—frequently suffices. The incidental nature of such kin relations may be seen in those instances in which an aunt and uncle drop in while one is visiting his parents or in which one goes to see a cousin while on a trip home for the purpose of visiting parents and siblings. The circumstantial side of secondary kin contact is well depicted in the "wakes and weddings" relatives of whom Schneider speaks. These are kin brought together by such circumstances as the marriage or death of a mutual kinsman.[47]

The notion of incidental or circumstantial contact is opposed to that of intentional or volitional contact, and fits quite well the character of most secondary kin in the United States. In the author's Greensboro study (see note 45), a few respondents were troubled by the weakness of secondary kin ties. The wife of a clerk explained: "It is distressing that distance is pulling families apart so. Seeing relatives was very important when I was young, and I miss it now. It bothers me that my children don't know their cousins and play with them like I did." However, a much greater proportion of respondents made this sort of comment: "My parents and sister mean a lot to me, but I simply don't have time to spend keeping up with a lot of kinsfolk that don't mean anything to me anyway." Or even more pointedly: "I have an aunt and one cousin besides my mother and brothers that mean a lot to me. As for the others—phooey!"

It should be noted that in the United States there are two prime exceptions to circumstantiality. One is grandparents of the young adult. It is, in fact, such aging grandparents who, along with females, form the hub of kin activity and involvement. However, by the time the young person reaches adulthood and marries, his grandparents are often no longer alive. The second exception to circumstantiality is the activity and mutual concern of the secondary kin of many ethnic groups. Their activities—originally means for ensuring mutual survival—are now more likely to be means for achieving individual success. We have mentioned extended kin ties among blacks; in addition, Hope Leichter and William Mitchell report a phenomenon that is somewhat prevalent among the Jewish families they studied in New York City:

---

[46] Coult and Habenstein, "Closeness to Non-Primary Relatives in the American Kinship System," p. 20.
[47] Schneider, *American Kinship*, p. 70.

Family circles and cousin clubs may also support occupational achievement by giving instrumental help as an organization: the group's loan fund may help to support children's education, or special collections may be taken up when there is particular need on the part of one member.[48]

Such secondary kin support has not automatically disappeared as the various ethnic groups have been incorporated into the dominant structures of U.S. society. Yet these exceptions do not alter the overriding generalization that, even in the lower and working classes, secondary kin ordinarily play a relatively minor role in the individual's social network.

In-Law Relations

"If I had it to do over again," remarks the weary American husband, "I'd marry a Japanese girl. They're pretty, graceful, obedient—and your mother-in-law's in Yokohama." So goes one of the many in-law jokes with its typical focus on mother-in-law troubles. As is often the case with jokes, these jokes have in them an element of truth, but the picture they present is incomplete and exaggerated as well. We shall, therefore, summarize what is known about in-law relationships in the United States, and in so doing perhaps clarify some popular impressions.

The discussion of in-laws, the relatives one gains by marriage, requires that several distinctions be made. First, it should be—but is not always—made clear whether one is referring to the spouses' relations with their in-laws or with the influence of the in-laws upon relations between the spouses. We shall attempt to deal with both. Second, investigations of in-law relationships should distinguish between specific in-laws, such as the husband's mother and the wife's mother, sisters-in-law, and so on. Such specification is as necessary here as it is in the discussion of blood kin. Third, the focus of in-law studies should be not only on the roots of trouble or conflict—which is the case for most such studies—but also on the conditions that make for satisfactory relationships. We shall examine both.

In her classic article on sex roles, Mirra Komarovsky hypothesized that as a result of the female's closer ties to her parents in-law troubles would more often involve the husband and the wife's parents than the wife and the husband's parents.[49] Later studies of working-class families by Komarovsky and by Young and Willmott have in fact discovered a substantial amount of conflict between the husband and the wife's parents. According to Young and Willmott, this relationship is *ordinarily* one of conflict; Komarovsky, in *Blue-Collar Marriage*, adds: "It now seems likely that when the mode of life

---

[48] Leichter and Mitchell, *Kinship and Casework*, p. 156.
[49] Mirra Komarovsky, "Functional Analysis of Sex Roles," *American Sociological Review* 15 (1950), 508–16.

forces husbands to associate closely with their in-laws regardless of personal congeniality, the chances of strain can be as great as for their wives."[50] Yet, despite these studies indicating a considerable amount of husband–in-law trouble, the majority of studies since Komarovsky's hypothesis was formulated have concluded that in-law troubles are generally more frequent between the wife and the husband's mother than vice versa.[51] This is the case in spite of the tendency of married couples to interact somewhat more often with the wife's parents than with the husband's.[52]

The specification of factors that give rise to in-law conflict or peace is not complete, but several factors have been tentatively isolated. Evelyn Duvall finds that older women have less in-law trouble than *younger* ones. Robert Blood and Donald Wolfe phrase it thus: "As young adult men and women transfer their loyalties from their parents to each other, some stress is inevitable and it shows in the concentration of in-law problems at the beginning of youthful marriages." Sheldon Stryker adds that the presence of offspring in the home is likely to improve relations, particularly between the two mothers.[53] Thus, the fact that younger marrieds appear to have more in-law troubles than older marrieds can be explained partially by the independence struggle that is completed during the early years of marriage and partially by the strengthening of bonds that results from the presence of grandchildren during the later years.

A second apparently necessary, but not sufficient, condition for in-law trouble is *proximity*. Young and Willmott report that, among working-class Londoners, there is likely to be trouble between the young husband and his mother-in-law unless one of three conditions is met—one of which is for the young couple to move away. Americans, Duvall claims, "really believe that the way to get along with our in-laws is to keep as far away as possible."[54] While this is an overstatement, it does point up the fact that few married couples have trouble with in-laws who are in absentia.

---

[50] Michael Young and Peter Willmott, *Family and Kinship in East London* (Baltimore: Penguin Books, 1964), p. 62; and Mirra Komarovsky, *Blue-Collar Marriage* (New York: Random House, 1962), p. 279.

[51] Mirra Komarovsky, "Continuities in Family Research: A Case Study," *American Journal of Sociology* 62 (1956), 46; Paul Wallin, "Sex Differences in Attitudes to 'In-Laws': A Test of a Theory," *American Journal of Sociology* 59 (1954), 466–69; Evelyn Millis Duvall, *In-Laws Pro and Con* (New York: Association Press, 1954), p. 187; Peggy S. Marcus, "A Study of In-Law Relationships of 79 Couples Who Have Been Married Between 2 and 11 Years" (Master's thesis, Cornell University, 1950); and Leichter and Mitchell, *Kinship and Casework*, p. 174.

[52] Reiss, "The Extended Kinship System," p. 334; Leichter and Mitchell, *Kinship and Casework*, p. 174.

[53] Duvall, *In-Laws Pro and Con*, p. 219; Robert O. Blood, Jr., and Donald M. Wolfe, *Husbands and Wives* (New York: Free Press, 1960), p. 248; and Sheldon Stryker, "The Adjustment of Married Offspring to Their Parents," *American Sociological Review* 20 (1955), 153.

[54] Young and Willmott, *Family and Kinship in East London*, pp. 62f; Duvall, *In-Laws Pro and Con*, p. 291.

Dependence upon parents is a third factor which, though not entirely separate from either age or proximity, seems to account for a portion of in-law conflict. While young adult females are more likely to manifest an emotional dependence upon their parents than males are upon theirs, a certain amount of female dependence seems to be acceptable in U.S. society. Thus, though female dependence is more prevalent, when male dependence does occur it is surer to cause trouble between the wife and the husband's parents.[55] The greater involvement of females in kin relations means that the wife and the husband's mother may very easily come into conflict over the young husband's time and interest. Another reason why wife–mother-in-law conflict is more prevalent is that the husband is very often incorporated into the wife's family as a virtual offspring. Komarovsky, for example, points out the positive value of the "ability of some in-laws to play the role of parent-substitutes to a man who has been deprived of parental affection."[56] In many families, says Paul Wallin, the husband is more attached to his wife's parents than she is.[57] In fact, after marriage men seem to count more of their in-laws as close than do women.[58]

Treating a daughter- or a son-in-law as one's own offspring is not the only mechanism for avoiding in-law conflict, particularly conflict with the mother-in-law. Irwin Deutscher points out that today the myth of the meddlesome, troublesome mother-in-law causes many mothers-in-law to resolve *not* to be that way, but rather to do everything they can to stay out of the way.[59] Alice Rossi, furthermore, feels that adult-to-adult relationships with parents may "be difficult to achieve even after marriage, while parents-in-law are met as adults, so that relations with them may take on some of the quality of relations with a friendly peer." Thus, the increased equalitarianism of the family may have improved in-law relations and weakened parent–grown-child relations.[60] Treatment as a blood offspring, efforts to disprove the mother-in-law myth, and equalitarianism may all have gone to improve in-law relations in recent years.

Age, proximity, and dependence, which were all discussed in relation to in-law troubles, are also related to husband-wife conflict about kin.[61] And,

---

[55] Komarovsky, *Blue-Collar Marriage*, p. 258; and Komarovsky, "Continuities in Family Research," p. 46

[56] Komarovsky, *Blue-Collar Marriage*, p. 278.

[57] Wallin, "Sex Differences in Attitudes to 'In-Laws.' "

[58] Coult and Habenstein, "Closeness to Non-Primary Relatives in the American Kinship System."

[59] Irwin Deutscher, "Socialization for Postparental Life," in Arnold Rose, ed., *Human Behavior and Social Processes* (Boston: Houghton Mifflin, 1962), p. 520.

[60] Rossi, "Naming Children in Middle Class Families," p. 512.

[61] Blood and Wolfe, *Husbands and Wives*, p. 248, indicate that "in-laws are an issue when the partners are young—indeed the younger the wife, the more often conflicts over relatives are mentioned." Adams' Greensboro study found that both proximity and dependence are quasi-necessary, but not sufficient, conditions for conflict between husbands and wives about their kin.

of course, conflict *with* and conflict *about* kin are both related to marital adjustment. In a sample of 544 couples in the early years of marriage, the Landises find that 67 percent of those who reported excellent adjustment to in-laws also reported very happy marriages, while only 18 percent of those who had fair or poor adjustments to their in-laws indicated that their marriages were very happy.[62] As we have noted so often in this volume, however, a simple relationship may be causatively interpreted only with great caution. Although it is easy to jump to the conclusion that in-law trouble causes marital difficulties, an equally plausible interpretation would be that marital difficulties disrupt the relations of couples with other members of their social network—including in-laws—as well. Yet, however one explains the relationship between in-law trouble and marital conflict, it is to be expected that there will be a relationship between them.

The least disrupted marriages, in terms of kin relationships, are those in which there are children and in which the couple live some distance from the two kin networks and manifest little emotional dependence upon kin, so that their attention is focused on their own family of procreation rather than on their kin of orientation or other relatives. Yet, such a conclusion assumes that a great amount of value is placed upon simply avoiding conflict, with the positive functions of kinship involvement considered insignificant. The literature on kinship in the United States seems to show that most people disagree with Barrington Moore's assertion that kinship is nothing more than a barbaric "obligation to give affection as a duty to a particular set of persons on account of the accident of birth."[63] Despite the emphasis society places on individualism and independence—which make the relations of couples with their parents, in-laws, and other kin tenuous at times—most people seem to prefer the sense of identity, emotional support, visiting, and emergency help that genealogically close kin provide, rather than the total independence and isolation that might be achieved if the couple truly desired it.

Compared to those of other societies, cross-culturally and historically, kinship ties in the United States appear insignificant and weak. There is little institutional embeddedness in the kin network, and personnel embeddedness in terms of solidarity exists only with the kin of orientation in most middle-class and some working- and lower-class families. But U.S. kin ties do have a form of viability that is positively valued by most Americans. Whether kin ties *should* "wither away" for the sake of other, more individualistic values, as Moore believes they should, is a question the reader may decide for himself.

---

[62] Judson T. and Mary G. Landis, *Building a Successful Marriage* (Englewood Cliffs, N.J.: Prentice-Hall, 1963), pp. 331–35.

[63] Barrington Moore, *Political Power and Social Theory* (Cambridge, Mass.: Harvard University Press, 1958), p. 163.

For married couples in the United States aging usually involves the relinquishing of two key roles—the parental and the occupational. Aging requires numerous decisions and a substantial reorientation of activity patterns. The discussion of aging in this chapter has four major foci: the theory of disengagement, socialization into old age, the issue of age grading and the social network, and disenchantment or satisfaction with marriage. In the concluding section, four activity patterns of the aged are summarized, and a brief comparison is drawn between old age and adolescence.

Aging and the Family in the United States

The typical couple of two generations ago had a life expectancy which enabled them to survive together for 31 years after marriage, two years short of the time when their *fifth* child was expected to marry. But "the decline in size of family and the improved survival prospects of the population since 1890 not only have assured the average parents of our day that they will live to see their children married but also have made it probable that they will have one-fourth of their married life still to come when their last child leaves the parental home."[1]

Throughout the history of mankind, aging has always meant losing hair, friends, illusions, and strength; and dealing with senescent or senile fellows has always been a problem for families and communities. However, in most known cultures, some sort of compensation to their inevitable losses and decrements had been devised and were available to the aging individuals. The aged have indeed very often been considered the more wise, influential, and honored people. We have within a few decades almost ruined such a conception of life. In the same time we have made old age a common and lengthier experience, and made it a period of isolation, anguish, boredom, and uselessness.[2]

---

[1] Irwin Deutscher, "Socialization for Postparental Life," in Arnold Rose, ed., *Human Behavior and Social Processes* (Boston: Houghton Mifflin, 1962), p. 507.

[2] Michel A. J. Philbert, "The Emergence of Social Gerontology," *Journal of Social Issues* 21 (1965), 5.

These two statements—the first by Irwin Deutscher (who quotes Paul Glick), the second by Michel Philbert—introduce us to the dilemmas of old age, a period that has decreased in honor as it has increased in prevalence in U.S. society. Longevity is currently approaching seventy for men and seventy-five for women in a society that emphasizes the achievements of the young adult years and glorifies youth. What is happening to the ever-increasing numbers of aged? are they adjusting easily or with difficulty to this stage of the life cycle? and what does that adjustment require? According to one recent theory, the adjustment is effected by the process of *disengagement*.

Section One

DISENGAGEMENT THEORY AND ITS CRITICS

Disengagement theory was first set forth by Elaine Cumming, Lois Dean, and David Newell in a 1960 *Sociometry* article, and was developed further in *Growing Old: The Process of Disengagement,* a book by Elaine Cumming and William Henry that was published in 1961. The study on which the theory is based involved 279 old people in the Kansas City area, ranging from working class to upper middle class—the same sample that formed the basis for the studies by Bernice Neugarten that are described in Chapter 11.[3] Very simply, disengagement is a universal theory of the reduction of one's life space and of the change to a positive orientation toward death in old age. But let us delineate the various aspects of the process.

At the heart of disengagement is the forfeiting of the individual's major life role: for the female this ordinarily means the parental role; for the male, the occupational role. "On the whole, men make an abrupt transition from the engaged to the disengaged state, but it is soon resolved; women have a smoother passage, which lasts longer."[4] A concomitant of the role loss at the launching of offspring and at retirement is the "decreased interaction between the aging person and others in the social systems he belongs to. . . . His withdrawal may be accompanied from the outset by an increased pre-

---

[3] Disengagement theory was first presented in Elaine Cumming, Lois R. Dean, and David S. Newell, "Disengagement, a Tentative Theory of Aging," *Sociometry* 23 (1960); see also Cumming and William Henry, *Growing Old: The Process of Disengagement* (New York: Basic Books, 1961). Neugarten's study is Bernice L. Neugarten, *Personality in Middle and Late Life* (New York: Atherton Press, 1964).

[4] Cumming and Henry, *Growing Old,* p. 159; also reported in Lillian E. Troll, "The Family of Later Life: A Decade Review," in Carlfred B. Broderick, ed., *A Decade of Research and Action* (Minneapolis: National Council on Family Relations, 1971), p. 198.

occupation with himself."[5] There are changes, say the authors, in the number of people with whom the aged person interacts and in the amount of his interaction. There are qualitative changes in interaction commensurate with decreased involvement. And there are changes in personality that cause decreased interpersonal involvement and result in increased preoccupation with self.[6] Preoccupation with self includes facing the inevitability of death. Any demoralization that results from the combination of role loss, withdrawal, and facing death, the authors feel, is only temporary. Older people eventually come to appreciate the disengaged state, and to orient positively to it.[7] One reason for this positive orientation, pointed out by Deutscher in his discussion of the postparental period, is that old age is

> a time of new freedoms: freedom from the economic responsibilities of children; freedom to be mobile (geographically); freedom from housework and other chores. And, finally, freedom to be one's self for the first time since the children came along.[8]

Thus, disengagement theory is, according to its proponents, a cross-culturally applicable theory that includes a generally positive orientation on the part of the aged to the loss of their major roles, to their withdrawal from the social world, and to their increasing preoccupation with self and death.

Criticism of disengagement theory has been both direct and indirect. The best example of direct criticism is a volume edited by Arnold Rose and Warren Peterson, *Older People and Their Social World*. Using the concept of "aging group consciousness," the editors assert that

> aging group conscious persons have not become disengaged from social roles as a result of aging or retirement. Rather, for most of them, aging and retirement have opened up new roles, because of the increase of leisure time *and* because of their aging group consciousness.[9]

In order to criticize disengagement theory, Rose and Peterson begin by describing it as follows:

> The Cumming and Henry theory of disengagement is that the society and the individual prepare *in advance* for the ultimate "disengagement" of incurable, incapacitating disease and death by an *inevitable, gradual, and mutually satisfying process* of disengagement. . . . Cumming and

---

[5] Cumming and Henry, *Growing Old*, p. 14. On role loss, see Cumming, "Further Thoughts on the Theory of Disengagement," *International Social Science Journal* 15 (1963), 377–93.

[6] Cumming and Henry, *Growing Old*, p. 15.

[7] Cumming, "Further Thoughts on the Theory of Disengagement," p. 385; and Cumming and Henry, *Growing Old*, p. 142.

[8] Deutscher, "Socialization for Postparental Life," p. 524.

[9] Arnold M. Rose and Warren A. Peterson, eds., *Older People and Their Social World* (Philadelphia: Davis, 1965), p. 26.

Henry say that the values in American culture of competitive achievement and of future orientation make this society especially negative toward aging and hence encourage disengagement. But the process itself must be understood to be inevitable and universal, according to the theory, and not limited to any one group in a society or any one society.[10]

The most direct criticisms made by Rose and Peterson are that the theory of disengagement is neither cross-culturally applicable nor universally applicable even in the United States and that the process of disengagement is not necessarily of positive value when it does occur.[11] The U.S. culture and economic structure have created conditions that lead to the disengagement of large numbers of the aged. Although disengagement may make for a sense of freedom (as Deutscher claims), Rose and Peterson cite evidence provided by Robert Havighurst and his associates

> that the engaged elderly, rather than the disengaged, are the ones who generally, although not always, are happiest and have the greatest expressed life satisfaction.[12]

Retreat, disintegration, devastation, threat, desolation—these are some of the terms used by various authors to describe the transition into old age. Disengagement, according to Ethel Shanas, is based on bereavement. "The kind of theory we need is one that suggests not the image of erosion but, rather, that of sudden, if partial, disintegration and patched-up reconstruction."[13]

How, then, did Cumming and her associates arrive at the conclusion that aging and disengagement are actually considered of positive value? This conclusion resulted in part from the fact that they sampled primarily healthy people. Once the old person finds himself staying well and outliving his peers, his satisfaction increases as he compares himself with others. He is grateful to be alive and well, disengaged or not. A more subtle reason, Rose and Peterson feel, is that this theory draws the functionalist conclusion that "what is, must be," or, to change it slightly, "what is, is good."[14]

If the theory of disengagement is not only *not* cross-culturally valid, but unable even to account for old age in U.S. society, how might it be corrected or expanded? For one thing, disengagement is psychologically continuous and

[10] Rose and Peterson, *Older People and Their Social World,* pp. 360, 361.
[11] Rose and Peterson, *Older People and Their Social World,* pp. 362, 363.
[12] Rose and Peterson, *Older People and Their Social World,* p. 363.
[13] Ethel Shanas et al., *Old People in Three Industrial Societies* (New York: Atherton Press, 1968), p. 285. Copyright © 1968, Atherton Press, Inc.; reprinted by permission of the publishers. All rights reserved. See also Cumming and Henry, *Growing Old,* p. 159; and Paul H. and Lois N. Glasser, "Role Reversal and Conflict Between Aged Parents and Their Children," *Marriage and Family Living* 24 (1962), 46–51.
[14] Rose and Peterson, *Older People and Their Social World,* p. 366.

gradual; early social attitudes are manifested behaviorally in the way one reacts to the departure of children and to retirement.[15] Thus, the socially active woman who wishes she could escape the entertaining and other responsibilities demanded by her husband's occupation may be positively oriented toward disengagement for many years before she can manifest this attitude in her behavior. Or the man who finds no meaning in his occupation may be oriented positively toward disengagement virtually throughout his work career. "In the working class," Irving Rosow finds, "there is initially more acceptance of aging."[16] Aging, yes, but not necessarily retirement. Lillian Troll, for example, points out that the retired working-class husband who spends much time with household chores, as many do, may find them demeaning. Seeing them as "woman's work," the ex–manual laborer who has few outside interests in old age may react negatively rather than positively toward disengagement from his work role.[17] Thus, in terms of roles, there may actually be three categories of elderly persons in U.S. society: (1) the positively oriented disengaged, who may have experienced "anticipatory disengagement" for many years prior to old age; (2) the negatively oriented disengaged, who, in relinquishing their dominant life roles, give up a highly valued part of their lives, or who find old age to be a period of domestic entrapment, sickness, bereavement, and loneliness, rather than one of freedom; (3) the aged who do not become disengaged at all. The self-employed male who never retires exemplifies the still-engaged aged. However, the numbers of still-engaged aged in the United States are small compared to the numbers of positively and negatively oriented disengaged.

Thus far, we have referred to the critics who have questioned the cross-cultural applicability of disengagement theory, and who, while admitting that most U.S. aged become disengaged from their major life roles, have noted that some react positively and some negatively to disengagement. A further criticism of the theory concerns the issue of withdrawal from the social network. While many of the aged do become cut off from other people and preoccupied with themselves, two other patterns also recur. Shanas et al. report that the aged tend to find themselves "nearer one of two extremes—experiencing the seclusion of the spinster or widow without children and surviving brothers and sisters, or pushed towards the pinnacle of a pyramidal family structure of four generations."[18] The pyramidal kinship structure, characterized by substantial contact with children and grandchildren, nephews and nieces, and other kin, is more prevalent among

---

[15] Neugarten, *Personality in Middle and Late Life*, p. 193.
[16] Irving Rosow, *Social Integration of the Aged* (New York: Free Press, 1967), p. 291.
[17] Troll, "The Family of Later Life," in Broderick, *A Decade of Research and Action*, p. 198.
[18] Shanas et al., *Old People in Three Industrial Societies*, p. 172.

working-class aged.[19] A third category of aged, described by Rose and Peterson, Rosow, and Mark Messer, are the aging group-conscious, who are neither isolated and withdrawn nor highly involved with kin or other members of the descending generation, but are age-segregated and in frequent contact with other aged.[20] Both Rosow's study in Cleveland and Messer's in Chicago indicate that age segregation is not necessarily negative in its effects on the individual's sense of social integration. Messer, for example, finds that:

> (1) age grouping is associated with less dependence on the family as a source of morale, (2) this is not accompanied by a feeling of familial neglect, and (3) age grouping serves as a mediator between the older individual and the overall society, providing a greater sense of social integration.[21]

Rosow, while agreeing that residential concentration of older people appears to be functional for their integration and support, admits that "some gerontologists strenuously object to such concentration as segregation which is implicitly invidious and anti-democratic."[22] Yet the main point is that many elderly people do not simply withdraw from social contact, but either continue (and even intensify) their contacts with kin and friends, or else become active in groups whose members are aware of their common age bond.

In conclusion, we can say that Cumming and Henry have isolated an important aspect of aging in the United States: the relinquishing of the crucial parental and occupational roles in old age. This role loss, however, may be viewed positively or negatively by the individual, and it may or may not be accompanied by a withdrawal from social interaction, a reduction of his life space, and a preoccupation with self. The debate regarding disengagement theory is reminiscent of the "isolated nuclear family" debate discussed in Chapter 13. Parsons said that kin are less functional in industrial society, and his critics responded: "But they do function." Cumming and her associates say that the aged are functionally unimportant, and their critics answer: "Yes, but they do things." The variety of responses to old age in the United States makes highly questionable a theory claiming that disengagement is a universal, positive fact of old age and that old age in-

---

[19] Shanas et al., *Old People in Three Industrial Societies*, p. 256.

[20] Rose and Peterson, *Older People and Their Social World*; Rosow, *Social Integration of the Aged*; and Mark Messer, "Age Grouping and the Family Status of the Elderly," *Sociology and Social Research* 52 (1968), 271–79.

[21] Messer, "Age Grouping and the Family Status of the Elderly," p. 279.

[22] Rosow, *Social Integration of the Aged*, pp. 323–24.

variably includes role loss, social withdrawal, and the facing of death. The various responses to aging are the result of a series of decisions, particularly with respect to retirement, that must be made as old age is reached.

Section Two

SOCIALIZATION: THE DECISIONS OF THE AGED

The departure of children and retirement from one's occupation are the kinds of changes in life situation which demand substantial reorientation on the part of individuals and married couples. According to Deutscher, there are several aids to parents in their preparation for the change that takes place when children leave home and postparental life begins.

> There is the underlying value in our society on change for its own sake—a value which can be applied to the particular case of change in the family structure; there are the temporary departures of children during the adolescent years for college, service in the armed forces, and a variety of other reasons; there is the modern complex of urban high school life, which can move children into a world which is foreign to their parents; there are the exigencies of the work situation which often remove the middle-class father from the family during the years when the children are growing up; there is the myth and the reality of the mother-in-law which some mothers internalize as lessons for themselves. In addition, remnants of the older extended family pattern which tend to reduce the impact of the transition cannot be ignored.[23]

This statement, while indicating the societal supports for child departure, ignores the fact that many parents are *never* really prepared for the postparental period. Nor, for that matter, are they prepared for many of the other changes that must be made in middle and old age. Nor is enough known about the actual transitions or processes of movement into old age. Rosow, for example, feels that a major focus for further study of the elderly should be socialization into old age. Old age, he says,

> represents a devalued, unstructured role with sharp discontinuities from middle age. Hence, the individual enters the situation with little incentive, role specification, or preparation. Effective socialization under these conditions is problematic and it is necessary to clarify both the conducive and inimical forces at work in the situation.[24]

---

[23] Deutscher, "Socialization for Postparental Life," in Rose, *Human Behavior and Social Processes,* p. 522.
[24] Rosow, *Social Integration of the Aged,* p. 326.

How difficult are the adjustments into old age? They are most certainly made more difficult than they would be otherwise by the fact that roles and norms, or expectations concerning what the aged should do and be, are so poorly spelled out. The greatest amount of difficulty, however, is likely to be experienced by two types of persons. The wife who has poured body and soul into her children, who had few outside interests except those that furthered her children's development, can very easily shrivel up mentally and even physically when her children achieve independence and she finds herself still "attached to her absent children's apron strings." Their very independence may drain the meaning from her life, which was sustained by nurturing them. And while Troll and others have noted that child launching is a gradual transition, Donald Spence and Thomas Lonner report that many women at this stage in their lives feel that they are failures, and are at a loss for something to do. What disturbs these authors most, however, is that the young married women whom they interviewed didn't seem to be making any better preparation for the postlaunching period than their mothers had.[25]

Likewise, many a man has died only a few months after retirement. If the entire significance of a man's life was wrapped up in working and earning, the physical and psychological adjustment necessitated by retirement may be too much for him. Thus, the family-oriented woman and the occupation-oriented man who have no alternative values to fall back on are likely to be poorly prepared for a *positive* disengagement from their major life roles.

In this problematic atmosphere, and with all too little information on the decision-making processes and outcomes of old age, what are some of the decisions that the elderly must make? First, they must make *residential* decisions. These include deciding whether to stay in the home in which they reared their children, for the sake of periodic family reunions, or whether to change residence completely.[26] Change of residence may mean deciding whether to move into an apartment, a trailer, or a smaller house in the same community (perhaps closer to the business district); whether to move to a retirement, or age-segregated, community; or whether to move to a community in which their children or other kin reside. Feature 9 presents one writer's view of the complexity of the residential decision in old age. Second, they must make *activity* decisions. They may continue to

---

[25] Donald Spence and Thomas Lonner, "The 'Empty Nest': A Transition Within Motherhood," *Family Coordinator* 20 (1971), 375–76.

[26] This is referred to in Reuben Hill, "Decision Making and the Family Life Cycle," in Ethel Shanas and Gordon F. Streib, eds., *Social Structure and the Family: Generational Relations* (Englewood Cliffs, N.J.: Prentice-Hall, 1965), p. 130.

pursue the same activities, or take up new ones. They may join new organizations—perhaps age-graded groups, such as golden age clubs—or continue their current affiliations with religious and other groups, or simply drop many old activities and organizations. Another set of decisions, which is related to the two already introduced, has to do with their *social networks*. How should they relate in terms of proximity and contact to age companions, children, and other friends and kin—or should they simply disengage from most social contacts?

The final set of decisions concerns *marital relations* (if, of course, the marriage is still intact). In which activities should the aged couple participate jointly, and in which as individuals? How should household responsi-

---

FEATURE 9

Two-thirds of Americans over age 65 own their own home, but with the family gone, the house may be too large, too expensive and too difficult to maintain.

Therefore, the question, "To move or not to move," looms large. Especially when you consider that a major share of retirement income goes into housing costs. . . .

Most older people prefer not to live with their child's family, and studies have shown that you may well stay healthier and live longer and happier if you maintain your own home, whatever it may be. . . .

Think twice about tearing up your roots; selling an old house can be a devastating emotional experience. . . .

If you are serious about making a change, spend some time researching the possibilities open to you. Don't be hasty. Visit the areas you think you might want to live in, get the feel for the new community. . . .

Also, think through the specific type of housing you would prefer: a small house, a co-op apartment, a condominium, a mobile home, or a "retirement" community. . . .

Questions to ask before deciding to move (add up the pluses and minuses):

√ Do my present home and community suit my notion of a good life in the future?

√ Do I now have convenient access to transportation, shopping, medical care, church, entertainment and recreation, educational and cultural facilities of interest to me?

√ Will I be embarrassed to live in my present home on retirement income?

√ Does the old house impose too much of a workload on me?

√ Should I move for health reasons?

√ Would I be able to adjust to a new situation at my age?

√ How much will I really miss my old friends?

√ Will I make new friends as easily as I used to?

√ What can I gain by moving—socially, economically, or otherwise?

√ What could I lose by making the change?

√ If the move doesn't work out, can I afford to relocate again?

Jack Gourlay, "Life After 65: To Move or Not to Move?" *Wisconsin State Journal*, March 6, 1974.

bilities be divided, now that the husband no longer goes off to work each morning? These last two decision areas—social network relations and marital relations in old age—have been the objects of substantial research. They are complex and important enough for us to take a more intensive look at them in Sections Three and Four.

Section Three

THE SOCIAL NETWORK AND AGE SEGREGATION

The social networks of the elderly consist of two categories of persons: *kin,* who are primarily children and others of the descending generation, and *nonkin,* who are for the most part of their own generation.

Kin Relations of the Elderly

The elderly are likely to keep in touch with whatever kin they have. This may mean considerable contact with their own aging brothers and sisters,[27] but more often the focus is on children and grandchildren—their family of procreation. Separate-but-near is the rule of residence in old age, as Troll states clearly: "While joint households are . . . the exception rather than the rule, related nuclear households tend to be near each other, particularly among urban working class families."[28] Shanas and her associates, in their excellent study of 2,500 aged in each of three countries—Denmark, Britain, and the United States—report further that there are some significant, class-related differences in contact with adult offspring.

> Middle class, white collar persons in both Britain and the United States are more likely than working class persons to have only a few children and to live at a greater distance from their children. The married children of middle class familes, both sons and daughters, tend to live apart from their parents, not only in separate households, but also at a greater distance from them. In some degree this physical separation of parents and children is compensated for by more overnight visiting on the part of white collar families. The average old person of white collar background maintains strong relationships with his children. He is more likely than his blue collar counterpart, however, to see his children infrequently or not at all. In the case of white collar parents, the patterns

---

[27] Elaine Cumming and David M. Schneider, "Sibling Solidarity: A Property of American Kinship," *American Anthropologist* 63 (1961), 498–507.

[28] Troll, "The Family of Later Life," in Broderick, *A Decade of Research and Action,* p. 190.

of help in old age flow from parents to children; in the case of blue collar parents, they flow from children to parents.[29]

The author's own study of young adults and their aging parents corroborates most of the above conclusions and adds a few details to the picture. When adult offspring—particularly middle-class offspring—are spatially separated from their parents, they keep in touch not only by periodic visits but also by telephone and letter. The last two forms of contact are one reason why Shanas et al. can say in one sentence that the white-collar aged "maintain strong" ties with their children and in the next sentence state that they may see them "infrequently or not at all." Also, the pattern of white-collar aid moves first toward equality—that is, it changes from aid given by the parents to the children to a mutual exchange of favors—and, in many cases, continues to change until services and even finances flow primarily from the middle-aged white-collar adult to his elderly parents.[30] The effect of the aged's need for care in sickness and for monetary assistance is a function, to some extent, of historical changes in relations between the generations. In 1900, says Meyer Nimkoff, the elderly were still more authorities and less playmates for their adult offspring than they are today.[31] But since that time, according to the Glassers, a role reversal has taken place, and the aging parents have become dependent on their adult offspring, with no power or authority base to offset their dependence. The result is conflict and psychological threat to the aged.[32] This, of course, would not be true of the high-status elderly who are overseers of an important symbolic family estate, or ancestral tradition, whose authority may be substantial.[33]

Other authors have also found that dependence on children in old age is alienative,[34] but Gordon Streib's early report on the Cornell study of aging and retirement agrees with Shanas' report that solidarity is generally quite strong between the generations.

Our analysis of around 1,500 cases has indicated that there is a higher degree of family solidarity as measured by our indices than has been

---

[29] Shanas et al., *Old People in Three Industrial Societies*, p. 256.

[30] Bert Adams, *Kinship in an Urban Setting* (Chicago: Markham, 1968), p. 46; and Adams, "Structural Factors Affecting Parental Aid to Married Children," *Journal of Marriage and the Family* 26 (1962), 327–32.

[31] M. F. Nimkoff, "Changing Family Relationships of Older People in the United States During the Last Fifty Years," *The Gerontologist* 1 (1961), 96.

[32] Glasser and Glasser, "Role Reversal and Conflict Between Aged Parents and Their Children," p. 50.

[33] On the symbolic family estate, see Chapter 13 of this book; and especially Bernard Farber, *Kinship and Class: A Midwestern Study* (New York: Basic Books, 1971), pp. 97–118.

[34] Robert M. Dinkel, "Attitudes of Children Toward Supporting Aged Parents," *American Sociological Review* 9 (1944), 370–79; and Bert N. Adams, "The Middle Class Adult and His Widowed or Still-Married Mother," *Social Problems* 16 (1968), 50–59.

noted by other writers. . . . The high degree of family cohesion between older parents and their children is . . . shown by the fact that there is a high degree of congruity between parental expectations for their children and the children's behavior. In the minds of older parents, affectional ties are more important than financial assistance, although, as one might expect in view of their greater economic deprivation, retirees tend to stress the importance of financial assistance more than older parents who are still working.[35]

Seven years later, however, in reporting on the panel phase of the same study, Streib noted that, while the retired stress affectional ties between themselves and their offspring, the latter see the relationship as dependent on both affection and their aged parents' need of help. "It appears," Streib concludes,

that from the standpoint of the adult child, family relations within the family of procreation take precedence over linkages to the family of orientation.[36]

In summary, then, relations between aging parents and their adult offspring are clearly based more on friendship than on authority; it is instances of dependence by the aged on their offspring that are most likely to cause intergenerational strain.

The grandparent role, which has been more discussed than studied, is of course intertwined with the intergenerational relationships just discussed. When relationships between parents and their offspring are authoritarian and formal, the alliance between grandparent and grandchild is likely to be quite strong. The reason for this is that in such instances the child can seek support from his grandparents when he is disciplined by or in conflict with his parents. In the United States, however, when the grandparent role is significant, it is generally a social-emotional role, though tending toward greater formality as both the grandparents and the grandchildren get older.[37] "Interaction includes visits, gifts, communication, interest in the progress of the young, and sharing of wisdom by the grandparents."[38]

---

[35] Gordon F. Streib, "Family Patterns in Retirement," *Journal of Social Issues* 14 (1958), 60.

[36] Gordon F. Streib, "Intergenerational Relations: Perspectives of the Two Generations on the Older Parent," *Journal of Marriage and the Family* 27 (1965), 475.

[37] Harold E. Smith, "Family Interaction Patterns of the Aged: A Review," in Rose and Peterson, *Older People and Their Social World,* p. 156; see also Ruth Albrecht, "The Parental Responsibilities of Grandparents," *Marriage and Family Living* 16 (1954), 201–4; and especially Bernice Neugarten and Karol Weinstein, "The Changing American Grandparent," *Journal of Marriage and the Family* 26 (1964), 199–204.

[38] Smith, "Family Interaction Patterns of the Aged," in Rose and Peterson, *Older People and Their Social World,* p. 156.

While the grandparents may interfere in conflicts between parents and children, this is less likely in the United States than in societies in which the family is more authoritarian. In the United States, Cumming and Henry assert,

> where the bonds between children and parents are defined as friendly rather than hierarchical, and where the generational difference is minimized, not only does the child not need a friendly ally but the grandparent presumably has maintained an unbroken friendly relationship with his own child, and thus does not need a mediating relationship.[39]

The position of grandparent, therefore, may involve any of four possibilities: authority, friendship, dependence, and inheritance. In working- and lower-class families, the aging parents are apt to provide important friendship relations for their descendants, but the likelihood that they will be dependent on their adult offspring strains the friendship to some extent. In the middle class, the aged are less likely to be dependent and more apt to control an inheritance; but their adult children tend to have more age-peer friends and are more likely to be residentially separated from their parents than working- and lower-class offspring, and thus they have less need for their parents' friendship. Even a prospective inheritance does not necessarily strengthen the friendship between the generations, but may instead give the relationship economic overtones. In other words, whatever role the aged play in the lives of their children and other kin is ordinarily based on social-emotional centrality; but this role is often tenuous, and the aged are simply not defined as *necessary* by their descending kin.

Nonkin and Age-Grading

Members of the younger generation tend to exclude from society not only their aged kin but all aged. This exclusion is based on the devaluation of the aged because of their loss of efficiency and on the lack of any special prestige marks for them. As a result of their devaluation by society in general and their "surplus" character in the eyes of kin, the aged tend increasingly to become a subsociety, with a few distinctive cultural elements. "Those in retirement communities, in rural communities from which younger people are rapidly emigrating, and in the central parts of big cities are most age-separated and hence are most likely to develop a subculture."[40]

One constraint upon assimilation into the aged peer group is the elderly person's marital status. Some subcommunities of the aged consist

---

[39] Cumming and Henry, *Growing Old*, p. 61.
[40] Rose and Peterson, *Older People and Their Social World*, p. 7.

of widows, especially in big cities, while others, such as retirement communities, are likely to involve couples. In her study of the elderly in New York City and Elmira, New York, Zena Blau points out the effect that a change in one's marital status has on his peer group affiliations.

> Since friends tend to be of the same sex and in a similar age group, a change in marital status that places an individual in a deviant position among his age and sex peers and differentiates his interests and experiences from theirs is likely to have an adverse effect on his friendships. When, on the other hand, widowhood becomes prevalent among others similarly located in the social structure it is the individual who is still married who occupies a deviant position and who, therefore, often sees less of his old friends.[41]

Thus, one of the bases for a residential or activity decision in old age may very well be the death of one's spouse, which may impel him to seek out age companions whose marital status is the same as his own.

Both Messer and Rosow have found that the age-graded elderly tend to feel a greater sense of integration into society than do those among the elderly who depend for social contact on kin of the descending generation. In fact, if children and other kin are not located nearby, the aged generally do not even feel dependent on them or greatly deprived by their absence. Messer puts it this way: "Older people living in a situation which lends itself to age-peer formation rely less on the family for social support, but at the same time do not feel more alienated from their families." And, speaking functionally, Messer concludes that this "situation seems appropriate for the predominant system of conjugal family organization in complex societies."[42]

The middle-class elderly fit Messer's picture of the ideally age-segregated more closely than do the working- and lower-class aged. Their kin tend to be more scattered than are those of the blue-collar aged, and they have more friends.[43] While those friends are also more scattered, the middle-class aged have a greater number of options open to them in terms of socialization into old age, due to their generally greater economic resources and their more cosmopolitan life orientations. This, however, does not necessarily mean a smoother transition into old age for middle-class persons, because they are more likely to have a strong positive orientation toward the major life roles which they must give up, and therefore to be negatively oriented toward disengagement.

---

[41] Zena Smith Blau, "Structural Constraints on Friendship in Old Age," *American Sociological Review* 26 (1961), 438.

[42] Messer, "Age Grouping and the Family Status of the Elderly," p. 276.

[43] Rosow, *Social Integration of the Aged*, p. 293.

Section Four

HUSBAND-WIFE RELATIONS IN OLD AGE

The shift of focus away from children and the incorporation of the husband *into* the home are the tasks which give married life among the aged in the United States its particular character. As the years go by, reports Harold Feldman, the conversation of couples shifts from the children toward home repairs and health.[44] Feldman, as reported by Lillian Troll, states: "Three themes seem to dominate the interactions of . . . aging couples: decrease in passion, increase in conventionality . . . , and concern with health."[45] The elderly, however, are not unhappy with their lot. Having disengaged themselves *into* the family, as Troll puts it, they are likely to report their marriages as happier than ever before.[46] One reason for this, as has been noted, is that they are still alive and married, having outlived many of their cohort. Thus, old age is not a period of marital disenchantment, as was the launching period, but of at least comparative satisfaction.

Some question must be raised concerning the universal applicability of the label "conventional," as applied to the aged. There are signs, though as yet no research results, that point to the increasing willingness of aging couples to experiment with alternative life-styles after their children have been launched. Cohabitation between single persons, a lower standard of living, and greater freedom—these and other changes in parents' lives have been reported by students and in the mass media. Such experimentation, often noted by the media before being uncovered by sociological research, is one aspect of what Peter Falkman and Donald Irish call reverse socialization.[47] Reverse socialization is the process whereby older people learn from younger people. It is as yet too early to tell whether such nonconventionality will become increasingly prevalent among middle-aged and aging persons, but it does deserve research attention.

Moving from the general nature of marriage in old age to some of its specific characteristics, we note a general tapering off of sexual activity, in

---

[44] Harold Feldman, *Development of the Husband-Wife Relationship* (preliminary report, Cornell Studies of Marital Development: Study in the Transition of Parenthood, Cornell University, 1964).

[45] Troll, "The Family of Later Life," in Broderick, *A Decade of Research and Action*, p. 197.

[46] Nick Stinnett, Linda M. Carter, and James E. Montgomery, "Older Persons' Perceptions of Their Marriages," *Journal of Marriage and the Family* 34 (1972), as reported in Troll, "The Family of Later Life," in Broderick, *A Decade of Research and Action*, p. 197.

[47] Herman M. Lobsenz, "Sex and the Senior Citizen," *New York Times Magazine*, January 20, 1974. On reverse socialization, see Peter Falkman and Donald P. Irish, "Socialization—Resocialization—Reverse Socialization: Analysis and Societal Significance" (paper presented to the Midwest Sociological Society, April 5, 1974).

some instances as a result of boredom. Sexually adjusted women show little abatement of their sex drive—but many women are not sexually adjusted. The sex drive of many aging males begins to abate. The result is that, even in the absence of physiological difficulties, sex become less frequent.[48] This, however, is not universal, and there are aging couples whose sex life is still as active as before.

In considering household responsibilities, we recall Ruth Cavan's point (summarized by John Ballweg) that retired husbands are more apt to take on a heightened role in household responsibilities than a "playboy" or social activity role.[49] Yet the home is presumably the wife's domain, and one might assume that the sudden availability of the husband might make for substantial marital conflict. Several reasons why this is not the case are indicated by Meyer Nimkoff and Ballweg. Noting historical changes, Nimkoff states that in 1900 the division of labor between the sexes was such that the "home was more exclusively the wife's domain" than it it today.[50] Thus, while retirement is more likely to be compulsory today than it was in 1900, this is somewhat counterbalanced by a normative change, especially in the middle class, toward greater acceptance of male involvement in household tasks. According to Ballweg, two factors lessen the possibility that the husband's involvement in household tasks will disturb the family equilibrium. His small-scale research showed that

> the retired husband did not share tasks with his wife to any greater extent than was the case during his work career. Rather than shared activities with the wife, the retired husband was more likely to assume full responsibility for a select group of tasks. Secondly, these tasks which the retired husband carried out appeared to be masculine or marginal in orientation, [such as burning trash, moving furniture, fixing faucets, or administrative tasks, such as paying bills,] rather than those which would have a significant influence on the self-conception of the wife. The supposed invasion by the retired husband thus became more of an emancipation from tasks which the wife could have relinquished at any time the husband was willing to accept them.[51]

It is interesting that the same pattern existed in Jacquelyne Jackson's sample of aging blacks. Here too the typical middle-class division of household tasks was apparent even in retirement. That is, wives still spent their time with

---

[48] W. H. Masters and Virginia E. Johnson, "Human Sexual Response: The Aging Female and the Aging Male," in Bernice Neugarten, ed., *Middle Age and Aging* (Chicago: University of Chicago Press, 1968).

[49] John A. Ballweg, "Resolution of Conjugal Role Adjustment After Retirement," *Journal of Marriage and the Family* 29 (1967), 277, 281.

[50] Nimkoff, "Changing Family Relationships of Older People in the United States During the Last Fifty Years," p. 92.

[51] Ballweg, "Resolution of Conjugal Role Adjustment After Retirement," p. 281.

the traditionally female chores, while their husbands did yard work and home repairs.[52]

When we turn from tasks to husband-wife power relations, we find an apparent contradiction in the literature. Harold Smith, on the one hand, asserts that, due to the relative scarcity of males, the wife whose husband has survived into old age tends to show deference to him and that the husband's withdrawal from his work role does not alter husband-wife power relations. Jackson's findings among Durham black couples agree substantially with those of Smith. Reuben Hill, on the other hand, finds in his three-generational study that there is "both a decline in husband dominance from the early stages represented by the married child generation and an increase in wife dominance into the last stage of the cycle."[53] It is at least possible that both are correct, but that they are talking about different phenomena. It may be, for example, that in old age the husband makes the major decisions, such as residential location, and has a considerable say-so in the running of the household, while the wife runs the social-emotional machinery of the couple, particularly as it relates to the social network. However, further work on the power, influence, and dominance of elderly husbands and wives needs to be done before this issue can be completely resolved.

Section Five

SUMMARY AND CONCLUSIONS

Socialization into old age includes decisions about residence, activity, the social network, and couple relations. Wayne Thompson and Gordon Streib, in their article "Meaningful Activity in a Family Context," summarize much of the foregoing discussion by means of a useful fourfold typology (see Table 8), focusing on the social network and marital relations.[54]

First (Type I), the adjustment of an aged couple may be characterized by high cohesion to each other and by close ties to their social networks. Such a couple finds meaning in shared activities and in continued contacts with persons outside the home, including friends and kin. Many of the couple's former role adjustments are maintained as they move together through

---

[52] Jacquelyne Johnson Jackson, "Marital Life Among Aging Blacks," *Family Coordinator* 21 (1972), 21–27.

[53] Smith, "Family Interaction Patterns of the Aged," in Rose and Peterson, *Older People and Their Social World*, p. 151; Hill, "Decision Making and the Family Life Cycle," in Shanas and Streib, *Social Structure and the Family*, p. 127; and Jackson, "Marital Life Among Aging Blacks."

[54] Wayne E. Thompson and Gordon F. Streib, "Meaningful Activity in a Family Context," in Robert W. Kleemeier, ed., *Aging and Leisure: A Research Perspective into the Meaningful Use of Leisure Time* (New York: Oxford University Press, 1961), pp. 177–211.

Table 8
Four Ways in Which the Aged May Relate to
Their Spouses and to Their Social Networks

	Marriage (Cohesion)	Social Network (Ties)
Types		
I	High	Close-knit
II	High	Loose-knit
III	Low	Close-knit
IV	Low	Loose-knit

their various joint activities, as well as separately within their individual networks.

Second (Type II), the aged couple's adjustment may combine high marital cohesion with a loose bond to extrafamilial persons. This is the prototype of what the popular press calls "togetherness." The couple share not only goals—a bond that may have characterized their earlier lives—but activities as well. This is a likely pattern for striving and successful couples who were too busy during their adult careers to develop strong ties to other persons.

The third possibility (Type III) is low couple cohesion in conjunction with close ties to members of the social network. This relationship is exemplified by the old man who spends most of his time with his cronies while his wife is busy with her clubs. The peer group reasserts itself, perhaps as marital disenchantment gives rise to a kind of mutual avoidance. Network relations may involve kin instead of friends; this type of adjustment in old age is most apt to be found among those couples who have experienced the greatest amount of role segregation or differentiation during their adult lives, that is, working- and lower-class couples.

Finally (Type IV), there is the low-cohesion couple that is loosely tied to the social network. This situation is especially troublesome for the retired male, whom it compels to find hobbies, such as the basement workshop or the garden, with which to occupy himself during his declining years. The wife, under these circumstances, may vigorously pursue every speck of dust in the home, and may think of her husband as in the way. The couple live together but are not really together.

In which of the four types is the desolation of one spouse likely to be the greatest at the death of the other? A Type II spouse, whose activity patterns in old age have involved doing things with his spouse, is obviously going to be profoundly affected by such a loss. However, substantial desolation also occurs when a member of a Type IV couple dies. For, while the old age of Type IV couples may have been spent in conflict and avoidance, their habit patterns are almost as interwoven as are those of Type II couples.

Thus, the bereavement of the surviving spouse, regardless of the specific character of the husband-wife bond, is likely to be greatest in those instances in which the individual lacks close social relationships not involving his spouse. Shanas et al. reported that "some of those who have experienced severe social loss are relieved by substitute or remaining contacts and relationships, particularly with members of their families. Companionship may thus prevent or mitigate loneliness," although the precondition for loneliness in old age is more often the loss of a spouse than the lack of extrafamilial companions.[55] The desolation of the surviving spouse, it should be added, can also be mitigated by remarriage, and there are an increasing number of studies of this phenomenon.[56] At present, the elderly widower is more likely to remarry than is the elderly widow, partly because of the low ratio of men to women at this stage of life.[57]

In this chapter we should by now have become aware that, even without the inevitabilities of sickness and death, old age is a period of uncertainty and loss in the United States, with few positive compensations. Even the reasonably satisfactory marital adjustments found among the aged are to some extent achieved "by default," by giving up other major life roles. And, of course, the many elderly who no longer have marital partners, though generally forced to give up their major life roles, cannot avail themselves of this compensating satisfaction. According to Leo Simmons,

> while we have made much ado over the discovery of adolescence as a unique stage in life experiences, and recognized it as quite different from adulthood, we are continuing—mistakenly—to regard aging as little more than a somewhat discredited extension of mid-adulthood. . . .
>   There are some quite justifiable reasons to assume that a shift from mid-life to old age can be as significant a change as that from adolescence to adulthood, and the range of variations in the successful fruition of life in old age may really be much wider than it is for youth.[58]

If one looks back over this chapter, at least three points of similarity between old age and adolescence in the United States become apparent. First, the

---

[55] Shanas et al., *Old People in Three Industrial Societies*, p. 285. In Willard Waller and Reuben Hill, *The Family: A Dynamic Interpretation* (New York: Holt, Rinehart and Winston, 1951), p. 482, the authors note that the desolation of the remaining partner is greatest when the couple's habit patterns are enmeshed, regardless of social network relations. They state it thus: "It is submitted that this account" of serious bereavement "is essentially correct whether the bereavement situation represents the loss of a person intensely loved or merely a greatly ramified loss entailing necessary readjustments in a number of phases of life."

[56] Helena Znaniecki Lopata, "Self-Identity in Marriage and Widowhood," *Sociological Quarterly* 14 (1973), 407–18; and Walter C. McKain, "A New Look at Older Marriages," *Family Life Coordinator* 21 (1972), 61–69.

[57] Troll, "The Family of Later Life," in Broderick, *A Decade of Research and Action*, p. 193.

[58] Leo William Simmons, "Social Participation of the Aged in Different Cultures," *The Annals* 279 (1952), 51.

multiple decisions that the aged must make parallel the multiple decisions of the adolescent and demonstrate that a vast amount of *socialization* takes place during both adolescence and old age. Granted, the decisions of adolescence are concerned with the "engagement" process, or the assumption of one's major life roles, while those of old age are related to disengagement, or their relinquishment, but the choices are numerous during both periods. Second, both the adolescent and the elderly person are presented with *unclear role options*. The question "How should the adolescent behave?"—posed in Chapter 8—may appropriately be applied to the aged as well. For, in U.S. society, the behavioral expectations for both young people and old people are not clear-cut, but are up to individual decision. As long as adolescents and the aged stay out of the way, they may determine their own social behaviors. This condition, "staying out of the way," brings us to the final similarity between the elderly and the adolescents. In many ways both groups have increasingly taken on the character of *minorities*. They are increasingly age-segregated; they have little social power as a group; and they are tolerated only as long as they keep to themselves. Even among the working classes, the aged are decreasingly embedded personnel-wise in their kin networks. An important reason for treating adolescents and the aged as subsocieties appears to be economic: both categories must be kept out of the occupational market—the adolescents by postponing their entry, the aged by hastening their departure—so that unemployment rates may be kept to a minimum.

Despite these similarities, old age is generally a more pessimistic and negative period than adolescence, for the adolescent has his adult future to look forward to, while the elderly must find comfort in thoughts of the past, while looking forward only to decline and death. Some of the aged may find satisfaction in leisure and "a job well done," as disengagement theory says they should, but many others in the United States simply cannot make their peace with this period of ill-defined choices, separation, and loss.[59]

---

[59] For more on the demographic characteristics of the aged, see Maria Davidson, "Social and Economic Characteristics of Aged Persons (65 Years Old and Older) in the United States in 1960," *Eugenics Quarterly* 14 (1967), 27–44.

Family life involves both pattern and change. Thus far we have concentrated primarily on the patterns that develop and persist in the modern family. In this chapter the foci of attention are the acts, events, and processes—such as unemployment, mental illness, alcoholism, and death—that require some form of adjustment on the part of the family. These topics and others like them are often discussed under such headings as crisis, disorganization, and dissolution. We shall attempt to develop a framework for distinguishing among the various changes and challenges that confront families and to summarize the conditions that determine different family responses. Finally, four specific events that affect families are discussed in some detail. These are unemployment, violence, divorce, and death.

Response of the Family to Change and Challenge

Life in the family is not just many years of habit and routine. Although some married people may complain that "nothing exciting ever happens," the fact is that transition and change are as central to family experience as are continuity and pattern. The gradual and abrupt transitions of parenthood, the departure of children, physical decline, and eventual death are expected and inevitable; in addition to such transitions, most families face unexpected challenges.

The literature on expected and unexpected acts, events, and processes as they relate to the family is voluminous. It includes studies of parenthood, infidelity, illegitimacy, departure, unemployment and economic setback, physical and mental illness, disability, retardation, alcoholism, drug use, violence, divorce, and death.[1] The terms that have been used to describe

---

[1] **Parenthood:** E. E. LeMasters, "Parenthood as Crisis," *Marriage and Family Living* 19 (1957), 352–55; Everett D. Dyer, "Parenthood as Crisis: A Re-Study," *Marriage and Family Living* 25 (1963), 196–201; Daniel F. Hobbs, Jr., "Parenthood as Crisis: A Third Study," *Journal of Marriage and the Family* 27 (1965), 367–72; and Hobbs, "Transition to Parenthood: A Replication and an Extension," *Journal of Marriage and the Family* 30 (1968), 413–17.

Infidelity: There are papers on this in Gerhard Neubeck, ed., *Extra-Marital Relations* (Englewood Cliffs, N.J.: Prentice-Hall, 1969); see also John Cuber and Peggy B. Harroff "Other Involvements," in Robert R. Bell and Michael Gordon, eds., *The Social Dimension of Human Sexuality* (Boston: Little, Brown, 1972), pp. 115–29; and Ralph E. Johnson, "Some Correlates of Extramarital Coitus," *Journal of Marriage and the Family* 32 (1970), 449–56.

Illegitimacy: William J. Goode, *The Family* (Englewood Cliffs, N.J.: Prentice-Hall, 1964), pp. 19–30; Alice J. Clague and Stephanie J. Ventura, *Trends in Illegitimacy; United States—1940–1965,* Department of Health, Education, and Welfare, Vital and Health Statistics, Series 21, No. 15 (1968); Clark E. Vincent, *Unmarried Mothers* (New York: Free Press, 1963); Robert W. Roberts, ed., *The Unwed Mother* (New York: Harper & Row, 1966); Reynolds Farley and Albert I. Hermalin, "Family Stability: A Comparison of Trends Between Blacks and Whites," *American Sociological Review* 36 (1971), 1–17; and Hallowell Pope, "Unwed Mothers and Their Sex Partners," *Journal of Marriage and the Family* 29 (1967), 555–67.

Departure: See Ernest W. Burgess, Harvey J. Locke, and Mary Margaret Thomes, *The Family,* 3rd ed. (New York: Litton Educational Publishing, 1963).

Unemployment and Economic Setback: Mirra Komarovsky, *The Unemployed Man and His Family* (New York: Dryden Press, 1940); Robert C. Angell, *The Family Encounters the Depression* (New York: Scribner's, 1936); E. Wight Bakke, *Citizens Without Work* (New Haven, Conn.: Yale University Press, 1949); Ruth Shonle Cavan and Katherine Howland Ranck, *The Family and the Depression* (Chicago: University of Illinois Press, 1938); see also parts of Earl Lomon Koos, *Families in Trouble* (Morningside Heights, N.Y.: King's Crown, 1946).

Physical and Mental Illness: Talcott Parsons and Renee C. Fox, "Illness, Therapy, and the Modern Urban American Family," *Journal of Social Issues* 13 (1952), 31–44; Ezra F. Vogel and Norman W. Bell, "The Emotionally Disturbed Child as the Family Scapegoat," in Bell and Vogel, eds., *The Family* (New York: Free Press, 1960), pp. 382–97; John A. Clausen and Marian Radke Yarrow, eds., "The Impact of Mental Illness on the Family," *Journal of Social Issues* 11 (1955), 3–64; Melvin L. Kohn, "Class, Family, and Schizophrenia: A Reformulation," *Social Forces* 50 (1972), 295–304; and Clark E. Vincent, "Mental Health and the Family," *Journal of Marriage and the Family* 29 (1967), 18–39.

Disability: Geoffrey Gibson and Edward G. Ludwig, "Family Structure in a Disabled Population," *Journal of Marriage and the Family* 30 (1968), 54–63.

Retardation: Irving Tallman, "Spousal Role Differentiation and the Socialization of Severely Retarded Children," *Journal of Marriage and the Family* 27 (1965), 37–42; Bernard Farber, *Family: Organization and Interaction* (San Francisco: Chandler, 1964); Joseph H. Meyerowitz and Farber, "Family Background of Educable Mentally Retarded Children," in Farber, ed., *Kinship and Family Organization* (New York: Wiley, 1966), pp. 388–98; and John B. Fotherington et al., *The Retarded Child and His Family: The Effects of Home and Institution* (Toronto: Ontario Institute for Studies in Education, 1971).

Alcoholism: Selden D. Bacon, "Excessive Drinking and the Institution of the Family," *Alcohol, Science, and Society* (New Haven, Conn.: Journal of Studies on Alcohol, 1945); Samuel C. Bullock and Emily H. Mudd, "The Interaction of Alcoholic Husbands and Their Non-Alcoholic Wives During Counselling," *American Journal of Orthopsychiatry* 29 (1959), 519–27; and Joan K. Jackson, "Alcoholism and the Family," in David J. Pittman and Charles R. Snyder, eds., *Society, Culture, and Drinking Patterns* (New York: Wiley, 1962), pp. 472–92.

Drug Use: Roslyn Ganger and George Shugart, "Complementary Pathology in Families of Male Heroin Addicts," *Social Casework* 49 (1968), 345–61; and Nechama Tec, "Family and Differential Involvement with Marihuana: A Study of Suburban Teenagers," *Journal of Marriage and the Family* 32 (1970), 656–64.

Violence: William J. Goode, "Force and Violence in the Family," *Journal of Marriage and the Family* 33 (1971), 624–35; Suzanne K. Steinmetz and Murray A. Straus, eds., *Violence in the Family* (New York: Dodd, Mead, 1973); George R. Bach and Peter Wyden, *The Intimate Enemy* (New York: Morrow, 1969); Craig Taylor, "The 'Battered Child': Individual Victim of Family Brutality," in Clifton D. Bryant, ed., *Social Problems Today* (Philadelphia: Lippincott, 1971), 210–16; John E. Snell, Richard J. Rosenwald, and Ames Robey, "The Wife-beater's Wife: A Study of Family Interaction," *Archives of General Psychiatry* 11 (1964), 107–13; and David G. Gil, *Violence Against Children: Physical Child Abuse in the United States* (Cambridge, Mass.: Harvard University Press, 1970).

Divorce: Paul H. Jacobson, *American Marriage and Divorce* (New York: Rinehart, 1959); William J. Goode, *After Divorce* (Glencoe, Ill.: Free Press, 1956); William L. O'Neill, *Divorce in the Progressive Era* (New Haven, Conn.: Yale University Press, 1967); and Michael Wheeler, *No-Fault Divorce* (Boston: Beacon Press, 1974).

Death: Willard Waller and Reuben Hill, *The Family: A Dynamic Interpretation* (New York: Holt, Rinehart and Winston, 1951); and Burgess, Locke, and Thomes, *The Family,* pp. 460f.

family responses to these changes and challenges are numerous and often vague; they have included, among other concepts, those of trouble, problem, crisis, stress, demoralization, deviance, disorganization, breakdown, maladjustment, disintegration, dissolution—and their opposites, such as organization, adjustment, and integration. William J. Goode, John Scanzoni, Jetse Sprey, and others have met with some success in their attempt to clarify this array of concepts by means of definitional distinctions.[2] Sprey, for example, distinguishes between deviance and disorganization in terms of the family's mutual role expectations. Thus, deviance is a family member's violation of his generally understood and accepted role in the family. And a family that lacks a set of understood and accepted roles, or "rules of the game," is said to be disorganized.[3] Yet, important as terminological clarity is, the present author will focus instead on: (1) a framework for organizing the various changes and challenges that may confront families, and (2) specification of the conditions for various family responses. Perhaps a by-product of these two concerns will be an increase in conceptual clarity as well.

Section One

A FRAMEWORK FOR ANALYZING CHALLENGES AND FAMILY RESPONSES TO THEM

Several authors have developed frameworks to deal with the processes of family reaction to various stimuli. Some of these frameworks have been derived from research on a specific problem. For example, E. Wight Bakke described the stages of the family's response to unemployment during the Depression as follows: (1) momentum stability, (2) unstable equilibrium, (3) disorganization, (4) experimental readjustment, and (5) permanent readjustment. Likewise, Joan Jackson traces the family's reaction to alcoholism through denial, admission, attempts to eliminate the problem, strain and disorganization, exclusion of the alcoholic, and reorganization of the family.[4]

Other frameworks, however, are not problem-specific, but are general descriptions of the process of family adjustment to crisis. According to Reuben Hill, following Earl Koos, the parts of the process are: "crisis—dis-

---

[2] William J. Goode, "Family Disorganization," in Robert K. Merton and Robert A. Nisbet, eds., *Contemporary Social Problems* (New York: Harcourt, Brace, 1961); John Scanzoni, "Family Organization and the Probability of Disorganization," *Journal of Marriage and the Family* 28 (1966), 407–11; and Jetse Sprey, "Family Disorganization: Toward a Conceptual Clarification," *Journal of Marriage and the Family* 28 (1966), 398–406.

[3] Sprey, "Family Disorganization."

[4] Bakke, *Citizens Without Work*; and Jackson, "Alcoholism and the Family," in Pittman and Snyder, *Society, Culture, and Drinking Patterns*.

organization—recovery—reorganization" (see Figure 12). Hill discusses the conditions that enable some families to react to a stressor, or crisis-provoking event, without disorganization.[5] Although Hill treats both the stressor and

Figure 12
Hill's "Roller-Coaster Profile" of Family Reaction to a Crisis-Provoking Event

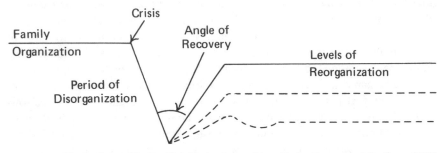

SOURCE: Reuben Hill, *Families Under Stress* (New York: Harper and Brothers, 1949), p. 14; and Earl Lomon Koos, *Families in Trouble* (Morningside Heights, N.Y.: King's Crown, 1946), pp. 108–11.

the family adjustment as variables, and spends considerable time discussing the factors conducive to a good adjustment to crisis, Bernard Farber feels that Hill's major attention is devoted to the period of disorganization. Thus, Farber indicates that an alternative to viewing crisis as a source of disorganization and a new equilibrium is viewing it as an impetus to a lengthy process of adaptation and reorganization. He labels this the "Crisis Process," though it is in reality the "Family Adjustment, or Reorganization, Process."[6] Changes that affect one family member, says Farber, affect other family members as well. Drawing upon Bakke, Jackson, and others who have described family response to specific crises, Farber defines the stages of family adjustment to crisis as follows. The first stage is an attempt to handle the challenge within existing role structures—combining the ideas of denial and momentum stability. A part of the rationale behind this approach is the hope that the condition is temporary and that restoration will soon occur. If the situation is not righted, the second stage, facing the problem, is reached— the result being a test of former family commitments. In the third stage, the problem becomes public and extrafamilial ties are altered. The fourth stage is role reorientation or, using the term in Sprey's sense, reorganization. That is, a new set of mutual expectations is developed and accepted by the family members. The fifth and final stage of the family's adjustment to crisis

---

[5] Reuben Hill, "Generic Features of Families Under Stress," *Social Casework* 39 (1958), 139–50.
[6] Farber, *Family: Organization and Interaction*, pp. 403–6.

is "freezing out," or the removal of the crisis-causing individual from the home so that the family unit can get on with the business of passing on its culture.

Although Farber's crisis process furnishes excellent conceptual tools with which to tackle the vast literature on family response, it has limitations in applicability that become apparent as one attempts to relate it to the various acts, events, and processes listed at the beginning of this chapter. Many crises never advance beyond stage one; that is, the crisis *is* temporary and the family is reconstituted in pretty much its precrisis state. Stages two and three frequently occur in reverse order, with a problem becoming public knowledge while the family continues to deny its existence. In fact, being confronted by a member of one's social network may trigger the family's admission that "we've got a problem." Finally, "freezing out" may differ in two ways from Farber's view of it as the last stage of the crisis process. In some instances, such as the launching of an offspring or the death of a family member, freezing out may be the *first* stage of the process, followed by admission of the crisis and reorganization. In other instances, instead of the individual being frozen out of the family unit, the behavior may be frozen out and the individual reinstated. A good illustration of this is when a middle-class family discovers that a daughter is premaritally pregnant, and sends her to a home for unwed mothers. After the child is born and adopted out, the young woman returns home from her "Mediterranean cruise," often with the proviso that she never discuss her illegitimate child. In this instance, it is the behavior, not the individual, which has been frozen out of the family unit.

Farber's crisis process does not, therefore, apply equally well to all the changes and challenges that may confront the family. For that reason, we shall introduce a somewhat more complex framework for viewing family responses to crises by first categorizing the stressors along two dimensions which, in light of the literature, seem to be crucial: (1) Is the stressor temporary or permanent? (2) Is it voluntary or involuntary? (See Figure 13.) With these two variables as the axes, it is possible to locate the stressor events within the quadrant in which they would typically appear. Two qualifications regarding the location of the stressors involve *variation* and *compounding*. Let us consider variation first. Physical illness is usually both involuntary and temporary; however, there are psychosomatic elements in many illnesses which make it difficult to distinguish the involuntary from the voluntary, and the most serious forms of illness may result in permanent disability. Another example of variation is the possibility of "drying up" the alcoholic; although he is not cured, he may nevertheless be reinstated in the family if he responds to treatment. Even divorce is temporary in those few cases in which the same individuals remarry. Thus, many stressors actually cover a wider

Figure 13
A Categorization of Changes and Challenges (Stressors)

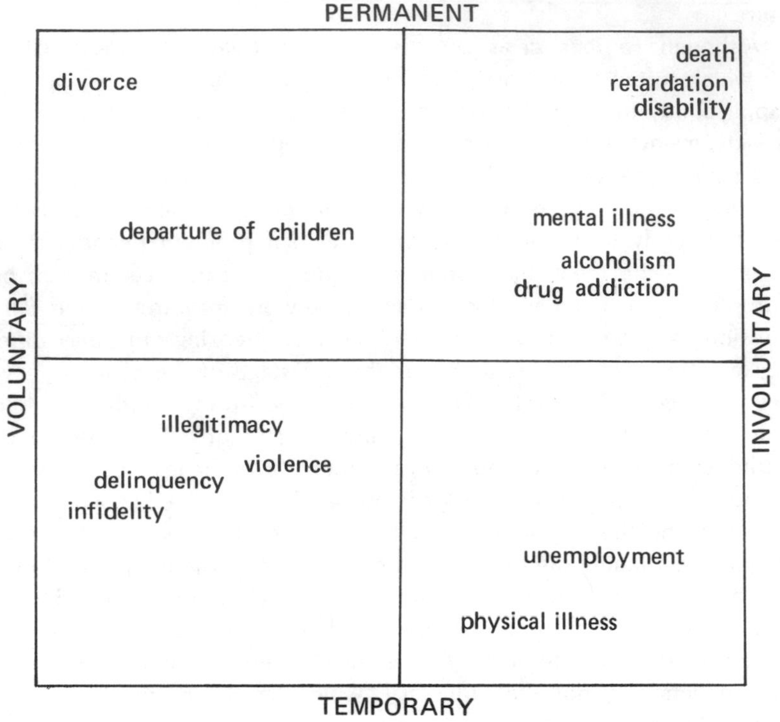

PERMANENT

divorce

death
retardation
disability

departure of children

mental illness

alcoholism
drug addiction

VOLUNTARY

INVOLUNTARY

illegitimacy

violence

delinquency

infidelity

unemployment

physical illness

TEMPORARY

range of possibilities than is indicated in Figure 13, and their placement in the figure has been based on their modal character as perceived by the author. The second qualification, the compounding of stressors, may be illustrated as follows: the infidelity of one spouse might contribute to the alcoholism of the other, with the eventual outcome of the process being divorce.[7]

We have, however, isolated the specific stressors in Figure 13 according to their modal character so that we may proceed to the more important question: How does the family typically respond to the various types of challenges? (See Table 9.) A voluntary-temporary stressor, which would include most forms of deviant behavior, may simply be frozen out of the family's thoughts and lives and the individual reinstated on the assumption that the behavior will never be repeated. This would apply as well to the sorts of family conflict mentioned in Chapters 11 and 12. It was stated, for example, that one way a married couple may resolve constant disagreements

---

[7] An article by Koos and Fulcomer, referred to in Hill, "Generic Features of Families Under Stress," p. 145.

Table 9
Most Likely Family Responses to Changes and Challenges (Stressors)

Type of Stressor (with Example)	Responses
Voluntary-Temporary (illegitimacy)	Freeze out behavior ⟶ reinstate person (if behavior persists, other stressors may follow)
Involuntary-Temporary (unemployment)	Ignore or deny; or else admit ⟶ temporarily reorganize ⟶ reinstate family role structure
Voluntary-Permanent (divorce)	Reorganize
Involuntary-Permanent (retardation)	Admit ⟶ freeze out person ⟶ reorganize (death: admit ⟶ reorganize)

about family finances is to make a basic decision about the distribution of income each month and subsequently "freeze out" that area of life from family communication. If, however, a voluntary-temporary stressor, such as infidelity, persists, the result may be disorganization in the sense of a confusion of expectations, a loss of consensus on "the rules of the game."

An involuntary-temporary stressor, such as unemployment, is apt to be met first with the assumption that it will soon be over, and therefore requires no family adjustment except a tightening of the family budget. If the situation is not immediately remedied, the family may admit its predicament, may reorganize temporarily (perhaps by the wife's getting a job), and may subsequently reinstate the former family role structure when the husband is once again employed.

The two permanent types of stressors ordinarily involve a freezing out of the individual. In divorce and the departure of children, the freezing out is voluntary and requires the reorganization of the remaining family members. The involuntary forms of permanent stress include death, which requires admission and reorganization, and retardation and mental illness, which are ordinarily responded to by eventually recognizing the problem, freezing out the person, and reorganizing the family.

The crises depicted in Figure 13 are not meant to be regarded as either static or as unrelated to one another, though such an impression is unavoidable. However, in "real life," violence in the family that is temporary (sporadic) initially may become permanent (chronic) subsequently, as one or more family members attempt to cope with their problems by habitually abusing other members. And a possible result of chronic violence may be divorce on the ground of cruelty—a quite permanent outcome.

Again, we have said that specific challenges result in specific typical responses: freezing out the behavior and reinstating the individual, or temporarily reorganizing and reinstating, or freezing out the individual and permanently reorganizing. However, this picture is oversimplified. It is quite possible that the same challenge may meet with different responses due to variables other than the two primary axes of Figure 13. These additional variables that may affect the character of the family's responses include: (1) whether the challenge was *expected or unexpected;* (2) whether the challenge originated outside or inside the family, that is, *externally or internally;* (3) how the *family* is *structured in* relation to *its environment* (Is it embedded in a large kin network? is it a large or small nuclear family in which the individuals are highly embedded? or is it a highly individualistic nuclear family?); (4) how the *family* is *organized internally* (Is it well organized and adaptable prior to the challenge, or is it disorganized or too rigid?); (5) *definition* of the stressor (Is it or isn't it defined as deviant or as a source of trouble?). Let us look briefly at each of these five variables as they affect the intensity of family crisis and disorganization in response to a challenge.

(1) Expected or Unexpected Challenges

"A crisis," say Burgess and Locke, "is any decisive change which creates a situation for which the habitual behavior patterns of a person or a group are inadequate."[8] Thus, E. E. LeMasters is able to speak of parenthood as a crisis, since it calls into play new role demands and alters a married couple's habitual interaction patterns.[9] Yet the crisis is not in the event but in the response to it, and the response to an expected event is likely to be substantially less severe and disorganized than the response to an unexpected one. Alice Rossi asserts that the birth of the first child is a more crucial marital transition than the marriage itself.[10] It is obvious, then, that the likelihood of crisis is substantially greater in the birth of a handicapped or retarded child (an unexpected event) than in the birth of a normal child (an expected event).[11] One reason why an expected event is likely to be less stress-producing than an unexpected one was pointed out in Chapter 11. There Wesley Burr was cited as saying that when an event is expected the individual—or the family—can engage in anticipatory socialization, or pre-

---

[8] Burgess, Locke, and Thomes, *The Family,* p. 415. Copyright © 1963, by Litton Educational Publishing; reprinted by permission of Van Nostrand Reinhold Company.

[9] LeMasters, "Parenthood as Crisis."

[10] Alice Rossi, "Transition to Parenthood," *Journal of Marriage and the Family* 30 (1968), 27.

[11] Hobbs, "Parenthood as Crisis," and Hobbs, "Transition to Parenthood," question whether becoming a parent for the first time very often causes a crisis in the family.

learning. This can, in turn, ease the transition and result in a lower level of crisis.[12]

(2) External Versus Internal Origin

The response of the family to a stressor event originating outside it—such as a natural disaster, a depression, or a war—may be either disorganization or increased solidarity, depending upon its internal resources. The likelihood of crisis and disorganization is greater, however, if the stressor event originates within the family. Compare, for example, the family which loses its belongings in a flood with the family whose resources are gambled away by the husband. Or compare the family in which the husband, like millions of others, loses his job in a depression with the family in which the husband loses his job because of excessive drinking. Or, again, compare the family disrupted by war with the family disrupted by the husband's desertion. In each of these paired instances, the latter eventuality is more likely to cause family difficulties since the blame cannot be placed outside the family.[13]

(3) The Family Structure in Its Network

"Compared with other associations in the society," says Reuben Hill,

> the average family is badly handicapped organizationally. Its age composition is heavily weighted with dependents, and it cannot freely reject its weak members and recruit more competent team mates. . . . This group is not ideally manned to withstand stress, yet society has assigned to it the heaviest of responsibilities: the socialization and orientation of the young, and the meeting of the major emotional needs of all citizens, young and old.[14]

The family is, however, better able to withstand internal stresses if it is embedded in a larger kin network that can absorb some of the shock. Researchers have found that, even when the family is not highly embedded in its kin network, it may call upon kin for assistance in times of external threat.[15] There is likewise a difference, according to Thomas Dow, in the

---

[12] Wesley R. Burr, *Theory Construction and the Sociology of the Family* (New York: Wiley-Interscience, 1973), p. 125.

[13] The effect of externalization of blame on the lessening of a crisis is discussed in Donald A. Hansen, "Personal and Positional Influence in Formal Groups: Propositions and Theory for Research on Family Vulnerability to Stress," *Social Forces* 44 (1965), 202–10.

[14] Hill, "Generic Features of Families Under Stress," p. 140.

[15] Thomas E. Drabek and Keith S. Boggs, "Families in Disaster: Reactions and Relatives," *Journal of Marriage and the Family* 30 (1968), 443–51.

ability of nonembedded families to withstand various challenges. While Dow admits that further research is needed, it is his view that "the affective, interpersonal, intrafamily crisis is better met by the large family structure, while the material, economic, instrumental crisis is more effectively avoided and/or coped with by the small family structure."[16] When the kin-embedded family (personnel-wise), the large nuclear family, the small nuclear family, and the individualistic family are compared, the small nuclear family appears to be most vulnerable to stressor events originating within the family unit itself. The intensity of emotional ties and the strength of mutual expectations in the small family make it quite likely that both deviant behavior and the freezing out of an individual will severely test its coping ability. While the least disorganization and crisis might characterize the response of a truly individualistic family to a stressor event, the fact remains that there are apparently few families in which the laissez-faire attitude regarding member behavior is so extreme that the family has *no* mutual expectations whatsoever.

(4) Internal Family Organization

Hill states that the various researchers who studied the Depression concurred that it is

> possible to explain the different reactions of crisis-proof and crisis-prone families to sharp decreases in income during the Depression by these twin factors of integration and adaptability, with a restudy [by Angell] suggesting the greater importance of family adaptability.[17]

Thus, the family with mutual role expectations, common goals, flexibility, and a sense of satisfaction in family experience is more adequately organized and less vulnerable to stressor events than are other families. While such variables are unquestionably important to family stability, there are two problems in their use as predictors of family response. First, they are somewhat *tautological* in their relation to the stressor events. For example, the family in which a member deviates from expectations can be said to have weak mutual expectations. Likewise, the family that is unable to adapt to the birth of a retarded child obviously lacks flexibility. In other words, the variable that is said to help the family withstand stress may also be considered part of the stressor syndrome itself. Second—and this is really inseparable from the first problem—such internal variables are almost inherently post hoc. How can it be determined whether a family is organized and adaptable until it has

---

[16] Thomas E. Dow, Jr., "Family Reaction to Crisis," *Journal of Marriage and the Family* 27 (1965), 366.

[17] Hill, "Generic Features of Families Under Stress," p. 144.

confronted an event that tests its organization and adaptability? Yet, despite these qualifications in their use, the internal characteristics of families are obviously important determinants of the families' responses to changes and challenges.

(5) Definition, or Perception, of the Stressor

Here is a variable that quite clearly overlaps with some of those already discussed. For example, when a family is able to define an external event as threatening to many people, it may be easier for that family to "ride it out." However, the condition under which this variable is best distinguished from the others is one in which a particular act, event, or process is simply not defined as a stressor. Perhaps the best example would be giving birth to an illegitimate child. When a family does not define this as deviant behavior, any crisis caused by the event will be a result not of internal stress but of the ostracism of people in the society who define the behavior as deviant.[18]

We have cataloged the stressors and the likely familial responses to them, and have outlined the conditions under which a family is apt to be more or less susceptible to crisis and disorganization. Given the variables that influence the *intensity* of family response, the *greatest threat* to the family is likely to result from the following combination of factors: a *small, non–kin-embedded, nuclear family lacking flexibility* confronts an *unexpected, internal* challenge that it defines as a stressor. The *least threat*, or greatest resilience, is likely to characterize the *adaptable, kin-embedded* family that faces an *expected* event, an *external* challenge, or a situation not defined as crisis-provoking. This section has pointed out that to speak of *"the crisis process"* is to oversimplify a complex set of stimuli and responses; the purpose of the framework presented above is to help to order a wide variety of materials concerning the nonroutine aspects of family life.

Section Two

FOUR CHANGES AND CHALLENGES BRIEFLY CONSIDERED

Having developed a framework for understanding family responses to various stressors, we shall describe briefly a few of the characteristics of family economics and violence as stressor events, and then review at somewhat greater length the prevalence and significance of divorce and death in the contemporary U.S. family.

---

[18] Pope, "Unwed Mothers and Their Sex Partners," 555–67.

Economics, Employment, and the Family

There is a close relation between marriage and divorce rates and the business cycle. On the basis of his analysis of the period from 1860 to 1956, Paul Jacobson asserts that

> the incidence of divorce, like that of marriage, closely follows the business cycle, running low in periods of depression and correspondingly high during years of prosperity. In general, however, the divorce rate is less sensitive to changes in economic conditions, due largely to the fact that a marriage cannot be dissolved as readily as it can be contracted.[19]

What this boils down to is that people can ill afford to change their commitments, either through marriage or divorce, when times are hard because the reorganization process itself costs money. Therefore, in such periods individuals tend to maintain their current interpersonal affiliations whenever possible. Although figures are lacking, it is also possible that in times of economic hardship an intolerable situation is more likely to be escaped by desertion than by the costly process of legalized divorce.

How does the individual family react to an economic setback, whether it be unemployment during a depression or loss during a natural disaster? The vast majority of families tend to look to their kin at such times.[20] Yet the problems in thus utilizing kin are twofold. First, the poor and unskilled, who are in greatest economic jeopardy because they constantly live close to the subsistence level, are likely to have kin who are no better off than they are. Thus, they may be forced to seek help from outside agencies rather than from kin. Second, members of the middle class and the stable segments of the working class, though more likely to have economically secure kin upon whom to call for help, are also more likely to be characterized by values that stress individualism and independence. As we indicated in Chapter 13, kin relations in U.S. society appear to operate most smoothly when the obligatory elements are kept in the background. Our family values give negative, not positive, sanction to such economic functions and obligations. Therefore, even though the kin network may provide a buffer against economic setback, if it is utilized in this way there is a likelihood of interpersonal strain and personal insecurity—an insecurity that results from the conflict between one's value system and the necessities of existence.

A large number of significant research projects grew out of the Depres-

---

[19] Reprinted by permission of the author, from Paul H. Jacobson, *American Marriage and Divorce* (New York: Rinehart, copyright © 1959), p. 95.

[20] Koos, *Families in Trouble*, p. 87; Drabek and Boggs, "Families in Disaster"; and Enrico L. Quarantelli, "A Note on the Protective Function of the Family in Disasters," *Marriage and Family Living* 22 (1960), 263–64.

sion in the United States during the 1930s. This research showed that the same stimuli—unemployment and financial loss—affected different families in different ways. Some families made temporary adjustments, such as moving in with relatives; others disintegrated; and still others (for example, 27 of the 100 families studied by Ruth Cavan and Katherine Ranck) reacted by rallying together and manifesting a more overt sense of family unity than ever before.[21] Part of the explanation for the various reactions to this specific challenge lay in the family's value system. If the family's major goals and values had been economic, the undermining of its economic position resulted in a severe disorganization of its values and norms, or behavior patterns. If, however, the family had other values—perhaps religion, perhaps service to others, perhaps experience and adaptation—these might serve as rallying points. The ability to adapt and cope is seldom developed overnight; the ability either is or is not developed by a family as a result of many experiences, and, as stated above, it is difficult to know whether a given family has developed this capacity until *after* the family confronts a challenge and demonstrates the adequacy or inadequacy of its preparation.

Unemployment and economic setback may, of course, be a consequence of internal rather than external factors. If the husband loses his job due to excessive absence from work, or if he gambles away the family's resources, it is relatively easy to pinpoint him as the chief cause of the difficulty; the likelihood of crisis, weakened solidarity, and at least temporary reorganization is much greater in such a situation than in one in which the threat can be "externalized" or generalized.[22] Here, then, once again we see a range of possible outcomes that depend both on the nature of the challenge and on the family's structure and values at the time of its impact.

Violence in the Family

The family in the modern industrial world, we said in Chapter 5, is supposed to meet the individual's need to be loved, understood, and treated as a whole person, and the ideology of the happy family encourages people to get married and stay married. Yet meeting such social-emotional needs is a heavy burden for any small group to bear, and the happy family ideology is a hard one to live up to. Thus it is that many married couples today, unable to bear that burden and meet those needs, feel free to "break ties and try again."

Divorce, however, is not always a prompt and automatic response to unmet needs. In many families there is an interim period between a failure

---

[21] Cavan and Ranck, *The Family and the Depression.*
[22] Koos, *Families in Trouble,* pp. 91–102.

to meet social-emotional needs and divorce, during which much conflict may occur, some of it violent. In other families there is no divorce, only the verbal and physical expression of dissatisfaction. "Violence," Suzanne Steinmetz and Murray Straus assert, "seems as typical of family relationships as love."[23] Ideologically, we prefer to ignore this fact, but social scientists, physicians, and social workers are making it increasingly difficult to do so.

How prevalent is violence in the U.S. family? That, of course, depends upon how violence is defined. If it is defined as any use of physical force by one person against another person, then it is extremely prevalent. If its meaning is restricted to the use of physical force which results in injury, then it is less prevalent. However, this redefinition leaves us with no clear "cutting point." Does a bruise qualify as an injury, or must there be more serious physical damage, such as a broken bone? Both William Goode and Steinmetz and Straus set their discussions of violence on a backdrop of any use of physical force.[24] On that basis, Steinmetz and Straus report a study which shows that during one year "62 percent of the high school seniors had used physical force on a brother or sister and 16 percent of their parents had used physical force on each other."[25] In addition, "data on students in three different regions of the United States show that half of the parents sampled either used or threatened their high school seniors with physical punishment."[26] George Levinger, in his study of causes of divorce, notes that 23 percent of middle-class and 40 percent of working-class couples gave "physical abuse" as the major complaint—which makes it highly probable that violence is a secondary issue in many other divorces.[27] In the ensuing discussion, we will restrict ourselves primarily to the more serious injury-causing forms of family violence, but we will do so in the recognition that, as the authors cited have made clear, our family system is "shot through" with the threat and the use of physical force.

Fights between family members are the largest single category of police calls, and "more murders are committed on family members than on any other type of person."[28] It is, furthermore, the physically stronger members of the family who are likely to abuse the weaker members. This means that the two major forms of serious family violence are wifebeating

[23] Suzanne K. Steinmetz and Murray A. Straus, "The Family as Cradle of Violence," *Society* 10 (1973), 50.

[24] Goode, "Force and Violence in the Family," pp. 624–35; Steinmetz and Straus, "The Family as Cradle of Violence."

[25] Steinmetz and Straus, "The Family as Cradle of Violence," p. 51.

[26] Steinmetz and Straus, "The Family as Cradle of Violence," p. 50.

[27] George Levinger, "Sources of Marital Dissatisfaction Among Applicants for Divorce," *American Journal of Orthopsychiatry* 36 (1966).

[28] Steinmetz and Straus, "The Family as Cradle of Violence," p. 51.

and child abuse. The *wifebeater* and his family setting are described by John Snell, Richard Rosenwald, and Ames Robey as follows:

> This structure is characterized by the husband's passivity, indecisiveness, sexual inadequacy; the wife's aggressiveness, masculinity, frigidity, and masochism; and a relationship between the two in which a frequent alternation of passive and aggressive roles serves to achieve a working equilibrium. The husband's drinking is often used as an aid to role alternation.[29]

A specific factor that contributes to wifebeating, Goode feels, is the unwillingness of human beings to terminate a conflict by either submission or escape. In fact, "fighting conversation" between intimates, says Goode, "being so unsatisfactory because it exposes still more disagreements and hostility as it progresses, does not easily lend itself to a safe completion."[30] Another factor in wifebeating may be the general competition and antagonism between the sexes in our society. In fact, the changes being preached by women's and men's liberation, while liberating in the long run, may in the short run produce just the sort of couples that Snell, Rosenwald, and Robey describe. This, however, is speculative and should not be overemphasized. What is not speculative is that socialization in U.S. society does teach the individual that force is effective in getting one's way.[31] While force may not be viewed as desirable, it is always "waiting in the wings" when needed. Here, then, is a situation in which a family is unable to adapt as an integrated unit to a stressor event and in which its individual members are unable to control a destructive emotion. In addition, there are often other contextual factors at work, such as the egging on of the combatants by kinsmen. We shall summarize what we have said about wifebeating with a formula which merits further research: socialization for violence + societal sex antagonism + encouragement from others + inadequate husband + aggressive wife + inability to terminate a verbal conflict = wifebeating.

Child abuse, claims Goode, is also a result not so much of the situation as of the parent's socialization for violence and of the inadequacy of his own childhood. The child abuser typically received little love or tenderness as a child, and as a parent combines a high level of demand with a great desire for response. Essentially, such parents

> approach the task of child care with the wish to do something for the child, a deep need for the child to fill their own lacks, to salve their

---

[29] Snell, Rosenwald, and Robey, "The Wifebeater's Wife," p. 112.
[30] Goode, "Force and Violence in the Family," p. 632.
[31] Goode, "Force and Violence in the Family," p. 630.

own hurt self-esteem, to give them love, and a harsh demand that the child behave in a certain way. Failing that, the child demonstrates thereby his lack of respect, love, affection, goodness, and so on.[32]

The context, of course, is not unrelated to child abuse. Very often the housewife who feels trapped, who feels that she has given up a career to be a mother, is apt to feel most threatened when the child does not respond as she desires. Likewise, the young or unsuccessful husband may respond to occupational frustration with child abuse.[33] Finally, the triggering mechanism for child abuse is often the child's failure to comply with parental insistence that he stop crying. While the crying may have a perfectly legitimate physical basis, the vulnerable parent construes it to mean that the child lacks self-control or is willful, unresponsive, and "bad."[34]

In general, wifebeating and child abuse are more frequent among low-status couples, poorly educated couples, and couples who married young. However, these types of violence are sufficiently prevalent throughout the United States family system to warrant further study.[35]

Divorce in the United States

A brief legend from nineteenth century India may serve to introduce one of the most frequently debated aspects of the contemporary family.

> In the first year of the reign of King Julief, two thousand married couples were separated, by the magistrates, with their own consent. The emperor was so indignant, on learning these particulars, that he abolished the privilege of divorce. In the course of the following year, the number of marriages in Agra was less than before by three thousand; the number of adulteries was greater by seven thousand; three hundred women were burned alive for poisoning their husbands; seventy-five men were burned for the murder of their wives; and the quantity of furniture broken and destroyed, in the interior of private families, amounted to the value of three millions of rupees. The emperor reestablished the privilege of divorce.[36]

Making divorce easy, some commentators would say, is just another compromise with the weaknesses of the flesh. To these authors, the rate of divorce in the United States is another sign of the imminent collapse

---

[32] Goode, "Force and Violence in the Family," p. 634.

[33] Taylor, "The 'Battered Child,' " in Bryant, *Social Problems Today*, p. 215.

[34] Taylor, "The 'Battered Child,' " in Bryant, *Social Problems Today*, p. 212.

[35] Murray Straus and others are continuing their research on family violence, and this should increase our understanding of both its prevalence and its causes.

[36] Nelson Manfred Blake, *The Road to Reno: A History of Divorce* (New York: Macmillan, 1962), pp. 80–81, quoted from 28 Niles Register 229, June 11, 1825.

of both the family system and the society. But how does divorce in the United States look in cross-cultural and historical perspective? Practically all societies, with the possible exception of the Incas, says George P. Murdock, have made some cultural provision for terminating marriage through divorce.[37] In a sample of 40 societies, he found that 16 had a lower divorce rate than that of the contemporary United States, and that 24 had a higher rate. In some of these 24 societies, divorce is a private matter, with informal social pressure rather than legal restrictions or contracts keeping most couples together. However, in 19 of Murdock's sample of 40 societies, the rate of permanent separations appears to exceed that of the United States. Murdock therefore concludes that, despite "the widespread alarm about increasing 'family disorganization' in our own society, the comparative evidence makes it clear that we still remain well within the limits which human experience has shown that societies can tolerate with safety.[38]

Given the cross-cultural evidence, why has the rate of divorce in the United States been viewed with alarm by many observers? The answer is that it has been so viewed, not by comparison with other countries, but by comparison with our own traditions and history. Max Rheinstein, for example, reports that in the West the family and the control of divorce first came under increasing religious domination and subsequently underwent a process of liberalization and secularization.[39] The Victorian nuclear family was simultaneously the end of the religious and institutional era and the beginning of the era of high expectations for families consisting of a small number of intensely involved persons. In his book *Divorce in the Progressive Era,* William O'Neill describes the close link between Victorian family expectations and the increase in the prevalence of divorce:

> When families are large and loose, arouse few expectations, and make few demands, there is no need for divorce. But when families become the center of social organization, their intimacy can become suffocating, their demands unbearable, and their expectations too high to be easily realizable. Divorce then becomes the safety valve that makes the system workable. Those who are frustrated or oppressed can escape their families, and those who fail at what is regarded as the most important human activity can gain a second chance. Divorce is, therefore, not an anomaly or a flaw in the system, but an essential feature of it. When

---

[37] George P. Murdock, "Family Stability in Non-European Cultures," *The Annals* 272 (November 1950), 195.

[38] Murdock, "Family Stability in Non-European Cultures," pp. 199, 197.

[39] Max Rheinstein, "Trends of Marriage and Divorce Law of Western Countries," *Law and Contemporary Problems* 18 (1953), 3–18; reprinted in Marvin B. Sussman, ed., *Sourcebook in Marriage and the Family* (Boston: Houghton Mifflin, 1968 ed.), pp. 543–54.

the modern family came to dominate society in the nineteenth century, divorce became common.[40]

As divorce has become more common, it has also been met with less alarm and more acceptance. Jessie Bernard says very simply that it may be "surprising to learn that the 'news' about divorce today is that it is no longer news."[41]

But, the alarmists would counter, doesn't divorce, even in a society whose family system appears to require it, eventually lead to the destruction of that society? To this question Morton Hunt responds:

> It is fairly well known that freedom to divorce has existed in certain deteriorating societies; this was the case in the later years of the Roman Empire. What is less well known, freedom to divorce has existed in certain stable and healthy societies—especially those which have mechanisms other than the father-mother family for insuring the well-being and socialization of the children.[42]

This latter situation is exemplified, according to Hunt, by the Hopi Indians. Yet he does not go on to compare the contemporary U.S. family with that of the Hopi in terms of its cultural mechanisms for coping with a high rate of divorce. We shall keep this issue in mind as we look more closely at divorce in the United States, beginning with the *prevalence* to which so many authors refer.

The classic work on the prevalence of divorce in the United States is Paul Jacobson's *American Marriage and Divorce*. Jacobson traces the rate of divorce per 1,000 existing marriages from 1860 to 1956. Combining his data with *Monthly Vital Statistics* reports issued since 1956, we are able to construct in Figure 14 the rate of divorce from 1860 to 1973 by five-year intervals. The two high points in U.S. divorce occurred in the years 1943–50 and from 1968 to the present. In 1946 divorces reached a peak of 18.2 per 1,000 marriages, and in 1973 they reached a high of 17.5. In fact, if the divorce rate is figured on 1,000 population instead of 1,000 marriages, the rate in 1973 surpassed that of 1946, by 4.4 to 4.3. The reason that the 1973 rate falls short of the 1946 rate when figured on marriages, is that a larger proportion of the 15-and-over population is married today than was the case in 1946. The upward trend in divorces is continuing, so that it now seems likely that the average divorce rate for the five-year period 1971–75 will be higher than that of any other five-year period in U.S. history.

---

[40] O'Neill, *Divorce in the Progressive Era,* pp. 6–7.

[41] Jessie Bernard, "No News, but New Ideas," in Paul Bohannon, ed., *Divorce and After* (Garden City, N.Y.: Doubleday, Anchor Books, 1971 ed.), p. 3.

[42] Morton M. Hunt, *The World of the Formerly Married* (New York: McGraw-Hill, 1966), p. 290.

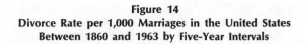

Figure 14
Divorce Rate per 1,000 Marriages in the United States
Between 1860 and 1963 by Five-Year Intervals

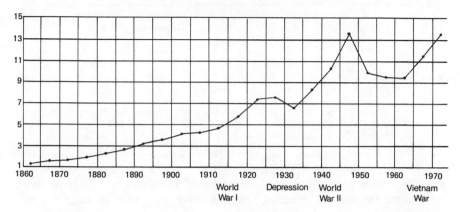

SOURCE: Computed from annual rates, by permission of the author, from Paul H. Jacobson, *American Marriage and Divorce* (New York: Rinehart, copyright © 1959), p. 90, table 42; and *Monthly Vital Statistics* (Rockville, Md.: U.S. Department of Health, Education, and Welfare), selected yearly reports, including that of February 28, 1974.

As Figure 14 illustrates, divorce rates declined during economic recessions and rose during and after wars. It is possible that, due to the extraordinary length of the Vietnam war, the entire period from 1968 to the present, during which the divorce rate has been rising, should be seen as a postwar period despite the fact that direct U.S. participation in that war did not end until 1973. This may mean that by 1975 the divorce rate will once again taper off. However, this assumes that no other important changes are taking place in U.S. society which might contribute to a continued rise in the divorce rate; as we shall see in the discussion of no-fault divorce and alternatives to the family, such an assumption hardly seems warranted. It is also instructive to relate the divorce rate to death and desertion. While the divorce rate has risen in 100 years from one per 1,000 marriages to 18 per 1,000 marriages, the death rate has declined during the same period by an even greater amount. Consequently, says Jacobson, "the annual rate of total marital dissolutions is lower now than it was 100 years ago; the combined rate has declined from an annual average of 33 per 1000 in the 1860s to about 27 per 1,000 at present [1956]."[43] Jacobson, however, was comparing the 1860s—a wartime period—with the mid-1950s—a peacetime period. In Table 10 we compare four selected years —1860, 1908, 1956, and 1963—in terms of their rates of death and divorce.

---

[43] Jacobson, *American Marriage and Divorce*, p. 143.

Table 10
Rates of Death, Divorce, and Total Marital Dissolution
per 1,000 Marriages for Selected Years, 1860–1963

Year	Death	Divorce	Total Dissolution	Percent Divorces
1860	28.4	1.2	29.6	4.1%
1908	24.4	4.4	28.8	15.4
1956	17.5	9.3	26.8	34.6
1963	19.1	9.6	28.7	34.0

SOURCE: Reprinted by permission of the author, from Paul H. Jacobson, *American Marriage and Divorce* (New York: Rinehart, copyright © 1959), p. 142, table 70.

It might seem reasonable to argue that one explanation for the rise in the divorce rate is that couples whose unhappy marriages would have been terminated by death a hundred years ago live long enough today to terminate them by divorce. Yet the problem with this explanation is that more than half of today's divorces occur during the first eight years of marriage; thus the explanation is partial at best.[44]

A second partial explanation offered for the rise in the divorce rate has to do with desertions. According to Doris Freed and Henry Foster, prior to 1900 "for the working man, desertion and heading west was the common way for husbands to escape from intolerable marriages."[45] To this, James Peterson adds:

> Whether, then, the increase in total divorce represents only the increased use of legal facilities by these classes we do not know. It is possible that a rising divorce rate may represent a more law-abiding population which signifies disruption with legal means, whereas, previously, the same disruption would have been accomplished by separation or desertion.[46]

Yet Freed and Foster indicate that today the annual number of divorces and desertions are approximately the same; legalized divorce has not entirely replaced desertion as a means of marital separation. It seems most probable that a tendency to legalize marital dissolutions accounts for less than half of the increase in the rate of divorce since the mid-1800s.

[44] Paul C. Glick and Arthur J. Norton, "Frequency, Duration, and Probability of Marriage and Divorce," *Journal of Marriage and the Family* 33 (1971), 307–17.

[45] Doris Jonas Freed and Henry H. Foster, Jr., "Divorce American Style," *The Annals* 383 (1969), 75.

[46] James A. Peterson, "Catastrophes in Partnership: Separation, Divorce, and Widowhood," in Seymour M. Farber, Piero Mustacchi, and Roger H. L. Wilson, eds., *Man and Civilization: The Family's Search for Survival* (New York: McGraw-Hill, 1965), p. 73.

A final issue concerning the prevalence of divorce involves, not the yearly divorce rate, but the number of U.S. marriages that eventually end in divorce. How can the yearly divorce rates from Figure 14 be related to the likelihood that a given marriage will end in divorce? The average length of marriages is about 25 years. Thus, if one projects the annual rate of 17.5 divorces per 1,000 marriages over the average length of marriages, it becomes apparent that *at that current annual rate* there would be 437.5 divorces per 1,000 marriages over a 25-year span. A 25-year projection of the 1965 rate would be 250 per 1,000. However, since the annual rate does change from year to year, these are only rough approximations, carried out to demonstrate the relation between annual divorce rates and the probability that a given cohort of married people will ever get a divorce.

For some years following World War II it was thought that somewhere between one-third and one-fourth of all married persons would experience divorce during their lifetimes. However, careful research by Thomas Monahan and others has shown that a portion of that apparent rate is accounted for by the greater likelihood that second and subsequent marriages would not last. In fact, Monahan found in an Iowa study that 16.6 percent of first marriages end in divorce, as compared to 34.9 percent of second marriages and 79.4 percent of marriages between persons who have been divorced two or more times.[47] Looking at a nationwide probability sample of 28,000 households, Paul Glick and Arthur Norton find that, of those 70 years of age and under who had ever been married, about 15 percent of the men and 17 percent of the women had been divorced.[48] Thus, viewed historically, the failure rate for marriages contracted in the United States since about 1920 is one in six. Even if the failure rate for post–World War II marriages is as high as one in five, this does not indicate, says Peterson, that we are moving toward serial monogamy (or, we might add, toward "permanent availability").

When we turn from the prevalence of divorce in the United States to its *causes,* we find two types of variables discussed in the literature. The first set of variables is arrived at by classifying the married population into certain basic categories, such as by age and by socioeconomic level, then noting in which categories the divorce rates are higher or lower. The second set of variables consists of the answers that divorced or divorcing persons give to direct questions about the causes of their marital difficulties. William Goode, Thomas Monahan, and J. Richard Udry all report that lower-status

---

[47] Thomas P. Monahan, "The Changing Nature and Instability of Remarriages," *Eugenics Quarterly* 5 (1958), 81.

[48] Glick and Norton, "Frequency, Duration, and Probability of Marriage and Divorce."

couples have higher divorce rates than do higher-status families. Monahan, for example, found in the mid-1950s that professionals, owners, and managers—who comprised 23.4 percent of his sample—accounted for only 9.6 percent of the divorces; skilled craftsmen, 22.7 percent of his sample, accounted for 21.2 percent of the divorces; and unskilled laborers, who made up 9.9 percent of his sample, accounted for 31.8 percent of the divorces.[49] A partial explanation for these figures is that low-status families are more susceptible to many of the stressors discussed above, including alcoholism and unemployment; possible outcomes of such stressors are disorganization and crisis and eventually divorce. In addition, "young marriages disproportionately involve persons from lower- or working-class backgrounds," and young marriages—specifically those in which one or both spouses are in their teens—are less stable than are those contracted later.[50]

"The divorce risk for teen-agers was said to be six times greater than that for adults," say Freed and Foster; because this is true at all status levels, the high divorce rate of teenagers cannot be entirely explained by the association between low status and youthful marriage.[51] Why, then, are youthful marriages on the whole less likely to last? Three partial answers to this are: (1) divergence in marriage, (2) marriage as an escape, and (3) premarital pregnancy. Some have claimed that in a society that stresses both personal choice of a mate and deferred adulthood, young people are not psychologically and intellectually prepared to make sound mate selections. While this assumption can easily be questioned by noting the way in which improved diet and the mass media help young people mature (physically and mentally) earlier than ever before, the fact remains that the earlier a couple marry the greater is the likelihood that there will be a *divergence* in their careers, interests, and personalities during the first few years of their marriage and that it will therefore end in divorce.[52]

A second possible explanation for the breakup of early marriages is that they are often as much an *escape from* something as a *commitment to* something. Young people who find themselves increasingly unable to put up with an unhappy home may see marriage as an opportunity to escape

[49] Goode, *After Divorce*, chap. 5; Thomas P. Monahan, "Divorce by Occupational Level," *Marriage and Family Living* 17 (1955), 322–24; J. Richard Udry, "Marital Instability by Race, Sex, Education and Occupation Using 1960 Census Data," *American Journal of Sociology* 72 (1966), 203–9; and Udry, "Marital Instability by Race and Income Based on 1960 Census Data," *American Journal of Sociology* 72 (1967), 673–74.

[50] Karen Winch Bartz and F. Ivan Nye, "Early Marriage: A Propositional Formulation," *Journal of Marriage and the Family* 32 (1970), 258–68.

[51] Freed and Foster, "Divorce American Style," p. 83.

[52] On this point, see Vladimir De Lissovoy, "High School Marriages: A Longitudinal Study," *Journal of Marriage and the Family* 35 (1973), 245–55; and Larry L. Bumpass and James A. Sweet, "Differentials in Marital Instability: 1970," *American Journal of Sociology* 37 (1972), 755.

and, therefore, may not allow sufficient time for unstable or unworkable dating relationships to run their course and dissolve. One way, of course, of escaping from home is to force parental acceptance of a marriage by means of a *premarital pregnancy*. This is the reason most often mentioned for the greater instability of youthful marriages, though Larry Bumpass and James Sweet find that, by itself, premarital pregnancy accounts for only a small portion of the variation.[53] There are two steps in the explanation of how premarital pregnancy increases marital instability. In the first place, a substantial proportion of teenage marriages involve a premarital pregnancy— 35–45 percent according to Freed and Foster and 30–60 percent according to Peterson. Samuel Lowrie finds that, in an Ohio sample of 1,850 first marriages, "70.9 percent of the premaritally pregnant brides were 18 or younger."[54] In the second place, most researchers agree that marriages characterized by a premarital pregnancy show a greater incidence of divorce than marriages not so characterized.[55] Though few writers attempt to explain why such marriages should be less stable, it seems likely that many of the couples who marry because of a premarital pregnancy would have weeded themselves out if they had been free from the pressure to marry that was occasioned by the pregnancy.[56] In other words, in such marriages the working of choice has been short-circuited.

This brings us to the second set of explanations given for divorces in the United States—the direct causes mentioned by divorced and divorcing persons. The wives interviewed by Goode gave as the causes of their divorces: nonsupport, arbitrary authority, complex reasons, drinking, personality problems, an unsatisfactory home life, value divergences, disagreements about consumption patterns, and the "triangle" or extramarital affair, as well as a scattering of other reasons. George Levinger, dividing his sam-

---

[53] Bumpass and Sweet, "Differentials in Marital Instability: 1970," p. 758; Bartz and Nye, "Early Marriage"; and L. Coombs et al., "Premarital Pregnancy and Status Before and After Marriage," *American Journal of Sociology* 75 (1970), 800–820.

[54] Peterson, "Catastrophes in Partnership," in Farber, Mustacchi, and Wilson, *Man and Civilization*, p. 75; Samuel H. Lowrie, "Early Marriage: Premarital Pregnancy and Associated Factors," *Journal of Marriage and the Family* 27 (1965), 48–56.

[55] Lowrie, "Early Marriage," p. 53; Lee G. Burchinal, "Trends and Prospects for Young Marrieds in the United States," *Journal of Marriage and the Family* 27 (1965), 252; Harold T. Christensen and Betty B. Rubenstein, "Premarital Pregnancy and Divorce: A Follow-Up Study by the Interview Method," *Marriage and Family Living* 18 (1956), 114–23; and Christensen and Hanna H. Meissner, "Studies in Child Spacing III—Premarital Pregnancy as a Factor in Divorce," *American Sociological Review* 18 (1953), 641–44. One researcher who disagrees is J. Ross Eshleman, who finds in a small Ohio sample that "contrary to most common notions about premarital pregnancies, the present study did not find pregnancy prior to marriage to be significantly related to either mental health or marital integration." See Eshleman, "Mental and Marital Integration in Young Marriages," *Journal of Marriage and the Family* 27 (1965), 257; on this, see the sources in footnote 53 as well.

[56] Coombs et al., "Premarital Pregnancy and Status Before and After Marriage," suggests this.

ple of 600 Cleveland applicants for divorce into lower-status and middle-status groups, reports the following differences by sex and socioeconomic status in reasons given for desiring a divorce:

> Lower-status wives were considerably more likely than middle-status wives to complain about financial problems, physical abuse and drinking. Middle-class wives were significantly more prone to complain about lack of love, infidelity and excessive demands. Middle-class husbands paralleled the wives in their significantly greater concern with lack of love; on the other hand, they were significantly *less* likely than lower-class husbands to complain of the wife's infidelity.[57]

The difference is, very simply, that lower-status marriages (and, therefore, complaints) are focused in the areas of physiological needs for food and safety or protection, while higher-status marriages tend to take these matters for granted and are thus more concerned about forms of emotional and psychological expression.

With some understanding of the prevalence and causes of divorce in the United States, it is possible to look now at the *significance, process,* and *effects* of divorce. First, what does divorce itself mean? As we stated above, the fact that 84 percent of first marriages in the United States remain intact seems to indicate that the country is not moving rapidly toward serial monogamy. Nor is the increase in the rate of divorce during the twentieth century necessarily a sign of moral degeneration. While the increase may be so interpreted, some writers would argue precisely the opposite. For example, Foster states that "sexual dissatisfaction in marriage today is more apt to lead to divorce and remarriage than to the acquisition of a mistress or a visit to a prostitute. In this sense, it may be argued, divorce promotes public morality."[58] What the higher divorce rate does unquestionably mean is that a lessened social stigma is attached to divorce than was the case in the earlier periods of U.S. history; divorce has become more acceptable as a "cultural alternative" to an intolerable marriage.[59]

Does the increase in the divorce rate indicate either a breakdown of the U.S. marriage system or a decrease in its popularity? "Despite the prevalence of divorce," say Freed and Foster, "marriage is more popular than ever before. In 1900 only a little more than half of all Americans above fourteen were married; today almost two-thirds are."[60] To this, Hunt adds that the "wide use of divorce today is not a sign of a diminished desire to

---

[57] Goode, *After Divorce*, p. 123; and Levinger, "Sources of Marital Dissatisfaction Among Applicants for Divorce," p. 806.

[58] Henry H. Foster, Jr., "The Future of Family Law," *The Annals* 383 (1969), 142.

[59] Goode, *World Revolution and Family Patterns* (New York: Free Press, 1963), p. 81.

[60] Freed and Foster, "Divorce American Style," p. 82.

be married, but of an increased desire to be happily married."[61] The effect of divorce upon the marriage and family system of the United States, O'Neill claims, justifies neither the expectations of the liberals, who thought it would act as a safety valve and solve all the internal inconsistencies in our family system, nor the fears of the conservatives, who believed that the availability of divorce would signal the disintegration of the family as we know it. What has happened is that what was "once a moral issue has become increasingly a clinical problem. That we have not solved it any more than the Progressives did" in the early 1900s "is probably less important than our abandonment of their utopian stance."[62] But the effect of divorce upon marriage and the family cannot be viewed apart from the process, including such issues as children and remarriage.

Divorce begins in marital conflict and ends in autonomy and perhaps remarriage. In between there are several overlapping experiences which, taken together, Paul Bohannon calls the six stations of divorce. These experiences are:

> (1) the emotional divorce, which centers around the problem of the deteriorating marriage; (2) the legal divorce, based on grounds; (3) the economic divorce, which deals with money and property; (4) the co-parental divorce, which deals with custody, single-parent homes, and visitation; (5) the community divorce, surrounding the changes of friends and community that every divorcee experiences; and (6) the psychic divorce, with the problem of regaining individual autonomy.[63]

In the remaining portion of this chapter we will speak to several of these issues, including remarriage as one factor in regaining autonomy.

Divorces increasingly involve couples with children. "In 1948," according to Freed and Foster, "only 42 per cent of divorcing couples had children under 18, but in 1955, the figure was 47 per cent, and in 1962 [it] reached 60 per cent, involving 537,000 children."[64] Goode, however, found that the divorced mothers he studied in Detroit were convinced that their children were better off than they would have been if their mothers had remained married to their first husbands.[65] While this may be partially a rationalization of the decision that these divorced mothers had made, their belief is generally corroborated by Ivan Nye in his study of children from broken homes and from unhappy unbroken homes. Using as his sample ninth through twelfth graders in three Washington schools, Nye discovered that

---

[61] Hunt, *The World of the Formerly Married*, p. 292.
[62] O'Neill, *Divorce in the Progressive Era*, p. 273.
[63] Paul Bohannon, "The Six Stations of Divorce," in Bohannon, *Divorce and After*, p. 34.
[64] Freed and Foster, "Divorce American Style," p. 84.
[65] Goode, *After Divorce*, p. 329.

in the areas of psychosomatic illness, delinquent behavior, and parent-child adjustment . . . children show better adjustment in broken homes. Children of homes broken by divorce in terms of the over-all adjustment picture do not have poorer adjustment than those from homes broken in other ways.[66]

One reason, Nye feels, that many studies have overemphasized the strains that children experience because of their parents' divorce is that these studies have concentrated on the period of the divorce process itself, rather than on the subsequent period of readjustment and reorganization. We should not, however, go to the other extreme of assuming that divorce has no damaging effects on the children. As Jack Westman and David Cline point out, after a divorce parents can continue to use their children in perpetuating their own conflict.[67] Futhermore, they may not have talked realistically with their children about the significance of the divorce. Thus, turbulence in the children's lives can be prolonged by an unsettled divorce "settlement."

As far as the postdivorce adjustment of the divorcee is concerned, Goode and others have reported that the prevalence of remarriage following a premature marital breakup (as opposed to a later breakup caused by death in old age) is such that it could be considered institutionalized.[68] Both this fact, and the fact that there are greater economic opportunities for women today, present alternatives to the divorcee which were much less available in earlier years. Though second and subsequent marriages are less stable than first marriages, the significance of this lesser stability seems to be that selectivity has occurred, so that those who have been willing to divorce once are the subcategory of married persons who are most willing to accept divorce as a working alternative to an unhappy marriage.[69]

In discussing the significance and process of divorce thus far, our tendency has been to minimize its tensions and problematic aspects, though we mentioned briefly the difficulties which can be caused when the conflicts of already divorced couples are perpetuated through their children. At this point we shall review three factors that serve to increase the *strain* of

---

[66] F. Ivan Nye, "Child Adjustment in Broken and in Unhappy Unbroken Homes," *Marriage and Family Living* 19 (1957), 361.

[67] Jack C. Westman and David W. Cline, "Divorce Is a Family Affair," *Family Law Quarterly* 5 (1971), 1–10.

[68] Goode, *After Divorce*, chap. 20. See especially Jessie Bernard, *Remarriage: A Study of Marriage* (New York: Holt, Rinehart and Winston, 1956).

[69] Hunt points out that simple figures such as those reported by Monahan should not necessarily be interpreted to mean that divorcees are unstable or "bad bets," but rather that they may have merely discovered that divorce isn't all that bad after all. See Hunt, *The World of the Formerly Married*, pp. 278–79. The factors that make for a successful remarriage among the elderly are discussed in Walter C. McKain, "A New Look at Older Marriages," *Family Life Coordinator* 21 (1972), 68–69.

divorce today. The first and most important tension-producing factor is the law. The history of divorce law in the United States is one of plaintiff and defendant, of perjury and legal skirmishing—all of which may add to the pangs of a process that could signify the "decent burial" of a dead marriage. Love is presumably the basis for marriage, but its mutual cessation is not a legal ground for divorce (see Table 11). The legal grounds in our fault-

Table 11
Grounds for Divorce, by Percent

Year	Cruelty	Desertion	Adultery	All Others
1867–70	12.4	35.4	26.4	25.8
1950	58.7	17.6	2.7	21.0

SOURCE: Reprinted by permission of the author, from Paul H. Jacobson, *American Marriage and Divorce* (New York: Rinehart, copyright © 1959), p. 121, table 58.

based system have changed over the years, but do not yet embody the mutual lovelessness of a dead marriage—the exception being California's recent move in that direction. The statutory grounds for divorce and the causes of marital breakdown have little relationship; and both Rheinstein and Freed and Foster point out the difficulty in getting legislators to bring the laws into keeping with the times. Freed and Foster put it this way:

> Even if judges and lawyers are convinced, for the most part, that marital fault is a difficult, if not impossible, thing to assess, legislators are most apt to be committed to the fault concept. In other words, the breakdown theory is a radical departure from prior law, and is not likely to appeal to most state legislators.[70]

The 10 percent of American divorce cases that were contested in the 1950s and 1960s seldom involved an individual trying to save his marriage, but quite often involved a spiteful, recalcitrant, or greedy spouse.[71] It is unquestionable that the present public, legal, and fault basis for the law serves to increase the strain of divorce rather than to alleviate it.[72] As Clifford Kirkpatrick asserts:

> There is a good chance that persons seeking divorce under present-day provisions will have contact with legal confusion, collusion, perjury,

---

[70] Freed and Foster, "Divorce American Style," p. 86.
[71] Freed and Foster, "Divorce American Style," p. 79; and Michael Wheeler, *No-Fault Divorce*, p. 4.
[72] Foster, "The Future of Family Law," pp. 137f; and Eugene Litwak, "Three Ways in Which Law Acts as a Means of Social Control: Punishment, Therapy, and Education: Divorce Law a Case in Point," *Social Forces* 24 (1956), 217–23.

degradation, humiliation, increased bitterness, and frustration, rather than professional help for the sickness of marital maladjustment.[73]

It is generally acknowledged that in most divorces both parties must shoulder part of the blame. However, the recrimination doctrine provides that if both parties are at fault, or have accused each other, there can be no divorce. This doctrine, says Michael Wheeler,

> forces unhappily married couples to remain married, if only in a legal sense. As a result, it encourages adulterous affairs, illegitimacy, and desertion, while preventing the stability which might come with remarriage.[74]

Likewise, the ease with which uncontested divorces are granted leads, Wheeler asserts, to an anomalous result:

> If the parties are still on good enough terms to work out an acceptable agreement on division of property and custody of children, they ordinarily will have no trouble getting a divorce on the basis of cruelty or some similar ground. But if the husband and wife have lost all respect for each other, if they want to use the courts to punish their spouse, if the divorce is contested, then there is a good chance the divorce will be denied.[75]

That there is "something wrong" with our divorce system, with its fault basis, its recrimination, and its contested or uncontested legalities is generally agreed, and is well illustrated by Feature 10. But what should be done about it?

One attempt to correct the inconsistencies in U.S. divorce laws has been the 1970 California law abolishing divorce. Replacing divorce with "dissolution," the

> legislature did far more than create a new name for termination of marriage. It also eliminated all fault-related grounds, such as adultery and extreme cruelty, and in their place substituted a no-fault standard, "irreconcilable differences, which have caused the irremediable breakdown of the marriage."[76]

Since the passage of the law, most lawyers have, very simply, assumed that irreconcilable differences exist if one or both spouses say they do. What has

---

[73] Clifford Kirkpatrick, *The Family as Process and Institution* (New York: Ronald Press, 1955 ed.), p. 547.
[74] Wheeler, *No-Fault Divorce*, p. 17.
[75] Wheeler, *No-Fault Divorce*, p. 8.
[76] Wheeler, *No-Fault Divorce*, p. 19.

been the effect of the "no-fault" statute upon the divorce rate in California? In 1970 the number of marital dissolutions jumped 46 percent. The figure dipped slightly in 1971, but it has headed back up since then, so that at present one out of five U.S. divorces takes place in California.[77]

Unquestionably, there are problems with the California law. One, which had been pointed out even before the law was passed, is the need for a family court to act as arbiter and counselor to would-be divorcees. Another is that the thorny issues of property settlement and child custody have not been resolved by the law.[78] Yet Wheeler feels that the law is a step in the right direction, a step toward consistency:

> So long as it is easier to get a marriage license than it is to get a driver's license, a high frequency of marital problems is inevitable. If we choose not to change our marriage laws, then our divorce statutes ought to reflect marriage as it really is, not as it ideally might be.[79]

---

[77] Wheeler, *No-Fault Divorce*, p. 27.
[78] Wendell H. Goddard, "A Report on California's New Divorce Law: Progress and Problems," *Family Law Quarterly* 6 (1972), 415–21.
[79] Wheeler, *No-Fault Divorce*, p. 49.

FEATURE 10

Ralph and Eva McNulty had been married twenty-three years, none of which had been happy. Both drank too much and they often fought. Occasionally they had come to blows. Eva suspected her husband of being unfaithful, and once she had attempted suicide. The McNulty marriage, which had always been precarious, broke down completely after Ralph was convicted of committing incest with their thirteen-year-old daughter. His sentence, three to four years of hard labor, was not particularly severe, since he might also have been tried for statutory rape and criminal adultery. While Ralph was in prison, Eva sought a divorce in Suffolk County (Massachusetts) Probate Court on the ground of cruel and abusive treatment. Ralph contested it because he was afraid that if it were granted, Eva would get sole title to their three-family house as a property settlement.

The trial judge denied Mrs. McNulty's petition for divorce. She appealed her case to Massachusetts' highest court. It upheld the denial, ruling that incest with the daughter was not cruel or abusive to the wife, in either a physical or emotional sense. Furthermore, the court declined to grant a divorce on the basis of adultery—even though the facts clearly warranted it—because adultery had not been alleged as a ground, though it was implicit in the facts. Since Eva McNulty had not requested a divorce based specifically on adultery, the court would not volunteer to give her one. Its decision may seem Victorian, both in its through-the-looking-glass logic and its apparent distaste for divorce, yet it was handed down in 1956 and has not been overruled since then.

Michael Wheeler, *No-Fault Divorce* (Boston: Beacon Press, 1974), pp. 2–3.

Several states besides California are currently trying some version of no-fault divorce,[80] but, as Freed and Foster noted, most states have been slow to change.

Legal obstacles are but one cause of strain in divorce. A second factor increasing the strain involves the expectations and intensity that characterize the U.S. family. We tend to expect love, understanding, happiness, and companionship in our marriages. Lincoln Day, comparing Australian and U.S. marriages, finds that the Australian male, far more than his American counterpart, "appears to obtain his recreation in the company of other men." In "mateship" Australian husbands find

> many of the satisfactions that a society characterized by more companionable marriages would expect them to obtain primarily in the company of their wives. . . . Compared with American couples, the Australian husband and wife seem to share fewer activities and to participate less often in joint decision-making.[81]

The results are, thus, higher marital expectations on the part of the U.S. couple, greater emotional intensity invested in the marriage, more opportunities for friction due to interaction, and, finally, a greater sense of personal failure if the marriage goes wrong. As has been pointed out, we have not moved in U.S. society to universal, permanent availability, but only as far in that direction as the companionship and neo-traditional family—that is, the family based on psychological involvement, adjustment, love, and a partial sharing of roles. Therefore, the damage to that adjustment and the death of that love which are indicated by divorce are regarded as signs of one's failure, of one's inability to live up to current expectations for the family, that is, the happiness of its members.

In addition to the difficulties generated by archaic divorce laws and the sense of personal and corporate failure fostered by the norms of our family system, a third factor intensifies the strain of contemporary divorce. An increased divorce rate is a fairly recent phenomenon. Thus, the U.S. family system has not yet developed institutionalized supports for the individual going through this process. In fact, remarriage following divorce has been institutionalized in U.S. society more fully than has the divorce process itself. Not only is the legal aspect of the process complex and confusing, but the friends and kin of a divorcing couple are unlikely to be highly supportive while the process is running its course. Burgess and Locke indicate the problem thus: "In our society divorced persons are presented with no

---

[80] Wheeler, *No-Fault Divorce,* includes a chapter on the other states with no-fault laws.

[81] Lincoln H. Day, "Patterns of Divorce in Australia and the United States," *American Sociological Review* 29 (1964), 521.

socially sanctioned means of adjustment such as those available to the bereaved."[82] It may not, of course, be feasible to develop a divorce ritual
similar to that surrounding death; yet it is significant that, while the frontier
of death has been slowly receding, the rate of premature marital breakup
by divorce has gradually risen. Thus, the mechanisms for coping with the
more frequent basis for premature marital breakup—that is, divorce—are not
as institutionalized and supportive to the people involved as are the mechanisms surrounding premature death.

Three factors, in summary, which make divorce more of a personal and
social problem in the United States than it might otherwise be are: outmoded laws, the psychological intensity and expectations that U.S. family
life entails, and the lack of institutionalized means for coping with the
divorce process. Those who feel that the individual should be embedded
in the nuclear family and serve its needs, assert that to lessen the strains by
simplifying the laws and institutionalizing emotional support for the divorce
is to invite more divorces. The strains, it is argued, are "functional" for
keeping down the rate of divorce. The individualistically oriented, on the
other hand, feel that divorce is a valuable safety valve for the U.S. family
system, and should be made as personally painless as possible. Regardless of
one's value position, there are signs that changes in the law, along the lines
taken in California, are the wave of the future—but when or how (or
whether) the other strains will be reduced is highly problematic.

Death and the Family

Even in the 1960s, approximately two marriages were terminated by death
for every marriage that ended in a divorce. However, if statistical analysis is
restricted to those marriages that are *prematurely* terminated by death or
divorce, for example, during the first twenty-five years of marriage, the ratio
is much smaller. Traditionally, the response to death has been supportive of
the bereaved in two ways. First, the institutionalized death ritual seeks to
help the individual *face the fact* of death. This is extremely important in
working through the grief process. The child, for example, who is allowed
to retain fantasies about the eventual return of a deceased father, may be
in for serious mental difficulties. Granted, there has been a substantial furor
in recent years over whether the removal of the critically ill from the home
and current U.S. funeral practices are helpful or harmful to the individual in
facing and admitting the death of a loved one. Nevertheless, the unmistak-
able finality of death is one of the points of greatest distinction between
death and divorce: "We are divorced now" is considerably less convincing

[82] Burgess, Locke, and Thomes, *The Family*, p. 462.

than "He is dead now"; as Paul Bohannon puts it, in divorce she becomes your "ex-wife," not your "non-wife." This distinction is particularly obvious when the ex-spouse remains nearby and interacts from time to time with the children.[83] In other words, working through the bereavement caused by divorce is more difficult than working through the bereavement caused by death.

A second difference between the responses to death and divorce is that friends and kin rally to the support of the individual bereaved by death. Both material and emotional support may be forthcoming in the event of death, while the effect of a divorce may be alienation from the members of one's social network. Says Bohannon: "The divorce (like the marriage) devolves on the stability and organizing sense of the people concerned—everyone else is likely to stand back."[84] Burgess, Locke, and Thomes summarize these and other distinctions between the attitudes toward death and divorce as follows:

> In bereavement there is a tendency to concentrate on the best traits of the departed and to give assistance to the survivors; in divorce there is a tendency to condemn the defects of one or both spouses, and possibly ostracize those involved. In bereavement the individual secures comfort and group support by the rallying around of his friends and relatives; the divorced may be confronted with gossip, unfriendliness, and the taking of sides by relatives. In bereavement it is expected that the normal person will show some signs of emotional disturbance; a divorced person who shows signs of emotional disturbance is given little consideration—in fact, he may be thought of as emotionally unbalanced. . . . In bereavement, catharsis is secured through participation in religious ceremonies; the divorced may experience an increase in emotional disturbance through the necessity of resorting to legal advice and court procedures.[85]

A third aspect of the resolution of premature death in a family is that a long period of institutionalized mourning is no longer expected to follow the death of a young parent. Instead, the remarriage of the remaining parent or spouse is accepted within a reasonably short period of time following the bereavement. This is, of course, the point of greatest similarity between responses to death and divorce.

The death of a young child or parent is less common and, therefore, more likely to be traumatic than was the case in the past. The trauma may

---

[83] On this, see Goode, *After Divorce*, chap. 20; see also Hyman Rodman's brief summary of Willard Waller's *The Old Love and the New* (Carbondale: Southern Illinois University Press, 1967) in Rodman, *Marriage, Family and Society: A Reader* (New York: Random House, 1965), p. 91; and Bohannon, *Divorce and After*, p. 283.

[84] Bohannon, *Divorce and After*, p. 286.

[85] Burgess, Locke, and Thomes, *The Family*, p. 468.

be greater in those instances in which the support of friends and kin is largely verbal and short-lived.[86] Ideally, however, society has devised a basic resolution consisting of assistance to the individual in facing or admitting the loss; support from one's social network; and, in the case of the death of a young parent, renewed courtship and remarriage for the remaining spouse.

Section Three

CONCLUSIONS

In a totally non–personnel-embedded, or individualistic, family system, deviance would cause no family crisis, and divorce and death would cause relatively little grief. But the U.S. family is characterized by strong bonds and frequently by strong norms as well. The embeddedness of individuals in the nuclear family has not yielded to individualistic pressures, with the result that the strains caused by many of the changes and challenges to which we have referred in this chapter are often devastating. Even divorce is neither as prevalent nor as nonchalantly confronted as the pessimists and conservatives of the early twentieth century predicted it would be.

Having said this, we must add that the concern today for personhood, individual adjustment, and psychological needs is resulting in a rethinking of the outmoded divorce laws of the United States. In addition, many people—old as well as young—are either advocating or experimenting with alternatives to the family. Each of these alternatives is meant to solve some problem or inconsistency in the typical family unit, and is aimed at meeting the needs of individuals. How do these alternatives relate to the future of the family? That is the subject of our closing chapter.

---

[86] For an interesting and insightful discussion of the problems of adjustment to widowhood, see Peter Marris, *Widows and Their Families* (London: Routledge and Kegan Paul, 1958).

Alternatives and the Future of the Family

The family in the United States provides affective ties for the individual, plays a direction-giving role in the socialization process, and constitutes the prime market for the economic system. Inconsistencies in and varieties of U.S. family experience are constantly in evidence. On each of the five continua presented in Chapter 5, the U.S. family is at present between the two extremes. But what of the direction and speed of change in the future? This will depend in part on the extent to which the alternatives to the traditional family now being proposed become legitimated. These alternatives include: (1) those outside and parallel, *such as the arrangement; (2) those* incorporable *into the contemporary family, such as "open marriage"; and (3) those* over against *or instead of the family, such as the commune. We close with the question: Will the family survive these alternatives?*

The first step in peering into the future would seem to be a brief review of where we have been. The family is characterized by both happiness and unhappiness. It is the cradle of love and of violence. It evokes feelings of unity and struggles for individuality. A large proportion of the U.S. population are getting married, but many are getting divorced or are experimenting with alternatives. It is this social unit, with its functions and inconsistencies, its ideal-type and its reality, that we shall now review.

Some aspects of the U.S. family system have either appeared for the first time or have increased in prevalence during the twentieth century, but have not yet produced institutionalized sets of expectations. Examples are the aged, the divorce process, and, to some extent, the dating system. Other aspects of the family were once institutionalized but have lost some of their predetermined character and are thus more open to individual choice. The best example of these aspects is marital-parental roles, especially in the middle-class family. In reviewing the characteristics of the contemporary family in the United States, it would seem profitable to employ as our bases for review the frameworks and continua developed in Chapter 5.

Section One

THE CONTEMPORARY U.S. FAMILY: A REVIEW

There are many kinds of family-kin systems in the world; the U.S. system is but one of them. It is impossible to assert that one type of family system is inherently "better" than the others, unless one is willing to go on and point out the ways in which that particular system functions to solve problems for both the individual and the society, and the ways in which it avoids strains and inconsistencies. This book has been but a case study—a look at the inconsistencies and functions that characterize one family system: that of the United States. It will be for others to ask the comparative value question of "goodness of fit."[1]

We have seen repeatedly that the family in the United States performs an important function in providing *affective* or primary relationship ties for its members. In the middle-class family, those ties are likely to be quite intense within the nuclear family, but not to extend very far out into the kin network, while in the families of the working and lower classes, the burden of love and understanding is more often shared by other kin as well. The same holds for the direction-giving function played by the family in *socialization:* much socialization takes place outside the U.S. home, but it is in the nuclear family that the individual acquires his cultural orientation, reinforced or contradicted by extrafamilial influences. Lower- and working-class children are somewhat more likely than are middle-class children to be influenced considerably by other members of the social network as well as by parents and siblings. Thus, affection and direction, or strong bonds and norms, are produced by family experience, and may be viewed as important aspects of the family's functioning in contemporary U.S. society.

The economic system and values of U.S. society are also related in a crucial way to the nuclear family. This unit seldom operates as a productive segment of the economy, but it does serve as a basic *consumer* of the goods of the market. Thus, it is not unexpected that the larger society would stress

---

[1] Functionalists, among them Talcott Parsons, have often written to show how well particular characteristics of U.S. family and kin behavior fit that society's needs. Three good examples are: Parsons, "The Kinship System of the Contemporary United States," *American Anthropologist* 45 (1943), 22–38; Parsons and Renee C. Fox, "Illness, Therapy, and the Modern Urban American Family," *Journal of Social Issues* 13 (1952), 31–44; and Elaine Cumming and William Henry, *Growing Old: The Process of Disengagement* (New York: Basic Books, 1961).

simultaneously the easing of divorce restrictions and the desirability of marriage and a family, for "the happy family is a 'consuming' family." The high rates of divorce and marriage are quite consistent with the needs of the U.S. economic system and the materialistic values fostered thereby.

In the course of time, the various parts of any given social system do not change at the same rate of speed or with the same degree of completeness. The result is that the same subsystem, such as the U.S. family, is simultaneously characterized by integration into the larger society and by inconsistencies and fragmentary changes. Such *inconsistencies,* notably in the middle-class family, have been quite apparent in the present volume. They include the following: (1) The U.S. family, particularly its middle-class variety, is currently walking a difficult line between stress on ego struggle and on conformity; parents teach the child to adapt and to assert his uniqueness, but also to comply with the strong family norms referred to above. That is, the family's attempt to "orderly replace" its culture in its offspring is somewhat inconsistent with the heterogeneous nature of the norms that the growing individual is likely to confront by the time he reaches adulthood. This is the socialization locus of the current struggle between individualism and nuclear family personnel embeddedness. (2) Young people are maturing earlier—in their awareness and even physiologically—and are, at the same time, being kept out of adult society longer than ever. Middle- and working-class young people are faced with other inconsistencies or fragmentary changes as well, such as the freedom from pregnancy fears accompanied by a still-substantial invocation of sexual absolutes by adults. One result of this inconsistency has been a considerable spread of "the arrangement," or living together prior to marriage, which we will discuss later. (3) In marriage, there is role choice without sexual equality. This is a partial change, leaving the wife's economic role and the husband's domestic role as supportive. One might say that having a door halfway open is more tension-producing than having it shut or all the way open—and thus it is with marital roles. The alternatives proposed by women's and men's liberation, and by what the Osofskys call "androgyny," are attempts to reconcile the current inconsistencies—to take the shift in roles all the way to equality or interchangeability. (4) In kinship relations, the norms of independence from parents and filial obligation often run at cross-purposes, serving to increase the ambivalence of such kin toward one another. (5) Divorce laws are inconsistent with attitudes toward and causes of marital breakup. While the grounds for divorce have multiplied, the "fault" system still predominates. There is no positive or supportive ritual through which the divorcing couple passes. It may be neither advisable nor possible to resolve all the inconsistencies within the U.S. family system. Yet it seems to the present author that the resolution of some of them would aid the individual, in both his intrapersonal and his interpersonal—especially his family —adjustments.

The *varieties* of U.S. families were the specific subject of Chapter 5, and differences between middle-, working-, and lower-class families in the United States have been referred to in virtually every chapter. The racial and ethnic subsocieties, dealt with principally in Chapter 6, mirror primarily the culture of the other families in the society which are of the same socio-economic level. There is, however, some cultural distinctiveness based on differences in traditions; in the case of the black family this distinctiveness is based on survival mechanisms against both prejudice and discrimination, such as extended kin ties, as well as on a current stress on ethnicity. It is worth noting that middle-class and working-class blacks seem to be concerned with the dominant forms of respectability and morality as much as or more than white families of the same social status are, since such blacks must continually seek to overcome the distorted white stereotype regarding behavior in the black community, while simultaneously and rightly demonstrating their concern with black cultural uniqueness and values. Thus, the U.S. family system includes diversity, inconsistency, and several important functions that it performs for the individual and the society.

In Chapter 5, five continua were presented upon which the characteristics of the U.S. family might be located. These continua pertain to mate selection, socialization, marital roles, institutional embeddedness, and personnel embeddedness. Each of the continua is, of course, a complex of variables; locating the contemporary U.S. family upon the continua is accomplished only by reducing its variations to zero. Thus, heeding the proper cautions regarding oversimplification, these continua may be profitably employed to summarize many of the findings reported in the preceding pages (see Figure 15). (1) *Mate choices* in the United States are based on personal desires, but are restricted considerably by propinquity and the salient family values concerning such issues as religion and race. (2) *Socialization:* the individual is influenced by both familial and extrafamilial socializing agents, with the direction-giving influence of parents still substantial. (3) *Marital roles:* there is modified role choice in marriage. Certain options are available to both sexes, though aspects of the old patriarchy and the economic-familial division of labor by sex are still openly operative in the working and lower classes and subtly operative in the middle class. (4) *Institutional embeddedness:* other institutions have become highly differentiated from the kin group and the nuclear family. The latter still specializes in primary relations, socialization, and economic consumption, and sometimes in recreation and religion. (5) Nuclear family *personnel embeddedness* (with the individual interacting intensely with family members, while being subservient to the family's norms and needs) and individualism (with the family

Figure 15
**A Tentative Location of the Contemporary U.S. Family on Five Ideal-Typical
Continua Concerning the Family and Its Characteristics**

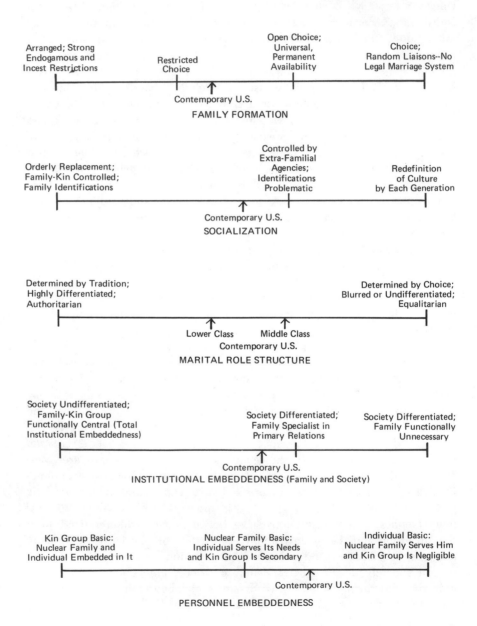

serving the individual's need for personality development and uniqueness) are currently vying for value ascendancy in U.S. society, with the kin network playing a supportive role in the background.

This, then, is what the family is expected to be, and how it is functioning currently in U.S. society. Its inconsistencies and its "midstream" position with regard to several changes have given rise to an increasing amount of experimentation with alternative ways of meeting people's needs. These alternatives are the subject of Section Two.

Section Two

ALTERNATIVE LIFE STYLES IN THE 1970s[2]

Three major types of alternatives to the family are currently being either experimented with or proposed. First, there are alternatives which are *outside* the family and *parallel* it. Since such alternatives do not challenge the family directly, they may be little threat to it. Second, there are alternatives which are *incorporable into* the family, which are meant to alter certain problematic aspects of family behavior without abandoning its basic nuclear structure. Third, there are alternatives *to,* or *over against,* today's family. We shall examine each of these types in turn.

Parallel Alternatives

The alternatives which are outside the family and parallel it are primarily concerned with the premarital—and, in some cases, the postmarital—period. The *arrangement,* or the nonlegalized heterosexual domestic unit, is the prime example, with the number of college students who try it apparently increasing each year. The research that has been done thus far on the arrangement shows that the combination of the birth control pill and the decrease in the attempt by colleges to play an in loco parentis role for their students have contributed to its spread. In addition, the arrangement is a result of the individual-adjustment and "do your own thing" orientations which were discussed in Chapter 9. In a small-sample study of students who had lived in arrangements, conducted by Eleanor Macklin at Cornell University, the majority of students indicated that if a couple had a strong affectionate relation and were not dating anyone else, living together was

---

[2] Much of the following discussion is adapted and expanded from Bert N. Adams, "Can the Family Survive Alternative Life Styles?" *Forum* (November 2, 1973), 4–8.

perfectly all right.[3] Those who had actually lived together indicated that the principal problems were of four types: loss of identity and a lessening of school activity; the feeling of being trapped or used due to the lack of a total mutual commitment; sexual maladjustment; and trouble with parents. However, it is important to note that almost all the students who had been participants in an arrangement felt that in terms of personal growth its benefits outweighed its drawbacks.[4] A majority even reported that their parents had learned to accept what they were doing. One-third of Macklin's sample had broken off their relationship with their partners, their arrangements having lasted, on average, about four and a half months; one-third had participated in arrangements that eventuated in marriage; and one-third were in the process of redefining their arrangement relationship.

Judith Lyness, Milton Lipetz, and Keith Davis, who studied the arrangement in Boulder, Colorado, noted the lesser commitment to marriage of those living together as compared to those simply going together. They further found that, while living-together men were more satisfied with their sexual adjustments than were going-together men, their greater satisfaction was unrelated to other aspects of the relationship, such as happiness and trust. The living-together man had less trust and respect for the woman he lived with than did the going-together man for the woman he went with, and the living-together man was considerably less committed to marriage than was the living-together woman.[5] These findings signify that many male participants in arrangements still hold to a Victorian mentality, and look with some disfavor on their female partners because they have entered into such a relationship. The result, then, is that at present the arrangement appears to be a learning and growing experience, but labors under the social and psychological stigmata which are still a part of many people's cultural heritage. Furthermore, most young people who participate in the arrangement see it, not as an alternative to marriage, but as an interim expedient.

Another expression of the parallel alternative is Margaret Mead's *"individualized"* marriage, which she distinguishes from what she calls the "parental" marriage.[6] The individualized marriage is a contract which would allow for experimentation prior to the conventional child-rearing marriage, but would entail a greater amount of commitment than does the arrange-

---

[3] Eleanor D. Macklin, "Heterosexual Cohabitation Among Unmarried College Students," *Family Life Coordinator* 21 (1972), 467.

[4] Macklin, "Heterosexual Cohabitation Among Unmarried College Students," pp. 468–69.

[5] Judith L. Lyness, Milton E. Lipetz, and Keith E. Davis, "Living Together: An Alternative to Marriage," *Journal of Marriage and the Family* 34 (1972), 305–11.

[6] Margaret Mead, "Marriage in Two Steps," in Herbert A. Otto, ed., *The Family in Search of a Future* (New York: Appleton-Century-Crofts, 1970), pp. 75–84.

ment. Still another parallel alternative is living together as a permanent arrangement, a choice which has received its strongest support from divorcees. However, this will be discussed under "remaining single" as an alternative to marriage itself.

Incorporable Alternatives

The *content* of marriage could be changed in many ways without directly tampering with its structure. First, the continuing *change in sex roles* could be carried to its logical extreme, that is, males and females could be freed from traditional sex-role definitions to be and do what is fulfilling for them. The androgynous society, say Joy and Howard Osofsky, will be a society with no sex-role differentiation. They do not mean by this that everybody will behave in the same way and carry out the same roles; what they mean is that the hereditary differences of individuals and the differences in their socially acquired interests will be given full freedom of expression. Some couples may live in accordance with the old sex roles, but others may choose to live by a precisely opposite model.[7] The androgynous alternative will require much social engineering, and many aspects of the necessary changes have already been referred to in Chapters 7, 11, and 12.

A second alternative which has been proposed to improve today's marriage is what Sidney Jourard calls the *"reinvented marriage."* Jourard feels that multiple arrangements within the same marriage might help keep marital interest alive. Perhaps the couple—even while on good terms—should live apart for a while just to rekindle their desire for each other. From time to time the children might be sent away, so as to facilitate the recapture of the "honeymoon feeling."[8] This, incidentally, should not be held off until the children are grown and gone—by that time it may be too late! Taken by itself, reinvented marriage is, of course, hardly a panacea for marital difficulties, but taken in conjunction with role freedom and other alternatives, it could have a salutary effect.

The resurrection of the *intimate network* has been proposed by a number of writers. It is not sufficient, they feel, to refurbish the marriage itself. What is needed are other intimate individuals with whom to share the nuclear family's excessive emotional load. Frederick Stoller, for example, believes that it would be possible to intensify compatible neighborhood ties, so that sharing could take place in all areas but sex. One of the great

---

[7] Joy D. Osofsky and Howard J. Osofsky, "Androgyny as a Life Style," *Family Life Coordinator* 21 (1972), 411–18.

[8] Sidney M. Jourard, "Reinventing Marriage: The Perspective of a Psychologist," in Otto, *The Family in Search of a Future*, pp. 47–49.

lacks of the contemporary family, he feels, is people with whom to communicate more than surface concerns.[9] The privacy of the nuclear family is also a lack, making for the violence and frustration discussed in Chapter 15. This, then, would be a pseudokin network consisting of neighbors and friends. A similar proposal by Sylvia Clavan and Ethel Vatter calls for linking a nuclear family with an elderly couple in a pseudograndparental relationship. This "affiliated family" unit would meet the needs of children for contact with the elderly, of adults for communication and the sharing of responsibilities, and of the aged for meaningful interaction with a family unit.[10] Some church groups have been trying to implement this suggestion—with some success.

The final alternative which could be incorporated into the existing family structure is *extramarital sex*. One theologian, for example, has argued that it might be possible to redefine marriage, not in terms of sexual exclusiveness, but in terms of dialogue or communication—for, after all, language is distinctively human; sexual intercourse is not.[11] Alex Comfort, in Feature 11, argues that "open sex" will be the norm in the future.

Sexual affairs are either short-term or long-term, fleeting or regular. The fleeting affair may be with a prostitute, a stranger, or an acquaintance, the last being the least frequent type. Prostitution is currently diminishing, while sexual contact with a stranger—which is most likely to occur when the individuals involved are away from home—is becoming more prevalent.[12] A fleeting affair with a person one already knows can be particularly troublesome, affecting either the marriage, or the mutual relationship between the acquaintances, or both.

Long-term extramarital affairs are also primarily of three kinds—the sexual liaison, the "other wife," and spouse swapping or group sex.[13] The sexual liaison may be based on a special meeting time and place, and lasts for varying periods of time. When one speaks of "having an affair," this is usually what is meant. Having a second wife is a much less frequent phenomenon, and involves supporting two different domestic units, usually with only one based on a legal marriage. In some instances each "wife" knows about the other, while in others only the nonlegal spouse knows

---

[9] Frederick H. Stoller, "The Intimate Network of Families as a New Structure," in Otto, *The Family in Search of a Future*, pp. 145–60.

[10] Sylvia Clavan and Ethel Vatter, "The Affiliated Family: A Continued Analysis," *Family Life Coordinator* 21 (1972), 499–504.

[11] Edward C. Hobbs, "An Alternative Model from a Theological Perspective," in Otto, *The Family in Search of a Future*, p. 39.

[12] On this, see Gerhard Neubeck, *Extra-Marital Relations* (Englewood Cliffs, N.J.: Prentice-Hall, 1968), pp. 4, 36; and Paul Kinsie, "Her Honor Pushes Legalized Prostitution," *Social Health News* (February 1967).

[13] Robert R. Bell and Michael Gordon, eds., *The Social Dimension of Human Sexuality* (Boston: Little, Brown, 1972), pp. 120, 126, 130–43.

that there are two households. The third type of long-term extramarital sex contact—and the one receiving the most attention today—is spouse swapping, or swinging. This is primarily a middle-class phenomenon, and often involves couples who strive to maintain "respectability," in middle-class terms, in the nonsexual areas of their lives, but are seeking fresh experience, relief from boredom, and recreation. They try to work out the "ground rules" of spouse swapping carefully, so that it will in no way damage their primary commitment to each other.[14] While Duane Denfeld and Michael Gordon see swinging as a substantial move toward the single standard and toward sexual freedom for women, Anne-Marie Henshel points out that it is generally the husband who brings a couple into a swapping club.[15] This,

---

[14] Among the many studies on swapping and swinging, see Duane Denfeld and Michael Gordon, "The Sociology of Mate Swapping: Or the Family That Swings Together Clings Together," *Journal of Sex Research* 6 (1971), 85–100; Mary Lindenstein Walshok, "The Emergence of Middle-Class Deviant Subcultures: The Case of Swingers," *Social Problems* 18 (1971), 488–95; Richard M. Stephenson, "Involvement in Deviance: An Example and Some Theoretical Implications," *Social Problems* 21 (1973), 173–90; Charles A. Varni, "An Exploratory Study of Spouse-Swapping," *Pacific Sociological Review* 15 (1972), 507–22; and Gilbert D. Bartell, "Group Sex Among the Mid-Americans, *Journal of Sex Research* 6 (1970), 113–30.

[15] Denfeld and Gordon, "The Sociology of Mate Swapping," pp. 92–93, 98; and Anne-Marie Henshel, "Swinging: A Study of Decision Making in Marriage," *American Journal of Sociology* 78 (1973), 885–91.

FEATURE 11

Friendship, more than kinship, will underlie future human relations, and tomorrow's couples will engage openly in sexual relations with friends and other couples, says a British biologist and medical researcher.

In an article entitled "Sexuality in a Zero Growth Society" in the December issue of Center Report, Dr. Alexander Comfort says today's trend toward swinging "marks the end, or the beginning of the end, of proprietary sexual attitudes."

Mate sharing, says Comfort, is a "realistic view of the needs of couples and individuals for variety" and a "recognition that the meeting of needs rather than their frustration is a gift which expresses love . . . and strengthens the primary bond."

Comfort says he expects "to see a society in which pair relationships are still central but initially less permanent, in which child-bearing is seen as a special responsibility involving a special life style and in which settled couples engage openly in a wide range of sexual relations with friends, with other couples and with third parties as an expression of social intimacy, without prejudice to the primacy of their own relationship."

The old have been increasingly isolated by the decline of the kinship family, says Comfort, and would benefit the most from "a 'spreading' of the couple-preoccupied family into something like a tribe of friends.

"We are not here talking about change which we can further or prevent, simply about changes which are now taking place."

"Tomorrow's Couples Will Have Open Sex," *Capital Times*, Madison, Wisconsin, December 11, 1972.

she feels, indicates that now, as before, males dominate in the sexual sphere and are the decision-makers when a couple embark on this form of middle-class deviance.[16]

What are the effects of swinging on the couples involved? Here, as in the case of most of the experimental alternatives, they may be positive or negative. Charles Varni, for example, says the "most often reported effect of swinging (by eight couples) was an increased feeling of warmth, closeness, and love between the husband and wife."[17] His couples reported greater honesty and openness with each other as a result of swinging. The sharing of a new interest, "which can be explored, observed, and discussed between themselves," is a positive function noted by Gilbert Bartell's informants.[18] However, these authors find that jealousy is an ever-present possibility, as is contact with couples and individuals who have sexual hang-ups. In fact, swinging may be a means of discovering one's own hang-ups, without providing a sure means of overcoming them. Likewise, the swinger may not be able to live up to his sexual myths and illusions, the result being frustration rather than satisfaction.[19]

According to the Kinsey reports, by the age of forty 26 percent of U.S. females and 50 percent of U.S. males have had extramarital intercourse. Most of the extramarital experiences recorded by Kinsey and his associates were fleeting or sporadic, and usually both of the persons involved were married. The reason for this is that such relationships must have no hint of commitment in them. The same holds for middle-class swinging, which, with its rules of propriety and mutuality on the part of couples, seeks to avoid anything that would be defined as "cheating." How many swingers are there? The Breedloves concluded that in 1964 two-and-a-half million U.S. couples exchanged partners more or less regularly. This was around 5 percent of the country's married couples.[20] Recent figures are unavailable, but it seems reasonable to assume that—if the Breedloves were correct for 1964—the proportion should be higher today.

An alternative which to a great extent encompasses all the alternatives that could be incorporated into marriage is what the O'Neills call *open marriage.* This means seeing marriage as an open system, in which the couple members do not lose their separate identities, but rather work together to accomplish both personal and interpersonal growth. Such growth may be furthered by all sorts of nonconformity to traditional ways, in-

---

[16] Denfeld and Gordon, "The Sociology of Mate Swapping," pp. 92–93, 98; and Henshel, "Swinging," pp. 885–91.
[17] Varni, "An Exploratory Study of Spouse-Swapping," pp. 518–19.
[18] Bartell, "Group Sex Among the Mid-Americans," p. 527.
[19] Varni, "An Exploratory Study of Spouse-Swapping," p. 512; and Bartell, "Group Sex Among the Mid-Americans," p. 528.
[20] William and Jerrye Breedlove, *Swap Clubs* (Los Angeles: Sherbourne Press, 1964).

cluding the role freedom and sexual freedom mentioned above. As an open system, then, marriage must be based on mutual commitment, but not of the exclusive sort that can make, and has made, marriage a prison for many people.[21] It is apparent that open marriage and the other alternatives discussed in this section are all oriented in some way toward increasing personhood or individual fulfillment, while continuing a certain amount of embeddedness of the individual in the nuclear family. We turn now to those alternatives that question nuclear family embeddedness directly—its structure as well as its traditional content.

Alternatives to the Family

When one introduces a discussion of "Alternative Life Styles," it is usually alternatives of this third type, namely, alternatives to the family, that come to mind. A frequently mentioned example is the commune. However, often ignored in such analyses of alternatives to the family is *remaining single,* with or without children. Traditional societal values are still such that the single individual is likely to be accused of one or a combination of the following: being undesirable, frigid, celibate, promiscuous, homosexual, or a mama's boy (or daddy's girl). However, this negative attitude seems to be changing. Rosalyn Moran points out that in 1971 there were 41 million single adults in the United States, of whom 15½ million males and 12½ million females had never been married. She feels that the social position of these singles is changing rapidly:

> A single person is a human being with drives and desires like everyone else. Before, he had to sublimate some of these desires in order to conform with society. Today, society has made a place for him, albeit a lesser role for the single female. Now, there is a choice for all. How one chooses is a strictly personal thing: and that, after all, is the way it should be.[22]

Moran is correct at some points and given to hyperbole at others. Clearly, the single female is still at a disadvantage, often being treated as little better than chattel. The result is that females are more locked into the marriage system than are males. Formerly, in most cases the single person did not, however, have to sublimate sexual interests. Rather, he or she had to get married. And even today free personal choice is more a future

---

[21] Nena O'Neill and George O'Neill, "Open Marriage: A Synergic Model," *Family Life Coordinator* 21 (1972), 403–9; and O'Neill and O'Neill, *Open Marriage* (New York: M. Evans, 1972).

[22] Rosalyn Moran, "The Singles in the Seventies," in Joann S. DeLora and Jack R. DeLora, eds., *Intimate Life Styles: Marriage and Its Alternatives* (Pacific Palisades, Calif.: Goodyear, 1972), pp. 338, 344.

goal than a reality. As Moran herself reports, many of the singles clubs, like those for divorcees, are primarily dating and mating organizations.[23] Further changes will have to be effected before remaining single can be considered a true cultural alternative to marriage.

We have been speaking of unattached singles, not of single persons with children. The latter, however, have received far more attention than the former. Carole Klein, in *The Single Parent Experience,* and E. E. LeMasters, in *Parents in Modern America,* have shown that, while the one-parent household may be voluntary or involuntary in origin, it should not be automatically assumed that it is an abnormal setting for child rearing.[24] Some of these units are formed by the never-married, others by the divorced or deserted. Altogether there are about five million single-parent families in the United States, the majority of them headed by a mother.

Henry Biller reports that, in the absence of a father, mothers may overprotect, or the mother-child relationship may be very intense, but in any case it is the mother's ego strength and resourcefulness in child rearing that determine outcomes. Carmi Schooler adds that, while there are signs of lesser intellectual development and a lesser sense of well-being among children raised in father-absent homes, the overall negative effects seem small and do not influence individuation.[25] After reviewing the literature in search of what he calls "pathological effects" of single parenthood, LeMasters concludes that "one *good* parent is enough to rear children adequately or better in our society."[26] However, if there is pressure on the single individual to get married, there is even more pressure on the single parent,[27] though finding a mate may be more difficult for the man or woman encumbered with children. Thus, while an increasing proportion of the U.S. population live as singles or as single parents at some point in their lives, remaining single still runs counter to the dominant nuclear family societal ethos.

Several redefinitions, not of the content of the marriage relationship, but of the *legal form of marriage* itself, are being proposed. Marriage could be redefined as a nonlegal voluntary association which lasts "for as long as we both shall love." Margaret Mead, as we have already mentioned, has proposed that a distinction be made between "individualized" and "parental" marriages, each of which would be bound by a different set of

---

[23] Moran, "The Singles in the Seventies," in DeLora and DeLora, *Intimate Life Styles,* pp. 338–39.

[24] Carole Klein, *The Single Parent Experience* (New York: Walker, 1973); and E. E. LeMasters, *Parents in Modern America* (Homewood, Ill.: Dorsey Press, 1970), pp. 157–75.

[25] Henry B. Biller, "The Mother-Child Relationship and the Father-Absent Boy's Personality Development," *Merrill-Palmer Quarterly* 17 (1971), 227–41; and Carmi Schooler, "Childhood Family Structure and Adult Characteristics," *Sociometry* 35 (1972), 255–69.

[26] LeMasters, *Parents in Modern America,* p. 167.

[27] Klein discusses pressures to get married in *The Single Parent Experience.*

legal and cultural obligations. A third way of redefining marriage is by means of the marriage contract, a method now being studied by Marvin Sussman and others. The contract may be renewable annually, or every three years, or may run until one signatory wants out. In any case the marriage contract ordinarily tries to build in a great amount of equality, and usually involves a definable period, after which the signatories must agree to continue. There is still some difficulty in making such contracts legally binding, since many states do not recognize them, but this has not kept them from proliferating.

An interesting proposal advanced by Victor Kassel suggests that longevity differences between the sexes in the U.S. society make *polygyny*, that is, one man and several wives, a logical alternative *after the age of sixty*.[28] This, he asserts, would solve some problems of the aged (discussed in Chapter 14) —loneliness, desolation at the loss of a spouse, being forgotten by a youth-oriented society.

The best known of the current alternatives to the nuclear family is the *commune*. There are many kinds of communes, ranging from the religious economy with sexual exclusiveness to forms of group marriage.[29] Some communes are primarily economic, with property held in common but with the responsibility for other aspects of life left to nuclear family units, which often include children. Other communes are political, their chief aim being some sort of revolutionary orientation, with other aspects of life subsidiary to that aim. Still others are noncreedal, their members' major concern being experience—perhaps with drugs, perhaps with sex—or the desire for intimacy, communication, and sharing with more than one other person. Many of these experiential communes, epitomized by the urban communes of the late 1960s, last but a short time. In fact, the average life of the urban commune is two years, and of the individual in it eight months. Two insightful comments by Joyce Gardener, one of the founders of Cold Mountain Farm, illustrate the problems of rural and urban communes alike:

> Slowly, all the stragglers had left—empty people who had come to fill themselves, sapping our energies, needing to be taken care of and giving nothing at all—and now there were only between four and six couples and a few single people left. . . . We didn't find a way of sharing our

---

[28] Victor Kassel, "Polygamy After Sixty," in Otto, *The Family in Search of a Future*, pp. 137–44.

[29] S. Levine et al., "The Urban Commune: Fact or Fad, Promise or Pipedream?" *American Journal of Orthopsychiatry* 43 (1973), 149–63; James W. Ramey, "Communes, Group Marriage, and the Upper-Middle Class," *Journal of Marriage and the Family* 34 (1972), 647–55; Bennett Berger, Bruce Hackett, and R. Mervyn Millar, "The Communal Family," *Family Life Coordinator* 21 (1972), 419–27; Sallie Teselle, ed., *The Family, Communes, and Utopian Societies* (New York: Harper & Row, Torchbooks, 1972); Rosabeth Kanter, "Communes," *Psychology Today* 4 (1970), 53–78.

visions . . . and we didn't have a shared vision to bring us and hold us together.[30]

The commune movement, then, is a quest for many things. It may be a quest for a revolutionary transformation of society, or for an economic alternative to capitalist accumulation, or for more meaningful relationships than the participants found in their own nuclear families, or for the healthful atmosphere that is absent in the suburbs as well as the cities, or for expanded experience. But, as Gardener points out, many communes fail to find what they are seeking. Sometimes the communes fail because their members have compounded their problems through interaction with others who are laboring under various difficulties. Sometimes the communes fail because their members try only to get but have nothing to give, the result often being, as in swinging, that the women are exploited by the men.[31] Sometimes the opposition of neighbors causes communes founded on weak commitment to fly apart. Sometimes communes fail because they lack a vision, a goal larger than themselves, to live and strive for. And thus the commune movement of the late '60s has subsided. The commune movement, however, has not died; only the superficial experiments have failed to survive. The promise of the ideal-type commune continues to give rise to new experiments, and there are sufficient successes to give proponents of the commune alternative continued hope.

Closely linked to the commune is *group* and *multilateral marriage*. Group marriage, say the Constantines, is primarily a living arrangement, while multilateral marriage is a family arrangement.[32] The multilateral marriage can include three-person marriages (of which the Constantines found only thirty-five examples), while group marriage classically means at least two of each sex. Group marriage, Albert Ellis feels, can combine the advantages of swinging with those of the intimate communication network.[33] Of course, in most states such units still lack the kind of legal acceptance which would change them from isolated experiments to an accepted alternative.

We have classified the alternative life styles into three major categories: those which parallel the nuclear family, those incorporable into it, and those opposed to it. Another way of classifying the alternatives we have analyzed

---

[30] Joyce Gardener, "Communal Living: Economic Survival and Family Life," in Gordon F. Streib, ed., *The Changing Family: Adaptation and Diversity* (Reading, Mass.: Addison-Wesley, 1973), pp. 117–18.

[31] Vivian Estellachild, "Hippie Communes," in DeLora and DeLora, *Intimate Life Styles,* pp. 332–37.

[32] Larry L. and Joan M. Constantine, "Group and Multilateral Marriage: Definitional Notes, Glossary, and Annotated Bibliography," *Family Process* 10 (1971), 157–76.

[33] Albert Ellis, "Group Marriage: A Possible Alternative?" in Streib, *The Changing Family,* pp. 81–86.

is into *experiential* and *programmatic* alternatives. By this we mean that some of them are currently being tried by considerable numbers of people, while others are basically in the proposal stage. In the former category are the arrangement, changing roles, extramarital sex, remaining single, and communes, and these are the alternatives to which we devoted the most attention in the foregoing discussion. In the light of these alternatives, we now face two final questions: What is the future of the nuclear family? Will the family survive the alternative life styles?

Section Three

FUTURE PROSPECTS FOR THE U.S. FAMILY

During the 1930s and 1940s, Carle Zimmerman, Pitirim A. Sorokin, and others analyzed the changes that had occurred in the U.S. family since the nineteenth century, and concluded that its future was one of *disintegration.* Zimmerman summarized such predictions in 1949:

> The influence of these gradual developments during several centuries, and the recent upheavals, have given us a plethora of unusual family behavior in recent years. Some persons see these changes as "progress," or the breaking through toward a new and more interesting family system. Others, including the writer, look upon it as a polarization of values typical of the breakdown of a family system....
> We must look upon the present confusion of family values as the beginning of violent breaking up of a system. The mores or social forces present when it rose to power now no longer exist. Negative polarization is here because the crisis is at hand.[34]

Just as Vance Packard speaks of changes in the sexual sphere as a "wilderness," and other authors describe today's marital role choices as "problems," "predicaments," or "dilemmas," so these earlier authors were convinced that changes in the nineteenth and twentieth centuries were negative in their import and signaled the disintegration of the family as we know it.

In the mid-1940s, Ernest Burgess and Harvey Locke responded to these dire predictions by asserting that the U.S. family was not disintegrating, but was *reorganizing* with characteristics that approximate the companionship family. "Family reorganization," the authors claimed,

---

[34] Carle C. Zimmerman, *The Family of Tomorrow* (New York: Harper and Brothers, 1949), pp. 200–210; see also Zimmerman, *Family and Civilization* (New York: Harper and Brothers, 1947); and Pitirim A. Sorokin, *Social and Cultural Dynamics,* 4 vols. (New York: American Book, 1937).

may be considered in its two aspects: (1) the checking of tendencies to disorganization in the individual family and its reshaping through the redefining of attitudes and values of the husband and wife and parents and children; and (2) the development in society of a new conception of the family which its members individually and collectively attempt to realize.[35]

The family would stabilize, they felt, within twenty to thirty years, due to education, more security in the economy, and a slowing down of immigration and population increase. This meant that stability would be reached between 1965 and 1975. In addition, Burgess and Locke saw certain trends of the early 1940s as continuing into the future, among them: (1) a declining birthrate and smaller-sized families; (2) an increase in the proportion married among those of marriageable age; (3) a lowering of the age at marriage, coincident with family life education; (4) an increase in the employment of all women, including married women; and (5) a decline in the family's historic functions in favor of emotional functions, such as happiness and companionship.

For some twenty years, the twin themes of disintegration and reorganization held sway within the family literature. During the 1960s, however, several authors once again took up the themes of projection and prediction, with the former based on current statistical trends and the latter on an informed survey of societal changes and their significance for the family. One of the more insightful projections was effected by Robert Parke and Paul Glick, working with 1960 census data. They agreed with Burgess and Locke's projection of the proportion married, and continued it into the future; they found the age at marriage *increasing* and projected this too; and they found family size small and likely to remain at about the current level. In addition, they projected other trends, such as the following:

> Over and above any general decline in mortality, the declines in the difference between the ages of the husband and wife will reduce the frequency of widowhood and increase the proportion of couples who survive jointly to retirement age.
> ... Declines in the relative frequency of divorce and separation should result to the extent that there are reductions in poverty and general improvements in the socioeconomic status of the population.[36]

While the projection of internal family trends performs a useful service for the student of the family, the more exciting and debatable predictions are a result of taking a holistic perspective and attempting to answer the

---

[35] Ernest Burgess and Harvey Locke, *The Family: From Institution to Companionship* (New York: American Book, 1945).

[36] Robert Parke, Jr., and Paul C. Glick, "Prospective Changes in Marriage and the Family," *Journal of Marriage and the Family* 29 (1967), 256.

question we have raised: Will the family survive the alternative life styles? Using the best evidence we can muster, we will pose three answers to this question, and will conclude with the writer's view of the probable outcome.

The first answer is: *Yes, the family will outlast the alternatives.* It will swallow up whichever of the first two types of alternatives, that is, those within and those parallel, seem workable. They will be added as the safety valves the family needs to retrench itself in a day of rapid change. This point is reminiscent of the turn-of-the-century debate concerning divorce. At the beginning of the twentieth century the radicals were saying that an increase in the flexibility of divorce laws would increase the divorce rate, thereby destroying the Victorian family—and that's good. The conservatives, concurrently, were saying that increasing the flexibility of divorce laws would increase the divorce rate, and thereby destroy the family—and that's bad. Both agreed on the outcome; they simply disagreed in their value positions. The fact is that both were wrong. Divorce merely became the safety valve which our family system needed at that time to "weed out the bad bets."[37]

In addition, the family will outlast the third group of alternatives, as long as they are just protests among a few disenchanted. As Rick Margolis[38] and Gardener have pointed out, communes are often formed by young people whose needs for understanding, love, and intimacy were unfulfilled within their nuclear families. They are seeking to resurrect a larger pseudokin network in the hopes of meeting those needs. It is no wonder that many such communes, consisting of young people who have brought their problems and bad experiences together in the new network, should fail grandly in a brief period. Likewise, swinging is frequently ineffective for growth because the parties involved have sexual hang-ups which inhibit them. Also, the family will outlast the alternatives as long as policymakers, lawmakers, moral leaders, and the helping professions continue to define the family as of intrinsic value and as worthy of perpetuation.[39] Such is likely to be a dominant orientation into the foreseeable future. Finally, as long as we are afraid of freedom, and are comfortable in our ruts, change will come slowly and painfully, if at all. Erich Fromm reminded us years ago how we escape from freedom,[40] and Jourard put it this way more recently:

> *Not* to capitalize on our increased release from economic necessity, *not* to "play" creatively with such existential forms as marriage, family life, schooling, leisure pursuits, etc., is a kind of madness, a dread of, and

---

[37] For more on divorce at the turn of the century, see William L. O'Neill, *Divorce in the Progressive Era* (New Haven, Conn.: Yale University Press, 1967).

[38] Rick Margolis, Institute for Policy Studies, Washington, D.C., January 1970.

[39] F. Ivan Nye distinguishes between the family as an intrinsic value and as an instrumental value. See Nye, "Values, Family, and a Changing Society," *Journal of Marriage and the Family* 19 (1967), 241–48.

[40] Erich Fromm, *Escape from Freedom* (New York: Rinehart, 1941).

escape from, freedom and the terror it engenders. . . . Not to legitimize such experimentation and exploration is to make life in our society unlivable for an increasing proportion of the population.[41] (Italics in original.)

Thus, these arguments would say that the family will incorporate some alternatives as safety valves and will outlive those which are but fleeting attempts to solve individual difficulties.

Yet in Jourard's statement we already have the seed for a second answer to the question: Will the family survive the alternative life styles? This answer is: *Yes, the family will continue to exist, but it will be alongside a series of increasingly legitimated alternatives.* Jourard implies that many people have found our family form unlivable or impossible. If there is one value demonstrated by our society over its long history, it is instrumentalism. That is, we are concerned with what works, or what functions best to solve our problems. As internal pressures build within our family system, increasing numbers of persons will begin to look for viable alternatives. And here is where today's movements, whether communalism or the feminist-humanist movement with its multiple goals, will provide increasingly legitimated alternatives. The reason is that the overarching value in our society is more and more the individual and his self-actualization. As concern for the individual and his happiness becomes increasingly dominant, so will a multiplicity of alternatives be needed to allow for the self-fulfillment of a great variety of individual personalities. Economic and familial values will give ground grudgingly, but the individual and his needs and wants in U.S. society cannot be denied.

This, then, leads to the threshold of a third possible answer to the question: Will the family survive the alternative life styles? This answer is: *No, the family as a legalized institution cannot stay alive in the face of the alternatives.* It is, slowly but surely, on the way out. Such an answer grows, as did the previous answer, out of the instrumental perspective, that is, what works best equals "the good." However, to arrive at this conclusion, a third factor must be added to the family's strains and to the alternatives' propaganda and programs. That factor is the biological advances now taking place in various laboratories. In 1950, and again in 1960, Meyer Nimkoff reviewed some of these advances in terms of their possible effects upon families. Improvements in contraception, artificial insemination, incubator birth (in which, after conception, the fetus resides outside the human body), control over the sex of the child, and work with hormones—all would seem to have implications for the contemporary family.[42] If preservation of the ovum were

---

[41] Jourard, "Reinventing Marriage," in Otto, *The Family in Search of a Future*, p. 46.
[42] Meyer F. Nimkoff, "Biological Discoveries and the Future of the Family: A Reappraisal," *Social Forces* 41 (1962), 121–27. For an interesting assessment of the possible

perfected, reproduction outside the human body would become possible. And if it were found, further, that incubator fetuses were able to avoid birth defects and were more uniformly able to maximize the positive hereditary features of the two parents, then instrumental values might lead increasing numbers of people to a new view of what works best. Granted, at this time it is unthinkable for most people to try to imagine society without our legalized form of monogamy. Yet this reminds me somewhat of the history of anesthesia in the 1800s. Anesthesia was usable medically for some thirty years—a generation—before it was accepted socially or ethically. From the pulpit and elsewhere people were reminded by devout clerics that women were meant to give birth in pain, and that to eliminate such pain artificially was immoral. It took a generation for an equally devout, but scientifically enlightened, cleric to discover the verse in Genesis which said: "And God caused a deep sleep to fall upon Adam, and he removed one of his ribs, and from it he made woman."[43] From that moment on, the "oughtness" battle was won. Our values may not be prepared when discoveries are made, but this answer to our question makes four assumptions: (1) the family does have internal strains; (2) alternatives are being pushed which may work for many people; (3) science does not take a vacation; (4) people's values eventually catch up with and incorporate scientific advances. On these assumptions it is possible to argue that somewhere out in the dim future the family we know will cease to exist. But that is all right, because by then we will no longer value it or see it as necessary any more than we currently value or see as necessary the feudal system or the notion that the earth is the center of the universe.

So there you have it, three answers to the question: Will the family survive the alternative life styles? Society's supports for today's family, the alternatives as reactions against it, our fear of freedom, the propaganda of the alternatives, instrumental and individual values, and scientific advances—it is the relative weight you assign to these factors that will determine your own conclusions as to the family's future.

Personally, I feel that evidence is easiest to muster for the first and third answers to the question, but if I were asked to hazard a guess, I would select the second answer for the foreseeable future. We do not like to choose, but we must do so increasingly; we do not like freedom, but we will exercise it increasingly. And our choices will gradually lead to the legitimation of several alternatives to legalized monogamy, but will not replace it. Which of the alternatives are most likely to receive such legitimation? That depends

---

effects of controlling the newborn child's sex, see Gale Largey, "Sex Control and Society: A Critical Assessment of Sociological Speculations," *Social Problems* 20 (1973), 310–17.

[43] Genesis 2:21.

upon which ones the experimenters find to work the best. Perhaps remaining single; perhaps the commune—these are, after all, opposing attempts (one more individualistic, one less so) to avoid the strains of our monogamous nuclear family.[44] Yet to push on beyond a period of multiple alternatives in our prediction would, I believe, carry us perilously close to that fine line which separates "informed conjecture" from science fiction.[45]

---

[44] For an interesting appraisal of the alternatives most likely to be incorporated into our family system in the future, see Suzanne Keller, "Does the Family Have a Future?" *Journal of Comparative Family Studies* 1 (1971), 1–14. For other recent sources on the family's future, see DeLora and DeLora, *Intimate Life Styles,* pp. 345f.

[45] For further discussion of this viewpoint, see Bert N. Adams, "Can the Family Survive Alternative Life Styles?" *Focus* 2 (1973), 4–9.

ANDROGYNY: A society with no sex-role differentiation; that is, a society in which there are no stereotyped differences between the roles of males and females on the basis of their sex alone.

CULTURAL ALTERNATIVES: Cultural traits which are shared by certain individuals but are not common to all the members of a society or even to all the members of any of its socially recognized categories.

CULTURAL UNIVERSALS: Ideas, habits, and conditioned emotional responses which are common to all sane adult members of a society.

CULTURE: The material and nonmaterial creations of man, which are passed on from generation to generation.

DEPENDENT VARIABLE: The factor, value, or behavior that is to be explained.

MIDDLE CLASS, WORKING CLASS, LOWER CLASS: The *middle class* consists of persons who are engaged in the professional, managerial, sales, and other "white-collar" occupations which are clustered in the upper portion of the prestige-income ladder. Such persons are not, however, at the top of the ladder—those at the top are generally labeled the "upper class." The *working class* consists predominantly of manual workers with steady employment and income, including foremen, skilled craftsmen, and industrial workers. The *lower class* comprises those who are at the bottom of the socioeconomic ladder, either due to handicap, lack of skill, or discrimination. Ordinarily, they are irregularly employed and have low incomes. Whether a family is designated as middle, upper, working, or lower class has traditionally depended on the occupational status of the household head.

MULTIVARIATE MODEL: A combination of three or more variables used to represent certain aspects of a social situation.

NORM: A standard or expectation of conduct. Norms are sets of rules specifying what may, or may not, be done in a particular situation.

QUASI-THEORETICAL FRAMEWORK: A framework that provides a basis for organizing the descriptive materials and also has a certain amount of explanatory usefulness.

ROLE: Normatively patterned action; a pattern of behavior that is associated with a particular position, such as that of husband or wife.

SOCIETY: People in relations and groups; a relatively self-sufficient unit consisting of a number of persons who carry on a common, interdependent life that has continuity through successive generations.

TYPOLOGY: A series of logically constructed points on a particular behavioral, normative, or positional continuum. Examples are typologies of *societies*, such as hunting and gathering, horticultural, agrarian, and industrial, or typologies of *familism*, including the nuclear familistic, kin of orientation familistic, and wider kin oriented.

NAME INDEX

SUBJECT INDEX